A Salvation Audit

A Salvation Audit

Colin Grant

Scranton: University of Scranton Press
London and Toronto: Associated University Presses

University of Scranton Press
Chicago Distribution Center
11030 S. Langley
Chicago IL 60628

Associated University Presses
P.O. Box 338, Port Credit
Mississauga, Ontario
Canada L5G 4L8

Material from *TRUTH AND DIALOGUE IN WORLD RELIGIONS: Conflicting Truth Claims*, edited by John Hick. Copyright © 1974 University of Birmingham. Published in 1974 in the U.S.A. by The Westminster Press. Used by permission of Westminster/John Knox Press.

The paper used in this publication meets the requirements
of the American National Standard for Permanence of Paper
for Printed Library Materials Z39.48-1984.

Library of Congress Cataloging-in-Publication Data

Grant, Colin, 1942–
    A salvation audit / Colin Grant.
    p. cm.
    Includes bibliographical references and index.
    ISBN 0-940866-34-X (alk. paper)
    1. Salvation. 2. Salvation—History of doctrines—20th century.
    3. Salvation—History of doctrines. I. Title.
    BT751.2.G65   1994
    234—dc20
                             92-62490
                                 CIP

To our mothers
and in memory of our fathers
Annie and the late Archie Crawford
Ida and the late David Grant

Contents

Preface

Judged by much of its recent production, theology could be seen as a discipline in search of a subject. Its central theme has been subjected to prolonged scrutiny in the debate about God, and as if this would not be damaging enough, that debate has been pursued with an air of abstractness that virtually assures its confinement to the precincts of professional theologians. The unreality of God in secular culture certainly has to be addressed in theology, but it must be recognized that this issue has two sides. To approach it as the question of an adequate understanding of God overlooks the way in which any understanding of God always entails an understanding of ourselves. This means that the fundamental issue is not an adequate notion of God, important though this is, but a sense of God that makes sense of ourselves and the world. In short, the formative theme of theology is not God *per se*, but salvation.

The shift in focus from a literal approach to theology as thinking about God, to the more indirect and confessional exploration of the meaning and shape of salvation by no means provides a panacea for theology. We can identify some of the factors that have undermined traditional confidence in salvation and suggest some of the dimensions that must be present for any recovery of a vital sense of its reality, but perhaps the most fruitful outcome of such reflections is the realization that the reality of salvation is no less elusive for theology than the reality of God as such. Salvation, like happiness, defies our attempts to possess it. The constructive role for theology might well be to seek to promote and articulate that sense of having and not-having which must characterize a genuine appreciation of salvation.

The work that resulted in this manuscript was begun during a sabbatical leave from Mount Allison University, spent at St. Mary's College in the University of St. Andrew's. I am grateful to Mount Allison for the leave and for funding to support it, and to St. Mary's College for the academic hospitality accorded to me during that year. I am particularly grateful to then Dean— now Principal—D. W. D. (Bill) Shaw, then Principal, William

McKane, the members of faculty and other visiting scholars who made the year a pleasant one, and to the principal's secretary, Maisie Blackwood, for incorporating me into the College physically and socially. If there is any wisdom in the reflections proposed here, it derives in some measure from colleagues among whom I have worked here at Mount Allison since 1971. I am grateful in particular to an interdisciplinary group, the Phoenix Club; although none of the matters presented here were aired in that august group, the arguments presented here would be even less cogent without that experience. My other immediate academic debt is to my departmental colleagues, Eldon Hay and Charles Scobie, whose most direct connection with this manuscript relates to Chapter 10, which was developed originally for a panel presentation in which the three of us participated at an annual meeting of the Canadian Theological Society. My most obvious debt in connection with this manuscript itself here at Mount Allison is to our department secretary, Robin Hamilton, who not only typed the entire manuscript, proofread it and secured permission to use material under copyright, but also pointed out awkward phrasing and grammatical offenses, not to mention challenging matters of substance.

Versions of three chapters appeared in theological journals: Chapter 3 as "The Abandonment of Atonement" in *King's Theological Review*, Chapter 7 as "The Threat and Prospect in Religious Pluralism" in *The Ecumenical Review*, and Chapter 10 as "Possibilities for Divine Passibility" in *The Toronto Journal of Theology*. I am grateful to these journals for permission to reprint this material here. I am also grateful to the University of Scranton Press and the Associated University Presses to which it belongs for publishing this manuscript, especially to Father Richard Rousseau who made the initial contact and ushered the manuscript through the examination that resulted in its acceptance, and to Julien Yoseloff who presided over the publication process. Thanks also to Joyce Brody, the copy editor, and Regina Phair, the production editor.

Of course, my greatest debt is to my family, to my wife Sheina and our sons, Scott and Neil, who have learned to live with "Dad's books." Without that, this book would not have been possible. It is dedicated to Sheina's parents and to mine.

* * *

Permission to reprint from the following is hereby acknowledged:

Hymns Today and Tomorrow by Erik Routley, © 1964 Abingdon Press;

Audacity to Believe by Sheila Cassidy, permission granted by Harper Collins Publishers;

Christianity and Other Religions, edited by John Hick and Brian Hebblethwaite, permission granted by Collins, Fount;

"On Freedom and Gratitude" by Elie Weisel, from *Luther Magazine* 18, no. 2 (December 1981): p. 6;

"Moral Arguments" by Philippa Foot, from *Mind* 67 (1958), by permission of Oxford University Press (Oxford);

Against the Protestant Gnostics by Philip J. Lee, by permission of Oxford University Press (New York);

Henry Alline, Selected Writings, edited by George Rawlyk, by permission of Paulist Press;

Truth and Dialogue in World Religions: Conflicting Truth Claims, edited by John Hick. © 1974 University of Birmingham. Published in 1974 in the U.S.A. by The Westminister Press. Used by permission of Westminster/John Knox Press.

A Salvation Audit

1

Introduction: The Dilemma of Salvation

There is good reason for concluding that salvation is the neglected preoccupation of the modern West. Many of the public concerns and private passions that characterize contemporary life can be understood as gropings after salvation, and yet few notions come closer to representing a broad popular consensus than the disavowal of any interest in salvation per se. A typical expression of this perspective occurred at a public meeting when one participant characterized a possible solution to a vexing problem as "our salvation," and another participant interjected with a note of resentment bordering on anger, "I'm not interested in salvation." The second speaker was no less intent on finding a solution than the first, but he gave articulation to a widely held sentiment in disassociating their predicament and prospects from any connection with that term.

The Suspicion of Salvation

POPULAR DISSATISFACTION WITH SALVATION

Aversion to the word *salvation* is indicative of connotations this term has acquired in popular understanding. At the very least, it signals an intrusion into what is generally perceived to be the private domain of one's fundamental allegiance in life. When this intrusion is sponsored, as it often is, by an insistent assurance about what that allegiance should be, nuisance becomes offense. The promotion of a neat solution to life's problems, even on a personal level, through the incantation of a sacred name and association with a select company of fellow subscribers, offends the intelligence. The complexity and enormity of the issues that face us in postindustrial society defy such simplistic perspectives. Only the naïveté of this outlook prevents the intellectual offense taking on

15

moral overtones. For if we take the proposal seriously, the promotion of salvation strikes at the core of our own existence, suggesting that we stand in need of parental advice and counsel and that the messenger of salvation is privy to the wisdom we lack. The air of smugness that can permeate this assurance may be what makes the notion of salvation particularly objectionable to the contemporary mind. It smacks of narrowness, naïveté, and self-righteousness.

The net result is that for the hypothetical average citizen of the developed world today, salvation probably conjures up visions of the television evangelist promoting divine acceptance like heavenly detergent or else elicits buried images from childhood or the media that define religious sensibility. Nor is the situation much better for the average churchgoer.[1] Salvation tends to be part of the jargon used in the religious context. But its significance in the ongoing involvements of life is far from evident. The more specific elements included in the religious connotations of the term hover in the air of secular culture like camouflaged birds, barely visible, and defying identification when they do come into view. Thus a character in T. S. Eliot's *The Cocktail Party* searches for a word to identify her sense of anxiety:

> It's not the feeling of anything I've ever *done*
> which I might get away from, or of anything in me
> I could get rid of—but of emptiness, of failure
> towards someone, or something, outside of myself;
> and I feel I must—*atone*—is that the word?[2]

Recognition of salvation and its components is fundamentally foreign to the vocabulary of contemporary life.

INTELLECTUAL DISPENSABILITY OF SALVATION

This fate to which salvation is subject thus appears to be a product of the spirit of the age. The *Zeitgeist* renders talk of salvation problematic to the point where it is in danger of falling off the index of intelligibility. It just does not fit life as we experience it. The residual meaning salvation does retain suggests a preoccupation with our own individual destinies, which appears trivial in comparison to the massive structural problems that threaten our whole world, problems of ecological imbalance that have the potential for vastly altering life as we know it, social imbalance through the massive disparities between the affluent who. make such demands on the natural environment and the impoverished for whom life itself is intensely precarious, and the ever-menacing prospect of nuclear catastrophe that could destroy life completely. "For postmoderns 'salvation' must include social strategies for preventing ecological disaster, nuclear holocaust, and oppression of the poor, and cannot be restricted to the imagery of interpersonal transactions between the Absolute king and his disobedient subjects, even though that imagery has honored place in the Bible and in the prayers and hymnody of the church."[3] If salvation is to effect any purchase on the mentality of the age, it must somehow encompass these prominent concerns that have to do with the very survival of life, rather than being associated with a retreat from all such issues to a private assurance of our own personal security.

This shift in consciousness might be attributed to the technological mastery that has characterized the modern era. This is what has made the massive ecological impact possible, has aggravated social disparities and made us aware of them, and has provided the unique possibility of geocide. Such attribution would not be without merit, providing it entails the realization that technology is not an external process confined to the perfecting of mechanical means and instruments, but rather involves a comprehensive development that portends a whole mentality and approach to life. It is far too simplistic to suggest that we must come to grips with our newfound mastery of the means of life and death. We only begin to appreciate the situation when we note the irony of that proposal in the way it exposes itself as a version of the technological mentality itself. To want to come to grips with something is to seek technological mastery. The naturalness of this reaction is an indication of how profoundly that outlook has captured our imaginations. Thus, what we are facing in the contemporary challenge to salvation is not an external threat as a kind of inference from technological mastery, but a whole shift in sensibilities that give us a different outlook on life from previous ages where concern for salvation was assumed. "When the universe seemed small and man the undisputed center of it, the purpose of God was generally believed to be fulfilled in the destiny of the human. soul."[4] Now that we live in an expansive universe, we do not find it so easy to assume that our own individual lives have great cosmic importance. This points to the paradoxical nature of the contemporary perspective. On the one hand, we have thrust ourselves into the center of life as technocrats, progressively reducing the areas that require appeal to

God, but at the same time we have felt ourselves demoted by the immensity of space so that we cannot imagine that our lives have any particular significance in the vast cosmic panorama.

As Promethean orphans we neither require nor recognize a savior. A savior is a bridge between the realms of divinity and humanity. "He is a divine or semidivine being, who descends from the domain of the gods to the dwelling-places of men, or who operates through other gods for the benefit of men."[5] Because we have taken charge of life ourselves, forcing nature to reveal its secret workings, we have emancipated ourselves from divine tutelage, and have fastened our sights on what we can do with the Promethean fire we have procured. Thus confining ourselves to the human, and having relinquished any firm sense of the divine, we have no need for a bridge to a region that is no longer on our psychic map. Insofar as we have experienced this shift in consciousness, salvation is bound to be a nonissue, so that there is considerable merit in the suggestion that any prospect for a positive appreciation of salvation must come to grips with the cultural watershed constituted by the Enlightenment.[6] The self-sufficiency of the modern anthropocentric perspective, whether experienced positively as the challenge to extend the range of human mastery or negatively as the sense of our ultimate insignificance in an impersonal, careless universe, precludes any serious entertaining of a significant concern with salvation.

THEOLOGICAL FAILURE TO CLARIFY SALVATION

The depth of the challenge this poses for theology cannot be overestimated. For in one sense, though it has never been subject to explicit doctrinal prominence in itself, belief in salvation might even be regarded as more important for Christian theology than belief in God. It is the dimension of faith that assures us that belief in God is significant. Without this assumption of salvation, belief in God becomes an academic affirmation of great theoretical import perhaps, but lacking that existential cement, which incorporates that belief in our lives, and which enables us to feel ourselves incorporated into an inclusive reality far greater than we can begin to imagine.

The most evident response of contemporary theology to this challenge has been to attempt some bridge building of its own, seeking to establish links between the traditional interest in salvation and the imminent pursuits, which have seemed to replace that concern. Those who promote this solution castigate fellow theologians for their tardiness in seeking to effect this linkage. "Theology has taken a long time, far too long, to realize and integrate into its researches the *epochal* gap or divide between traditional belief in redemption and man's quest (both explicit and implicit) for salvation today."[7] The plethora of political and liberation theologies that have emerged in recent years might be seen as instances of this endeavor to articulate versions of salvation that are relevant to present experience and commitments. These reflect the self-conscious awareness, which has developed over the last century, whereby we recognize the importance of the social in establishing who we are and what possibilities are open to us. Although there are basic differences between this present approach and the social gospel movement from the earlier part of this century, the fundamental direction that guides both movements, the recognition of the formative importance of social arrangements, is indicated by the father of that earlier movement, Walter Rauschenbusch. "A realization of the spiritual power and value of these composite personalities [organizations] must get into theology, otherwise theology will not deal adequately with the problem of sin and of redemption, and will be unrelated to some of the most important work of salvation which the coming generations will have to do."[8] The understanding of salvation must change as our understanding of life changes. Our recognition of the importance of social arrangements must be incorporated into the understanding of salvation not only for the sake of the understanding of salvation itself, which will tend to recede in significance as a private concern for individuals, but also for the sake of the reality of salvation that must embrace the social dimension in order to penetrate life as we know it in this century.

In his day, Rauschenbusch struck a responsive cord, sometimes hostile, sometimes appreciative, just as liberation and political theologians have done in the decade of the 1980s in which they have become prominent. The appreciation stems from the recognition that this basic approach makes contact with life as we find it today. But that very relevance also accounts for the hostility, or at least reservation, which represents an expression of the concern that the contemporary horizon may be allowed to dissipate any distinctive connotation for salvation by assimilation just as surely as it does by exclusion. To baptize social concerns with the label salvation does not necessarily rejuvenate the lost sense of the significance of salvation, nor does it noticeably add anything to the importance of these causes in their own right. If recognition of the importance of social arrangements as vehicles for sin and avenues for salvation is to offer any significant prospect for revitalizing the appreciation for salvation, it must involve more than a relabeling of contemporary concerns, which commend themselves in their own right. It must come to grips with that basic shift in consciousness that has rendered salvation unintelligible. In itself, the attachment to the social may represent a further intensification of that alienation from salvation constituted by the Promethean grasp of modernity. "If it could, the world of the New Testament would rise up and convict our generation of a massive corporate *hubris*, an attitude of proud challenge to God which can only result in disaster."[9] This is the issue that must be faced if we are to address the matter of salvation. "In a setting so utterly different, how on earth is salvation to be proclaimed?"[10] The shift to the social will hold no promise of alleviating the dilemma for salvation unless this underlying shift in consciousness is addressed. For not only is it baffling as to how salvation can be proclaimed in our age of *hubris*, but also it is not clear how the notion can even be intelligible.

Although salvation has thus been the victim of the anthropocentric shift signaled by the Enlightenment and the successive ripples that have emanated from that impetus, theology cannot be absolved of responsibility for failure to clarify this central aspect of its focus. Even in the legacy of liberal theology there has been the lingering sense that Christianity has to do particularly with the event of the cross, but just why and how this is so is not clear. More traditional approaches are more vocal about the centrality of the cross, but their volubility has tended more to repetitive jargon than toward illuminating exposition. A general survey of Christian doctrine sums up the disappointing results of theological work in this vital area:

> Many Christians, myself included, are impressed by the failure of the church to give any effective witness concerning the cross of Christ. Its meaning is easily lost in cliches which seem remote from the realities of human life. The word "salvation", which is often used among Christians to express the meaning of Christ, has become so stereotyped that it is no longer a useful term. The question often posed in evangelical fervour "Are you saved, brother?" leaves us with the impression that to be saved is to embark on a parochial and unexciting life. The situation is tragic in view of the fact that the message of the cross actually touches the most profound levels of human existence.[11]

If "salvation" is to recover from its present relegation to the preserve of fanatics and idle dreamers, it will only be because it is seen to touch profound levels of human existence. This will require a more compelling articulation of the meaning of salvation than theology has yet been able to achieve and a challenge to the prevailing understanding of human existence that sponsors the air of *hubris* that precludes recognition of the need for, or significance of, salvation.

The Sense of Salvation

Insofar as we are children of modernity (and postmodern sensibilities do not abolish that influence, however much they may modify it), we will regard the word *salvation* as a quaint reminder of a simpler era. However, anyone who has read this far is not likely to have succumbed completely to this relegation of salvation to antiquarian realms. Some positive connotation for the term remains, however resistant to articulation that may be. If then we try to develop that articulation, and ask what might possibly be meant by salvation, it would seem that the main variations on this theme can be organized under three broad headings.

SALVATION AS DELIVERANCE

The biblical understanding of salvation centers on the assurance of deliverance. The experiences of Israel to which the Old Testament narratives testify revolve around the deliverance from Egypt in which Yahweh became known to the people and the people became a people, the delivered community. Prior events of the patriarchal period are seen as a preparation for this formative event, and post-Exodus happenings are measured by their faithfulness to, or betrayal of, the allegiance established in the deliverance from Egypt. The theme is renewed in the New Testament where the deliverance of a people from foreign bondage is broadened into the claim of universal deliverance of humanity from the bondage of sin. Through proclamation and pictures, the early Christians portrayed the event of Christ, and particularly his death, as a decisive turning point in the divine–human drama, which provides the basis for the assurance of divine forgiveness and acceptance. Down through the centuries this remained the focus of the Church's celebration and proclamation. As the core of the gospel of salvation, this claim of deliverance is also at the heart of the contemporary suspicion of salvation.

One suggestive reading of this situation is represented by the contention that the identification of salvation with deliverance is a mistake, and that this is responsible for the suspicion to which salvation has become subject. "The equation of deliverance with salvation has narrowed the whole message of the Gospel and has brought it to stagnation, making it impotent and irrelevant in terms of the common aspiration and hopes of human society."[12] The deliverance focus involves attributing decisive importance to divine involvement in particular historical activity, the deliverance from Egypt or the sacrifice of Christ, and consequently neglects the prominent presence of God in the natural processes of creation.[13] This position derives from the Old Testament scholar, Claus Westermann, in his contention that the identification of salvation with deliverance obscured the other important biblical motif of blessing. He sees this process being facilitated by the fact that the Latin *salus* and the German *Heil*, which originally both bear the connotation of blessing, as evidenced in their use as greetings, were adopted as designations for the message of deliverance. In this way, the dimension of blessing was absorbed and the words that had designated this state become associated with the act of salvation.[14] The net result is that salvation comes to be thought of as an intervention by an absent god, whereas one of the persistent themes of the Bible is that life is only possible because of the ongoing sustenance of God who is ever present. "The God who saves is the God who comes; the one who blesses is the one who is present."[15]

The crux of Westermann's position seems to be that salvation should be seen to encompass blessing as well as deliverance, the ongoing providence of God as well as transformative intervention. However, although his statements imply this, the direct meaning they convey is more ambiguous. In the last reference cited, he himself clearly contrasts blessing and saving. His central concern would seem to dictate a differentiation between blessing and deliverance, and a parallel insistence that these two forms of divine activity must be recognized as integral in salvation. Yet he himself seems to remain tied to the identification of salvation with deliverance. His considered position would seem to be that the one who is present saves as well as the one who comes, and saves in the presence of blessing as well as in the coming to deliver. Yet Westermann implicitly identifies salvation with deliverance, even when he is intent on broadening it to include blessing. "The distinction between God's work of deliverance and his work of blessing has its effect in a total theology of the Old Testament in such a way that God's saving actions can no longer be reduced to soteriological terms because they are not identical with his work of deliverance."[16] Here he seems to put himself in the untenable position of rejecting a tautology. If "saving acts can no longer be reduced to soteriological terms" what can they be reduced to? What he seems to mean is that soteriology must not be confined to acts of deliverance, but also must encompass the ongoing activity of blessing.

This confusion in the statement of his position is symptomatic of Westermann's implication in the more pervasive ambiguity in the contemporary understanding of salvation as such. The clue to this wider context is provided by the editors of the series in which his book is issued. They suggest: "Westermann offers what may be a quite fresh interfacing between *liturgy and secularization.*"[17] This raises the possibility that Westermann's motivation is not simply to promote a neglected strand in the biblical fabric, but also to develop a theological stance that is more congenial to the modern secular perspective than the deliverance understanding of salvation can be. The notion of blessing is certainly far less threatening than that of some kind of external intervention. Although he notes that the Deuteronomic history links blessing with the events of history, under the influence of the prophetic tradition, so that the blessing that comes with obedience is balanced by the curse that accompanies disobedience,[18] this prophetic note of judgment seems to disappear by the time of the New Testament since Jesus the deliverer is presented as the agency of blessing with no suggestion of any significant negative note of rejection of any kind.[19] Thus, whereas Westermann identifies a neglected theme in both testaments, his promotion of blessing as a counterbalance to deliverance gives the appearance of succumbing to the modern secular *Zeitgeist* in affirming not only the God who is present, in contrast to the God from whom we are alienated and by whom we require deliverance, but also the God whose presence to us is essentially positive, totally confirming, blessing, rather than judging.

Westermann does not deny the deliverance understanding of salvation. His recommendation seems to involve a balancing of that interventionist theme by a recognition of the neglected theme of blessing. The difficulty is that these two themes do not easily go together. Deliverance presupposes an unsatisfactory state from which rescue is required. Blessing, on the other hand, implies an endorsement of the status quo, or, at most, a perfecting of it:

> The idea of salvation, and especially Christian salvation, presupposes some kind of dualism in the human condition. If there were no split, if people were all already whole, there would be no need for salvation and religions and churches would simply go out of business.[20]

Deliverance constitutes the clearest expression of dualism under-lying salvation. The Hebrews are delivered to freedom from bon-dage in Egypt; in Christ, humanity is delivered from the enslave-ment of sin to the liberty of the Kingdom of God. But it is precise-ly this notion of dualism that is unintelligible to the modern mind because it involves not only the deliverance from the state of sin to that of salvation, but also the dualism of the external agency by which this is effected. It is this underlying dualism of the interven-tionist God that causes particular problems for moderns accus-tomed to thinking in terms of secondary causes. Westermann typifies the reaction of mainline theology to this problem in advo-cating a recognition of the presence of God, rather than trying to account for the intervention of God who is otherwise absent. His emphasis on blessing reminds us that life is possible only because of the abiding and sustaining presence of God. However, the prob-lem is not really the absence of God from us, but our absence from God, our state of alienation, as depicted in the suggestion of the fall story of Genesis 3—it is the desire to replace God ourselves which is the source of our difficulties. However we understand the metaphysical dualism of God and humanity, this spiritual dualism of sinful humanity before the holy God stands as the indispensable background for any understanding of salvation as deliverance. The extent to which Westermann can allow for this in conjunction with his promotion of the motif of blessing will depend upon the extent to which he would subscribe to either of the two other broad ways in which salvation may be understood.

SALVATION AS HEALING

The embarrassment of metaphysical dualism is alleviated some-what by shifting to the historically oriented moral and spiritual dualism between the way we actually are and the way we could be. Here, hints of medieval supernaturalism are replaced by intima-tions of deficiency, which imply possibilities missed that might somehow be recouped, rather than flaws requiring external in-tervention. Westermann himself notes that the original reference of *salus* and *Heil* is to "the state of being 'whole', 'healthy', 'intact'."[21] This offers scope for an understanding of salvation as healing, which is more congenial to contemporary consciousness than the more traditional interventionist image of externally effected deliverance. However, once again this very relevance may be indicative of compromise with the requirements of modern secularity.

The shift from deliverance to healing as the formative model for salvation represents a shift from the context of holiness to one of wholeness. Not only does this ameliorate the problem of metaphysical dualism, but also it tends to minimize the significance of moral and spiritual dualism. Although focusing on the unity of reality (so that God is understood from within the processes of life rather than as hovering somewhere above and beyond them) reflects a more biblically compatible understanding of God as involved in the world (thus representing a corrective to the deistic direction that emerged with the mechanistic universe of the early stages of modern science), this assumption of the immanence of God invariably shades over into a qualitative reduction in awareness of the otherness of God. The God who is with us in life is the God of blessing, in contrast to the God who stands over against us across the qualitative gap of divine holiness. The shift is a subtle one, but no less dramatic. Any sense of the need for healing presupposes some gap or deficiency, which should be put right. "The place where God is known and His offer of salvation received is always some place where men either know that their humanity is threatened, distorted, oppressed, or some place where they become aware of the offer of a greater humanity than they yet enjoy."[22] It is where such sense of inadequacy is lacking that salvation becomes completely unintelligible. "Those who are whole have no need of a physician" (Mt. 9:12). But there's the rub. The ironic note sounded in that summation is missed precisely by those who consider themselves whole, and in so doing expose their desperate state in being unaware of their need for healing. Complacency is the practical orientation of which disinterest in salvation is the intellectual expression.

One major difficulty with the healing model for salvation is this circularity implicit in it. The need for healing is really recognizable only on the basis of the experience of health. We are troubled by a toothache only because of its contrast with the normal experience of healthy teeth. When we move to moral and spiritual health, the recognition of ill-health becomes much more precarious. For here, part of the disease is its own camouflage as health. The obvious sins which prick the conscience are far less potent than the dispositional and attitudinal sins that come equipped with self-justifying mechanisms so that they are not associated with sin at all. This is why Jesus insisted on going behind the deed to the underlying motive, behind murder to anger, behind adultery to desire. This is also why when an alcoholic can say, "My name is John, and I am an alcoholic!" the battle is more than half won. In the moral and spiritual domain, diagnosis must be made by the patient. But if one recognizes one's self as a patient, the healing process has already begun.

The circularity of salvation as healing hinges on the question of recognition of the need for healing, and this in turn depends on the criterion by which our condition is assessed. This is where the shift from holiness to wholeness becomes particularly significant. Traditionally, the sinfulness of humanity was recognized against the background of the holiness of God. But as the last quotation indicating the kind of recognition that is involved in appreciating the need for healing suggests, the criterion has shifted from the divine to the human. The need for salvation is an expression of the recognition that our humanity is "threatened, distorted, oppressed," or of a glimpse of a "greater humanity" than is presently realized. Implicit in this change of criteria are two developments that characterize modern sensibility. One is the secular thrust of modernity whereby the divine is displaced by the human. The other is the historical consciousness that has served to underwrite the assumption of progress so that deficiencies are associated with the past and inherent superiority is assigned to the future. Together these assumptions transform the residual meaning of salvation identified in terms of healing. From a sense of having offended the holiness of God, sin now becomes a matter of failing to realize our full potential. Of course, this is not entirely a modern invention. One of the fundamental New Testament designations of sin, *hamartia*, carries the sense of missing the mark, falling short of the goal, as an archer's arrow that fails to reach the target. But the myth of progress, along with its secular context, gives this a new meaning implying that there is a certain inevitability in this because of the residual impediment of our prehuman inheritance and a certain mitigation of responsibility because the target is only an ideal that will continue to elude us because it too is subject to progress.

The net result of the view of salvation as healing is an approach that is more congenial to modern sensibility than to the notion of external divine intervention. According to the healing view, "salvation can indicate a reverence before the mystery and wonder of the universe of which we are a part, and a whole and healthy attitude toward our own existence and growth."[23] The appeal of this vision of salvation as harmony between ourselves and the universe and within ourselves might be totally convincing if we had not seen that the problem with a healing version of salvation is the intimate correlation between the effectiveness of healing and the recognition of disease. Who among us would not like to think that their attitude is "whole and healthy?" But in thinking this, we may well be settling for an understanding of salvation that is really an intensification of the disease, an acquiescence in the status quo. This would accord well with the following academic definition of salvation: "Salvation is a state of cognitive and affective well-being within the currently available system of world interpretation."[24] Or, as the same author puts it, even more formally, and even more thoroughly indicating the endorsement of the prevailing situation: "Salvation is that state of sufficiency of durable plausible existing for an individual or group, under given ideological and social structural conditions, such that no alternative is sought."[25] This suggests that salvation is not so much healing as a state of perfect health where no healing is required. In light of what we have seen about the subtlety of sin, we have to wonder whether this is not rather a description of double perdition, where the understanding of salvation itself serves to obfuscate a recognition of the need for salvation.

This danger of complacency to which the healing model is subject must not be permitted to detract from an appreciation of the importance of the ideal of wholeness with which it is allied. No other image of salvation may be quite so powerful in the context of the fragmentation of contemporary life. "The universalistic task of the religious leader in our society is to answer its overemphasis on professional specialization with credible discernment of the meaning and the arts of human wholeness, but it is a large and difficult task."[26] The whole is also a crucial consideration for theology proper. The Tillichian ontology and process theology represent two prominent forms of the suggestion that God is to be understood in terms of wholeness, rather than separateness. "Perhaps our question today is not whether or not we believe in God but how we understand inclusive reality and whether within that understanding we find it appropriate to designate the whole or some element as God."[27] However, recognizing the relevance of this approach does not dispense with the suspicion that in the transition from holiness to wholeness something is lost, with the result that we may be parodying salvation rather than participating in it. That danger becomes manifest in the third general way in which salvation is understood.

SALVATION AS ENDORSEMENT

The shift from understanding salvation in terms of reconciliation with the holy God to regarding it in terms of seeking wholeness in our own lives involves the fundamental implication that salvation is thereby inclined to appear more as a project to be achieved than as a gift to be appropriated. This exposes the inadequacy of spiritual quietism, which looks to God to right wrongs. As a process theologian puts it, "There will be more basis for hope for this world when more people perceive that God's *modus operandi* is to save us *through* our activities, not in spite of them."[28] This recognition counters the "verticalism" which understands salvation as a divine accomplishment directed to the isolated individual.[29] It restores the balance between the two tables of the law, insisting that the love of God is experienced and expressed through the love of neighbor. It also punctures the myth of the isolated individual, replacing it with the recognition of the primacy of community.

The outstanding example of this corrective in theology is the variety of political and liberation theologies that have emerged in recent years. It has even been suggested that this approach to theology represents a new lease on life for salvation as the determinative theological theme. "Probably its most significant contribution has been the recovery of the soteriological motif as central to the entire theological enterprise, a motif that has been smothered in theology for too long."[30] Others are equally convinced, however, that this theological orientation runs the very serious risk of going to the other extreme, so that instead of achieving an integrated balance to quietistic verticalism, it can appear to favor a reactionary "horizontalism", in which salvation is equated with social programs for achieving justice and freedom from oppression.[31] While liberation theologians themselves insist that it is not their intention to reduce salvation to political and economic terms, the confidence that God can be identified with particular political and economic positions puts the onus on liberation theologians to show that their concern for the political and economic dimensions is an integral part of, rather than a substitute for, a more comprehensive understanding of salvation.

Whereas political and liberation theologians are the most obvious source of suspicion of a reductionist treatment of salvation, some of the clearest statements of an immanentist, humanistic view are to be found in versions of theology that are committed to comprehensive visions. The insistence that salvation is effected only through our action cited from a process theologian may be reinforced by a representative of narrative theology Sallie McFague. "Any notion of salvation which presumes that individuals can be rescued *from* the world; that does not take seriously our necessary efforts to participate in the struggle against oppression and for well-being; or that allows us to abjure our responsibility by appealing as children to a father who will alone protect and save—any such notion must be seen as immoral, irrelevant and destructive."[32] In itself, this may be read as a further unexceptionable rejection of the passivity and complacency of a quietistic understanding of salvation and an insistence that genuine salvation must involve the ways we live together. However, this statement is particularly interesting because it leads to a positive articulation of an understanding of salvation, which suggests that we are reaching the opposite extreme from the traditional deliverance perspective. "At the most a credible view of salvation can only be that God is *with us*—on our side—as we suffer through and work towards overcoming these evils and the perversity of our hearts from which they come."[33] Here the concern that salvation engages us where we really live threatens to shade over into a Pelagian assumption that salvation is essentially our project for which God is seen, as we have come to see nature and our fellow beings, as a resource. We have to wonder whether there is much prospect for really appreciating "the perversity of our hearts" when the governing assumption is that God is "on our side."

Insofar as the recent concern that salvation be practical and effective does represent a Pelagian direction, it suggests that the understanding of salvation has moved from deliverance through healing to direct endorsement. Correspondingly, the characterization of God has shifted from the austerity of holiness through the comprehensiveness of wholeness to the innocuousness of blessing. With this development, it is not much wonder that salvation has tended to become a nonissue for contemporary sensibilities.

The Significance of Salvation

Opinion polls are not the most reliable gauge of truth. One does not have to take a cynical view of human nature to suspect that the majority are more apt to endorse the expedient and the convenient rather than the true. The fact that salvation does not readily accord with the temper of the age may be more detrimental to the temper of the age than to the real significance of salvation. We shall consider three ways in which, despite its obvious difficulties, salvation remains a matter of vital significance.

THE SIGNIFICANCE OF SALVATION FOR CHRISTIANITY

It is hardly accidental that the loss of interest in salvation coincides with a decline in the status and impact of Christianity. The

Zeitgeist that has rendered salvation problematic is the same one that has relegated Christianity to the status of a private option for those who have this particular interest. The coincidence between these two developments is due to the fact that Christianity is so inextricably identified with the salvation theme. In one sense, this can be said of all religions. As one introductory text in world religions puts it: "Religions may be approached as ways of salvation."[34] This raises further questions which will have to be confronted, but for now we shall confine ourselves to the importance of salvation for the identification and endurance of Christianity.

It is not surprising to find a specific treatment of the salvation theme asserting that theme's centrality. "Of all theological themes, perhaps soteriology has raised the question of relevance most acutely; nor would it be an exaggeration to say that in soteriology the relevance of all theology is at stake."[35] But even stronger sentiments, asserting the significance of salvation not only for the relevance of theology but for its very existence, can be found in treatments not explicitly focused on salvation per se, and in the writings of theologians from both ends of the theological spectrum. Thus in endorsing a return to a more traditional theological orientation, such as that promoted by the Hartford Appeal, Thomas Oden contends: "It is this pardoning event of cross and resurrection that is printed indelibly on the mind of the Church as the crucial moment in history where we are met once for all by the redemptive God who suffers for us and delivers us from sin and death."[36] From the other end of the spectrum, in explaining the contemporary process of *Taking Leave of God*, Don Cupitt contends that it is possible to say what would spell the end of Christianity. It is not the loss of belief in God, but the failure to experience salvation. "If a time were to come when people no longer found salvation in Christianity, no longer heard a divine call in Jesus' words, no longer experienced conversion through union with Jesus in his death and no longer received the divine spirit, then in that time Christianity would indeed have died."[37]

While the fate of Christianity in the modern era has been determined by the process of secularization, Christian theology must share the responsibility for this fate because of its failure to develop an intelligible articulation regarding the matter of the salvation it proclaims. Undoubtedly there is some excuse for the inadequacy of accounts of the meaning of salvation that constitutes the Christian gospel. The vast range of interpretations to which this gospel has been subject over the centuries and the diversity between conservative and liberal versions of Christianity today testify to the impossibility of capturing the Christian notion of salvation in any direct formula. What is more, the subject itself, by its very nature, defies delineation in any straightforward sense. Its transcendent scope involves a totality that evokes symbolic, rather than directly descriptive, representation, and on the personal level, this entails a confessional sensibility that defies the possessiveness of any creedal formula or theological explanation that might be passed around as an adequate impersonal statement of what is involved. These difficulties render the task of depicting Christianity as one of several world religions particular precarious. In texts that try to do this, the result is apt to suggest something of a caricature,[38] an impression that takes on the air of the comic the more seriously the depiction is meant. The comedy rapidly turns to tragedy, however, when tired cliches and pious phrases are repeated as the substance of the gospel. A more appropriate response is surely the lament cited earlier from the introductory text in Christian theology,[39] which deplores the failure of Christian theology to provide challenging articulations of the meaning of the salvation it proclaims.

There is no question of requiring some firm and final statement of the Christian meaning of salvation. The scope of religious themes and the symbolic nature of religious language renders any such expectations infantile. But if there is any point at all in speaking of a Christian understanding of salvation that must be amenable to some exposition that is more than repetition of cliches. "God is ultimately unknowable in this life, but that which Jesus Christ has done for us must be capable of being understood to some extent if we are to respond to it."[40] The challenge is to articulate an understanding of salvation in a discipline which has specialized in avoiding the issue to an age which is largely convinced that it is a nonissue. But the difficulty of the task is matched by its potential significance. "There are few ways in which the Church could better serve this generation than by a recovery, a translation into modern idiom, and a bold proclamation of the wonderfully comprehensive message of salvation contained in the Scriptures."[41] The future of Christianity depends on such a translation. The failure to achieve it, however approximately, not only will confirm the secularly perceived irrelevance of the Christian faith, but it will testify to a lack of confidence within the Christian community itself. "The understanding of God's salvation through Jesus remains the central task of Christian theology."[42] Salvation is what Christianity is all about. Without some firm sense of what that means, Christians do not know what they are about.

THE SIGNIFICANCE OF SALVATION FOR THE WORLD

One of the principal obstacles to gaining a hearing for any reinterpretation of salvation is the sense of the precarious state of the world in light of ecological imbalance, social and economic imbalance, and the ominous threat of nuclear holocaust. Even those who retain some sense of significance for salvation may well be inclined to find concern with ultimate destinies trivialized by these immediate threats to survival. Or alternatively, the question of survival itself may tend to become the form that the question of salvation takes. Thus, in light of the environmental concerns, one writer advocates the establishment of a university that will be dedicated to teaching survival skills as a means of salvation:

> Let's call it Survival U. It will not be a multiversity, offering courses in every conceivable field. Its motto—emblazoned on a life jacket rampant—will be: "What must we do to be saved?" If a course does not help to answer that question, it will not be taught here.[43]

To survive is to be saved.

This equation of salvation with survival is understandable in the context of these massive threats to survival. To challenge this equation is somewhat like challenging the tendency of liberation theologians to concentrate on the economic in light of the massive structural poverty prevalent in Latin America. However, to accept this equation is to settle for the reductionistic kind of account like that advanced by sociobiologists who suggest that the point of life is reproduction. Although the threat to world survival and the more direct threat to particular segments of humanity cannot, by any means, be taken lightly, it is another matter to find these challenges exhaustive of the meaning of life. At the very least, preservation of sheer quantity of life, without any sense of the quality of life, may be understandable in circumstances where survival is such a pressing issue as to constitute an obsession, but where there is any scope at all for ceasing from the struggle momentarily, the issue of the quality of life, the why of survival, must emerge. "In essence, quality of life refers to the degree to which people live in harmony with their inner spirit, their fellow man, and nature's physical environment."[44] Survival is threatened by disharmonies between us and nature, among us collectively, and within us individually. Reductions of these disharmonies that will make survival possible themselves represent aspects of the quality of life. Thus, the prospect for sheer quantity of life depends on achieving some measure of quality of life.

Further, as the last writer cited recognizes, even in considering the role of contemporary business, once the importance of quality of life considerations emerge, we have opened ourselves to an expansive perspective. "It is . . . a utopian concept in the sense that most people use it as an ultimate goal that they realize probably will never be obtained absolutely."[45] But this recognition represents an unstable middle ground between the reductionist assumption that we can deal with life purely in quantitative terms and a full recognition of the theological dimension. And just as the assurance of continuing quantity of life depends on our ability to achieve a certain quality of life, so that achievement may in turn be contingent upon our sense of cosmic holiness and wholeness. The Eastern Orthodox tradition may have retained a firmer sense of this pervasive holiness than we have generally managed in the West:

> A totally fresh attitude is necessary, one which is different from our objectifying–analyzing technique. We shall call it the *reverent–receptive* attitude. It is the attitude of being open to fundamental reality as it manifests itself to us through visible, audible, sensible realities in the creation. This fresh attitude is not to be adopted as an alternative to the scientific–technical attitude but as a necessary complement. Without this combination the scientific–technical attitude becomes as harmful as the other attitude becomes obscurantist and self-deceiving.[46]

Although the equation of survival with salvation must be questioned for all but those whose survival is immediately at stake, it is not unreasonable to suggest that the prospects for survival ultimately depend on an appreciation of salvation, not only from the utilitarian point of view of its requirement to underwrite the reconciliations necessary between us and nature, and among and within ourselves, but also from the point of view of the intrinsic significance of salvation itself. However inadequate our articulation of it, the will to survive bespeaks some sense of significance in life, which transcends mere survival for its own sake.

THE INTRINSIC SIGNIFICANCE OF SALVATION

The survival of Christianity may well depend on a renewed appreciation of salvation, and the survival of the world may well depend on realizing a measure of cooperation in place of the stress and strife that threaten its destruction, but the ultimate significance of salvation does not reside in such utilitarian benefits. Indeed, such benefits are not apt to be achieved unless salvation is seen to possess intrinsic significance in its own right. As such, it will have a specific focus, such as that provided by the Christian tradition, and encompass the pressing problems of the present, but in itself it will entail a vision and venture which exceeds these particular perspectives and problems.

By its nature, salvation is elusive. The idea that salvation could consist in a state of realized satisfaction represents an external social science perspective in contrast to the internal view of theological sensitivity:

> Salvation as I understand it is in its most comprehensive sense the final goal to which God wills to bring his creatures in relation with himself in the eschatological state. As such it remains to some extent unknown to us between the times, and all our images of it are provisional.[47]

Salvation is the known unknown that provides a sense of direction, or at least the sense that there is direction, in life, however dimly we may see it refracted in our finitude and frailty. The elusiveness is fundamental to the reality of salvation. This has important implications for our expectations regarding it.

The comprehensive scope of salvation requires that our articulations of it be proleptic, poetic, symbolic.[48] It has become conventional wisdom in non-fundamentalist theological circles to assume the symbolic nature of theological language. Nowhere is this more vital than in this matter of salvation. Too strident claims for particular visions of salvation can trivialize the whole issue; whereas too nebulous views of what is involved can dissipate any interest and concern. As a matter subject to symbolic representation, salvation involves a particular sense of what is finally important and dependable in life, which includes the built-in realization that expressions of that sense are inevitably inadequate and provisional. The significance of any renewed theological appreciation of salvation will depend on its ability to convey such a sense of the living reality of salvation that it overflows the images and stories by which it is articulated. Only thus is there any prospect of salvation regaining credibility in the wake of secular cynicism and the bewilderment of religious pluralism.

As salvation must overflow our language, simultaneously authenticating it and exposing its inadequacy, so too, it must encompass and transcend the engrossing problems and projects that have come to occupy such a prominent place in contemporary neoliberal theological circles. To identify salvation with social causes is as detrimental to salvation as equating it with particular images by which it has been identified. Yet many who would be horrified at the thought of literalizing symbols perform this parallel operation by absolutizing a cherished social cause. John Updike notes this contemporary transference of religious fervor: "This generation, which by and large has lost all inculturated instinct for the Judaeo–Christian sacral, has displaced much of its religiousity onto antipollution, ranging from the demand for smoke-free zones in restaurants to violent demonstrations in front of nuclear power plants."[49] The Judaeo–Christian sacral casts a long shadow over the way we live and organize our lives, but that shadow is not the substance. The reality to which it testifies ultimately transcends even the injustices that loom so large in our present. Any renewal of appreciation of salvation will depend on recovering something of the Judaeo–Christian sacral itself, the sense of salvation as a comprehensive destiny that informs, but exceeds, the involvements and frustrations of the present.

Salvation may have desirable repercussions, rendering us better people, inspiring more just social structures, eliciting greater sensitivity to the world that sustains us, but these results are secondary. It would be disastrous to promote salvation as the means to these desirable, and perhaps even necessary, ends of human life. The only essential argument for salvation is the reality itself. This is the experience of people of the major religious traditions. Whatever its bearing on what we do or what we believe, salvation is first and foremost a compelling comprehensive reality.

Part One
The Salvation Legacy

2

Salvation and the Bible

It is surely beyond dispute that the Bible as a whole is preoccupied with the topic of salvation. The Old Testament in its history, hymns, and prophetic challenges constantly harkens back to the deliverance from Egypt as the saving event that established the people Israel and looks forward beyond the disastrous history climaxed in the Babylonian exile to a new age when the day of the Lord shall come to establish justice and peace. In the New Testament eschatological hopes and apocalyptlc visions narrow down to focus on the individual Israelite, Jesus of Nazareth, and these broaden out again in the claim that through Him God offers salvation to the whole world.

Apparently from a very early stage, the first Christians identified the gospel by this term *salvation*. In testifying before the spiritual leaders in Jerusalem in the embryonic stage of the Christian community, Peter is presented as assuring these leaders that "There is salvation in no one else, for there is no other name under Heaven given among men by which we must be saved" (Acts 4:12). Not surprisingly, Paul also is presented as referring to his proclamation as "the message of salvation" (Acts 13:26) and seeing His mission as being to "bring salvation to the outermost parts of the earth" (13:47). In his own letters, Paul describes the gospel as "the power of God for salvation to everyone who has faith" (Rom. 1:16) and assures the Corinthians that "if we are afflicted it is for your comfort and salvation" (II Cor. 1:6) which affliction is a sharing "in Christ's sufferings." The Thessalonians are assured that "God chose you from the beginning to be saved" (II Thess. 2:13).

It is difficult to avoid the conclusion that salvation was a pivotal expression for the early Christians. "It became, probably very early, a technical term to sum up all the blessings brought about by the gospel."[1] Yet although the term occupies a central place in the early Christian vocabulary, there has not been unanimous agreement that it occupies a legitimate place. Since the emergence of modern historical consciousness in the last century, there have been influential complaints that, rather than representing a summation of Christian faith, the concept of salvation has functioned to obscure and displace the original gospel proclaimed and practiced by Jesus. One of the most dramatic versions of this charge identifies Paul as the villain of the piece. Whereas Jesus proclaimed and lived a straightforward message of the love of God that evokes a responsive love to God and neighbor, Paul replaced this by an elaborate scheme involving a preexistent being coming to earth and appeasing divine displeasure over sin so that we might be forgiven. As salvation has come to be identified with this latter transaction, the personal gospel of divine love, which speaks to us directly, and challenges our actual living, has been displaced by this theoretical explanation of the significance of Jesus. Thus, rather than expressing the reality of the experience of the gospel, salvation has been relegated to the realms of abstract orthodoxy.

The Recovery of Jesus Behind Paul

The Christian faith is centered in a massive transformation. It is not the transformation of the individual from unrepentant sinner to believer saved by grace, or the transformation of unjust social structures to forms that are institutional expressions of fairness and opportunity, but rather a transformation that underlies both of these latter types insofar as they claim Christian sponsorship. It is the shift in the understanding of Jesus whereby he is transformed from the proclaimer of a message to the subject of a message. The amazing fact at the heart of the Christian phenomenon is that the early Christians did not concentrate on promoting the teachings of Jesus. They did this to some extent, of course, and the Gospels provide some reflection of this dimension of early Christian concern. But insofar as the teachings of Jesus are presented, this is done in the context of a more fundamental presentation regarding Jesus himself. He is proclaimed as the Messiah, the Son of God, the Savior. It would seem that this development is unique in religious history. Even in the cosmopolitan atmosphere of the present, where we are wary of the potential parochialism of distinctively Christian claims, it is difficult to avoid the conclusion that the claims made about Jesus by early Christians have no parallel in pre-Christian religion and hence post-Christian approximations have to be suspect of coming under Christian influence.[2] The point of stressing this uniqueness is not to foster claims of superiority, but to appreciate how integral this is to the development of Christianity itself. In large measure, Christianity is a religion about Jesus rather than a religion of Jesus.

But this difference is precisely what critics of the gospel of salvation view of Christianity find offensive. They regard this transformation of the gospel of Jesus into a gospel about Jesus as an illegitimate fabrication on the part of the early Church. Under the inspiration of modern historical sensibility they have attempted to get behind this doctrinal church gospel to the genuine living gospel of Jesus.

THE HISTORY OF RELIGIONS VERSION

The apex of confidence in historical method as the avenue to understanding, and, in particular, to understanding the essential nature of the Christian religion, was probably reached in the History of Religions School, which emerged in Germany toward the end of the nineteenth century. Seeing Christianity as one instance of the wider phenomenon called religion, this school tended to account for the more distinctive features of Christianity in terms of beliefs and practices in other contemporary religions in the immediate surroundings in which Christianity developed. "Through the creative imagination of the community, under the spell of the Hellenistic Mysteries, the gospel of Jesus has been replaced by a religion of salvation centering in a mystery cult of the Christ as *Kyrios*."[3] The direct impact and message of Jesus has been all but obliterated by the early Christians succumbing to the influence of neighboring mystery cults and transforming Jesus into the heavenly Christ who comes to earth like the dying and rising gods of these mystery rites. The person held most responsible for this perversion of the gospel was the Apostle Paul, and the History of Religions charge against Paul is articulated most succinctly and forcibly by William Wrede.

So great is Paul's influence on the development of the Christian faith that, according to Wrede, he can be regarded as *"the second founder of Christianity."*[4] Citing some of the most influential molders of Christian thought from the early Fathers through the Reformers, Wrede contends: "The backbone of Christianity for all of them was the history of salvation; they lived for that which they shared with Paul."[5] What Paul added was this understanding of Christianity as a religion of salvation. "Paul's whole innovation is comprised in this, that *he laid the foundation of religion in these acts of salvation, in the incarnation, death, and resurrection of Christ.*"[6] Wrede concedes that Paul cannot have been totally original. There must have been similarities with the early Christian community in Jerusalem, but he contends that while the latter was centered on the "event of salvation" constituted by the confirmation of Jesus as the Messiah through the experience of the resurrection, Paul developed this common conviction in a particular mythical direction.[7] The confirmed Messiah becomes a heavenly being who "forsakes heaven, veils himself in humanity and then dies, in order to ascend again into heaven."[8] In place of the moral challenge presented by Jesus, we have a religion of salvation focused on concepts like incarnation and atonement.[9] The result is an unbridgeable gulf between Jesus and Paul.

Where Jesus focused on individuals, seeking to expose them to the direct claim of God upon them, Paul interposes his elaborate scheme of salvation. "In Paul the central point is a divine act, in history but transcending history, or a complex of such acts, which impart to all mankind a ready-made salvation."[10] Salvation no longer consists in knowing and obeying God as known in Jesus, but in believing certain things about Jesus himself, that he was divine, that he achieved reconciliation between God and humanity so that forgiveness of sins and eternal life are thereby assured. Wrede asks and immediately answers the question as to what the scheme of salvation has to do with Jesus himself. "Of that which is to Paul all and everything, how much does Jesus know? Nothing whatever."[11] In fact, as Wrede sees it, Paul is further from Jesus than Jesus is from Judaism.[12] Thus, what Wrede is really saying is that Jesus is perfectly understandable against the background of Judaism, and would probably have remained thus understood had not the apostle to the gentiles launched his mission in the wider gentile world and developed a theology to match. There can be no doubt about the success of Paul's formulation. Wrede insists that it must be respected in light of its massive influence over the centuries.[13] But this does not make it any less devoid of legitimacy as an interpretation of the significance of Jesus. If we start from the other end and consider the teachings of Jesus, it would never occur to us, Wrede suggests, to develop a schemata such as Paul elaborates. "No one who set out to describe the religion which lives in the sayings and similitudes of Jesus could hit by any chance on the phrase 'religion of redemption'."[14] The irony is that in developing this "religion of redemption," and its being endorsed by the councils and creeds of the Church, Paul has in fact displaced Jesus rather than promoting him; "he has thrust that greater person, whom he meant only to serve, utterly into the background."[15]

How was it possible for Paul to effect this massive transformation, to create Christianity as a religion of redemption in unwitting defiance of the directness of Jesus himself? The answer Wrede thinks is that Paul had his scheme in place before he encountered the Christian message. If not in detail, at least in basic direction, the Pauline Christology must be seen to predate Paul's own embracing of Christianity. Thus "the Pauline Christ cannot be understood unless we assume that Paul, while still a Pharisee, possessed a number of definite conceptions concerning a divine being, which were afterward transferred to the historical Jesus."[16] The explanation of the significance of Jesus advanced by Paul was in no way drawn from Jesus himself. Whether from Jewish apocalyptic or Hellenistic Mysteries, Paul had in some way acquired this vision before he encountered Christianity. Indeed, the fact that he did not encounter Jesus, but was encountered by the risen Christ, is the source of his opportunity to impose this alien framework on the original gospel. "The 'revelation' freed him from the fetters of tradition in which the members of the mother community were bound; it gave him the power to make a new beginning."[17] It is thus that Paul became the "second founder of Christianity," and, by far, the more influential one in molding the gentile religion, which has prevailed over the centuries. But in so doing he obscured the direct and challenging original gospel of Jesus.

THE LIBERAL VERSION

Although Wrede represents the more radical return to the historical Jesus, the better known version is that of Adolf von Harnack. Harnack is generally taken as the epitome of the liberal quest of the historical Jesus that dominated the nineteenth century. He himself did not produce yet another life of Jesus in the train of biographies that emerged throughout the century, but he did espouse the historical method and gave it theological dignity by making it central for the reconstruction of the whole sweep of Christian thought.

The generally endorsed reading of Harnack sees him promoting Jesus the Teacher against Jesus the Savior of ecclesiastical orthodoxy. The original message of the authoritative Teacher, obscured by Christian dogma, is found in his *Das Wesen des Christentums* (1900), in which Harnack professed to indicate the *essence* of

Christianity, although the English translation loses this in rendering the title in interrogative form, *What is Christianity?* (1901):

> If . . . we take a general view of Jesus' teaching, we shall see that it may be grouped under three heads. They are each of such a nature as to contain the whole, and hence it can be exhibited in its entirety under any one of them.
> *Firstly, the kingdom of God and its coming.*
> *Secondly, God the Father and the infinite value of the human soul.*
> *Thirdly, the higher righteousness and the commandment of love.*[18]

The suggestion that any one of these three basic affirmation entails the others and thus epitomizes the whole gospel indicates the central thrust of Harnack's position. Jesus the Teacher serves to bring together God and the individual soul. A familiar summary of the gospel is provided by Harnack in the first volume of his seven volume *History of Dogma.* "The Gospel is the grand message of the government of the world and of every individual soul by the almighty and holy God, the Father and Judge."[19] This is the kingdom Jesus proclaimed. It is not essentially a political entity, but a personal one:

> The kingdom of God comes by coming to the individual, by entering into his soul and laying hold of it. True, the kingdom of God is the rule of God; but it is the rule of the holy God in the hearts of individuals; *it is God himself in his power.*[20]

This brings us to a dimension of Harnack, which may be missed, or at least minimized, in the contrast between Teacher and Savior. To identify Jesus as Teacher tends to focus attention on his message. Thus the essence of the gospel proposed by Harnack tends to be equated with the three basic principles already mentioned. However, to stop at this level is to attribute to Harnack precisely what he wished to avoid. "It is not a question of a 'doctrine' being handed down by uniform repetition or arbitrarily distorted; it is a question of a *life* again and again kindled afresh, and now burning with a flame of its own."[21] This is Harnack's central concern. This is the essence of Christianity. "The essence of the matter is a personal life which awakens life around it as the fire of one torch kindles another."[22] In fact, the teaching of Jesus is not particularly original at all. "It is the Person, it is the fact of his life that is new and creates the new."[23]

If the essence of Christianity is to be found in the person of Jesus, rather than in his teaching, where then is the quarrel with the traditional interpretation? Harnack can hardly castigate Paul for transferring attention from the message to the person of Jesus, as Wrede does, when he himself insists that it is the person which is central. And in fact, Harnack does not castigate Paul at all. Rather, in Harnack's writings, Paul comes across as the great interpreter of the faith, the first Protestant, rather than the second founder of Christianity. He is affirmed as "the one who understood the master and continued his work."[24] Paul's essential contribution was not to transform Christianity but to transplant it, moving it beyond the confines of Judaism into the wider Greco–Roman world. And he accomplished this without compromising the essence of the Gospel. "Without doing violence to the inner and essential features of the Gospel—unconditional trust in God as the Father of Jesus Christ, confidence in the Lord, forgiveness of sins, certainty of eternal life, purity and brotherly fellowship—Paul transformed it into the universal religion, and laid the ground for the great Church."[25] This is where the problem emerges. The distortion of Christianity is essentially due to the emergence of doctrine, and this in turn is traced to the influence of the Greco–Roman environment into which Christianity spread, that is, to the process of Hellenization. In this context, another name for Hellenization is dogmatization; "the philosophical means which were used in early times for the purpose of making the Gospel intelligible have been fused with the contents of the Gospel and raised to dogma."[26] It is important to note, however, that Harnack does not simply equate Hellenization with dogma. In protesting that in his definition, which stipulates that "dogma in its conception and development is a work of the Greek spirit on the soil of the Gospel," the words "on the soil of the Gospel" are often overlooked, Harnack insists that "the foolishness of identifying dogma and Greek philosophy never entered my mind."[27] The problem is not simply that the original gospel has been displaced by Greek dogma, but that the dogmas used to express the gospel, inspired by the Greek spirit, have become the centre of attention as ends in themselves, rather than functioning as vehicles for articulating the gospel, as originally intended. This is what allows Harnack to absolve Paul of direct responsibility for this state of affairs.

As Harnack sees it, there have been two major transitions in the understanding of the gospel, the transition from Jesus to the first generation of believers, including Paul, who were themselves Jews, and the transition from this first generation to Gentile Christians.[28] It is this latter transition which has been most disastrous for Christianity. It has led to the ecclesiastical dogmatism of Catholic Christianity that veils the impact of Jesus through insisting on affirming correct dogmas about his person as the Christ.[29] This transition was a rather protracted process, culminating in the councils and creeds of orthodox Christianity.[30] Paul's complicity in it is confined to the role of unwitting catalyst. He himself was little influenced by the Greek spirit, but he used Greek ideas for apologetic purposes, and these ideas came to have greater intrinsic significance for Paul's successors than he himself intended.[31] The fact that Paul's writings were included in the New Testament canon gave the theological concepts he used legitimacy in the formative period of Christian dogma.[32] It was the failure of gentile Christians to distinguish between these concepts and the reality they were meant to convey, which was a misunderstanding of Paul, which resulted in the distortions of dogmatism.[33] Where Paul recognizes the foolishness of dogma on its own, gentile Christians came to prize it for its own sake. "The characteristic of this dogma is that it represents itself in no sense as foolishness, but as wisdom, and at the same time desires to be regarded as the contents of revelation itself."[34]

The difficulty then is not dogma per se, which is necessary to give expression to the gospel if we are to think about it at all, but the equation of dogma with the gospel. However, this distinction is not as simple as it might appear because it has two elements, the second of which brings us back to dogma itself. The initial concern is that dogma not be allowed to foreclose "the sphere of personal experience and inner reformation."[35] But to avoid this in the case of the Christian gospel involves concern about particular dogmas themselves, and not just the abuse of dogma. It is not enough that the experience of redemption retain preeminence over its articulation:

> If redemption is to be traced to Christ's person and work, everything would seem to depend upon a right understanding of this person together with what he accomplished. *The formation of a correct theory of and about Christ threatens to assume the position of first importance, and to pervert the majesty and simplicity of the Gospel.*[36]

With this, Harnack approaches the most distinctive aspect of his own position. The "simplicity of the Gospel," which is threatened by concern over "the formation of a correct theory about Christ" is the gospel of Jesus himself that has been displaced by the development of Christology. The starkest, and probably the best known statement of this in Harnack runs as follows: "*The Gospel, as Jesus proclaimed it, has to do with the Father only and not with the*

Son."[37] Jesus' concern was to bring people into personal relation with God. Christian orthodoxy diverted that purpose by focusing on Jesus himself, and making belief in him as Son of God and Savior the central issue. In summation of the tradition of liberal protestant theology from Schleiermacher, Harnack identifies the meaning of referring to Jesus as Son of God with his consciousness of God. "The consciousness which he possesses of being the *Son of God* is, therefore, nothing but the practical consequence of knowing God as the Father and as His Father."[38] The gospel is the good news that God was really known by Jesus and through him can be known by us, if we give ourselves to the direction proclaimed and practiced by him. Unfortunately, Christian orthodoxy focused attention on Jesus himself and blocked rather than promulgated this gospel by the dogmatic abstractions of Christology.

THE LIBERATION VERSION

The concern to get back to Jesus behind the theology of the early Church in general, or Paul in particular, which characterized the nineteenth century, has suffered what would appear to be fatal blows in this century. However, in recent years a new variation on the nineteenth century concern has emerged in the form of Latin American liberation theology. One survey of the leading pioneers of this theology, for instance, notes how liberation theology concentrates on the Jesus of history rather than the Christ of faith.[39] This author goes on to quote one of the more radical of these pioneers of liberation theology: "Assman is absolutely accurate, then, when he says that Christology is one of the most dramatic of the gaps in the theology of liberation in Latin America."[40] The only sustained venture in systematic Christology is Jon Sobrino's *Christology at the Cross Roads: A Latin American Approach*,[41] which attempts an inductivist Christology from the synoptics.[42]

To Harnack's concern with Hellenization, and to Wrede's with Pauline speculation, liberation theology adds the suspicion of ideology. The historical consciousness that led the nineteenth century to look for origins has been turned upon ourselves in this century so that we have become acutely self-conscious about our own historicity. We have learned that we see life as we do because of our particular location, and that the understanding we develop is inevitably shaped by the interests of that position. Since theology has been the preserve of favored Westerners, it has served to bolster and sacralize Western imperialism. The problem with Paul and orthodoxy in general is not simply abstraction, but naive abstraction. In diverting its energies into the pursuit of doctrinal accuracy, the Church lost sight of the interests this direction was serving. The result was that the Church developed as an institution serving its own interests; not simply representing a preserve removed from the ongoing concerns of human life, but an elaborate system of polity and doctrine that rapidly became an end in itself. This naïveté really involved a double blindness because in not noticing the dominance of its own interests, the Church readily succumbed to the interests of the political powers of the day and so forged alliances which served short-term ecclesiastical interests of security in return for providing a veneer of divine endorsement for political regimes.

The irony of this route that Christianity has taken is that it represents the very opposite direction to that portrayed in the Gospels. "Jesus categorically refused to inaugurate a kingdom based on power and its use."[43] The way of Jesus is the way of service; not the way of domination. Liberation theology thus represents yet another version of a return to the gospel of Jesus behind the gospel of ecclesiastical theology. The focus is not on Jesus' person and work, as in traditional Christian theology, but on what Jesus himself was concerned about, the kingdom. In this respect, liberation theology is an extension of nineteenth century protestant liberalism. Thus, in what is generally regarded as the charter document of Latin American liberation theology, Gustavo Gutierrez's *A Theology of Liberation*,[44] the index lists various references under "Jesus" and also under "Christ", but the only reference to Paul follows the heading "Paul VI, Pope".

However, liberation theology cannot simply be equated with the historical return to Jesus of nineteenth century Protestant liberalism. As an essentially Catholic movement, liberation theology draws on a fundamental sacramental base. Thus we find Gutierrez saying things like the following: "The first task of the Church is to celebrate with joy the gift of the salvific action of God in humanity, accomplished through the death and resurrection of Christ."[45] Liberation theology shares with liberal theology the concern to take the humanity of Jesus with utmost seriousness. Descriptions of Jesus in terms of a God-consciousness, which render him a virtually transparent manifestation of the love of God,[46] could have been lifted wholesale from prominent liberal theologians. But just when the link with liberalism seems most strict, the sacramental base erupts with an implicit recognition of the inadequacy of the dedication to historicism that characterized the nineteenth century. Yet whatever we finally make of liberation theology, it ensures that the interest in the historical Jesus is still very much with us.

The Recovery of Paul Between Us and Jesus

Insofar as liberation theology advocates a return to Jesus' gospel of the kingdom behind the ideological gospel of the Church, it ignores some very dramatic reversals suffered by the attempt to found Christianity on a secure historical base. From several directions, it has been argued to the point of widespread consensus from the end of the nineteenth century on that this historical project failed, that its failure was inevitable, and that it was misguided in principle.

THE FAILURE OF THE RETURN TO JESUS—SCHWEITZER

The attempt of the nineteenth century to apply the new historical consciousness to the origins of Christianity has come to be known by the title of the English translation of a book by Albert Schweitzer surveying that attempt, *The Quest of the Historical Jesus*.[47] In the original edition of this work in 1906, Schweitzer examined some 250 authors who, in one way or another, had attempted to get back to the historical Jesus. His conclusion is that this quest has turned out to be the epitome of negative theology. "There is nothing more negative than the result of the critical study of the Life of Jesus."[48] Rather than recovering Jesus as he actually was, what has been produced is a series of lives of Jesus which are more indicative of the biographers themselves than of their subject:

> The Jesus of Nazareth who came forward publicly as the Messiah, who preached the ethic of the Kingdom of God, who founded the Kingdom of Heaven upon earth, and died to give His work its final consecration, never had any existence. He is a figure designed by rationalism, endowed with life by liberalism, and clothed by modern theology in an historical garb.[49]

The search for the first century Jesus found a nineteenth century rationalist who confirmed the most cherished insights of the age, the Messiah of the Moral Kingdom.

The problem with the quest was that it unwittingly but ardently cut the pattern of Jesus to fit its own humanistic cloth:

> The mistake was to suppose that Jesus could come to mean more to our time by entering into it as a man like ourselves. That is not possible. First because such a Jesus never existed. Secondly, because, although historical knowledge can no doubt introduce greater clearness into an existing spiritual life, it cannot call spiritual life into existence.[50]

The attempt to capture Jesus in the snares of modern historical science failed because it could only capture a being of modern historical proportions. It could not deal with the spiritual being who reaches out to us across the centuries. However, in asserting this, Schweitzer himself is attributing a certain success to the historical quest. Although the biographies of Jesus it produced were variations of nineteenth century versions of Jesus, this exposes the elusive greatness of Jesus as a figure transcending historical categories:

> He was not a teacher, not a casuist; He was an imperious ruler. It was because He was so in his inmost being that He could think of Himself as the Son of Man.[51]

Historical research brings us to this being who transcends history. The resulting portrait is sketched by Schweitzer in the memorable closing words of his book:

> He comes to us as One unknown, without a name, as of old, by the lake-side, He came to those men who knew him not. He speaks to us the same word: "Follow thou me!" and sets us to the tasks which He has to fulfill for our time. He commands. And to those who obey Him, whether they be wise or simple, He will reveal Himself in the toils, the conflicts, the sufferings which they shall pass through in his fellowship, and as an ineffable mystery, they shall learn in their own experience Who He is.[52]

Schweitzer himself had more specific ideas about Jesus, which depicted him in terms of the eschatological expectations of his age. But leaving these aside, this basic suggestion of an understanding of Jesus, which runs into "ineffable mystery," sounds very similar to the language of Paul. Schweitzer himself did not develop this theologically so much as existentially in obeying the "Follow thou me!" to the point of locating in the jungles of Africa and through the "trials, the conflicts, the sufferings" of a medical missionary learning "in his own experience Who He is." It was left to others to develop the theological implications of the failure of the quest of the historical Jesus.

THE INACCESSIBILITY OF THE HISTORICAL JESUS—KÄHLER

Although Schweitzer's demolition of the quest of the historical Jesus was more acclaimed, it had been preceded by another work that proposed an even more radical assessment of the movement and in the long run exerted more influence on the further development of Christian understanding. This was Martin Kähler's *The So-called Historical Jesus and the Historic, Biblical Christ*, first published in German in 1896.[53] Where Schweitzer documented the failure of the nineteenth century quest, Kähler asserted a dogmatic rejection of the whole attempt as misguided in principle. "I regard the entire life-of-Jesus movement as a blind alley."[54]

The reason the quest is a blind alley is that we do not have the evidence on which to base a historical reconstruction of Jesus' person and activity. In Kähler's words: "We have no sources for a biography of Jesus of Nazareth which measure up to the standards of contemporary historical science."[55] The problem is not the stringent requirements of modern historiography, but the sheer paucity of evidence. What we have is from followers of Jesus. There is virtually no independent documentation of his existence. Even the evidence we have cannot be traced with assurance to eye witnesses. And if this were not enough, such evidence as there is deals only with the latest stages of the life and career of Jesus. From a strictly historical point of view, it could even be doubted whether Jesus actually existed. "He could be taken for a product of the Church's fantasy around the year A.D. 100."[56] Kähler is not particularly disturbed by this situation, because it is implicit in the nature of the Gospels themselves. "What we do have is simply recollections, which are always at the same time confessional in nature since in presupposition and intention they always witness to something which lies beyond mere historical factuality—something which we call revelation or salvation."[57] The Gospels are kerygmatic, preaching documents rather than historical ones. "The purpose is to report not so much *what* happened as *who* acted, and *how*."[58] With this, we reach the central significance of Kähler's title.

The original title contrasted two German words for the historical, *historisch* and *geschichtlich*, rendered by the translator as historical and historic. The historical refers to an account of what happened, the facts of history; historic to a sense of significance in what happened. In contrast to the nineteenth century concern to get the facts, to recover the real historical Jesus, Kähler is contending that the only Jesus we know is the historic, biblical Christ. "The risen Lord is not then the historical Jesus *behind* the Gospels, but the Christ of the apostolic preaching, of the *whole* New Testament."[59] This is the range of data to which Kähler appeals, the whole New Testament, and, indeed, the whole of Christian tradition.[60] Rather than the isolated documentation of incidents or sayings, the evidence on which Christianity is based is that of the total impact of Jesus. "The real Christ, that is, the Christ who has exercised an influence in history, with whom millions have communed in childlike faith, and with whom the great witnesses of faith have been in communion—while striving, apprehending, triumphing, and proclaiming—*this real Christ is the Christ who is preached.*"[61] The historic, biblical Christ is the subject of the tradition, and it is impossible to go behind that to a recoverable historical Jesus.

The import of Kähler's position is that the questers, for all the appeal of their project, really had things backward. It might be impossible for us to appreciate fully the excitement with which those scholars, imbued with the spirit of modern critical history, anticipated recovering the reality of Jesus as he actually was.[62] Our inability to share their enthusiasm is due not only to their failure to deliver the historical Jesus, but also to the recognition that there is no historical Jesus to deliver. This is not to deny the historical existence of Jesus, but rather to recognize that we only know about Jesus because of the conviction that he is the Christ. If Jesus had matched nineteenth century expectations and turned out to be a teacher of extraordinary moral insight who disclosed the direction that God really intends for us to take as builders of the Kingdom, we might not be aware of him today; and if we were, it would undoubtedly be in a different form from that in which the New Testament and Christian tradition have proclaimed him. From the beginning, the disciples presented Jesus not as a Teacher with a crucial message, but as the Savior in whose person God had acted decisively. "It is clear that they did not later go forth into the world to make Jesus the head of a 'school' by propagating his teachings, but to witness to his person and his imperishable significance for every man."[63] It is the modern historical temper, which leads us to assume a foundational stage of Jesus as teacher, promulgating his message of the Kingdom, to which the early Christians added by inference the superstructure of the theological interpretation of him as savior. If there was some transition point at which the disciples' convictions shifted from regarding Jesus as an impressive prophet to recognizing him as the Messiah, this is lost in the mists of history. The most primitive historical fact is the proclamation of Jesus as the Christ to which the whole New Testament testifies.

"That is the situation; for the fact that we know of no form of Christian preaching older than our Bible is, from the standpoint of *historical science*, more certain than the fact that Jesus of Nazareth ever lived."[64] We cannot get behind the kerygma to some firmer historical foundation. The documents do not permit it, and the gospel does not require it.

Kähler illustrates the difference between his holistic approach and the assumptions involved in the pursuit of some independent historical foundation in terms of the way the key phrase "God is love" would be understood by each.

> We like to summarize our faith and the New Testament revelation in the words: "God is love." How did we learn to make this confession? It was not through the preaching which sounded from the Galilean hillside and was carried by messengers throughout the towns of Israel; it was not from the preaching of the Kingdom of God, however much God's love may be contained therein. This obscure metaphor—"God is love"—was first to acquire its full meaning through Christ's deeds and life. "God shows his love for us in that while we were yet sinners Christ died for us," we are reminded by Paul.[65] (Rom 5:8; cf. 8:32–39)

This reference to Paul indicates the direction that is being promoted. The hint of Pauline Christ–mysticism evident in Schweitzer is here outstripped by a more full-bodied endorsement of the Pauline gospel of salvation in Christ. This brings us to the climax of this development, the full scale vindication of Paul in contrast to the nineteenth century attempt to dispense with him in the interests of getting back to the real Jesus whom Paul had so badly misrepresented and distorted in his gospel of salvation.

THE VINDICATION OF PAUL—BULTMANN

In addition to lurking in the background as a major source of the substance of Kähler's position, Paul also fills an important function in providing the form. The English translator of Kähler's book, Carl E. Braaten, confirms this in an introductory essay, if we supply the obvious premise that Paul is the chief source of inspiration for the Reformers. "To my knowledge Kähler is the first Protestant theologian to develop a theological methodology out of the reformation doctrine of justification through faith alone."[66] In this respect, Kähler stands as one of the most underrated influences behind the giants of Protestant theology in the first half of twentieth century. In the present context, we may confine ourselves to the way in which this legacy was developed by one of those giants,

Rudolf Bultmann. Bultmann is best known for his proposal for demythologizing the New Testament. What he intends by this is contingent upon his understanding of myth. His range of references from the contrast between world views of the first century and the twentieth and the forms of expression for the central affirmations of the gospel have occasioned intense debate as to the meaning and significance of his demythologizing program. In one sense, the issue is one of translating the gospel from first century categories to those of the twentieth century. Thus, talk of divine transactions affected supernaturally is replaced by anthropological categories concerned with possibilities for authentic human existence. However, Bultmann also insists that in Christ, God acted decisively to change the human condition. His concern is that this act of God be understood eschatologically rather than mythologically. One dimension of this, the one which is most relevant here, is a protest against identifying this decisive act with any account of it. What is involved is an experiential reality, which must address us personally rather than a supernatural achievement, which can be captured in doctrinal categories. In this respect, Bultmann's dissatisfaction with mythology may appear to be very similar to Harnack's suspicion of dogma. Both are concerned with the living reality of the gospel, which is all too easily obscured by abstract conceptualizations. Yet whatever common ground Bultmann and Harnack may share, the directions of the resolutions they propose are virtually diametrically opposed. Where Harnack sought a secure foundation in the historical Jesus, Bultmann has been warned of the illusory security this offers by people like Schweitzer and Kähler, and turns in the other direction toward a reinstatement of Paul and a kerygmatic foundation in the preached message of the Christ of faith.

This restoration of Paul entails a strong reaction against the historical interest, which had underwritten the return to Jesus. What is at stake in Christianity for Bultmann does not concern the realm of history itself at all. "Christ's death and resurrection, accordingly, are cosmic occurrences, not incidents that took place once upon a time in the past."[67] This kind of phrasing has prompted considerable misunderstanding of Bultmann's position. He is often taken to be denying the historicity of the cross. But this is not his intention. His point is that as a historical event the cross is neither interesting nor accessible to believers. The cross is only significant because of its endorsement by the resurrection. But this is not accessible as an event of history either. It is available only as eschatological event. "Indeed, *faith in the resurrection is really the same thing as faith in the saving efficacy of the cross*, faith in the cross as the cross of Christ."[68] The appeal to the resurrection as a historical claim cannot be used to establish the significance of the cross because that is not where the dividing line falls. The distinction is not between the routinely historical incident of the cross and the extraordinary event of resurrection. Rather cross and resurrection belong together as eschatological events in contrast to historical claims of any kind. Thus, the person who is of interest is not the historical Jesus but the Christ of the kerygma. "Christ meets us in the preaching as one crucified and risen. He meets us in the word of preaching and nowhere else."[69]

To want to meet Christ elsewhere, such as in the precincts of historical scholarship, is not only precluded by the nature of the New Testament documents, as Kähler argued, but also is indicative of a failure of faith. Faith must rest on and in the eschatological event. Just as the cross cannot be established by the testimony of the resurrection, so our faith in the resurrection cannot rest on the faith of the first Christians who claimed to have witness it.

> We cannot buttress our own faith in the resurrection by that of the first disciples and so eliminate the element of risk which faith in the resurrection always involves. For the first disciples' faith in the resurrection is itself part and parcel of the eschatological event which is the article of faith.[70]

It is important to recognize that Bultmann is not denying the historical dimension. This is one thing that distinguishes Christianity from other religions of the ancient world. Its lord is really a historical figure. Christianity could never be purely mythical because of this rootage in history. But what Christianity actually involves can no more be derived from, or assured by, the findings of historical research than faith can be vindicated or eliminated by scientific expertise. What is at stake in Christianity, and faith itself, which are virtually two ways of saying the same thing, are eschatological matters. The Christian kerygma centers on a historical person, but it understands him as an eschatological figure. "For the kerygma maintains that the eschatological emissary of God is a concrete figure of a particular historical past, that his eschatological activity was wrought out in a human fate, and that therefore it is an event whose eschatological character does not admit of a secular proof."[71] And this is finally what preserves Christian faith from succumbing to mythology. It is concerned not with the kind of transactions that can be dealt with in historical terms, but with the

eschatological dimension that is present in but overflows historical categories. "It is precisely its immunity from proof which secures
the Christian proclamation against the charge of being mythological."[72] As a matter of faith and eschatology, the Christian
proclamation confronts us with the claim of the living God. To
want to bolster this challenge of faith with historical knowledge is
the other side of compressing the eschatological dimension of its
kerygmatic substance into the confines of mythology.

Once again we note the similarity between Bultmann and Harnack. As each was opposed to second order abstractions, whether
seen in terms of dogma or myth, so too their positive concern was
to open the way to the claim of God on the life of the believer. But
this common concern finds expression in diametrically opposite
conclusions about what Christianity involves and how that is
known. Whereas Harnack is convinced that the essence of Christianity is to be found in the gospel preached by Jesus in reflection of
his intimate awareness of God, and that this is accessible through
the methods of critical historical scholarship, which can get us behind the theological obfuscations of Church dogma, Bultmann is
equally confident that if there is any such simple gospel of Jesus,
we cannot and should not want to know it, because what the gospel involves is the eschatological claim of God on us which transcends history while participating in it. This claim is exerted on us in
the gospel of the Christ proclaimed by Paul as the expression of
the full significance of Jesus recognized by faith.

> One cannot flee from Paul and return to Jesus. For what one encoun
> ters in Jesus is the same God who is encountered in Paul—the God
> who is Creator and Judge, who claims man completely for himself, and
> who freely gives his grace to him who becomes nothing before him. All
> that one can do is to go to Jesus *through* Paul; i.e., one is asked by Paul
> whether he is willing to understand God's act in Christ as the event that
> has decided and now decides with respect both to the world and to
> us.[73]

Thus, from the expectant probings of the historical evidence that
were to get us back to the real Jesus behind the distortions of the
Church's gospel of salvation, we have come full circle back to that
gospel of salvation as the key to what Christianity really involves.
From this position reached by the middle of the twentieth century,
the succeeding decades have been occupied with resolving the
stalemate between these essentially mutually exclusive positions.

The Dialectic of Jesus and Paul

The recovery of respect for the kerygmatic Christ exposed the attempt to get back to the real Jesus as a rather crass, and even positivistic, project that was sponsored by a reductionist view of history and a misunderstanding of the nature of the gospel. Far from being subject to objective documentation, history ultimately involves the level of personal events that engage us as whole persons and not simply as academic scholars. It is not simply *Historie* but *Geschichte*, and, when the religious dimension is at stake, the personal dimension is further caught up in the eschatological. Similarly, the gospel is not a perpetuation of the message of Jesus but a proclamation about Jesus himself and the activity of God that was effected in him. Thus, the developments that have dominated the first half of the twentieth century have amounted to a recovery of the breadth and depth of historic Christianity, which was so severely undervalued by the nineteenth century enthusiasm over the prospect of documentable history.

This recovery, however, has not been entirely problem free. When Kähler says of Jesus, for example, that "He could be taken for a product of the Church's fantasy around the year A.D. 100,"[74] we might see in this an indication that the corrective has become reactionary. In contrast to the nineteenth century assumption that the origins of Christianity are to be found in the historical Jesus, the recovery of the Pauline type of gospel has so focused on the early Christian community as the molder of the message that one is often left with the impression that Jesus must have been the most unoriginal person who ever lived. The kerygma is so associated with the early Church that Jesus recedes into the background often to the point of disappearing, as Kähler's reference indicates. Not surprisingly, this swing of the pendulum has evoked a response since the midpoint of the twentieth century from scholars who insist that there has been an overreaction to the quest of the historical Jesus, and that the preoccupation with the kerygmatic Christ must be balanced by some chastened kind of quest of the Jesus who is the subject of the kerygma.

THE NEW QUEST ATTEMPT TO BALANCE PAUL AND JESUS

Critics, and in many cases students, of Bultmann have attempted to establish links between the *kerygma* of the early Church and the historical Jesus. Dissatisfied with procedures that either absorb or displace the historical Jesus by the kerygma, they have attempted to detect approximations to the kerygma in the sayings and behavior of Jesus as this comes through in the Gospels. In some cases the link that is established is very direct. Joachim Jeremias, for example, finds the kerygma contained in the teachings of Jesus himself.

> Every verse of the Gospels tells us that the origin of Christianity lies not in the kerygma, not in the resurrection experiences of the disciples, not in a "Christ idea." Every verse tells us, rather, that the origin of Christianity lies in the appearance of the man who was crucified under Pontius Pilate, Jesus of Nazareth, and in his message.[75]

The gospel is not the product of the early Church. Nor can it be attributed to the dramatic impact of the resurrection on the first disciples. Still less is it to be considered on the level of ideas as though it were some variation on ancient philosophies. The source of the gospel is located in the person of Jesus himself, especially in his teaching, where the whole of the kerygma can be seen in embryo.

The direct link Jeremias argues for between the early Christian kerygma and the historical Jesus may be too powerful for the requirements of the position he wishes to promote. It assumes that the gospel derives from Jesus himself, but it virtually equates the gospel with the teachings of the historical Jesus. This does not allow much scope for the "historical" events of the crucifixion and resurrection of Jesus, which however understood, must be regarded as experiences that impinged on the early community in ways they could not have affected Jesus himself. As a more direct representative of the new quest of the historical Jesus, Ernst Fuchs, puts it: "As soon as the interest of research is concerned with the historical Jesus, one must basically reckon with the fact that the early Christian kerygma of the crucified and risen Lord not only says something that Jesus did not say, but also adds something new that Jesus could not have said."[76] Whereas the reaction against the reductionist tendency in the original quest went too far in the other direction in its inclination to attribute the gospel to the early Church, the role of the community must not be overlooked, particularly when the gospel centered so definitely in claims about the significance of Jesus himself. The new quest does not typically expect to establish direct continuity between Jesus and the Christian kerygma. Rather it seeks hints of the kerygma in the teachings and actions of Jesus as these are conveyed by the evangelists.

The difference between the new quest and its nineteenth century predecessor is categorical. Where the original quest attempted to establish discontinuity between the theology of the Church which focused on Jesus as the Christ and the historical person of Jesus himself, the new quest seeks to determine whether there are hints of continuity so that the proclamation of the early Church can be seen to be grounded in Jesus himself. "Hence the purpose of a new quest of the historical Jesus would be to test the validity of the kerygma's identification of *its* understanding of existence with *Jesus'* existence."[77] Besides attempting to identify continuity between Jesus and the kerygma, the new quest differs also in that it assumes a gestalt type of picture of Jesus that comes through the Gospels, rather than the strictly inductivist piece by piece accumulation of isolated fragments of information prized by the nineteenth century veneration of facts. Not that this holistic vision is directly accessible. It can only come through the reports of individual teachings and encounters. But it is the total impression that gives the individual instances meaning just as it is these instances which provide the material for the overall picture.

> One seeks an encounter with the whole person, comparable to the totality of interpretation one has in the *kerygma*. Yet the totality of the person is not to be found in terms of chronological and developmental continuity, which is not only unattainable, but also is a different order of "wholeness" from that needed to draw a comparison with the *kerygma*. Rather the whole person is reached through encounter with individual sayings and actions in which Jesus' intention and self-hood are latent. Hence the relation of each saying or scene to the whole would be a problem of constant relevance.[78]

The general result of this pursuit of an overall impression of Jesus is a sense of someone who could carry the weight of the kerygma. Rather than finding its origins in the convictions of the early community, or the dramatic reversal of the resurrection, important though these factors may be, the new quest finds a basis in Jesus himself for the claims that were made about him.

Implicit in the words and actions of Jesus is an embryonic Christology. At a minimum, this is there in the basic challenge Jesus presented to his contemporaries, for "nothing has been more characteristic of recent research in the past generation than the growing insight that 'Jesus' call to decision embraces a christology.'"[79] This assurance, deriving from no less a skeptic regarding the prospects for historical quests of Jesus than Bultmann has been filled out in various ways by exponents of the new quest.

Some focus on the words attributed to Jesus and find there a distinctive note of authority, which provides a connection between the claims made for Jesus and Jesus himself. Thus, for example, his distinctive use of the word "amen" in which, contrary to the conventions of his day and ours where it was and is used at the end of a prayer or reading to connote assent, he used it to preface his statements with a note of authority, "*truly*, I say to you. . . ." The same sense of mandate is evident in Jesus' behavior in the way, for example, in which he assumes the prerogative to forgive sins. At the same time this sense of divine commissioning is balanced by a constant deferral to the Father who alone is "good."

The general impression conveyed by the leading developers of the new quest is that of a Jesus who could inspire the confidence and convictions that marked the birth of the Christian faith. However, the significance of this conclusion is by no means obvious. On the one hand, it tends to place the origins of the gospel in Jesus himself rather than in the experiences or reflections of the first Christians. But if this means finding the source in the man Jesus, is this any significant advance on the position that locates it in the early community? In both cases, what we come to is a human person or persons. But is this enough to underwrite the claims of the Gospel? This is the concern that animated Bultmann. "Bultmann denies not the historical continuity between the Jesus of history and the *kerygma* but the essential continuity between the Jesus of history and the Christ of the *kerygma*."[80] Bultmann's concern is that there is a qualitative gap between the historical Jesus and the kerygmatic Christ. This cannot be bridged by historical scholarship because, for one thing, we do not know how Jesus regarded his own death. The closer we get to a position that entails an overall assessment of the significance of Jesus, such as the kerygma entails, the more difficult it is to credit Jesus with the perspective to make that overall assessment. If we object that he was not bound by the restrictions of finite mortals, then we have left the realm of historical research. From the point of view of the historian, the problem is that it is precisely those points where the words of Jesus are most in line with the message of the early Church that we have to be most suspicious of their originating with the early Church rather than with Jesus himself.[81] New questers generally accept Bultmann's criteria of eliminating sayings and teachings that could be derived from contemporary Jewish sources and those that bear an obvious stamp of the early Christian community. Even with these standards, they find an undercurrent of historical impression that speaks of the formative impact of Jesus on the followers who reported and articulated his story. Bultmann's concern with this recalcitrant historical element is that it may just as easily undermine faith as secure it If we can explain why the first Christians developed the convictions they did about Jesus, this may be a way of exposing their naïveté rather than of accrediting their wisdom.

This disagreement between Bultmann and the advocates of the new quest, many of whom are his former students, over the relation between faith and history, finally amounts to a divergence over the understanding of the nature of faith itself. Bultmann's perspective requires that faith be totally autonomous, unsupported by any external pillars such as historical scholarship. If faith could be substantiated by scholarship, then theologians would occupy a favored position, whereas the truth is that theologians have something of a liability in that there is the constant temptation to make their scholarship the ground of faith rather than its means of clarification. This reversal was exemplified by the nineteenth century attempt to get back to the historical Jesus and, for Bultmann, advocates of the new quest have failed to appreciate the dangers implicit in this interest. To want to shore up faith with historical evidence is itself a sign of lack of faith. The final inspiration behind Bultmann's position is thus, the apostle Paul. The suspicion of historical research is not ultimately grounded in the lack of documentation or the nature of the Gospels' accounts, but in the Pauline contrast between faith and works. Bultmann and other contemporaries such as Paul Tillich may be understood more accurately than they often are if it is seen that they are motivated by a concern to develop the epistemological implications of justification by faith. Just as Luther renewed the Pauline concern that the justification by the grace of God known in faith not be compromised by the attempt to justify ourselves by good works, so these twentieth century heirs of the Reformation have become aware that this very concern is subject to a more subtle perversion in the form of an intellectual variation. The centrality of faith in the justification by faith emphasis can encourage a preoccupation with correct belief, which is really an intellectual form of pursuing good works. If we are justified through faith, this must be pure faith, uncorrupted by the compromises of scholarly pretensions.

Practitioners of the new quest are not necessarily any less admirers of Paul than Bultmann was. They certainly do not contrast Jesus and Paul as did many exponents of the original quest. As we have seen, their aim is rather to seek points of continuity between impressions we can glean about Jesus himself and the gospel proclaimed by the early Church. Many would even endorse Bultmann's basic contention that the appreciation and acceptance of the gospel is finally a matter of faith, and that this cannot be guaranteed by any kind of evidence. It is a total commitment, which embraces us, and which we embrace, ultimately indivisible into components like evidence and probability estimates. However, they insist on the legitimacy of a new quest because they contend that although faith is total and ultimate in its own right, it does not occur in a vacuum. Furthermore, it is not Paul who is the chief inspirer of faith but Jesus. Consequently, any endorsement of Paul must be seen to be finally grounded in the reality of Jesus himself.

CONTINUITY AND CONTRASTS BETWEEN JESUS AND PAUL

Accepting the fact that we only know Jesus through the accounts of believers who proclaim him as the Christ, and that as a consequence it is impossible to say with certainty that an account of any particular teaching or action is an accurate reflection of the historical Jesus, it is nevertheless possible to gain an overall impression of the figure who launched the faith and to detect a fundamental kinship between him and the gospel proclaimed by the supposedly second founder of Christianity, the apostle Paul. To discount this possibility would entail attributing the distinctive features of the gospel to the early community itself. This would amount to identifying central themes and forms as communal products. The incredulity this fosters is due to the unity of these central themes and forms. It is much more reasonable to see them as reflections of a single source, namely the person to whom they are attributed, Jesus of Nazareth. Such a central theme, for example, is the Kingdom of God, which recurs again and again in sayings attributed to Jesus. A central form is the parable in which the homeyness of the teaching makes it understandable that the common people would have heard him gladly. In order to establish connections between themes prominent in Jesus' teaching and the claims made by the gospel of the early community, as articulated especially by Paul, we might consider a more directly pertinent theme such as the "Son of Man" references, which occur almost exclusively in sayings attributed to Jesus himself. However, rather than become involved in the controversy surrounding this term, in questions as to what Jesus meant by it, and whether and how he meant it to be applied to himself, we shall focus on the less abstruse theme of the kingdom and the parable format by which it is often described.

At first glance Jesus' teaching about the kingdom and Paul's gospel of salvation in Christ do not appear to have much in common. As some of the more prominent advocates of the return to the historical Jesus would have put it: The kingdom refers to the recognition of the immediate claim of God on our lives, whereas Paul developed an abstract theology of salvation that ascribed divine status and significance to the person and accomplishment of Jesus himself. And yet, if we consider the images of the kingdom offered by Jesus' parables, the gap between Jesus and Paul may not appear so formidable. Taking kingdom in the conventional sense of territory or duly constituted authority, the central message would appear to be that God is about to take over the wayward creation and the gospel then appears as the invitation to get on the winning side. But, of course, this is not the kingdom proclaimed in the parables of Jesus. Quite the contrary, it challenges our basic assumption about what winning entails. The kingdom is a kind of rule that accepts the wayward without question to the horror of conscientious elder brothers, a way which delights in the humble penitence of the confessing sinner and is offended by the pretensions of innocence by the pillars of righteousness. When we consider this inversion of our normal perspective that the kingdom proclaimed in the parables of Jesus entails, the language of Paul does not appear so foreign. It is, perhaps, more accurately regarded as Paul Ricoeur presents it, as "translation language," which renders the kingdom language of the parables more general.[82] Paul's gospel of divine acceptance to be received by grace is particularly compatible with Jesus' parable of the pharisee and the publican.[83] In Pauline terms, the pharisee is putting his trust in his own righteousness whereas the publican is appealing to the righteousness that is available only to faith. A similar reading could be taken from the parable of the prodigal son and the elder brother, and be extended to most, if not all, of the remaining parables.

But if there is such compatibility between the teaching of Jesus and the gospel of Paul, why all the fuss about Paul obscuring or perverting the gospel of Jesus? And what did Paul actually add to what Jesus had already said? If Paul's theology could simply be equated with the message of Jesus, the significance of Paul would be reduced to his historical role of extending the nascent Christian movement to the wider gentile world. But, of course, Paul's significance is much wider than this, important though his apostolic role is. He was also highly influential as a theologian. Although it is extravagant to call him "the second founder of Christianity" in light of the continuity between the basic thrust of his gospel and the teachings of Jesus, it would not do either to minimize the uniqueness of his contribution. There are those who come close to echoing the epitaph assigned by Wrede, seeing in Paul the transfórmation of Christianity through its transplantation into the gentile thought forms as well as into the gentile areas. "The theology of the Jerusalem church had, of course, no future and certainly cannot be revived today, whereas the theology of Paul triumphed to such an extent that it is only with difficulty that we can recover the theology of Jerusalem."[84] We must wonder that there could be such accord between Paul and the leaders in Jerusalem, if there was such a contrast in their theologies. Johannes Munck suggests that the point of division is not between Paul and the early Jewish band of Christians, but between Paul and his fellow Christian Jews on the one hand and non-Christian Jews on the other. "It comes to this, that they represented an entirely Jewish point of view, which could not be Jewish at all if they believed that the crucified Jesus was the same as the coming messiah."[85] To recognize the crucified as the Messiah, the Christ, was to transcend the stumbling block that the cross represented for Jewish understanding. It was, in effect, to be no longer simply Jewish, but Christian. That Paul was particularly influential in formalizing this break through establishing the new religion in the gentile world should not be expanded into the attribution of the break itself to Paul as a second founder of Christianity. Munck contends that Pauline studies have remained mired in this contrast between Paul and early Jewish Christianity because of the uncritical acceptance of the distortions of F. C. Bauer and the Tübingen School, in their positing of a Petrine–Pauline antithesis between Jewish and gentile factions in early Christianity. However, as we have suggested, Paul's significance is not confined to his apostleship, but extends to his theological formulations. Although the singling out of Paul as the theologizer of the otherwise simple gospel has been overdone, his contribution in giving expression to the understanding of the Gospel toward which the community that knew the crucified as the messiah was groping must not be underestimated.

Although Paul did not singlehandedly transform the message of Jesus about the kingdom into the gospel of God's action through the Christ, he gave powerful expression to this wider perspective, which the early Christians felt constrained to embrace. It was not enough to repeat the parables and precepts of Jesus. The significance of Jesus extended beyond his words to his deeds and ultimately to his very being. In him God acted to restore alienated humanity. This is why the parable of the prodigal son is inadequate as a statement of the full depth of the Gospel. As P. T. Forsyth says, in the cross "the father not only says but pays."[86] Whatever authenticity we attribute to the passion predictions of Jesus, insofar as he was a real human being, and the Church has always insisted on this, however inadequate its implementation of that insistence, it strains the imagination to think of Jesus approaching his own death with the understanding that it had the ultimate soteriological significance attributed to it in the letters of Paul or the Epistle to the Hebrews. It seems wise to concede with Bultmann that we simply do not know how Jesus thought of his death. This is, perhaps, the point where the congeniality of the statements attributed to Jesus and the convictions of the early Church is most intense. However, this does not necessarily imply a gulf between the simple gospel of Jesus and the kerygma of the early Christians. What it does imply is a difference. In Jesus, God was acting, as Forsyth says, whereas the early Christians found their role in testifying to that action. "It was the disciples who *proclaimed* the truth of the cross. Jesus himself could not adequately speak about this—he only *acted* it."[87]

It was, in retrospect, in light of the experience of forgiveness by Peter for his denials, by Paul for his persecution of the Church, and of the experience of the resurrection that the early Christians arrived at the gospel of the cross. How much that interpretation can be attributed to Jesus himself is subject to endless debate. It may be that he gave the clue, for example, in his handling of the Last Supper. "It was not primarily their own theological reflections, but above all the interpretative sayings of Jesus at the Last Supper which showed them how to understand his death properly."[88] It would be foolish to discount such a connection between Jesus and the kerygma. If his death had the significance the early Christians claimed for it, it is not unreasonable to expect Jesus to have some inkling of that himself. However, to attribute the fully developed theology of atonement to Jesus is somewhat like accepting that Moses wrote the Pentateuch, including the account of his own death. The early Christians, including Paul, say something about Jesus that he could not say about himself. "It would be as foolish to argue for no development from Jesus of Nazareth to Paul as to suppose that Paul betrays the simple gospel of Jesus."[89] Both extremes miss something vital, the nineteenth century attempt to get back to a simple gospel of Jesus behind the speculative theology of Paul and the twentieth century insistence that Paul and the kerygma of the early Church are all we have. The truth is more prosaic, and, at the same time, more exciting than these polarities allow. What we have in the gospel is an

understanding of life and especially of God in which there is a
basic continuity between the teachings of Jesus and the developed
theology of the early Church as reflected in Paul. However, that
continuity finds expression in different ways not only because Paul
and the early Church represent the second stage after the ministry
of Jesus is past, but also because they have different roles. The
mission of Jesus, irrespective of how clearly he understood this
himself, is to be the Christ. It is for those who recognize this, by
the grace of God, to proclaim it. Thus, the significance of Jesus exceeds his own message and embraces his life and death and his
very being. A strong case can be made then for a basic continuity
between Jesus and Paul, and by implication, the early Church
generally, with the difference between them being attributable to
their different roles of being the savior and being proclaimers of
the savior. But would Jesus himself endorse the Pauline gospel?

SALVATION AND THE NEW TESTAMENT

In spite of the apparent links in spirit between the basic tenor of
Jesus' teaching and the early Church's gospel of salvation, we must
confront the possibility that the fully developed claims of that gospel do finally represent an imposition on the demonstration of the
claim of the living God in Jesus himself. "Given its currency in
Christian history as a description of the basic content of the gospel,
the vocabulary of *salvation* and *saving* is used to a much less extent
in the New Testament than might be supposed."[90] In fact, the title
savior (Σωτήρ) only occurs 24 times, and 15 of these are in the Pastoral Epistles and II Peter.[91] Even the noun *salvation* occurs con-
siderably less frequently than the verb *to save*. In Acts and the
Pauline Epistles, *salvation* occurs almost as often as the verb,
which appears over 50 times, whereas the title *savior* is only about
half as frequently used. But in Revelation, *savior* never appears,
although James uses the verb *save* 5 times. Hebrews has 7 references to *salvation* and one to *save* but with no mention of *savior* at
all. II Peter moves even further in the substantive direction with 5
occurrences of *savior*, only one of *salvation*, and no use of the
verb *to save*. Perhaps most striking is the fact that, leaving aside
the pastorals, Paul only uses the title *savior* twice.[92] The upshot
would seem to be that emphasis on salvation and especially the designation of Jesus as savior was subject to development in the early
Christian community. The early speeches in Acts, for example,
proclaim the resurrection rather than salvation. But to jump from
this evidence of development to the position that the whole emph-

asis on salvation is to be attributed to Hellenistic influence in general and Paul's contribution in particular is hardly warranted. For in spite of the indication that it took time to come to the full-blown doctrine of Jesus as the savior who reconciled us to God, the direction of that interpretation is evident early,and in sources other than Paul. "For example, it is striking that two writings, which according to the tradition of the early Church—in my view completely reliable—must be assigned to the Petrine sphere of tradition, Mark and I Peter stress the soteriological interpretation of the death of Jesus as an atoning death in a marked way, I Peter by explicit citation of Isa. 53 (2.17ff., 3.18f.; cf1.18), and Mark in two places in an archaic Semitic linguistic form."[93] The most satisfactory conclusion would seem to be that the triumph of the fully developed doctrine of the atoning death of Jesus took some time, in spite of its early articulation by Paul, but that its eventual official endorsement reflected a consensus toward which most Christians were drawn from the earliest stages of wrestling with the meaning of the crucified messiah.

Yet even if it is conceded that the gospel of salvation is a reflection, rather than a distortion, of the central Christian kerygma, there is still the question of the relation of that kerygma to Jesus himself. For, besides the ethos of kinship between Jesus' teachings about the kingdom and the gospel of salvation by grace, there are also currents that might signal an even more profound divergence. For example, his criticism of the pharisees did not so much advocate a priestly alternative, as the parable of the Pharisee and the Publican might suggest, but rather a prophetic one. His response to the criticism of the pharisees that he ate with tax collectors and sinners was "go and learn what this means, 'I desire mercy, and not sacrifice'" (Mk. 9:13). Or when they challenged him for allowing his disciples to pluck grain and eat it as they passed through the grain fields on the Sabbath, Jesus pointed out that David ate the sacred temple bread because he was hungry (12:3, 4), and again the prophetic pronouncement of God's desire for mercy rather than sacrifice is reiterated (v. 7). To the scribe who agreed with Jesus' summation of the law in the great commandments of love for God and love for neighbor, Jesus offered the assurance that he was not far from the kingdom of God (Mk. 12:28ff.). These and similar references[94] suggest that Jesus is to be located in the tradition of the prophets in contrast to the gospel of salvation that has more in common with the priestly confidence in sacrificial ritual. The complaint of the nineteenth century about Hellenization and the contemporary insistence on the primacy of praxis might finally come down to this: The moral challenge inherent in the confrontation with the living God mediated by Jesus is formalized and domesticated by the development of an elaborate cultic ritual that glosses negligence and injustice through a sacramental assurance of forgiveness bolstered by an equally elaborate theology of atonement, which displaces the living challenge of the way of the kingdom by a representative endorsement of Jesus. If Jesus were to return to earth today, would he apply the type of criticism he directed against the pharisees to his own church? Would we be subject to the prophetic reminder that God's desire is not basically for sacrifice but for mercy?

There can be no doubt that the nineteenth century protest against the formalism of theological abstraction and the more recent protest against the perversity of ideological abstraction have their point. Insofar as salvation theology serves as a means of avoiding the personal challenge of the gospel to our own lives and its social challenge to the way we organize our economic and political structures, it is completely vulnerable to these forms of critique. However, if these critiques displace the gospel of salvation with a gospel of personal integrity or of social justice the critique has then become another form of abuse. For in themselves personal integrity and social justice remain essentially on the moral level. Their appeal is essentially an imperative one concerning what we should be doing individually and corporately. It reminds us that God desires mercy more than sacrifice, but the mercy is essentially directed to others. On this basis we need not see ourselves as recipients of mercy, or as standing in need of it. In short, the danger of the prophetic stance is that it may not transcend the moral plane where we are challenged to get on the divine side and in this preoccupation prevent us from seeing that the only basis for our being on God's side is through the gracious condescension by which God has come to our side. If this latter appreciation is more evident in the words of Paul than it is in the words of Jesus that should not be surprising. As we have seen, Jesus' mission was to be the Christ. It was for Paul and other Christians to proclaim the Christ:

> The contrast between Jesus and Paul is essentially the contrast between the love of God and the pain of God. But does this contrast mean an *opposition* between the two? Here lies the crux of the problem. Does Jesus' teaching on the love of God originate in the pain of God which Paul saw in Jesus? The pain of God which Paul saw implies the *person* of Jesus. Therefore, to say that the teaching of Jesus is based on Paul's

teaching shows that Jesus' teaching is based on his own person. This is "love rooted in the pain of God". Nothing could be more natural than this—the teaching is based on the person who taught it.[95]

Jesus proclaimed the love of God. In Jesus, Paul sees that the depth of that love issues in the pain of God, revealed especially in the cross. This comparison from Kazoh Kitamori makes sense of the contrasts and kinship we have seen between the teachings of Jesus and the Pauline theology. However, when he goes on to suggest that the Pauline assessment should be natural to Jesus himself, this is another matter. The theocentric and altruistic directions of Jesus' orientation would rather seem to render any concentration of Jesus on his own person inherently unnatural. That is why, in spite of its heights of spirituality, the way in which the Fourth Gospel presents Jesus proclaiming himself grates on Christian sensitivity. Nor is this totally alleviated by the qualification whereby Jesus repeatedly follows these "I" sayings with a deferral to the Father, assuring his hearers that it is not himself who is the final focus of attention but the Father for whom he is the vehicle. Given the basic thrust of the Gospel evident in the parables of Jesus and the theology of Paul, there is something incongruous about a self-proclaiming Christ. What seems perfectly natural is the lack of self-consciousness whereby Jesus lived the gospel and the disciple consciousness by which Paul, and the other early Christians, proclaimed him as the Christ because of how he lived and died. This makes the contrast and comparison between Jesus and Paul perfectly understandable. It does not guarantee its truth. As Bultmann contended, that is ultimately a matter of faith. It also lends credence to Harnack's contention that the gospel as Jesus proclaimed it has to do with the Father only and not with the Son. What it does not authorize is the conclusion that therefore the followers of Jesus made an illegitimate move in proclaiming the gospel of the Son. It seems much more plausible to conclude that that proclamation was making explicit what was implicit in Jesus in the very obedience by which he rendered all to God.

It is not surprising that the attempt to understand this person who burst the bounds of his own message to become the center of a gospel about him led Christians to talk of him as being both human and divine and to become embroiled in the complex deliberations of the Trinitarian and Christological Controversies. Given the transition from proclaimer to proclaimed, this, too, seems completely natural. Of course, the resulting formulations had a tendency to become ends in themselves and to displace rather than to re-present the amazing person in whom this union of God and humanity was seen to have been effected. But if this temptation can be resisted so that we confront Jesus as the epitome of the divine–human encounter we may be able to glimpse something of that living reality precisely through these categories which nineteenth century scholars were so convinced could only distort it. This would involve seeing Jesus as the person in whom God most directly reached out to humanity and as the human being who most completely responded to God's presence. We have long been accustomed to regarding Jesus as the coming of God to us, but are we ready to consider the full dialectic of these two natures as living realities and see Jesus as the "prototype of the justified person?"[96] The hardening of metaphysical categories in the two natures doctrine has its anthropological counterpart in the dogma of the sinlessness of Jesus. Insofar as this connotes an ahistorical superiority to temptation, the result can only be a docetic christology. If Jesus really constitutes that point where God and humanity have had their most intimate contact, the humanity must be genuine and, in some sense, Jesus would have to be seen as the prototype of the saved person as well as being the savior. If we could manage to attain some sense of such a living encounter taking place in Jesus, this could give life to the theological language of Paul and even of the historic creeds in a way, that, in turn, could disclose depths of meaning in the gospel that will remain inaccessible so long as it is approached as a moral challenge only and Jesus assumes the role of teacher and example. Only thus can there be a transformation profound enough to change us and our world.

3

Salvation and Theology

Salvation constitutes the central substance of Christian faith so that it represents a perennial theme running through all aspects of Christianity, rather than standing on its own as a distinct doctrine. However, theological articulation of this theme has focused on one article of belief in particular, the doctrine of atonement. Unfortunately, as we have seen, this articulation has not been particularly successful. The inherent ambivalence between comprehensive theme and particular article of belief might help to account for the unsatisfactory nature of the articulation, but there are also more specific reasons associated with the development and form of the articulation itself.

There is widespread agreement that there never has been, and never will be, one orthodox doctrine of atonement. While the issue of the person of Christ provoked the intense debates and debacles which resulted in the two-natures Christology of Chalcedon, the work of Christ never elicited such focused attention, and consequently never received a corresponding authoritative formulation. Some would suggest that this is so much the better because the work of Christ must necessarily shatter any concepts that would seek to contain it; though why this is not equally true of the person of Christ is passed over in discrete silence. The consensus rather goes on to enumerate a list of generally accepted theories of atonement, among which pride of place (although in view of the inevitable inadequacy of theoretical constructs in this area, it is a dubious distinction) is awarded to St. Anselm, whose *Cur Deus Homo* is reckoned as the first sustained statement of an atonement theory. Amid the concern of the feudal age with integrity and honor, Anselm concluded that sin was such an affront to God's honor that it could only be dealt with if, in some way, that affront could be recompensed. Because only man should, but only God could accomplish this, that costituted the explanation for the God-man. Thus the first explicit theory of atonement suggested that

71

God facilitated forgiveness with integrity through the sacrifice of the God-man.

From the vantage point of this explanation, it is possible to identify other prominent theories of atonement, pre- as well as post-Anselm. In what has probably been the single most influential book on the subject in this century, Gustaf Aulen's *Christus Victor*, the suggestion is made that there is a general understanding of atonement in the early centuries that is quite distinct from Anselm's theory. This understanding Aulen calls the classical or dramatic view of atonement, according to which the accomplishment of Christ was seen as the classic victory of God over Satan in the great cosmic drama of the clash between the forces of good and evil. On this side of Anselm, a very different understanding of atonement has emerged from the consideration that the problem that prompts the need for atonement is not God's but ours. It is we who are estranged; it is we who are sinners. Consequently what is required is not a change in God, but in us. And this is what God offers in Christ. In revealing His love in the cross, God elicits our responding love so that reconciliation is effected. This moral influence approach, broached by Abelard shortly after Anselm's theory was formulated, has tended to dominate modern thinking on the subject.

These three main conceptions of atonement may be supplemented by recognition of the juristic perspective of the reformers, which Aulen's impartial Lutheranism notwithstanding, draws on Anselm as well as on the early Fathers. Two other underlying motifs which have exercised varying degrees of influence on atonement articulations are the Greek concept of divinization, according to which the incarnation itself constitutes a kind of atonement, hints of which may be detected in someone like McLeod Campbell, and the cultic approach of sacrifice, which is presupposed in varying degrees by the more explicit theories.

This consensus about main types of atonement theories is seen to entail the corollary that this plurality of theories precludes any one theory gaining ascendancy to the exclusion of the others. At certain times it seemed inevitable to understand atonement in terms of one particular dominant motif. However, the advantage of hindsight shows that that understanding was, at best, partial. Anything approaching an adequate understanding of atonement must allow for the variety of expressions to which this diffuse reality has given rise. The various theories all have their contribution to make to a comprehensive appreciation of the meaning of atonement.

The obviousness of this conclusion and the ease with which it is reached is only exceeded by its uselessness as a contemporary perspective on atonement. The theoretical advocacy of a sophisticated openness that is appreciative of various approaches translates into the concrete practice of the total avoidance of the whole issue. Thus the persistent recommendation of such pluralism amounts to little more than lip service paid by theologians to a doctrine whose abandonment is too unthinkable to be acknowledged explicitly. The shallowness and absurdity of this solution is particularly glaring at that point where it derives its initial credibility, in its proposal for combining objective and subjective approaches to atonement. The superficial plausibility of this proposal is dissipated as soon as it is recognized that far from representing different emphases on a continuum, the objective and subjective approaches reflect the diverse world views of different historic epochs. At the very least, anyone who advocates their harmonization is undertaking to combine the ancient and modern worlds.

Deficiencies in Modern Subjective Theories

ELIMINATION OF ATONEMENT

Any attempt to combine elements of objective and subjective views of atonement runs into an immediate obstacle in that, from the point of view of the objective approach, subjective views are not views of atonement at all.[1] The final contention of subjective views is that atonement is not necessary because God is love, and forgives freely. However, rather than putting it so bluntly, advocates of the subjective approach continue to refer to this free forgiveness as atonement. We could find no clearer example of this stance than the following statement by one of the most influential exponents of the subjective view, Hastings Rashdall: "The atonement is the very central doctrine of Christianity insofar as it proclaims, and brings home to the heart of man, the supreme Christian truth that God is love, and that love is the most precious thing in human life."[2] Not all advocates of the subjective approach are so casual. Its leading American exponent, Horace Bushnell, was more aware of the cost of forgiveness to God,[3] and the alleged originator of this view, Abelard, may well be misrepresented in being identified with the view as it came to be articulated by later enthusiasts.[4] However, there can be no doubt about the triumph of this approach in modern theology.

The father of modern theology, Schleiermacher, entitled the 100th section of his major doctrinal work: "The Redeemer assumes believers into the power of His God-consciousness, and this is His redemptive activity.[5] Earlier he had diagnosed the problem which makes redemption necessary as "God-forgetful-ness"[6] which he warns must not be taken to mean "a state in which it is quite impossible for the God-consciousness to be kindled."[7] The possibility of its being rekindled is ever present. What it requires to actualize it is the ignition of someone who has that consciousness, and this is what is effected in Jesus. Thus for Schleiermacher, atonement refers to a reorientation in human consciousness whereby the awareness of God is recovered, at-one-ment is effected, apparently with little or no difficulty for God.

> The grace and love of God are reduced to sentimentality if the tension between judgment and grace, righteousness and love is not properly maintained. In Schlelermacher's theology this tension is presented only in weakened form. . . . The omnipotence and authority of God's sanctifying and transforming love are so strongly sounded that sin seen from God ' s side dissolves into nothing.[8]

This direction is further refined by Albrecht Ritschl by his expansion of the God-consciousness motif on both ends, in reference to Jesus and to ourselves. In Jesus, the God-consciousness takes the specific form of a consciousness of vocation.[9] "Jesus' *vocation to found the kingdom of God* is for Ritschl *the* key to every phase and detail of his life and ministry."[10] This object of Jesus' vocation, the kingdom of God, constitutes the significance of Jesus for us in the form of its ethical challenge, and provides the direction for reconciliation in that it opens the way through the ethical to the religious because it is also God's "eternal self-end."[11] The prospect of growing reconciliation in the advancing kingdom, which has come to light in Jesus, thus supplants the historic concern with justification in a further unfolding of the abandonment of atonement.

Perhaps the most concise certification of the new view is to be found in the statement of Harnack that came to be regarded as a central slogan of liberal theology: "*The Gospel, as Jesus proclaimed it, has to do with the Father only and not with the Son.*"[12] The "essence of Christianity", to follow Harnack's original German title, centers in the revelation that God is father and not the stern judge who demands the sacrifice of the son. The sacrifice of Jesus is essentially a human event. For "it was by the cross of Jesus Christ that mankind gained such an experience of the power of purity and love true to death that they can never forget, and that it signifies a new epoch in their history."[13]

The reaction against this direction represented by neo-orthodoxy, and by Barth in particular, can be seen as a recovery of an appreciation of the need for and reality of atonement. In Christ God pronounces His judgmental "No!" as well as His accepting "Yes!" Yet, even here, the direction away from the centrality of atonement is implicit in the continuing predominance of the consciousness motif in the form of the centrality of revelation.[14] Thus, even with Barth, it can be charged that atonement is finally a matter of the revelation of the grace of God in Christ, rather than something actually effected in the concrete reality of Christ.[15] At any rate, insofar as a restoration of concern with atonement was involved in neo-orthodoxy, it was short lived. For virtually all major movements in theology since the middle of the twentieth century have found it possible to accord the issue scant attention at best.

Neglect is difficult to document. Perhaps the best that can be done is to point to the absence of concern with atonement at those places where it might be most expected to emerge, and to elicit some confirmatory endorsements of this impression. One such place where it might be expected to have some prominence is in the recent controversy over christology.[16] However, apart from passing references, as in testimonials to the importance of atonement from Frances Young and to his aversion to the traditional accounts from Michael Goulder in the original volume, the only direct treatment of the subject is a scant twenty-five pages in the third volume on the controversy.[17] The fundamental focus is provided by modern academic interest in questions of history, myth and metaphysics, and in contrast to the classical christological controversy where the ancient counterparts of these issues were under debate, the atmosphere this time does not suggest an underlying assumption of soteriological significance.

The direction that seems to be the single most dominant one in contemporary theology manages to avoid atonement by focusing on the promotion of liberation. It emulates liberal theology in turning from the cross toward the whole life of Jesus and especially his message of the kingdom, but where liberals found in this confirmation of the inherent value of the individual, liberation theology sees it as the evidence of God's siding with the poor and oppressed. Consequently, any questioning of this theology invariably invites accusation of siding with the privileged and oppressors. Yet this accusation must be risked, as it is by Schubert Ogden when he asks how liberation can be motivated and sustained apart from redemption.[18]

At the other end of the spectrum, the personal approach of the theology of story has equally little difficulty bypassing atonement.[19] Even the theologians who most directly inherit the mantle of the neo-orthodox revival of interest in classical themes, such as Moltmann and Pannenberg, present "remarkably little of salvific value, of the reconciling love of God acting in atonement in Jesus,"[20] and this summation is proposed in spite of the fact that Moltmann has produced a book on *The Crucified God*.

Insofar as the atonement issue is even approached in contemporary theology, it tends to be assumed that it involves the recognition of the free and automatic acceptance of God. Perhaps the only atypical element in the following articulation of this stance is the fact that it is stated so explicitly:

> The revelation of God in Jesus is the developmental unmasking not of a terrible God, but of a God who would "wipe away every human tear," of a God who is radically personal and communal in knowledge love and free creation. God would have us "fear not."[21]

From the traditional point of view, this represents the elimination, rather than an articulation, of atonement.

MOTIVATION BEHIND SUBJECTIVE THEORIES

It must be recognized, however, that this modern approach to atonement is not without its merits. For one thing, it reflects the literal meaning of the term. The word *atonement* is unique in being the only major theological term of English origin. Its original meaning is precisely what its component elements suggest: at-one-ment. It refers to the achieving of at-one-ment between estranged parties. Thus, its primary reference is to reconciliation, and any suggestion that such reconciliation is achieved by making amends for the offenses which caused the estrangement in the first place, is a secondary development.[22] The strength of the liberal approach is that it reflects this priority. "The significance of the nineteenth century in the history of atonement doctrine is the new prominence given to such relations as that between father and son or between mother and child, to such concepts as personal sympathy and personal identification with others."[23]

Even more significant than this reflection of the root meaning of the term is the fact that the modern understanding of atonement is motivated by distinctly theological concerns. Aulen suggests that the subjective view represents a reaction against what he calls the Latin theory, originated by St. Anselm.[24] It takes issue with this theory's apparent assumption that atonement consists in appeasing God so that the divine attitude toward us is changed from wrath to grace. Against such a perspective, it insists that, far from being a trophy marking our successful propitiation of God, atonement is rather a gift of God's grace. Thus, one of the earliest proponents of this argument, Faustus Socinus, insisted toward the end of the sixteenth century that forgiveness is not achieved by satisfaction being provided to God, but rather issues from God himself of his own volition. "For God can, especially since he is Lord of all, abandon as much of his rights as he pleases."[25] Socinus suggests that if God cannot forgive without satisfaction, he has less power than humans.[26] Forgiveness must be of God, and not a response to which God is cajoled by the sacrifice of Christ.

In fairness to the traditional accounts of atonement, it must be noted that no serious exponent of them ever meant to suggest that this was how atonement was effected. In this regard, Aulen's reading of Anselm is highly misleading. The latter's explanation of atonement, in terms of the satisfaction of God's honor which allows God to forgive with integrity, presupposes that God is the source as well as the object of this satisfaction. This is the whole point of this treatise, *Cur Deus Homo*, as suggested most succinctly in the heading of Chapter Six of Book Two: "That the satisfaction whereby man can be saved can be effected only by one who is God and man."[27] Only the God-man can provide satisfaction because as God he can effect it and as man he represents the side from which it is due. In the dialectic of the incarnation, God satisfies His own honor from within estranged humanity. We shall see that this model of atonement is not without its own problems, but anthropocentrism is not one of them. Contrary to Aulen, Anselm does not see man propitiating God, but rather this office is, and can only be, executed by the God-man.

Still, the question that troubles modern sensibility is why there is need for satisfaction. In the tradition of Socinus, we wonder about the power and supremacy of God if there is some constraint to which God is subject. If God is God, then requirements of honor must surely be negotiable for God. If God is bound by these requirements, then such requirements are superior, and God is not really God. The point is nowhere expressed more clearly than by a theologian whose fame and influence have least to do with his pronouncements on atonement, St. Thomas Aquinas, in his explanation of how God could have forgiven without satisfaction and not thereby impugned the cause of justice:

> If God had wanted to free man from sin without any satisfaction at all, he would not have been acting against justice. Justice cannot be safe-guarded by the judge whose duty it is to punish crimes committed against others, e.g. against a fellow man, or the government, or the head of the government, should he dismiss a crime without punish-ment. But God has no one above him, for he is himself the supreme and common good of the entire universe. If then he forgives sin, which is a crime in that it is committed against him, he violates no one's rights. The man who waives satisfaction and forgives an offence done to himself acts mercifully, not unjustly.[28]

Because God is Lord of all, there is an inherent guarantee of the maintenance of justice in divine forgiveness. But this seems to assume that justice is a concomitant of authority and power. It is because of God's sheer supremacy that forgiveness should be possible without questions of compensation or satisfaction. But is justice guaranteed by authority and power? Is it not rather assured by impartiality and consistency? But in that case, forgiveness as a concession of supreme authority appears arbitrary and problema-tic. If God can forgive because of sheer supremacy, how does this differ from a capricious despot who might display indulgence one moment and vengeance the next? It seems that forgiveness itself, if it is to be genuine and worthwhile, must entail the affirmation of the truth or right offended.

LOSS OF DIALECTICAL DEPTH

The affirmation of truth and right was one of the main concerns be-hind the traditional models of atonement. It has been suggested that the strength of that version, which is prime candidate for the epitome of satisfaction models, the penal theory of atonement, lies in its concern for the sanctity of the moral law.[29] As is often the case in this area, sources of strength very easily revolve into points of weakness. Concern for the moral law can very easily result in its elevation over the personal reality of divine forgiveness. The con-cern for atonement, which validates the moral dimension, can dis-place the quest of at-one-ment, which is the goal of the whole pro-cess. Along with this, there is also the implication that somehow the moral law is superior to God. Its requirements have to be sat-isfied before God can forgive. Yet, recognizing these dangers in satisfaction perspectives, there is something in this outlook which will not be denied:

> The consciousness of guilt cannot be overcome by the simple assertion that man is forgiven. Man can believe in forgiveness only if justice is maintained and guilt is confirmed. God must remain Lord and Judge in spite of the reuniting power of his love.[30]

There can be no real at-one-ment without atonement. This is not due to the inviolability of some abstract reality such as the moral law, but rather has to do with the very nature of God.

The moral influence approach, as it is generally understood, sees atonement as the at-one-ment that can be realized through the recognition of God's graciousness which freely forgives us and accepts us as we are. As far as it goes, it is difficult to fault such an interpretation as an accurate portrayal of the fundamental thrust of the gospel. But to stop there, as much contemporary Christian rhetoric does, is to settle for a half-truth, which can only serve to undermine that very gospel. For as characterized by sheer forgiving acceptance, God cannot fail to appear as an arbitrary power representing indiscriminate indulgence for whatever transpires. Such a sentimentalization and trivialization of the gospel of divine love can be avoided only by acknowledging another side in the divine character, that side which traditionally has been designated as holiness:

> Love is not love of God if it is not holy. At the same time, holiness is not really holy if it is not love. Holiness is the presupposition of love, while love is the fulfillment of holiness.[31]

Because of this, the original meaning of at-one-ment expanded to include reference to the atonement that made at-one-ment possible. Consequently, a full appreciation of atonement must encompass this sense of making amends, which gives substance to the accepting love. The sentimentalization of accepting love on its own is dissipated through the recognition that it is holy love that thus accepts. This has at least two crucial implications. On the one hand, it dispenses with the suggestion of compromise that is implicit in the isolation of love as the sole ingredient in forgiveness.[32] At the same time, it provides an assurance that the acceptance of divine love is genuine and will be sustained.[33]

Thus, in spite of a fundamental concern to identify God as the source of forgiveness, the moral influence approach so portrays this as straightforward acceptance that it tends to eliminate the fundamental tension between acceptance and rejection, grace and wrath, love and holiness to which the traditional atonement models pointed:

> The "love of god" of liberal theology since Schleiermacher is nothing but the "soprano" of these happy people. They did not have the ears to hear the bass which is the pain of God sounding out of the depths.[34]

The easy acceptance by God coincides with an essentially easy understanding of life, which in the words of D. M. MacKinnon, "ignores altogether the dimension of the irrevocable; in the end, it comes perilously near taking refuge in a false optimism, which supposes all for the best, in the best of all possible worlds."[35] MacKinnon concludes that whatever their inadequacies, the traditional treatments of atonement insisted that the work of Christ concerned the deepest contradictions of human life. These contradictions are the human experiences that constitute glimpses of the conflict theology points to in terms of the dialectic of the holiness and love of God. It is out of that conflict that atonement emerges. When the dialectic is short-circuited, as it is in much contemporary religious and theological affirmation of the love of God, in complete disregard of God's holiness, atonement is replaced by an at-one-ment, which is as inconsequential as the arbitrary God who sponsors it.

Deficiencies in Traditional Objective Theories

THE FOREIGNNESS OF OBJECTIVE THEORIES

If the moral influence approach proves forbidding because it loses the depth of the gospel with which traditional atonement models were concerned, those models themselves fall far short of providing an acceptable alternative. "Their transactional character, whether expressed in terms of propitiation, substitution or payment of a debt, make them an easy butt for criticism."[36] In fact, the criticism is so easy that it readily degenerates into caricature, as in the following dismissal of traditional models of atonement by Michael Goulder:

> Alas for those whose task is the defence of the traditional doctrines of atonement! Better Skid Row than the endless round of empty speculations that run from the implausible to the irreligious: the theories that point to demons more powerful than God (unless he can cheat them),

and those that posit a faceless justice more powerful than God; those that make Christ a whipping boy, and those that make him an international banker in merit, with resources enough to pay off the world's balance of payments deficit. Many such expositors end their labours with the complacent reflection, "all these pictures are inadequate: we need them all to do justice to the greatness of the facts": but rubbish added to rubbish makes rubbish.[37]

The complacency implicit in the blanket endorsement of all accounts of atonement because none is adequate to the reality itself is precisely the index of inadequacy we are following here. Yet, it is hardly an improvement to react in the opposite extreme by simply rejecting all these versions. Without accepting Goulder's blanket dismissal of traditional accounts of atonement as being any more adequate than their blanket endorsement, we can agree that, even on the most sympathetic reading, these accounts do have an unfortunate tendency to trivialize the reality they attempt to present. Paul van Buren's assessment of Anselm's position that it portrays the cross "as a great transaction carried out over our heads,"[38] might be applied to any of the objective views of atonement.

THE IMPERSONAL NATURE OF OBJECTIVE THEORIES

It is not just the foreignness of talk of transactions between God and Satan, or between the Father and the Son, which makes these accounts problematic, but the very suggestion of an "objective" transaction that is somehow supposed to have an inherent significance for us. We could translate the ancient mythology of deals with Satan into the contemporary idiom of psychological conflict within God. Aulen asserts of the classical view of atonement: "God is at once the author and the object of reconciliation; He is reconciled in the act of reconciling the world to himself."[39] And we have seen that, contrary to Aulen's own interpretation, Anselm maintains this dialectic, and, indeed, facilitates a theopsychological type of interpretation even more directly by eliminating the external reference to Satan and concentrating the transaction internally in the Godhead between the Father and the Son. From a perspective as indebted to Luther as Aulen's, Kazoh Kitamori effects the transition to contemporary psychological terms by describing atonement in terms of a struggle within the divine psyche, which he characterizes as the pain of God resulting from the conflict in which the divine love conquers the divine wrath so that sinners might be acceptable in spite of their sin.[40] This psychological account is less jarring to modern ears than talk of treacherous deals with Satan, but the familiarity of the idiom does not dispense with the sense of an alien transaction to which we are not party.

The legacy of this theopsychic approach to atonement surfaces in the concern, particularly prominent in neo-orthodox theology, to isolate the significance of Christ, especially of his death, from the rest of life. "Theologians have commonly imagined that they are under obligation to make a complete isolation of the sacrifice of Christ from the heroic self-offering of other noble souls; and this has vitiated most of the classical attempts to produce a doctrine of atonement."[41] The concern that it is really God with whom we have to do in Christ easily slips over into the insistence that we have to do with God only in Christ. Thus Brunner emphasizes the once-for-allness (*Einmaligkeit*) of the event of Christ, contending not simply for its uniqueness but its absolute uniqueness.[42] Such insistence on the completeness of the work of Christ serves to confirm the sense of an alien transaction, which places such an encumbrance on any attempt at an appreciation of atonement that it is not likely to be surmounted.

MISREPRESENTATION OF GOD

Beyond the abstraction of essentially objective theories of atonement which give the impression of reporting celestial transactions which have little or nothing to do with us, an impression reenforced by the isolation of the work of Christ from the rest of our experience of life, the fundamental difficulty with objective theories is located in the same place as that of the subjective moral influence approach, in the understanding of God. Where the moral influence view sentimentalizes the love of God through a failure to appreciate and affirm divine holiness, the objective satisfaction theories fail to do justice to the love of God because of a one-sided obsession with divine holiness. Even if we were not put off by the transactional atmosphere of the traditional accounts of atonement, we would find ourselves brought up short by the understanding of God implied in them. Not only does God come off as something of a wheeler-dealer, but also as a wheeler-dealer of questionable credentials.

Beyond the deceitful treatment of Satan in the classical theory, which might suggest that it was really Satan who prevailed through the endorsement of his methods, the satisfaction theory, especially in its stronger penal-substitutionary form, raises basic questions about the sheer morality of the whole operation. The central assumption of the traditional accounts was that atonement was the method by which God was able to forgive with integrity. But the penal-substitution explanation suggests that this was made possible by allowing, if not causing, the innocent to suffer for the guilty. How is integrity maintained by such a reversal of just deserts? There would seem to be some point to Bushnell's conclusion: "The justice satisfied is satisfied with injustice!"[43] At the very least, it is ironic that the approach to atonement that puts the premium on moral integrity should be accused of portraying the atonement in immoral terms.

An immediate answer to this charge of immorality against the penal theory is to point out that God does not require Jesus to become the substitute for the guilty, but rather that it is God the Son who takes this judgment upon Himself in the mystery of incarnation. Thus, Moltmann contends that it is the cross that evokes the doctrine of the Trinity as its only adequate interpretation, according to which the Father sacrifices the Son through the Spirit.[44] However, far from exonerating God, such a perspective could, in fact, be seen to confirm the suspicions of those who challenge the God who requires satisfaction. Thus, Dorothee Soelle contends that Moltmann's position is an example of that understanding of God that actually glorifies suffering and really amounts to a theological sadism which ends up "worshipping the executioner".[45] Christians manage to live with this astounding concept of God because it is tempered with the conviction that God is loving as well as just, thus adding the note of masochism.[46]

> But the cross is neither a symbol expressing the relation between God the Father and the Son, nor a symbol of masochism which needs suffering in order to convince itself of love. It is above all a symbol of reality. Love does not "require" the cross, but *de facto* it ends up on the cross.[47]

Or, as Soelle puts it more crisply elsewhere: "Christ came to the cross because he went too far in loving people, not because a heavenly father elected him as the special victim to be punished."[48]

Thus, Soelle raises questions about the understanding of God implicit in traditional satisfaction theories of atonement, which are just as debilitating as the innocuous picture of God that results from the modern moral influence tendency to lose sight of holiness through the sentimentalization of divine love. The connotation of sadism and the legitimation of suffering are issues that must be faced by any account of atonement which would expect to be taken seriously today. On the other hand, Soelle's own position does not provide much help toward a positive understanding of atonement for today. Her concentration on the problem of suffering prescribes a different orientation:

> In the face of suffering you are either with the victim or the executioner—there is no other option. Therefore that explanation of suffering that looks away from the victim and identifies itself with a righteousness that is supposed to stand behind the suffering has already taken a step in the direction of theological sadism, which wants to understand God as the torturer.[49]

Blessed are those who can distinguish so clearly between victims and executioners! Doubly blessed are those who can be sure that they are on the side of the victim! Those of us who find life more ambiguous may continue to draw consolation from the traditional conviction, however inadequately expressed, that God is to be found in the midst of that ambiguity as certified by the cross. This consolation does not provide any excuse for not siding with the victims insofar as they can be identified, but it does submit our failures in identification and in recognition, as well as our complicity in the role of executioner, to the healing power of divine holiness and love.

Deficiencies in Attempts at Amalgamation

INCOMPATABILITY OF OBJECTIVE AND SUBJECTIVE APPROACHES

The off-setting deficiencies of the subjective and objective approaches to atonement make the tendency to propose an amalgamation readily understandable. Because the subjective focus on experience compensates for the abstraction of the objective theories, and the divine sponsorship of atonement in the objective theories supplies the substantive gap in the subjective approach, it seems obvious that the solution to the atonement issue lies in some combination of the two approaches. The traditional concern with the holiness of God and its satisfaction constitutes a corrective to the sentimentalization of love in the modern approach, whereas the emphasis on the love of God in this approach recovers the essential thrust of the gospel threatened by the narrowly fastidious preoccupation with divine integrity in the traditional approaches. Similarly, modern sensitivity to the realities of suffering expose the suggestion of sadism in a view of atonement that sees God regarding suffering as acceptable and even compensatory, whereas traditional theories maintain an appreciation of the complexity and depth of suffering threatened by the modern assumption that it should be susceptible to the remedial action of social engineering.

However, in spite of the obviousness of this direction and the frequency with which it is promoted, serious attempts to effect such a harmonization have not been particularly successful. The Erlangen school in Germany did not really manage to integrate the classical concern with redemption into the modern emphasis on reconciliation;[50] and Moberly's *Atonement and Personality* fails in its attempt to combine subjective and objective concern, according to critics from both sides of the spectrum.[51]

It is not surprising that advocates of objective or subjective views of atonement should find that comprehensive approaches, which attempt to combine elements from both sides, do not do justice to the distinctive concerns of their own position. From their respective points of view, their own positions are themselves comprehensive. The subjective approach cannot accept that it is lacking in its appreciation of a fundamental dimension of the divine reality which traditional approaches called the holiness of God. On its own terms, its understanding of God is complete. It simply has a more mature understanding than the traditional outlook was able to manage. In order to see these respective approaches as partial, and thus amenable to harmonization, we have to be standing on a more abstract level of theological reflection. Thus, it is not surprising that such attempts at amalgamation have not been successful. If objective theories of atonement strike an inevitable note of abstraction in their depiction of some kind of remote divine transaction, proposals for combining objective and subjective approaches only aggravate the problem by intensifying the degree of abstraction. Their product is a theological construction rather than a reflection of living reality.

What makes combination proposals abstract is their neglect of the rootedness of appreciation of atonement. They proceed as though the subject simply involved theoretical differences that should be subject to mutual adjustment. However, far from representing extremes on a continuum, which might lend themselves to harmonization, the objective and subjective approaches to atonement reflect basically different world views. They carry conviction not simply because they present atonement in a certain way, but because they reflect a certain mentality. It is not accidental that the objective theories emerged in premodern eras, while the subjective approach has gained prominence in the modern period. "The major shift in the symbolism of salvation took place in the age of the Enlightenment as a shift from a theocentric to an anthropocentric focus."[52] This is what separates objective and subjective approaches to atonement. In the language of the philosophy of science, the gap between them is not merely that of a variation between different models depicting a common reality, but rather constitutes what Thomas Kuhn has designated a paradigm shift.[53] The difference between these approaches is akin to the difference between the approaches of Newtonian and Einsteinian physics to the natural world. Just as the awareness of relativity raises questions and opens perspectives never dreamed of from the Newtonian vantage point, so too the self-consciousness of the modern outlook results in an entirely different perspective from the immediacy of the ancient and medieval worlds. It is this self-consciousness that is reflected in the emergence of the subjective approach and in the decline in interest in objective views of atonement.

This revolution in perspective from theocentric to anthropocentric focus not only explains the emergence of the subjective approach, but also goes a long way toward accounting for the dissolution of the atonement issue through this approach. Because the orientation is from the human rather than from the divine, concern with the requirements of divinity very easily recedes, to be replaced by an essential confidence in humanity, which not only makes appreciation of any need for human justification difficult, but also encourages the assumption that the problem is rather one of divine justification. "The enlightenment, therefore, began a process in which humanity no longer felt the need to justify itself before God; it was God who had to justify the divine existence to humanity."[54] This is the gap that proposals for amalgamating objective and subjective views of atonement would have to bridge.

THE NATURE OF THEOLOGY

What is at stake in the issue of atonement today is not a question of the compatibility of different versions of a theological doctrine, but rather the question of the viability of theology as such. What is required is nothing less than an understanding of atonement that reaches to the fundamental questioning of God characteristic of the contemporary outlook. An imaginative proposal in this direction is presented by Robert S. Paul in a book, which contrary to the more specific suggestion of its title, *The Atonement and the Sacraments*, also provides one of the most illuminating historical surveys of the doctrine.

The older ransom theories thought of atonement in terms of the debt for sin being paid to the devil; the satisfaction theories explained it as penal suffering inflicted to satisfy God's justice. But to give a content to the atonement that every generation can understand (and to get nearer to the passion narratives), we should perhaps think of it as a penalty or debt demanded by and paid to man. That measures the enormity of the deed that was perpetrated by our Lord's accusers, but it is also the measure of the goodness that was prepared to pay the price. The miracle of miracles is that in Christ God meets the charge that man makes against him and proves its falsity in the very act of taking the judgment for human sin upon himself. Here we are in the realm of pure grace.[55]

This interpretation cleverly combines the traditional concern with satisfaction with the modern questioning of the goodness of God. God satisfies this questioning by falsifying the judgment implicit in it through the very acceptance of that judgment in the cross. The answer to the theodicy question is "Yes"—God is responsible for evil. God accepts that responsibility in Christ, in submitting to the judgment of humanity. Yet by that very submission, the injustice of that judgment is exposed and the graciousness of God in submitting to that false judgment is exhibited, and in its light the real cause for atonement in human sinfulness is disclosed.

Yet in the light of what we have seen about the abstractness of comprehensive treatments of atonement, the very cleverness of Paul's proposal should raise a note of caution. Even more alarming is his stated aim—"to give a content to the atonement that every generation can understand." The price of such a universal perspective would seem to be an inevitable abstractness. However, that need not detain us, because it is equally evident that that aim is not realized. Far from giving "a content to the atonement that every generation can understand," it is highly unlikely that this interpretation would be understood by advocates of the traditional objective theories of atonement. They were not particularly troubled by the theodicy question. On the contrary, their concern was how they could be acceptable to God, rather than the modern question of whether God can be acceptable to us. Insofar as they would find it intelligible, they would undoubtedly find it lacking in that the penalty or debt referred to is prescribed by humanity, and indeed sinful humanity, the very antithesis of the traditional assumption of a prescription sponsored by the holiness of God.

Not only does this explanation fall short of meeting traditional concerns, but also it is doubtful whether it really speaks to modern sensibility either. For in spite of failing to do justice to the concern for the holiness of God in traditional versions of atonement, it nevertheless retains the form of that concern. Talk of debt and penalty is precisely what modern sensibility finds unintelligible. Thus, instead of achieving a comprehensive interpretation "that every generation can understand," what we seem to have is a theological hybrid, impressive in the theological greenhouse, but doomed to be scorched under the searching rays of the traditional concern with the holiness of God, or washed away completely in the showers of blessing from the modern God who, if credible at all, can only be entirely on our side.

Yet the failure of Paul's interpretation is as instructive as the interpretation itself is imaginative. His recognition of the extent of the gulf, which an understanding of atonement must bridge, makes the failure of his attempt to bridge it particularly poignant. It shows that the precariousness of atonement extends to theodicy as well. Paul's confidence that atonement can be approached through theodicy reflects his own prior appreciation of atonement. P. T. Forsyth may be taken as an illustration of this direction. He contends: "Christ is the theodicy of God and the justification of God and the ungodly."[56] The basis for this contention is his confidence that "the supreme theodicy is atonement."[57] This is not a conclusion to puzzlement over theodicy, but rather an application of an appreciation of atonement.

> We are bidden to recognize that God's demand on man takes the lead over man's demand on God. And both are over-ruled by God's demand on God, God meeting his own demand. And we learn unwillingly that only God's justification of man gives the secret of man's justification of God.[58]

From within an appreciation of atonement, atonement can be seen to address the theodicy problem. But it is another matter to assume that theodicy will open the way to atonement, as Paul implies. The likelihood is that the scales will tip in the other direction, toward the abandonment even of the question of God. For that is the direction which modern culture has taken in its march from theocentrism to anthropocentrism. And this is what is at stake in the atonement issue.

THE NATURE OF LIFE

The air of unreality that attaches to accounts of atonement is thus symptomatic of the foreignness that characterizes theology as such in the atmosphere of the present. In fact, this subject appears par-

ticularly esoteric in light of the alienation of our age from theological sensibility. This, no doubt, accounts for the attempt on the
part of those who remain under the influence of that largely van-
quished sensibility to concentrate on addressing that problem of
theological alienation directly. There would not seem to be much
scope for considering esoteric theological themes, like atonement,
when theology itself is so inherently problematic. And yet this
eminently reasonable approach might be sealing the fate of theology as well as of the subject of atonement, for not only does this
direct consideration of the feasibility of theology never get to the
subject of atonement, but in this neglect, it also might be missing
the essential ingredient without which theology is doomed to remain unappreciated.

The reasonableness of the contention that there must be some
acknowledgment of God before any sense can be found in worry-
ing about being reconciled with God rests on the assumption that
what we are to make of God is entirely at our disposal and that we
ourselves are not at all seriously at stake in that determination.
This is what is implied in the ongoing debate about whether or not
talk of God is meaningful. In a sense, this is one step beyond the
theodicy question, where the issue is whether or not it is possible
to believe in God in light of the way life is actually experienced.
Here the issue is whether or not the notion of God can make any
sense to us at all. From a serious theological perspective, formed
and informed by an appreciation of atonement, this question of
the meaningfulness of God is bound to appear unanswerable, or
perhaps even answerable only in negative terms. For the intrinsic
implication of this position is that the determinative requirement is
that God be acceptable to us. But, from the atonement perspective, the matter appears the other way around. Far from our questioning the meaningfulness of God, it is we who are questioned.
No one in the modern era was more aware of the dynamics of
atonement than Rudolf Otto. As he saw it, Christianity was particularly characterized by the prominence it accorded this dimension
and this in turn assured the significance of the Christian faith. "No
religion has brought the mystery of the need for atonement or expiation to so complete, so profound, or so powerful expression as
Christianity."[59] This is the case, according to Otto, because of the
basic sense of the holiness of God that permeates the gospel. It is
the divine holiness that makes atonement necessary and credible.
The necessity consists in the fact that the holy God cannot simply
ignore sin, but can forgive with integrity only through atonement.
The credibility derives from the recognition that it is precisely the

holy God who forgives. The holiness makes the divine acceptance amazing and captivating. Conversely, the loss of this amazement in the modern assurance of a virtually automatic divine acceptance results in a Christianity, which for Otto, is "slack and superficial beyond recognition."[60] The further step of concentrating on the question of the meaningfulness of God would probably be seen by Otto as an abandonment of theological sensibility altogether, totally lacking in prospects for amazement.

How that sense of amazement without which atonement is a foreign concept, or at best a collection of ridiculous antiquated myths, is to be recovered is thus something of a catch-22 situation. Appreciation of atonement depends on a sense of the holiness of God, but not only is this sense precluded by uncertainty even as to the meaningfulness of "God," but also concentration on this uncertainty virtually assures that the sense of holiness will never be achieved because this concentration assumes and endorses our own independent integrity. The theoretical solution to this predicament obviously resides in the recognition that our understanding of God and our understanding of ourselves are two sides of the same coin. We do not recognize the holiness of God, or even the meaningfulness of God, because of our sense of our own holiness, our own completeness and sufficiency. Conversely, confession of the holiness of God is possible only in conjunction with an awareness of our own sinfulness. How that theoretical explanation relates to the first hand experience of life, to the sensibilities that actually animate concrete persons, is the difficult question. It might be possible to get a step closer to this living reality through consideration of another theme that has dominated much recent theology, and in so doing has provided a further means for avoiding the atonement issue.

After musings about the meaningfulness of God, the topic which has received the most sustained attention in recent theology is that of Christology. The protracted debate about how the classical claim that Jesus is to be understood as God incarnate is to be interpreted has focused on the question of whether or not incarnation is to be regarded as myth. Much of the ensuing heat and lack of light that this focus has generated may be due to the failure to explore the question of the nature of myth itself. The assumption that seems to prevail is the one proposed, but hardly expounded, much less defended, in the initial volume, *The Myth of God Incarnate*, in which myth is seen essentially as expressions of personal preference in contrast to the objective concepts and conclusions of modern science. It is not surprising that this treatment evoked immediate reaction, because this subjectivizing of matters of faith is no more adequate than the outdated positivistic concept of science that prompts it. That the debate has tended to focus on this objective/subjective axis, with one side contending that convictions like incarnation are expressions of the subjective reactions of believers and the other side contending that they are claims about the object of the beliefs, in this case Jesus as God incarnate, is to some extent due to failure to clarify the inclusive nature of myth, but this can also be seen to entail neglect of the inner dynamic of atonement. This neglect is one of the generally unnoticed features that distinguishes this current debate from those of the classical Christological controversy, and it may also account for the professional and specialized nature of the contemporary debate itself. In spite of the constant castigation of the classical controversy as an exercise in abstract metaphysics, the debates that constituted that controversy were animated by profound soteriological concern. It was important to have some clear idea of how Jesus could represent both God and humanity because in him reconciliation between the holy God and estranged humanity was effected. The motivation for the recent controversy has much more to do with modern epistemological interest in what is intelligible to us on our own. This represents a further intensification of the dilemma of modern theology. Now the significance of Christ as well as the meaningfulness of God is a matter for our independent assessment. This treatment of myth does get away from the rationalistic stance that tended to dominate reflection on the meaningfulness of God, but it does this only by way of reaction. Myth is equated with our private preferences and predilections. A more adequate recognition of the comprehensive scope of myth would require consideration of the demands of atonement, because it would disclose how we ourselves are at stake in such ultimate matters. Far from God being a question of what is meaningful to us or the significance of Christ being a matter of what we happen to find congenial, the scope of these issues defy abstract rational or personal preferential resolution. We only really face these questions seriously insofar as we find ourselves questioned by them. In theological terms, they involve the issue of atonement.

How this theological topic takes root in the arid soil of modern anthropocentrism is the question. It is the question of the reality of theology itself in modern secular culture. But it is also a question of ourselves, of the nature of the life we find ourselves living. The modern sensibility which finds debates about the meaningfulness of God less and less interesting, and for which questions about the categorization of Christ are totally off the psychic map, renders theology precarious to the point of irrelevance. However, rather than bemoaning this situation, it might be more honest, and it certainly would be more constructive, for theology to consider its own complicity in this situation through its failure to pierce the abstraction of the questionableness of God with a vital sense of the holiness of God which questions us and to penetrate the metaphysical obscurity of classical Christology with an engaging vision of the paradigmatic encounter of creature and creator in the person of Jesus. The one consolation in this abject failure of theology to locate its own centre of gravity is the consideration that theology itself is a secondary activity. Its failure to articulate a credible account of the amazing acceptance of the holy God and of the divine condescension and human heroism evidenced in Jesus does not destroy the reality itself that has been experienced and celebrated first hand over the centuries to this day.

4

Salvation and the Church

The susceptibility of the Bible to different interpretations, supportive of different visions of salvation, and the generally acknowledged inadequacy of theological attempts to articulate a doctrine of salvation in terms of theories of atonement, may be less detrimental to the meaning and significance of salvation than might at first appear to be the case. For contrary to the negative impression the lack of precision and clarity conveys, these circumstances may be regarded as testimony to the comprehensive and transcendent nature of the issue involved. A salvation subject to consensus and clear definition would, by that very token, be too bland and parochial to be really interesting. Far from detracting from the importance of salvation, the elusiveness of the reality is rather indicative of its depth and value.

Because of its pervasive nature, salvation has lent itself to artistic expression much more readily than to intellectual articulation. Thus, although the vast majority of Christians might never have heard of the different theories of atonement that theologians have developed in an attempt to explain the significance of Christ, apart from very extreme advocates of the modern liberal direction, and their even rarer predecessors, all Christians have celebrated the salvation offered in Christ in liturgy, music, and through contemplation of the plastic arts. In this, theology is presented with a vivid reminder of its secondary and derivative status. It is by no means the creator of its subject, although we theologians are apt to forget that. What theology seeks to understand, in some measure, has its existence beyond and beneath the level of theological articulation. The understanding theology achieves is ancillary to the awareness of salvation celebrated in symbol and sacrament, sculpture and song.

The Celebration of Salvation

That the central raison d'être of Christianity has been the celebration and realization of salvation seems to be beyond dispute. Although there has certainly not been anything like unanimity on what that might mean for worship and practice at any given time, much less over the total expanse of Christian history, the theme emerges as the unifying thread linking liturgy and architecture, painting and music. We shall consider some of the more prominent instances as reminders of this pervasive presence of the sense of salvation.

HYMNS

In the late twentieth century, the most likely association to be evoked by the term *salvation* is that of the soap box or television evangelist pleading for lost souls to accept the Lord Jesus as their personal savior or soliciting donations so that the vital television ministry can afford to stay on the air to solicit donations, etc. Between these extremes of fanaticism and commercialization, there lies a vibrant tradition born in the recovery of a personal appropriation of the gospel, which transformed early industrial England and moderated the more inhospitable dimensions of the North American frontier. Whereas the most enduring institutional legacy of that eruption of modern evangelicalism is represented by Methodism in its various forms, the most direct link remains in the hymns of salvation, which continue to be sung, even in churches that would not own the evangelical label.

In moving from paraphrases of Psalms and other texts of scripture, the Congregationalist minister, Isaac Watts, is credited with reviving the older practice of creating spiritual songs and accordingly is credited with the title "The Father of Modern English Hymnody."[1] The hymn identified as the transition point from paraphrase to hymn proper, because it incorporates a paraphrase of Galatians (6:14), is his well-known "When I Survey the Wondrous Cross":

> See from His head, His hands, His feet,
> Sorrow and love flow mingled down!
> Did e'er such love and sorrow meet,
> Or thorns compose so rich a crown?

Of this verse, Alexander Macmillan asks: "Is not this sublime verse a high water mark of English hymnody?"[2] Erik Routley calls this the second greatest hymn on the atonement written since the Reformation. The one he places first was also penned by Watts, but it has suffered the opposite fate, being largely relegated to obscurity.

> Nature with open volume stands,
>   To spread her Maker's praise abroad;
> And every labour of His hands
>   Shows something worthy of a God.
>
> But in the grace that rescued man,
>   His brightest form of glory shines;
> Here, on the cross, 'tis fairest drawn,
>   In precious blood and crimson lines.
>
> Here his whole Name appears complete:
>   Nor wit can guess, nor reason prove,
> Which of the letters best is writ,
>   The power, the wisdom, or the love.
>
> Here I behold his inmost heart,
>   Where grace and vengeance strangely join,
> Piercing his Son with sharpest smart
>   To make the purchas'd pleasures mine.
>
> O the sweet wonders of that cross,
>   Where God the Savior loved and died!
> Here noblest life my spirit draws
>   From His dear wounds, and bleeding side.
>
> I would forever speak His Name
>   In sounds to mortal ears unknown,
> With angels join to praise the Lamb
>   And worship at His Father's throne.[3]

Routley speculates that this hymn has remained obscure because it withholds the image of the Crucified until the fifth stanza, whereas "When I Survey the Wondrous Cross" sets it forth from the opening words.

Watts receives Alexander Macmillan's vote as the greatest hymn-writer because of this single hymn, "When I Survey the Wondrous Cross," but he suggests that "if the greatest hymn-writer is he who has given the largest number of hymns of a high order, then undoubtedly the palm must be given to Charles Wesley."[4] The opening lines of some of Wesley's oft-sung hymns are indicative of this same focus on Christ the savior: "O for a thousand tongues to sing my great Redeemer's praise," "Jesus, lover of my soul." The centrality of this theme is totally explicit in the second verse of a less well-known hymn that invokes guidance on the church's preachers: "Help them to preach the truth of God, Redemption through the Savior's blood."

This preoccupation with the cross, which animates evangelical Protestantism, leaves no doubt about the centrality of salvation in its scheme of things. For many people, however, that is a liability, rather than an asset. George Bernard Shaw spoke for many when he called it "Crosstianity."[5] The significance of Jesus is so focused on his death that the cross threatens to become a self-sufficient icon to the exclusion of the encounters and teachings of Jesus' life, not to mention, the wider presence of God in the world. There is no doubt that this focus is presented in uncompromising vividness especially in the eighteenth century.

> They speak freely and repeatedly of bowels, cavities, blood, incisions, and flesh. The singer yearns to "fly to the bosom of Jesus", to "drink the living water", to "wash in the fountain of blood."[6]

However, beneath what may appear to be a morbid fascination with the details of the crucifixion, there runs the current of modern self-consciousness, which in this context emerges as the sense of our responsibility for the death of Christ. "Self-abasement of a different kind from the rhetorical prostration of Calvinist hymnists before God the Father resulted from the sense of personal responsibility for the passion."[7] That sense of responsibility is further internalized in the nineteenth century as the emphasis on the physical imagery gives way to lyrics that "tended to be more mawkishly sentimental."[8] In this general direction, Protestant worshippers' glorifying "Crosstianity" in song not only reflected the general development of self-consciousness characteristic of the modern Western outlook but also the shift we saw in the treatment of atonement from the traditional objective views to the modern subject-centered, moral influence approach.

> Between the fourth and the nineteenth centuries, the hymnody had evolved from objective representation of God's creative and redemptive action, through human response and inward realization, to ideas and feelings of mid-Victorians, prompted by mythical or historical incidents long ago and far away.[9]

Although the focus on our personal implication in the crucifixion and on the significance of the response the awareness of this evokes in us represents a subjective focus which is different from previous sensibilities regarding salvation, Shaw's charge of "Crosstianity" is misleading if it is taken to mean that this veneration of the Crucified is a novel development.

In their cruciolatry, Methodists and Evangelicals were not alone. Witness the Catholic cult of the Sacred Heart and the Precious Blood, and especially the pietism of the prayer "*Anima Christi*," "Water from the side of Christ, wash me" and "Within Thy wounds, hide me."[10]

What is more, the contemplation of the passion in modern hymns is not at all without precedent. Consider the following example:

> Jesu, crowned with thorns for me,
> Scourged for my transgression,
> Witnessing through agony
> That thy good confession:
> Jesu, clad in purple raiment,
> For my evils making payment;
> Let not all thy woe and pain,
> Let now Calvary be in vain.[11]

If you were to conclude that this was a fairly typical modern hymn, this would be understandable, and you would be right to the extent that this verse is a modern translation, provided by John Mason Neale, spearhead of the Cambridge wing of the Oxford Movement. In its origin, however, this verse is from the ninth century "Suppliant Canon of Jesus," written by one Theoctistus. A similar situation pertains with regard to the familiar "O Sacred Head, sore wounded," which is a nineteenth century translation of a hymn of the twelfth or thirteenth centuries composed of seven parts, "each consisting of an apostrophe to one of the seven members of the body of Jesus, as he hung upon the Cross—Feet, knees, hands, side, breast, heart, and head."[12] And it is surely not insignificant that what is probably the oldest extant hymn is called "Hymn to the Savior Christ." It was found appended to *The Tutor*, a work attributed to Clement of Alexandria (c. 170–c. 220).[13]

This musical celebration of salvation is by no means confined to the domain of popular hymns, although it is particularly evident there. The modern translation of the twelfth or thirteenth century hymn mentioned previously, "O Sacred Head now wounded," is usually sung to the tune of Bach's "Passion Chorale."[14] Some of the most sublime music the world has known has been inspired by the salvation theme. Many would say that the Swedish bishop,

Nathan Söderblom, is not extravagant in his designation of musical representations of salvation as "the fifth gospel."

> I would not hesitate to give the name "the fifth Gospel" to the musical interpretation of the story of redemption, which reaches its highest point in John Sebastian Bach. Very deeply do the *Passion according to St. Matthew* and the *Mass in B minor* enter into the mystery of suffering and redemption.[15]

The total impact of Christ ultimately communicates at a level deeper than the poetry of song, touching chords that vibrate only to the mystical tones of the transcendent reach of great music.

If it be true that the Church has come down the ages singing, it is no less true that the song she has sung at any given time is more apt to celebrate the salvation rooted in Christ than any other theme. However inadequate the understanding of that accomplishment may have been, its gripping reality received abundant testimony in poetic phrase and musical praise. It was a true sensibility that led the congregationalist minister of Carr's Lane, Birmingham, R. W. Dale, to propose: "Let me write the hymns of the Church, and I care not who writes the theology."[16] It is also a true sensibility on the part of worshippers that leads them to sing the hymns of Zion, many of which are cosmologically archaic and some of which reveal less than healthy fascination with the gruesome intricacies of the crucifixion, because they sense in these a note of eternity which is missing in our highly abstract or overly practical theologies.

> It is no mean tribute to the innumerable poets who over almost two millennia have expressed in song the central beliefs of the Christian faith, that their accumulated handiwork, though of "mere human composition" has at different times inspired believers of every tribe, rank, and avocation, playing a major part in the Lutheran, Methodist and Evangelical, Abolitionist, and Ecumenical movements, and in no small measure keeping alive during the nineteenth and early twentieth centuries beliefs that scientists, scholars, and even theologians were on every side forsaking.[17]

Among the beliefs that hymns have kept alive in the twentieth century is the central belief in salvation, the sense that in Christ God has reached out to humanity with a depth and significance that defies our theological explanations and transcends our social programs. The poetry of song allows us to celebrate this comprehensive vision that embraces us through the gospel sung down through the centuries. The majesty of music strikes this note at an even more profound level.

LITURGY

In spite of its noble heritage, of which the foregoing has offered only the barest sketch, the centrality of salvation in the hymnody of the Church is eclipsed by its prominence in the Church's liturgy itself.

> Historians of doctrine continually face the problem of trying to determine what the average person was thinking while the erudite theologians were discussing profound issues. We have a glimpse into the mentality of early Christians by looking at the liturgies, which were a part of their daily life. It was here, rather than in theological essays that the average person caught a vision of the meaning of salvation.[18]

While the liturgy that was part of the daily life of ordinary believers might often have taken a quite specific form such as a version of the cult of Mary, or the veneration of patron saints of clan or craft, there can hardly be any question that the fundamental source of liturgical inspiration lay in the sacrifice of the mass. Through eastern orthodoxy and classical Latin Christianity, the animating spirit of the faith has been derived from the re-enactment of the sacrifice of Christ on the sacred altar.

The sacredness and solemnity with which the Eucharist came to typify the essence of the Christian faith is attested by the eastern *Commentary on the Divine Liturgy*, by Nicholas Cabasilas, and the significance of this commentary, in turn, is attested by the wide endorsement it has received, and continues to receive, in both East and West. The seriousness of the sacrament is indicated right from the start in the elaborate preparation of the elements, the *Prothesis*,[19] in which the celebrant cuts off the part of a loaf marked with the monogram of Christ and pierces the side of it in reenactment of the piercing on the cross. Only this portion, the Lamb or the Seal, will be consecrated on the altar. Of the remainder, a piece is cut out in honor of Mary and is placed on the right side of the Lamb; three rows of three small pieces are placed on the other side of the Lamb in honor of the apostles, the saints, and martyrs; two rows of pieces for the living and the dead are placed in front of the Lamb. These portions of the loaf become the *antidoron* "instead of the gift," and as such are distributed to the people following the Eucharist itself. This is generally seen as a relic of the primitive *agape* feast in which the early community is thought to have joined as a common fellowship meal.[20] The prothesis and the Eucharist itself are separated by the Liturgy of the Catechumens, readings and prayers intended especially for those who have not yet been admitted to the ranks of the faithful. In earlier times the Catechumens were dismissed at this point; the modern practice has been to permit them to observe the celebration of the Eucharist itself, the Liturgy of the Faithful.[21]

The whole celebration, from the Prothesis through to the thanksgiving and closing prayers, which conclude the Liturgy of the Faithful is understood as a celebration of salvation. So even of that preparatory stage, Cabasilas' comments regarding the actions of the priest: "Thus they are all, as it were, a dramatization of Christ's sufferings and death."[22] The act of piercing the side of the loaf is a vivid example of this, in its own way as dramatic as the most descriptive evangelical hymn. However, the climactic moment of the drama is not reached until the Liturgy of the Faithful in the *epiklesis* or prayer of consecration, where through the invocation of the priest the elements are transformed into the body and blood of Christ. In wondering how this can be a true sacrifice, and not simply symbolic, in view of the fact that the sacrifice of Christ was made once and for all, Cabasilas arrives at his explanation for this focal point of the Eucharist:

> Is there an answer to these problems? Yes: the sacrifice is accomplished neither before nor after the consecration of the bread, but at the very moment of consecration itself. It is necessary thus to preserve all the teachings of our faith concerning sacrifice, without overlooking any. What are these teachings? In the first place, that this sacrifice is not a mere figure or symbol but a true sacrifice; secondly, that it is not the bread which is sacrificed, but the very Body of Christ; thirdly, that the Lamb of God was sacrificed once only, for all time.[23]

The mystery of the Eucharist thus combines the apparently contradictory factors of the one, final, and sufficient sacrifice of Christ himself and the manifold sacrifices of the altar, which are also sacrifices of the body and blood of Christ.

The logical dilemma raised by this insistence on the full reality of the sacrifice on the altar and the equally strong affirmation of the sufficiency of the historic sacrifice of Christ shades into the theological dilemma of the threat to that sufficiency posed by the emphasis on the real sacrifice of the mass which has been of particular concern within Protestantism. From this latter point of view, the solutions proposed appear no more satisfactory than the sacramental dissolution of the logical contradiction. For, on the one hand, in the usual Catholic rationale of the Mass, the traditional Protestant concern with the sufficiency of the cross is affirmed:

> In one sense it is quite certain that the Mass adds nothing to the Cross. It is the same sacrifice, one which was perfect in its historical realization.[24]

But at the same time this is qualified by the contention that the Mass does add something to the Cross.

> Nevertheless she [the Church] does renew it [the sacrifice of Christ] and on the explicit instructions of her Master: that cannot be a pointless thing to do. In this indirect manner, which must be correctly understood, it would be correct to say that the Mass does add something to the Cross.[25]

What it is seen to add is the concrete application of the fruits of the cross and also the offering of the Church in which the priest and the faithful "add to Christ's work that human participation which he desires."[26] This Catholic explanation will not satisfy Protestant suspicions, which are aroused by any talk of "adding to Christ's work." However, this logical and theological dilemma in Catholicism, East and West, is compensated for by the uncompromising concreteness of the sacrament. Where Protestants hymn the savior, Catholics taste salvation in receiving the broken body and shed blood. Whatever difficulties may be endemic to the doctrine of transubstantiation, the sense of the reality of salvation conveyed by the sacrament thus understood is beyond question.

The role of the Eucharist itself has, by no means, been constant over the centuries. Apart from Protestantism's challenge that the sacrament had been absolutized so that the institution, of which it constituted the center, far from dispensing Christ, had in fact dispensed with Christ, the approach to the Eucharist itself had changed over the centuries so that it became more remote from the worshipping community and more exclusively the property of the priest. In the fourth century the *disciplina arcani*, the duty to preserve the mystery of liturgical forms and actions by requiring secrecy about them, seems to have infiltrated the Church through the influx of members from the ancient mystery cults. One of the most visible results of this, in the East, was the shift from an open celebration where the priest said the prayers aloud, and the people owned the celebration with their assenting "Amen," to a whispered celebration where the people stood by as passive spectators at a priestly function.[27] This transition was resisted in the West until about the year 1000.[28] When it did develop, this change of focus from a communal to a sacerdotal celebration was reinforced by the change in position of the priest from behind the altar, facing the people, to a position in front of the altar with his back to the congregation.[29]

A further innovation can be attributed to the monastic movement, the rise of the private mass. The original monasteries, as lay communities, were hesitant about accepting priests into the community because their office gave them an authority which represented a potential clash with the authority of the community. Saint Benedict of Nursia solved the problem by allowing proven monks to be ordained priests. With the missionary efforts of the seventh and eighth centuries, the number of priests grew dramatically. The net result was the development of the practice of priests saying mass privately so that the people became dispensable even as passive observers.[30] With this the act by which the community had celebrated the reality of salvation was withdrawn from general currency, and regarded as the exclusive property of the clergy.

This might not have constituted such a dramatic change as we would be inclined to think. It may rather have simply confirmed what was a generally prevalent tendency for most worshippers in their inclination to pursue their own devotions in conjunction with what was happening at the altar.

> The devotion to the Son of God, present in the tabernacle on the altars, to his most Sacred Heart, and to His Passion, and equally the almost infinite number of forms of devotion to Our Lady—all these were more congenial to the pious than the existing forms of the liturgy which for the most part were not probably understandable, especially as the liturgy of the Middle Ages onwards was looked upon as the exclusive concern of the priest. Hence while the celebrant 'read' the mass at the altar with his back to the people, the faithful were busy with other devotional exercises, mostly of a subjective nature.[31]

Relics of the communal celebration intruded only as the three main parts of the Eucharist—the offertory, the consecration, and the communion—were signalled by the server's bell and the worshippers were momentarily directed to what was taking place at the altar.[32] However, this should not be taken to mean that the sacrament was peripheral for the typical worshipper of the Middle Ages. On the contrary, although its mode of celebration left the worshipper on the periphery, there is good reason to think that for the worshipper it was accorded a place of primary reverence. The immediate focus of devotion to the Sacred Heart or the Blessed Virgin were sustained by the underlying conviction that at the altar the priest was celebrating the fundamental element of salvation, the reenactment of the sacrifice of the cross. The centrality of this reverence for the Eucharist itself is attested by the emergence of the *Corpus Christi* procession. "People's longing for a 'saving look' at the eucharistic bread, and the delight the Middle Ages took in public processions led to the practice of the eucharist being carried around in a triumphal procession on *Corpus Christi.*"[33]

There can be no doubt then about the centrality of the Eucharist in medieval Christianity. What can be questioned is whether this emphasis itself was too confining for the reality it celebrated as the later evangelical emphasis on the horrors of the crucifixion and the personal appeal to the conscience of the sinner can be held to be. It seems clear that the scope of thanksgiving assayed by the Eucharist was subject to restriction in the medieval period.

> In medieval and Reformation rites that thanksgiving is concentrated on the cross; but while that has always been the focus, some of the earliest recorded liturgies show a much wider range of thanksgiving, incorporating the whole story of God's creation and of his dealings with the people. This fuller range of thanksgiving is a characteristic also of more recent revised or constructed rites.[34]

It does seem clear that medieval liturgy and modern hymnody each reveal a preoccupation with the crucifixion, which tends to isolate it, with the result that salvation tends to take on a magical quality as a sacramental priestly prerogative or a personal pietistic experience. And yet, just as modern evangelical hymns have their predecessors in early expressions of Christian praise of the crucified, so too the liturgical focus of the Middle Ages represents a constriction of the definitive focus of Christianity rather than a novel innovation.

EARLY CHRISTIAN ART

Although the crucifixion has been the focal point for Christian understanding and celebration, it does not figure prominently in the earliest representations. In fact, the available evidence indicates that not only was the crucifixion not a prominent subject of early Christian expression, but also that, in fact, the whole life of Christ was downplayed in the first centuries of the common era. "Very few episodes drawn from the life of Christ exist from pre-

Constantinian times, and the Passion and Crucifixion seem to have been almost totally excluded."[35] This lack of explicit representation of the life of Christ in early Christian art carries the surface connotation that the Christological focus was a later development, and perhaps an unwarranted one. However, a more immediate explanation for this reticence is at hand in terms of the circumstances in which the early Christians found themselves. The image of enthusiastic confessors of the faith rushing headlong toward martyrdom must surely be qualified by an expectation of a fairly general reluctance on the part of a minority movement to identify itself conspicuously for authorities that might be inclined to suspect it of seditious intent. To identify themselves as the followers of one who was executed, for supposedly monarchical ambitions, makes the absence of depictions of the cross particularly understandable.

> Stigmatized as atheists, as morally depraved, and even as cannibals through pagan misunderstanding of the Eucharist, the faithful had to be very circumspect and to avoid flaunting their religion. Thus the cross, now the universal symbol of Christianity, was at first avoided not only for its direct association with Christ but for its shameful association with the execution of a common criminal also.[36]

It would be a mistake, however, to assume that this lack of overt depiction of the cross implies its absence in the understanding and orientation of the early Christians. The opposite is almost certainly the case. "The doctrinal stress of the first Christian art was on deliverance."[37] This was presented through images of Old Testament figures like Daniel, Jonah, and Noah, but for the early Christians themselves, these heroes of the more publicly acceptable Hebrew faith no doubt spoke of the deliverance in Christ. It is impossible to imagine, for instance, that they could have meditated on the portrayal of the sacrifice of Isaac without seeing in that the sacrifice of the cross. This is confirmed by the earliest firmly dateable Christian art, paintings in the Christian complex at Dura Europus, which were completed around 240 C.E.[38] The two paintings displayed most prominently are one of Adam and Eve beside the tree of knowledge and the other of the Shepherd and his Flock. It is difficult to imagine a more vivid attestation to the centrality of the salvation theme for early Christians, given the constraints under which they operated.

Evidence of this centrality is provided by the use of the fish symbol as a means of identifying early Christian dwellings and places of worship. It is generally held that the explanation for this usage is that the Greek word for fish also constituted the initial letters of the confession ᾿Ιησοῦς Χριστὸς θεοῦ Υἱός Σωτήρ, Jesus Christ, son of God, Savior.[39] Those who object that this must represent a later more sophisticated interpretation of what must have been a much simpler symbol in its original intention, are left with the challenge of providing a simpler interpretation, which is consistent with the prominence of its employment. That the risen Christ joined the disciples for a meal of fish, according to the Fourth Gospel, hardly seems to provide an adequate base, in light of the fact that this did not receive any recognition in the tradition in any degree comparable to the perpetuation of the Last Supper. The fact that fish were involved in the accounts of the feeding of the multitudes also seems too peripheral to be a serious candidate. The encounter on the lake where Jesus directed the disciples to a successful catch seems equally incapable of bearing this weight. Even the designation of the disciples as fishers for the kingdom hardly seems adequate. And even the cumulative effect of all these references falls short of that comprehensive designation of what really distinguished the early Christians, the conviction that Jesus was the Christ, the Son of God, the Savior. It can hardly be held that this is a late development when the earliest gospel begins with the words "the beginning of the gospel of the Jesus Christ, the Son of God."

There can be no doubt, then, that from earliest times, Christian faith has been grounded in the celebration of salvation. That celebration has issued in works of art, simple and sophisticated, in music and song, equally diverse in quality and appeal, and in the shaping of the most characteristic forms of Christian worship. Although these expressions have sometimes approached the macabre, and thereby undermined the appreciation of the wider significance of the salvation being celebrated, they also preserve that central focus of the faith, which more explicit attempts to understand what Christianity involves have sometimes had a tendency to minimize.

The Legitimacy of the Celebration of Salvation

Although salvation enjoys an indisputable prominence as a communicator of what Christianity is all about, that that reality has been adequately addressed, even in the more symbolic and dramatic forms of representation, leaving aside the more conceptually oriented attempts at theological articulation, is not at all so evident.

In particular, it is suggested that the comprehensive thrust of the gospel was short-circuited by the restriction of focus to the passion, and especially the cross of Christ, as this was celebrated in the Eucharist and that this, in turn, was subjected to further artificial isolation with the Constantinian settlement.

THE LIETZMANN THESIS

The centrality accorded the Eucharist in Christian tradition is challenged by H. Lietzmann, in his *Messe und Herrenmahl, Eine Studie zur Geschichte der Liturgie* (1926). In this he identifies the fourth-century Egyptian liturgy of Sarapion and the third-century Roman liturgy of Hippolytus as the two sources of all later liturgies. He says the Egyptian liturgy is dependent on the *Didache*, ultimately deriving from the "breaking of bread" in Acts 2:42–46. This represents the continuation of the fellowship meals the disciples enjoyed with Jesus. It is characterized by joy, and has no connection with the death of Jesus or the Last Supper. The liturgy of Hippolytus, by contrast, reflects the Hellenistic sacramental Eucharist, which Paul developed as the memorial of Christ's death.[40] The central thesis, then, is that the somber, passion-focused Eucharist represents an imposition on the original joyous fellowship meal characterized by expectation.

> There are many who think that this is where the significance of these meals in the early days of the Palestinian Christians ends. They were simply fellowship meals of those who shared together in a loyalty to Jesus and His way of life. Any connection with the Last Supper and the death of Christ belongs, it is alleged, only to the cultic meals of the later Hellenistic Christian communities.[41]

The Lietzmann thesis has enjoyed considerable influence in molding scholars' opinion about the origins of the sacrament, which has occupied the focal point of Christian consciousness. No less a scholar, than Oscar Cullmann endorses the view that the generally accepted understanding of the Eucharist as the memorial of the passion of Christ, whatever that might be taken to mean in more precise terms, represents a later imposition on the originally eschatologically oriented fellowship meal.[42] Cullmann contends that the original Christian celebration was characterized by joy and expectation in contrast to the somber recollection, or re-presentation, of the passion of Christ.[43] But where Lietzman could find no source to account for the origins of this joyous celebration,

Cullmann locates its basis in the fact that the risen Christ appeared in the context of meals according to the Fourth Gospel account of the breakfast appearance by the seaside and the Lukan account of the risen Lord being recognized by the travellers to Emmaus in the breaking of bread.[44] This association was reinforced by "the cultic experience, constantly renewed since then, of the Lord's presence in the midst of the faithful assembled for the brotherly love-feast."[45]

This explanation derives plausibility from the transition that shaped early Christian understanding prompted by the delay of the parousia. It seems clear that as the early expectation of an imminent return of Jesus was frustrated, the first Christians found more and more significance in his original appearance. From this general perspective, it is entirely credible that an originally joyous celebration, anticipating the return of the risen Lord, could have become transformed into a retrospective re-enactment of the sacrifice, which is seen to typify his whole life as climaxed in the cross. However, this initial plausibility is threatened as soon as it is subjected to closer examination. One fundamental difficulty that arises immediately is the adequacy of the basis proposed for the fellowship meal. The dominant note of joy and expectation can be attributed to convictions about the risen Lord, but that direction is seen to qualify a practice of common fellowship meals. At its strictest, the contrast is between a Hebrew tradition of fellowship meals, which for the early Christians took on connotations associated with the resurrection and return of Jesus, and a later Hellenistic influence through which a cultic focus redirected Christian celebration toward a memorial of Christ's sacrifice. The immediate difficulty is that the evidence for such Hebrew fellowship meals is lacking.

> Certainly 'fellowships' are occasionally mentioned in connection with ritual meals, but these 'fellowships' were *haburot miswah*, i.e. 'fellowships for the observance of a commandment', and the *haburah* meals in which they took part, and to the cost of which they subscribed, were exclusively *duty* meals, such as those connected with betrothals, weddings, circumcisions, funerals, in which participation as a paying guest was considered meritorious. That these fellowships, which, moreover, were of a charitable nature, or other 'communities of friends' met at any time 'whenever they felt the need to do so' to hold a ritual meal, let alone a sacramental meal, cannot be proven.[46]

The main support for the notion that the first Christians assembled for fellowship meals at which they celebrated the resurrection of Jesus and anticipated his imminent return in a mood of jubilation and triumph that totally displaced the apparent defeat of the cross is to be found in the reference in Acts 2:42,46 to the Christians assembling for "the breaking of bread." There the regime of the believers is described thus: "And they devoted themselves to the apostles' teaching and fellowship, to the breaking of bread and the prayers" (2:42). And in slightly more specific terms: "And day by day, attending the temple together and breaking bread in their homes, they partook of food with glad and joyous hearts" (2:46). The fact that there is no reference here to either the cup or the atoning death of Jesus is, at best, an argument from silence. " 'Breaking of bread' may be a sort of technical term for the whole meal."[47] One could certainly conclude from Paul's description of practices in the Church in Corinth that there was not much consideration of the sacrifice of Christ, but neither does there seem to have been any clear note of eschatological expectation. The general impression is one of indulgence. Apparently, each individual or family brought their own food and drink, and those who had ample provisions ate and drank heartily, often to excess and resulting drunkenness, while those who lacked even went hungry. "When you meet together, it is not the Lord's supper that you eat. For in eating, each one goes ahead with his own meal, and one is hungry and another is drunk" (I Cor. 11:20,21). In these circumstances, Paul is not imposing a novel sacramental Eucharist on a previously joyous fellowship meal, but rather recalling the church in Corinth to the established meaning of the "breaking of bread." "What Paul did was to lay a renewed emphasis on the remembrance of the death of Christ which was already present, but which in Corinth was in danger of being forgotten—not to mention brotherly generosity and good manners."[48]

Slender textual evidence is not the only problem with the interpretation that assumes a joyous fellowship meal to which the sacramental memorial of the death of Christ was later added. There is also the difficulty of imagining the early Christians assembling in joyous celebration of the risen Christ and in continuation of the meals they had enjoyed together with no significant recollection of his shocking death and the last meal which preceded it. "But is it conceivable that that other memory—the memory of the Last Supper—was not also vivid at the very first—indeed, at its most vivid then?"[49] It seems incredible that the early Christians could have assembled for meals and not recalled the last meal Jesus shared with his disciples, unless it is held that that meal itself is an invention of the sacramental turn.

A less extreme alternative is represented by those who contrast the Markan and Pauline accounts of the Last Supper. The Markan account does not have the command to repeat this act of eating and drinking as a memorial, which Paul records: "Do this in remembrance of me" over the bread (I Cor. 11:24), and "Do this, as oft as you drink it, in remembrance of me" over the cup (I Cor. 11:25). Conversely, the Pauline account is not as explicit about the context of eschatological expectation associated with the Last Supper as Mark is: "Truly, I say to you, I shall not drink again of the fruit of the vine until that day when I drink it new in the kingdom of God" (Mark 14:25). However, it is a huge step from the recognition of this difference to the contention that Mark reflects a primitive eschatological celebration, anticipating the imminent return of Jesus, while Paul represents a backward looking fixation on the death of Jesus. For one thing, the eschatological note is by no means absent in Paul. His version of the institution of the Lord's Supper concludes with precisely that note. "For as often as you eat this bread and drink the cup, you proclaim the Lord's death until he comes" (I Cor. 11:26). Even more significant is the fact that understanding the Lord's Supper as the continuation of the Last Supper can hardly be confined to Paul's explicit reference to the command to so repeat it, and the parallel in Luke (22:19).

THE LAST SUPPER AND PASSOVER

The memorial character of the Lord's Supper is related to the link which can be established between the Last Supper and the Passover. The controversy over whether or not the Last Supper was a Passover meal has focused particularly on the contrast between the synoptic indication that it was and the suggestion in the Fourth Gospel that it occurred on the evening preceding the Passover. The most credible resolution seems to be to accept that the author of the Fourth Gospel retarded the whole chronology by twenty-four hours so that the crucifixion would coincide with the slaying of the Pascal lambs. But then the result is that the Fourth Gospel is actually intent on emphasizing the link between Jesus and the Passover, rather than undermining it.[50] What is more, the Fourth Gospel account can even be seen to assume, and thus to substantiate, the synoptic identification of the Last Supper as a Passover meal. When Jesus tells Judas to get on with what he must do, according to the Fourth Gospel, some of those present thought that because he was the treasurer of the group that Jesus was saying "Buy what we need for the feast" (13:29). But this was taking place during the feast itself. This inconsistency could suggest that the author has retained something of the recognition that the Last Supper was a Passover meal into which he has inserted his own decelerated chronology.[51]

This interpretation is further corroborated by characteristics of the Last Supper that suggest parallels to salient features and requirements of the Passover. Jeremias identifies fourteen such aspects among which the following appear particularly significant. The Last Supper was held at night, which was contrary to the prevalent custom of a simple breakfast meal in the late morning followed by the main meal of the day in the late afternoon. The only other place in the gospels that refers to an evening meal is the feeding of the five thousand (Mt. 14:15), but there it is explicitly asserted that the time for eating had already passed. The reason the Last Supper was held at night is readily available in the requirement that the Passover be held after sunset.[52] Another factor is the unanimous agreement of all the gospels that Jesus and the disciples reclined at the Last Supper. The custom for ordinary meals in Jesus' day was to sit. But it was a ritual duty to recline at the Passover as a symbol of the freedom it celebrated.[53] The fact that Jesus broke bread during the course of the meal is also contrary to the normal practice where meals began with the breaking of bread, but is perfectly consistent with the Passover celebration where one of the children's questions about the meaning of Passover was stimulated by having a dish before bread was provided.[54] The drinking of wine was also confined to festive occasions and the evidence that red wine was required for Passover fits with Jesus' association of the wine with his blood.[55] The Last Supper concluded with the singing of a hymn, which could well be the second half of the Passover *hallel*.[56] Most significant of all, Jesus' interpretation of the bread and wine as representing his body and blood is perfectly consistent with, and may well have been suggested by, the element of interpretation that constituted an integral part of the meal as the father in the family setting explained the significance of the different ingredients in the meal.[57] A full treatment of this issue would require consideration of the objections to this identification of the Last Supper as a Passover meal, which Jeremias also examines, but since these are largely arguments from silence, concerned with elements of the Passover observance that are not indicated by the accounts of the Last Supper, such as there being no mention of a lamb, we shall forego this otherwise essential dimension of a balanced approach and rest content in the overwhelming impression of an undeniable link between the annual celebration of the Passover and the Last Supper.

As a reinterpretation of the Passover, the Last Supper entails the note of remembrance as an inescapable dimension. The actual command "Do this in remembrance of me" may be a Pauline addition, although it can be argued that his contribution has been to add the command following the taking of the cup, and that he based this on the command regarding the bread that was in the early tradition which he received.[58] In this way Paul can be regarded as having Rabbinized the tradition[59] in the sense that he drew out elements, which were there at least implicitly, and made them explicit. He can be seen to have done this by adding the command to repeat the taking of the cup to the tradition he received which contained such an imperative in relation to the bread, or he can be seen to have made the whole memorial element explicit, in which case it can be seen to be present implicitly in Mark as the other main source of the Last Supper tradition. It hardly seems credible that the link between the Last Supper and the Lord's Supper can be attributed to Paul, as Cullmann suggests in his contention that Paul found these two elements in the primitive community and "added as a third element the idea of the link connecting them"[60] on the basis of his theology of redemption centering on the death of Christ. Far more credible is the contention of C. F. D. Moule that the connection between the Lord's Supper and the Last Supper was one that Paul received from early Christian practice.[61]

> In any case, even if we were to omit the allusion to a dominical command to commemorate the death of Christ, and ignore the peculiarly Lukan (Lk. 22:19) and Pauline (I Cor. 11:17ff.) material, there would still remain in the narratives of the Last Supper alike in Paul, Luke, Matthew and Mark a reference to the blood of Christ shed for many; and it is exceedingly difficult to escape the conclusion that in all available references to the traditions there is at least a linking of the idea of the death of Christ on behalf of others with this fellowship meal.[62]

Then rather than assuming a primitive fellowship meal on which a later sacramental rite was grafted, which would imply that the early Christians shared meals that reflected the fellowship meal of Jesus and his disciples and of the disciples and the risen Christ but which were essentially devoid of any reference to the cross and the Last Supper, what we have to consider is the much more likely possibility that these early fellowship meals included a remembrance of the cross and the Last Supper.

The understanding to which we are being impelled is virtually the converse of the Cullmann-type perspective, which sees the sacramental retrospective celebration of the passion as a modification of the primitive prospective fellowship meal, eaten in joyous anticipation of the return of Jesus. That anticipation almost certainly never entailed a complete obliteration of the recollection of the cross, and it is equally difficult to imagine that that recollection could have persisted in isolation from the interpretive perspective available in the accounts of the Last Supper. Thus, rather than the sacramental reading being imposed on the fellowship meal, it is more plausible to assume an original comprehensive celebration from which the fellowship meal and the Eucharist became detached.

> It was because Jesus was recognized by Christians as God's chosen King, because His death and the solemn meal anticipating it were seen to be the inauguration of the New Covenant sealed by His blood, that every meal together was at least capable of meaning for the Christians a renewal of their commitment as true Israel, as the real People of God. There is no need to believe that every meal explicitly carried this significance: no doubt there was an uninstitutional freedom and flexibility. But if the Pauline tradition is a true one, it is difficult to believe that there was not, from the very first, a vivid awareness of this aspect of the Christian breaking of bread also, and to concede this is to recognize something *sacramental* as an original element in distinctively Christian worship.[63]

The problem Paul encountered in Corinth assumes a common meal which supposedly celebrated the Lord's Supper. What he sees himself doing is not imposing a Eucharistic celebration on a simple fellowship meal, but rather reminding the Corinthians that the meal is meant to celebrate the Lord's death "till he comes" (I Cor. 11:26), and that the gluttony and drunkenness of some combined with the hunger of others is a violation of that celebration. In this way, Paul may well be regarded as a prime instigator of the separation of the sacrament from the full meal. Thus, rather than bringing them together, Paul's role is more likely to have been that of promoting their separation. This may be reflected in the contrast between I Cor. 11:25 and Lk. 22:21, on the one hand, where the cup comes "after supper," and the apparently more refined sacramental balance in Mark and Matthew where the bread and the cup appear in more direct parallel.[54]

THE EUCHARIST

The contribution of Paul, then, to the establishment of the Eucharist may well have been very significant, but this would not amount to anything like a novel invention. His effect rather had more to do with the promotion of the separation between the Eucharistic celebration and the fellowship meal. However, the realization of that separation took some time. Some would even place it as late as the third decade of the second century.

> Evening assembly to celebrate the Lord's Supper in connection with a regular meal is the usual form in the New Testament. Not until Justin is the ritual of the bread and cup separated from the meal as the "Eucharist" and incorporated into Sunday morning worship.[65]

Although the focus of the Eucharist can be seen to be present from the first, there is no doubt that the process of separation by which it came to stand on its own also involved a significant transformation in the understanding of the nature of the Eucharist itself.

One of the principal elements in the transformation is the transition from the understanding of the Eucharist as a memorial of Christ's sacrifice toward what we have seen to be the developed doctrine of the Middle Ages, which regarded the Eucharist itself as in some sense constituting a sacrifice. Thus, *The Didache* gives a prescription for the Eucharist that regards it as a sacrifice offered by the worshipper in line with the direction for sacrifice announced by Malachi (1:11,14).

> Assemble on the Lord's Day, and break bread and offer the Eucharist; but first make confession of your faults, so that your sacrifice may be a pure one. Anyone who has a difference with his fellow is not to take part with you until they have been reconciled, so as to avoid any profanation of your sacrifice. For this is the offering of which the Lord has said, *Everywhere and always bring me a sacrifice that is undefiled, for I am a great king, says the Lord, and my name is the wonder of nations.*[66]

The further shift from this general sacrificial understanding of the Eucharist to the more specific identification of it as a sacrifice in itself entails another crucial element in this postcanonical development, the formalization of the roles of leadership as liturgical and institutional authorities. Thus Ignatius admonishes the Philadelphians:

> Make certain, therefore, that you all observe one common Eucharist; for there is but one Body of the Lord Jesus Christ, and but one cup of union with His Blood, and one single altar of sacrifice—even as also there is but one bishop, with his clergy and my own fellow–servitors the deacons. This will ensure that all your doings are in full accord with the will of God.[67]

The practical point is spelled out in *Ignatius' Letter to the Smyrneans*: "The sole Eucharist you should consider valid is one that is celebrated by the bishop himself, or by some person authorized by him."[68] For Ignatius, this source of validity is not confined to the Eucharist, for he also requires the same authorization for the love feast. "Nor is it permissible to conduct baptisms or love-feasts without the bishop."[69] However, the Eucharist and the love feast are clearly two different things, and the basis for the exultation of the Eucharist, which followed its isolation, and which characterized the medieval sacerdotal sacrament, is already evident.

Further development of the medieval sacrament entailed two refinements. On the one hand, the eschatological note that continued to characterize the eucharist as well as the fellowship meals was largely displaced by a retrospective preoccupation with the past. This historicizing of the liturgy was part of a wider tendency to dwell on the details of the life of Christ without regard for the promise of a future fulfillment, the clear emergence of which has recently been held to be as late as Theodore of Mopsuestia in the early fifth century.[70] The lateness of that strong focus of the sacrament on the past in itself not only implies a clear vindication of Paul in this regard, but it is also indicative of the crucial shift that occurred from the early part of the fourth century onward with the Constantinian endorsement of Christianity as the religion of the empire. The concern about institutional control of the Eucharist, evident in Ignatius, is augmented by the triumphalism attendant upon the status accorded the church in the Peace of Constantine. The move to the sacerdotal sacrament, which clearly preceded the Constantinian endorsement of Christianity, is reinforced and further refined by that dramatic reversal in the public fortunes of the Christian cause. From being the celebration of a minority movement, which, however securely structured through its own institutional forms, was exposed to threat and even overt persecution, the Eucharist became the sacrament of the official religion of the empire. The legacy of that shift is hinted at today in the archaeological evidence of the fate of other religious rites and sacraments: "broken buildings, burned-out buildings, hastily buried icons and sacred vessels."[71]

A strong case can be made for the contention that it was the Constantinian embrace, rather than early eschatological fervor, which led to an essentially triumphalist celebration. Ironically, this happened not by forgetting the cross and the nascent hermeneutic of it provided by the Last Supper, but precisely by so emphasizing that element in the monopolistic sacerdotal sacrifice of the mass that the Eucharist came to represent virtually the reverse of its original direction. As the dominant and dominating religious institution "the Church now turned from sharing the sufferings of Christ, and set its eyes on the glory already revealed in Constantine."[72] This direction was reflected in the isolation of the mass as a priestly rather than a communal celebration, the logical outcome of which is the totally private mass. This direction bespeaks not only an isolation of the celebration of salvation from the wider involvements of life but also a possessive manipulation of the sacrament which represents the opposite of the self-giving it was originally understood to connote. This institutional inversion of the sacrament, rather than its supposedly secondary origins, constitutes the chief basis of concern regarding the way in which salvation has been celebrated in Christianity.

Limitations in the Celebration of Salvation

The limitations imposed on the celebration of salvation in the Middle Ages constituted the direct background for the revolt that became known as Protestantism. Luther's objection to indulgences sent shock waves through the whole medieval sacramental system. The option of reducing purgatorial sentences through direct cash payments was the tip of an iceberg that included the comprehensive sacramental system which represented the heart of the medieval church. In substituting the authority of the Word for the authority of the institutional church, the reformation was not simply going behind the magisterium to the testimony of the scripture. The effect of that shift was to challenge the credibility of the whole sacramental system. In particular, this involved the assumption that salvation is a commodity presided over by a priestly caste.

PRIEST AND PROPHET

From this point of view, the Reformation can be regarded as the reassertion of prophetic concern against priestly monopoly. The nature of that concern is epitomized in the Protestant critique of Catholicism presented by Reinhold Niebuhr: "Catholic Orthodoxy robbed prophetic religion of its interest in future history and destroyed the sense of the dynamic character of mundane existence."[73] Niebuhr's complaint is twofold. He sees the priestly focus replacing the temporally oriented prophetic proclamation of a coming kingdom with a spatially rooted supernaturalism in which the priest mediates between the mundane order and a supernatural realm to which he has special access. This has the effect of depreciating the ordinary involvements of life because these recede before the one place of access to the divine, the priestly sacrament. This further confirms the conclusion reached in the previous section that the loss of the eschatological note in the Eucharist does not occur in its origin as an imposition on an otherwise totally future oriented joyous fellowship meal, but in the proprietary direction it took as the Church developed in the second century and as this was reinforced with state recognition. "The medieval understanding as to what was the essential nature of the Eucharist became more and more aligned with the image which dominated Western interpretation of Christ's saving work, namely the offering of himself in propitiatory sacrifice to the Father; so that the mass was seen chiefly as the Church's propitiatory offering of Christ in sacrifice to the Father and it was hardly understood as the meal that is the sign of the feeding and feasting of the kingdom."[74] The renewal of the sacrifice of Christ, effected at the altar by the priest, thus becomes the sole assured point of contact between the mundane order and the divine. The sense of an all-encompassing presence that might at any moment transform the ordinary was displaced by a kind of tunnel vision focused on the priestly altar.

The prophetic alternative to the altar has several interconnected but distinguishable aspects. In general terms, the priestly and prophetic visions are fixed in opposite directions. Where the priest focuses on the past and sees the sacrifice of the altar renewing the sacrifice of the cross, the prophetic pronouncement looks to the future in anticipation of what God will do and what God expects. This contrast in orientation is by no means peculiar to Christianity. It can be argued that it represents a generic feature of the priestly and prophetic stances. The difference is apparent in Christianity's parent faith. In the New Testament era, the legacy of Judaism had crystalized into the priestly direction represented by the Sadducees and the prophetic perspective that informed the orientation of the Pharisees. Although neither of these might stand out as sterling examples of these respective approaches, this very fact may serve to underline the fundamental difference in direction each entails. As members of noble priestly families, the Sadducees were dedicated to preserving the position of advantage and consequently were characterized by a backward orientation and an arch conservatism.[75] They treated the written law, for example, with the kind of absolute reverence the medieval church assigned to the sacrifice of the mass. The connection between the Pharisees and the way of the prophet might seem less obvious. Their heritage would seem to be more that of the law than that of the prophets. However, the prophetic orientation emerges precisely in their approach to the law. Where the Sadducees prized the fixed and settled written law, the Pharisees were champions of the oral tradition, intent on refining the tradition so that it applied to every contingency. In doing this, their orientation was forward rather than backward, anticipating the day when the law would be kept so perfectly that the kingdom would come.

The contrast between past and future orientations is one dimension of a more fundamental divergence, which also includes the difference between a strict demarcation between the sacred and the secular, on the one hand, and an equally strong insistence on the importance of their mutual interpenetration, on the other. The priestly approach not only focuses on the past, but also does so in the conviction of its possession of a sacred deposit from that direction. Similarly, the prophetic approach does not simply look to the future, but does so in expectation of an alignment between the sacred and everyday realities through more holy living on the part of those to whom the prophet speaks, through the intervention of divine judgment or through some other form of eschatological consummation. From this latter perspective, the segregation of a sacred priestly realm from the rest of life is a source of great suspicion.

The prophetic concern to bring all of life under the sway of divine judgment must regard the claim to deal with God through a special area of cultic activity as highly dangerous, if not completely misguided. Thus Ferdinand Hahn contends that early Christian worship was "absolutely 'anti-cultic'."[76] As evidence, he contends that not only is *latreuein*, "serve," not limited to worship, but it is sometimes used in deliberate antithesis to cultic tradition, and that *leitourgia*, "service," is never used as a special term for worship.[77] He further contends that *thysia*, "sacrifice," and *prosphora*, "offering," are used only metaphorically until the late New Testament documents. Hahn sums up his findings with a classic statement of protestant suspicion of priestly religion.

The terminological evidence means not only that any cultic understanding of Christian worship is out of the question, but also that there is no longer any distinction in principle between assembly for worship and the service of Christians in the world. Here we clearly find an echo of Jesus' transgression of the boundary between the sacred and the profane.[78]

In its origins, divine service could refer to how Christians lived in the world just as readily as to explicit acts of worship. When worship is isolated from life in the world, the inevitable result is a formalism in which worship tends to become an end in itself rather than celebrating the common life of the people as liturgy was originally meant to do.

The danger of formalism attendant on the identification of the sacred with a particular segment of life readily shades over into the risk of idolatry as the custodians of the sacred inevitably seem to come to regard themselves as its possessors. This is where the eschatological note becomes prominent in the prophetic alternative. Priestly possession shatters on the recognition of divine sovereignty acknowledged in an eschatological orientaticn. This is the fundamental vision that informs Hahn's rejection of the cultic. "The worship of Christians is dominated by God's eschatological gift of salvation, and remains open to God's future acts."[79] As spokesperson for God, the prophet seeks to discern where God is leading and what God expects, with the awareness that any sense of direction attainable will be fragmentary and provisional. It is this awareness of the call and demand of the living God that makes any tendency to profess to be in possession of some established medium of divine access appear suspect to the point of abhorrence.

The one-sidedness of this prophetic rejection of the priestly direction is relieved somewhat when we recognize that the protestant critique, which represents the most dramatic instance of this reaction for modern westerners, is subject to a massive irony in that, on its own, the prophetic approach is very apt to degenerate into the very moralism so abhorred by Protestantism. Prophetic concern with living, and especially with right living, could easily result in a kind of works-righteousness in which it is assumed that it is up to us to earn divine acceptance through our moral performance. The biblical prophets were preserved from this by their spiritual sensitivity. "Such incipient doctrines of merit are the danger of an earnest moralism, but the intense religious feeling and sense of dependence upon Jahveh which the prophets and psalmists possessed and preached were an effective safeguard against an undue glorifying of human achievement."[80] But if the biblical prophets and psalmists were protected from committing the ultimate protestant sin, Protestants themselves might not be so favored; and the reason for their greater exposure to the moralism that is the theoretical antithesis of Protestantism itself may be precisely its suppression of the priestly dimension. It could be argued with con-

siderable plausibility that it was the balance of the priestly cult that
prevented prophetic religion from degenerating into moralism, just
as it, in turn, constituted the corrective for priestly formalism.
"The prophetic movement, by its emphasis on morality as the content of God's will, saved the religion of Israel from formalistic
ritualism, and the priestly revival under Ezekiel and his successors
saved the prophetic movement from degenerating into humanistic
moralism."[81] In its reaction against cultic abuse, Protestantism
embraces its own mortal enemy, moralism, as the perennial danger
of a prophetic stance that tries to go it alone.

Hahn's contention that early Christian worship was "absolutely
anti-cultic" must be seen in this context. It owes at least as much to
its Protestant sponsorship as it does to New Testament exegesis.
Indeed, it is interesting that he virtually reverses the anticultic
polemic we saw directed at suggestions of a direct connection between the Eucharist and the Last Supper. Although endorsing the
main plank of the anticultic position that the Lord's Supper originally, and he contends throughout the New Testament period,
took place outside the sacred and cultic sphere, "despite the
sporadic application of cultic terminology to the worship of the
community,"[82] he attributes cultic influence not to Hellenistic mystery cults but to the temple and other ritual traditions of Judaism.
"While the Hebrews still recognized the temple as God's house
and place of prayer, the Hellenists considered the temple eschatologically superseded."[83] Where Jewish Christians might be tempted
to slip back to cultic forms,[84] gentile Christianity was firmly set on
a path of spiritualizing any lingering cultic reference.[85] Hahn finds
confirmation of this even in a place, which on the surface, seems to
represent such a total endorsement of the cultic, the Letter to the
Hebrews. He insists that the designation of Christ as the perfect
high priest, in contrast to the approximations of the sacrifices
offered by the Levitical priesthood (7:1–10:18), must be read in
light of the ecclesiastical conclusions drawn from this (12:18–29),
according to which the sacrifice of Christ is understood in eschatological terms as the affirmation of God as a consuming fire whose
presence is not located in the past, or the preserve of a cultic
sphere, but in the living present and the in-breaking future, a
direction that is confirmed by the admonition to offer a "sacrifice
of praise" (13:15) and to go outside the camp in emulation of Jesus
who suffered outside the gate (13:12f.).[86] The Protestant reading
Hahn promotes is epitomized, curiously enough, in a verse that
he does not highlight himself. "Do not neglect to do good and to

share what you have, for such sacrifices are pleasing to God" (13:16). It would be difficult to imagine a more succinct statement of the prophetic alternative to cultic abuse.

It may be that Hahn does not emphasize this verse, which is so congenial to the position he affirms, because he is aware that it also represents the Achilles' heel of that position. For all its insistence on justification by faith and castigation of any hint that we might be able to render ourselves acceptable to God through our own efforts, Protestantism's suspicion of the cultic has left it exposed to that very danger. The eschatological God who is everywhere escapes the threat of idolatrous captivity to which the cultic God is subject, but by that very token this transcendence also entails an elusiveness to which the corresponding reality on the side of the believer is a sense of insecurity about whether they truly believe, whether their profession and practice is really acceptable. For all its dangers and potential for abuse, the cultic focus provides that concrete means for giving assurance and sponsoring participation in the holy. Although Protestantism has not dispensed with that element entirely, its relegation to the periphery in deference to the living Word can be seen in retrospect to constitute an impoverishment of religious sensibility.

THE SIGNIFICANCE OF SACRIFICE

One of the most significant instances of this impact is precisely this matter of sacrifice:

> Today we live in a culture in which the practice of sacrifice is totally foreign—no doubt largely because of the influence of Christianity down the centuries. But the result is that we no longer seem to be in a position to know *instinctively* what the sacrifice language of our traditions really means.[87]

When we consider the medieval emphasis on the sacrifice of the mass and its legacy in modern Roman Catholicism, we might be inclined to sharpen Frances Young's summation by the qualification that the loss of awareness of the importance and meaning of sacrifice in modern Western culture must be attributed particularly to the cultic suspicions of Protestantism. Young suggests that the residual meaning that sacrifice retains is that of "giving up something that we value," in contrast to that which has been lost is the original meaning of "to make an offering to God" or "to sanctify."[88] Her central contention is that religious sensibility depends on recovering an appreciation for sacrifice in its original sense. "In fact, sacrifice is integral to the religious response to the universe."[89]

The importance of sacrifice as a religious category can be approached on two levels. In terms of theological understanding, which we have insisted is secondary, but by no means dispensable because of that, it could be held that sacrifice represents the key category among those which have been used in attempts to articulate the significance of what was accomplished in Christ. "But when all is said and done, however much we may be helped by considerations drawn from battlefields, law courts, or elsewhere, it is in the sphere of religious worship that God in Christ is most directly revealed to His disciples."[90] It may be its obviousness that prevents us from noticing that religious categories are the most appropriate ones for conveying religious meanings. It seems to be a matter of common sense that the notion of sacrifice, peculiar to the religious concern to be acceptable to a god or God, should be more directly relevant for explicating religious meaning than legal analogies of justification in spite of guilt or military images of cosmic victory of good over evil. Of course, there are negative elements in the sacrifice analogy. One reason it has not enjoyed as prominent a position as it might have in Christian theology is the connotation of propitiation it bore from its earliest usage, and which was often reinforced by Christian priestly practice. The protestantlike suspicion of a concept that would suggest that somehow God had to be won over by humanity might have bothered as early an ancestor of the Reformation as St. Anselm. However, as criticisms of Anselm's own solution in terms of the feudal concern with satisfaction of honor show, no category is immune to this kind of interpretation, and the association with propitiation clinging to the sacrifice approach can be remedied by shifting the focus from propitiation to expiation. It is not that we must propitiate an angry God, but rather that God has provided the expiation for our sins in Christ.

The motivation for giving renewed consideration to the category of sacrifice for theological purposes lies in the other dimension in which this category has particular significance. Young laments the loss of recognition of the importance of sacrifice not because it impedes theological understanding but because it effects what we know "instinctively." Theological explanations will make sense only insofar as they give expression to something we know at an inarticulate level. Our basic problem is not that we do not understand sacrifice, but that we do not approach life in these terms. The foreignness of sacrifice to us is confirmed even in Young's own treatment. Her complaint that "giving up something that we value" is a modern meaning of sacrifice in contrast to the original religious meaning of "to make an offering to a God" itself reflects a diminution of the comprehensive thrust of the meaning of sacrifice. The worshipper who made an offering to a God was giving up something that they valued. This is reflected in the Old Testament requirement for the sacrifice of the first fruits, for example, whereby the worshipper was expected to sacrifice the best of the crop in recognition of the source of the whole crop. Or again, it is evident in the requirements of animal sacrifice that the sacrificial victim be without blemish. It is particularly evident in the practice of child sacrifice, the surrendering of the firstborn, echoes of which are evident in the near sacrifice of Isaac. It was this cost that made the sacrifice of the worshipper real. It is also this cost that makes the sacrifice of Christ real as God's own sacrifice for us. In promoting an exclusively religious meaning of sacrifice, apart from the ordinary meaning that it retains, Young flirts with a cultic isolationism, which might well justify the protestant fear of formalism and idolatry. It is clear, however, that she herself does not intend to advocate any such cultic isolation. Her plea is rather for a renewed sense of the importance of sacrifice as a fundamental element of the divine reality celebrated in cult and emulated in life .

It is in such terms that Young sees the significance of sacrifice for the first Christians:

> The sacrificial language of the early church represented not merely response to, but participation in the sacrifice of Christ. Worship, service, and atonement were inseparable. The same should be true for the Church today.[91]

The most ardent anticultist could hardly find reason to take exception to this. Her more direct focus on the present makes the organic connection between the sacrifice of Christ celebrated in worship and the impact of that sacrifice on the life of the world even more inescapable. "The place of Christ's continuing sacrificial work is in the sacrificial worship and sacrificial living of the Christian community, and in involvement like his in the sufferings of the world."[92] Appreciation of the sacrifice of God in Christ for us provides the motivation for us to emulate the sacrificial way of life accepted by Jesus. That emulation, in turn, extends the effectiveness of the sacrifice of Christ in the world today. The difficult question is how we are to recapture this appreciation of sacrifice. There is no doubt that it represents the antithesis of the way of the world to which we so readily sacrifice ourselves. It may be that the appreciation can only come through a real attempt at sacrifice in worship and in daily living. Rather than assuming that worship is something we should enjoy, perhaps we should approach it as a discipline, a sacrifice of time and effort. Similarly, in the normal routine of daily life we might, with a little imagination and sensitivity, find ways to give up something that we value for the benefit of someone else. It may be that only through such deliberate acts of sacrifice in what Young calls the ordinary sense of the word will we come to some appreciation of the more inclusive religious sense that it held for people in less secular times. And yet, if this does in any way rekindle a sense of the reality of the gospel that will only be because that reality was there all the time and was in no way created by our worship or work. The irony is that the gospel of Grace which the Protestant anticultic polemic was designed to protect may be protected best by a cultic celebration of this sacrifice that encompasses us.

THE CONCRETENESS OF SACRAMENT

Philip J. Lee has recently raised the alarm that Protestantism has come decisively under the sway of gnostic tendencies. He sees this in its individualism and otherworldliness, but above all in its avoidance of the concrete. "Gnostic syncretism . . . believes everything in general for the purpose of avoiding a belief in something in particular."[93] This provides an illuminating perspective on the protestant opposition to the concreteness of the sacrament. By contrast, it can be seen to be advocating a faith that is so pure and rarified that it defies embodiment. The reason for this, of course, is that it is reacting against abuses of the medieval sacramental system. That system can be seen to be subject to the danger which constitutes the other side of gnosticism. "That which separates the gnostic from the ordinary person is the conviction that the eternal is in his or her own hands."[94] Could there be a more accurate description of the medieval priest effecting the transformation from bread and wine to the body and blood of Christ? In the celebration of the sacrifice of Christ, Catholic concreteness and Protestant purification encounter one another, each exposing the strengths and weaknesses of the other. It is much too easy to pronounce the inevitable academic expedient of "not either/or, but both/and," and yet it is equally difficult to avoid this conclusion in the present context. What the long history of attempts to celebrate the sacrifice of Christ seem to show is that that celebration must be rooted in a givenness of the sacrifice, and of the sacrament that celebrates it, to which the Catholic concern for concreteness testifies, and yet if that celebration is to be genuine it must expose the worshipper to the pervasiveness of the sacrifice, which far from accommodating any will to priestly prerogative over it, rather brings priest and penitent into the presence of the living God in renewal of the gift of life and inspiration for the living of it in conformity to the sacrificial self-giving it celebrates.

One fact that appears to be beyond dispute is the centrality of this participation in the sacrifice of Christ as constitutive of the heart of the gospel.

> Failure to understand that the Church exists by continual participation in the atoning action of God in Jesus underlies many of the illusions in conventional images of the Church. Let us describe the Church as the community which lives by participation in the atonement.[95]

The other conclusion, which seems to force itself upon us, is the comprehensive nature of that participation, such that our theological formulations, our moral efforts, and our worship itself, can only grow out of and return to that sense of participation for judgment, direction, and affirmation. "If this divine action is at the heart of the gospel, then in interpreting it we are in the realm of epic and drama rather than of definition and formula, the realm of worship rather than of pure theology."[96] We have some sense of the gospel only insofar as we are claimed and cleansed by the sacrifice of God in Christ. At its best, worship affords the opportunity for that encounter which our theologies, our moral principles, and practical programs, and our liturgies, important though these all are, can only serve, and on which all these activities depend for whatever vitality and veracity they possess.

Part Two
The Problematic of Salvation

5

Salvation and Secularization

No other single factor can begin to compare with the comprehensive phenomenon we term *secularization* in accounting for the fate of interest in salvation in the contemporary setting. The celebration of salvation under ecclesiastical sponsorship appears parochial in the wake of secular interest in the world. The note of abstraction that modern theology has sensed in traditional concern over the price of sin is due, in no small measure, to secularity's disdain for the past and preoccupation with effecting immediate improvement. The shift in biblical hermeneutic from participation in the divine drama to inspiration for the human project is also clearly indebted to the influence of secularization. The scope of this influence would seem to suggest that the phenomenon of secularization should be amenable to precise identification and assessment, but the reality is that its very ubiquity makes for imprecision and elusiveness. Thus, before we can begin to consider the significance of secularization for a contemporary understanding of salvation, it is necessary to attempt some clarification of the phenomenon itself.

The Scope of Secularization

The widespread acknowledgment that we live in a secular age may be due in large measure to the ambiguity implicit in this designation. More careful consideration of what is meant by this epithet will disclose not only a variety of meanings attaching to it, but also even some question as to whether it is a very meaningful designation at all.

THE "FACT" OF SECULARIZATION

There seems to be little room for doubt that there is a widespread consensus that we have well and truly entered an era of secularity.

"The modern world is secularized: everyone takes that for granted now."[1] If this is not regarded as an obvious empirical generalization about the present situation, it is at least held to be indicative of the direction in which we are headed. The following prognostication from the heyday of secular theology in the late sixties would still find widespread assent:

> Bonhoeffer, as we have seen, looked on modernity as the time of man's "coming of age" and learning to live *as if* God did not exist. It is becoming increasingly obvious as the years pass that he was right: the secularized society, the society that carries on its affairs *as if* God did not exist, appears to be the pattern for mankind's future.[2]

This outlook assumes that there is a general public consensus about what is significant, or at least that there can be such a consensus, in contrast to which religious concerns are relegated to the domain of private preference. From the religious perspective, this amounts to living *as if* God did not exist, but insofar as the secular perspective itself does prevail the situation is the reverse. It is religious faith that is the exception in acting *as if* God does exist.

The implication of this type of generalization about secularization is that there has been a wholesale shift in public sensibilities from a religiously oriented outlook to one that requires no reference to religious concerns. Whether secularization can be understood in such stark and absolute terms, however, is a matter of some controversy. The English sociologist, David Martin, for example, contends that such a sweeping generalization represents a vast oversimplification of what is really a very complex development. "The most important point which I would urge is that there is no unitary process called 'secularization' arising in reaction to a set of characteristics labelled 'religious'."[3] He argues that far from an obvious "master trend of social development," what can be identified is particular shifts in perspective in specific times and circumstances:

> What *is* true is that given careful definitions of "secular"—notoriously an omnibus word—some shifts can be discerned away from the "religious" over particular periods of time in given cultures under specified circumstances. For instance, if religion is identified as stressing the limits on human achievement then men in advanced industrial societies have become less religious. Or if it is defined as regular institutional participation then in specified societies undergoing particular types of social change a decline in "religion" can be documented. Or again, if secular is defined as the making of autonomous decisions and exclusive

reliance on the empirical mode as a basis for decision, then one can inquire to what extent this is true. And as a matter of fact assertions about the "autonomy" of modern man, his rejection of authority, his exclusively empirical frame of reference are both woolly and doubtful.[4]

This call for a more disciplined understanding of secularity arises out of a demonstration that discloses just how ambiguous this whole idea is. Martin identifies this ambiguity in terms of four themes that tend to figure prominently in generalizations about secularization.[5] The first is the appeal to the "natural," which is inherently ambiguous, because either this is a comprehensive term which takes in everything, so that religion would be included, or else only some things are held to be natural, in which case the designation is an expression of a metaphysical perspective, which is, in principle, itself of religious proportions. This makes it impossible to regard secularization as simply a neutral alternative to religion, and leads to a second general ambiguity in the recognition of an inevitability of religious elements in antireligious positions. A third area of ambiguity is in the statistical accounts of decline in religious practices, which assumes significant overt involvement prior to the decline but, in fact, the announced decline may amount in large measure to an abandonment of conventional conformity. The final source of ambiguity Martin identifies is the duplicity attached to the phenomenon of temporal religious power, which may be viewed as the supreme recognition of the importance of religion, or as its most total capitulation to secularization. As a result of this last source of confusion, there is considerable room for debate as to which of either the Middle Ages or the modern era is the more religious and the more secular. If we consider the eruptions of religious fervor that have dominated the headlines since the high point of secular enthusiasm in the sixties, we will have evidential endorsement of Martin's theoretical reservations about assuming that we are subject to a monolithic, irreversible process of secularization.

With Martin's warning ringing in our ears, we must recognize, nevertheless, that something has taken place in the modern period which distinguishes our age from previous periods, and no designation for this seems more appropriate than the one of secularization. Thus, Martin's caution should be supplemented by Owen Chadwick's proposal that this term be retained even though its full implications remain obscure. "I do not think it an abuse of such a term to call this radical process, still in part so obscure to the inquirer, still in part undefined and possibly in part undefinable, by

the name of secularization; on the one condition (and it is an absolute condition) that the word is used, neither as the lament of nos-
talgia for past years, nor as propaganda to induce history to move
in one direction rather than another, but simply as a description of
something that happened to European society in the last two hun-
dred years."[6] This ideal of neutrality is, no doubt, much more easily announced than attained. As Chadwick recognizes himself, we
are much too close to this phenomenon to be able to classify it with
scholarly precision. The attempt to come to grips with secularization is "like trying to write the history of the Reformation in the
year 1650—everyone is still committed."[7]

Thus, as we strive to understand secularization, we are pulled in
opposite directions by forces that insist that it entails a shift in consciousness which renders everything that went before foreign, if
not finally obsolete, and by advocates of the opposite persuasion
equally convinced that the whole business has been vastly exagger-
ated. When we add to this perspectival tug-of-war the consideration that either direction can be affirmed with regret or unbounded
optimism, the prospect for any significantly objective assessment of
secularization appears particularly remote. Perhaps the most realistic perspective to adopt at the beginning of an attempt to come to
grips with this putative process is a comprehensive one such as that
which is entailed in William F. Lynch's suggestion that there is
something good and something bad in the contention that secularization is a totally new development.[8] The good part consists in the
recognition that we are facing "a qualitatively new and overwhelming situation for the religious imagination," but this recognition in
itself is bad insofar as it fails to appreciate that "we are in a sharply
and qualitatively new form of a permanent human situation." In
these terms, secularization appears as a massive intensification of
the perennial struggle with the limits and range of our humanity.
In its absolute forms, it seeks to dispense with the recognition of
any divine qualification on humanity at all. The question of the
significance of secularization is, in large part, a matter of the extent
and variety of this attempt to dispense with divine reference.

THE RANGE OF SECULARIZATION

In our preliminary identifications of the parameters of secularization, it has become clear that the elusiveness of the evidence for
this phenomenon is due, in part, to its comprehensive nature.
Rather than dealing with some process that might lend itself to
direct access, we are confronted by an atmosphere that penetrates

different areas of life. At the very least, secularization involves a political dimension and also an intellectual one. It refers to the development by which modern states have emancipated themselves from divine tutelage, or at least from alliances with religious institutions other than ones in which the state is firmly and officially in charge. This political process is accompanied by a shift in world-view whereby the fundamental sense of a transcendent power tends to recede before the prospect of immediate possibilities for our own exercise of power, collectively and individually.

The order of these developments is a subject of considerable debate. A strict Marxist reading, for example, would accord primacy to the political process. The achieving of political freedom, a primary component of which is economic emancipation, eliminates the need for the theoretical superstructure of religion. If we take charge of our own destinies, we will have overcome that alienation which locates the disposition of our fate in a transcendent power. Marx himself, however, particularly in his earlier writings, can be seen to be open to the opposite reading that sees institutional changes as expressions of shifts in understanding. The question of which of these directions is basic is the question of the respective significance of the methodologies of the social sciences and the humanities. If there is nothing to impede the social sciences from attaining a comprehensive grasp of reality, in principle, then the primacy of structure and institution is assured. If there is something about life that ultimately resists such management, then the more traditional and personal approach will be vindicated and will have proven to be indispensable. That neither of these approaches is susceptible to conclusive demonstration is indicative of the ambiguity that characterizes secularization. The process has political and perspectival dimensions, but how these relate is itself part of the difficulty in clarifying what secularization involves.

The depth of this ambiguity is disclosed by the ways in which these two dimensions of secularization can contradict and yet also reinforce one another. Denys Munby characterizes a secular society in terms of three principal features: (a) it excises commitment to any particular view of reality as such; (b) it accepts pluralism in belief among its members; and (c) it promotes toleration of different beliefs.[9] On the surface this appears to offer a coherent package. A secular society leaves beliefs entirely to its members; it is officially beliefless in itself. This is the theoretical account of secular society. The practice, however, may be another matter. If we consider a particularly controversial subject that demands a recognition of convictional pluralism, such as the issue of abortion, the appropriate stance of a secular society would seem to be to leave this matter to the individual. Those who favor abortion should be free to obtain abortions, whereas those opposed need feel no compulsion to avail themselves of this option. The difficulty with this solution is that rather than being neutral and convictionless, it is really an expression of the proabortion position, and, as such, cannot possibly satisfy antiabortionists. The fundamental issue is not simply whether or not abortions should be available. Particularly for antiabortionists, the issue is the nature of abortion. From this point of view, it cannot be condoned, except perhaps, in exceptional circumstances, because it is tantamount to murder. To allow abortion as a matter of individual choice in such a spirit of pluralism and tolerance is not different, in principle, from a lack of public interest in murder. If secular society is truly convictionless, pluralistic, and tolerant, will it not have to allow murder as an individual option?

The answer that has emerged to this dilemma is the contractual, utilitarian one. In principle, there is no reason for excluding murder any more than any other activity. But in practice, it must be excluded in the interests of society itself. It is impractical to have the members of society eliminating each other, not to mention the inconvenience of the constant threat to which members would feel exposed. But the abortion debate challenges the attribution of this social stance to a purely practical, utilitarian base. A society can only prohibit murder, if it knows what murder is. This is why there is a debate over abortion. Some members of society think it is murder and others do not. In promoting this controversy, the abortion issue serves to challenge the claim to convictional neutrality on the part of our supposedly secular society.

This recognition may be met, in turn, by the contention that the beliefs entailed by any social arrangement are not those of society but of the individuals who compose it, or, at least, of some influential portion of these. In itself, secular society is simply a mechanism for facilitating collective action. But the difficulty with this claim is that the society then does not represent a neutral arrangement which treats all of its citizens alike, with true pluralism and tolerance, but rather responds precisely to some, rather than to others. If the secular society in question is a true democracy, it will reflect the will of the majority. If we are talking about the real world, it will reflect the interest of opportunistic politicians and the powerful and wealthy lobbies that seek to capitalize on their opportunism. In either case, the society can hardly appear neutral and convictionless. It will reflect the convictions of those with the most influence, or where it is deemed inexpedient to endorse any particular lobby, the alternative may well be to pursue the lowest common denominator solution in an effort to arouse least offense.

In this way secular society betrays its implicit convictions precisely in its practicality. The characterization of pluralism and tolerance is a theoretical construction that cannot survive the practical requirement for decision and action. In its own operations, secular society renounces pluralism with policies that favor some and discount others. Insofar as these policies reflect religiously motivated concerns, they can even be held to instantiate religious belief to some extent. And when secular society acts most directly in its own capacity to attempt to foster the widest possible pluralism of outlook and tolerance of difference, it can be seen to be articulating its own beliefs most clearly. Prominent among these is the belief in minimalism and the positivistic perspective that entails. In this way, it can appear that far from representing a neutral, convictionless approach, secular society rather entails very definite convictions which may be all the more potent for the denial of their existence.

VARIETIES OF SECULARIZATION

Any attempt to delineate the beliefs implicit in a secular outlook will be compromised unless it is recognized that the most effective forms of secularization do not operate in this overt way. People generally do not decide to adopt a secular outlook or to fashion society along secular lines. The former tends to happen without deliberate intent, and the latter seems to be demanded by the circumstances. In retrospect, the Renaissance and the Enlightenment appear to have a certain inevitability, the former in the recovery of classical culture, and the latter in its response to the initial phase of modern science. The American and French Revolutions had their progenitors, their Voltaires and Thomas Paines, but again, in retrospect, there appears to be a certain inevitability about the secular direction in light of the religious monism of France and the religious pluralism of America.

Insofar as modern secularity was promoted by explicit analysis and argument, this was successful not only because of its cogency but also because it seemed to fit the way life was experienced. As the secularization process has gone on, it appears more and more to take on the quality of a fate, to be "not so much a purposive or consciously directed movement, as a condition of life that befalls a people."[10] To accept this is not necessarily to endorse the Marxist primacy of institutions and to relegate understanding to a peripheral role, or at least, not necessarily to do so in principle. It is sufficient to recognize that, in practice, reflection may not be a high priority for many people. Thus once established, the secular outlook may be absorbed through the pores rather than as a deliberate creed or self-conscious practice.

As a fate, secularization not only imposes its peculiar beliefs, contrary to its professed neutrality, but also those beliefs turn out to be virtually the opposite of its supposed endorsement of tolerance and pluralism.

> Science and industry, working together, provide the tools, machines, and resources for carrying on the activities of a technological society, but they also provide consumer products on a mass scale which must be marketed; and this requires a mass market, which in turn gives rise to what has been tentatively termed "a mass culture." Wherever a "mass culture" arises in response to the mass appeal of industries, the note of selectivity and sensibility in judgment tends to go out of a culture.[11]

In this way, secularization as a fate promotes uniformity and even mindless consumption rather than representing a neutral base that makes possible a rich plurality of choices. This suggests that secular society may well appear to be convictionless because its convictions are never officially confronted. If an attempt is made to ferret out the covert assumptions which underlie secularity, indications are that these will not correspond to the "non-beliefs" which secular society can acknowledge in its professed endorsement of pluralism and toleration.

The secularization that appears as a fate not only imposes a uniformity that is the antithesis of the free-wheeling pluralism which it supposedly facilitates, but also this uniformity itself will inevitably bear specific characteristics. Otherwise it would not be a uniformity. And in this regard, indications are that that characterization is inherently reductionistic. Not pluralism, but positivism, is the perspective that surreptitiously informs the secular mandate. Rather than dealing with a neutral base on which any and all convictions can be erected, recognition of secularization as fate suggests that this base is destined to take over, so that more wide ranging convictions will be progressively marginalized as private indulgences which will not be permitted to intrude on the omnivorous maw of secularization.

If secularization does represent positivism rather than pluralism, it is important that this be recognized, but by the same token, if this is true, that recognition will have to be gained against the fate-like sufficiency of secularization. It will be important to keep this in mind as we attempt to identify and assess the central currents of secularization because such identification may not touch the most effective well springs of this pervasive atmosphere. Thus, the delineation of the components of secularization, or even an exposition of the inadequacy of any or all of these as accounts of contemporary life, may not really come to grips with the reality of secularization as an experienced fate. This is especially important for the consideration of attitudes to salvation because the effects of secularization on these attitudes may have less to do with perceived inadequacies in received accounts of what salvation involves than with a fundamental sense of unreality about the whole subject.

The Impact of Secularization on Salvation

Although secularization as our modern fate may be too comprehensive and immediate to permit any fully satisfactory description or assessment of it, the designation enjoys the acceptance it does because it is indicative of certain features that seem to dominate modern sensibility. In identifying and explaining some of the more prominent of these, we may be able to delineate the general contours of secularization. But in light of what we have noted about its fatelike impact, we may expect that these features will be most significant, not in terms of any singular persuasiveness that might be seen to characterize any of them individually, or even any aggregate of them, but rather these features will probably be appreciated most accurately if they are regarded as component elements of that comprehensive and elusive atmosphere which is as difficult to pin down as it is impossible to evade.

THE LOSS OF TRANSCENDENCE

The most obvious feature of secularization is its dispensing with the conception of God, and ultimately with the whole notion of transcendence. The shot that launched the widespread public awareness of secularization in the English-speaking world, John A. T. Robinson's *Honest to God*,[12] was heralded in *The Observer* with the headline "Our Image of God Must Go." Nor was this merely a further instance of sensationalist journalism. The pivotal question is the one Robinson poses in the title of chapter two of the book, "The End of Theism?" The image of God that must go is the image of a transcendent being who is accountable for the world and to whom we are accountable for our lives. Robinson draws on Rudolf Bultmann's demythologizing program in its attempt to translate the supernatural categories of traditional Christianity into existential categories more congenial to contemporary sensibility, Paul Tillich's transposition of theology from metaphors of height to depth in its attempt to point to ultimacy, and Dietrich Bonhoeffer's call for a worldly Christianity to replace the God of the gaps appealed to to salvage Christian faith in the wake of its displacement by modern science. The appeal to these theologians, all of whom had gained international recognition before the midpoint of the century, is indicative of the fact that Robinson was not advancing a new thesis. He was presenting, in popular form, a concern that had preoccupied theology for some time, the concern with an understanding of God in an age that seems to have less and less need for any such understanding at all.

In retrospect, and despite the furor *Honest to God* caused when it was published in 1963, Robinson's concern seems rather mild. Others had been challenging the theistic understanding of God with at least equal vehemence, and the prospect of the meaninglessness of God was to find much more radical advocates than Robinson among the ranks of theologians in succeeding years. Robinson's concern was with the image of God. He confesses:

> However much I find myself instinctively a radical in matters theological, I belong by nature to the 'once-born' rather than to the 'twice-born' type. I have never really doubted the fundamental truth of the Christian faith—though I have constantly found myself questioning its expression.[13]

By contrast, Paul van Buren reacted against the substantially traditional affirmations of Barth's neo-orthodoxy not only to challenge the images in which God was portrayed but in defiance of the whole notion of God. *The Secular Meaning of the Gospel*[14] attempted the ambitious, not to say astounding, project of articulating the Christian gospel without reference to God. The consideration that the promotion of human freedom through the historical phenomenon of Jesus could stand as an adequate contemporary variation on what Christianity had always proclaimed with reference to God is perhaps less significant than the fact that it seemed necessary to search for such an alternative. The felt need for a secular meaning of the gospel not only testifies to the extent to which secularity had penetrated theological consciousness, but the proposal for meeting that need by eliminating all reference to God from the gospel also confirms the centrality of the sense of the loss of a meaningful notion of transcendence to the thrust of secularity itself.

The apex of this Christian abandonment of transcendence was reached with the phenomenon trumpeted on the cover of *Time* magazine, "The Death of God." William Hamilton affirmed the death of God as the distinctive experience of our time. "We are not talking about the absence of the experience of God, but about the experience of the absence of God."[15] Like the watchers who are waiting for Godot, Hamilton holds out some shred of hope that there might be some directive from on high provided in the future, but the present is characterized by the total silence of God. All that is available now is the example of Jesus as an indication of how life should be lived, but why the example of Jesus should be particularly significant, Hamilton cannot say. This lack of rationale, which might be expected to compromise the credibility of Hamilton's position, was not as damaging as would first appear because in that very lack of cogency he struck a chord with many readers. This sense of the death of God seemed to articulate the experience of a significant number of people in the second half of the twentieth century.

A more positive version of the death of God was proposed by Thomas J. J. Altizer. "We must realize that the death of God is an historical event, that God has died in our cosmos, in our history, in our *Existenz*."[16] The death of God is not just an experience that we have of the absence of God, but an event of which we are only now really becoming aware. In one sense, Altizer radicalizes the Christian conception of incarnation, claiming that it must be understood in cosmic terms as the self-emptying of the transcendent God into the immanence of the world. This death of God was recognized by Nietzsche in the nineteenth century, but it is only now coming to general consciousness. However, just as Altizer radicalizes the meaning of the death of God in shifting the focus from our experience to a cosmic event, he also radicalizes the note of hope. This descent of God into the world is one side of a dialectic, the other side of which is the divinization of the world. In this way, Altizer returns to some of the earliest Christian themes and to a vision that embraces the religions of the Far East as well.

One of the most interesting features of this intensification of the secular thrust that characterizes the theology of the sixties is the absence of reference to salvation and its reemergence in the most radical version of this thrust. As we saw, Robinson's problem is largely conceptual. He is claimed by the Christian gospel, but is troubled by the conventional accounts of God. His aim is the intellectual one of exposing the inadequacy of conventional understandings of God and of seeking an alternative more congenial to the changed perspective of the contemporary world. Van Buren's attempt to determine the secular meaning of the gospel is a response to the demands of analytic philosophy.

> For the particular language-game which we are playing, imprecisely identified as 'seeking the secular meaning of the gospel,' the heart of the method of linguistic analysis lies in the use of the verification principle—that the meaning of a word is its use in its context. The meaning of a statement is to be found in, and is identical with, the function of that statement. If a statement has a function, so that it may in principle be verified or falsified, the statement is meaningful, and unless or until a theological statement can be submitted in some way to verification it cannot be said to have a meaning in our language-game.[17]

With this curious blend of the broader language-game version of linguistic philosophy and the earlier empirically oriented logical analysis,[18] Van Buren reconstructs the Christian gospel as the account of the captivating freedom of Jesus which swept others into its contagious embrace. In place of a gospel of divine acceptance, which is held to defy verification, we are offered a perspective on life based on the historical impact of this amazing individual. Whether or not this version is any more subject to verification than more traditional accounts, it does apply this epistemological concern to the question of the meaning of the gospel. Not only is the essentially theoretical question of how we might envisage God necessarily left behind in the dismissal of God-language, but the replacement that is offered attempts to articulate the central significance of Christianity without that reference. In this way, the more deliberate turn from God entails a more direct consideration of the whole meaning and point of the Christian faith.

The irony of this situation reaches a climax in Altizer's version of the death of God in which concern with what Robinson referred to as "An Exercise in Re-Centering"[19] is largely displaced by a vision of a new eschatological era in which the rejection of the transcendent God in the name of the profane world is completed in a reaffirmation of the eternal through this acceptance of the temporal. Without professing to understand the full extent of Altizer's vision, it is clear that he is preoccupied with a search for wholeness which can only be regarded as a variation on the concern with salvation, in contrast to the more abstract concerns with images of God which have preoccupied a great deal of contemporary theology.

THE AUTONOMY OF THE WORLD

The loss of transcendence in general and the dissatisfaction with what are characterized as theistic images of God in particular represent the negative side of a wider orientation that includes as its positive dimension a basic confidence against which the notion of transcendence and images of God appear problematic. This basic confidence is grounded in a self-sufficient view of the world. One of the principal intellectual sources of secularization is the *Weltanschauung* arising from the impact of modern science in which explanation is seen to involve the identification of links in a chain of causal sequence, a chain which is assumed to be expanding with precise and inexorable logic. This scientific world provides less and less scope for God, and less and less need for recourse to God, so that God has become the endangered species Bonhoeffer called "God as a stop-gap for the incompleteness of our knowledge."[20]

Although this understanding of science is more Newtonian than Einsteinian, it continues to prevail in spite of such complications as relativity theory and the indeterminacy principle. The realization that the gaps in our explanations might be more endemic than the accepted view of science allows has not significantly punctured the confidence in a self-sufficient world which neither requires, nor permits, reference beyond itself. The resiliency of this sense of the independent intelligibility of the world in spite of the recognition of the inadequacy of closed systems of explanation is testimony to the dominance of the secular perspective. It also raises the aspect of ambiguity in secularism which attaches to what David Martin calls "naturalism".[21] What that amounts to, in the present context, is that either secularism clings dogmatically to the early modern view of the world as a mechanistic chain of cause and effect, in which case it is on a par with the most dogmatic versions of religious stances, or else it acknowledges the open-ended perspective that is required by the more sophisticated physics of this century. But if it does make this latter acknowledgment, then it is difficult to see how it can remain dogmatically secularist. The indeterminacy of modern physics places us back in a mysterious universe much more elusive than the mechanistic one whose basic principles we thought we had firmly and securely mastered.

This challenge to the dogmatism of the secular outlook constituted by the more recent developments in science might offer some
breathing space for religious sensitivity, but it is no more congenial
to religious than it is to secular dogmatism. The perspective for
finding room for God in the indeterminate spaces of modern physics leaves us still with Bonhoeffer's stop-gap God. We would be
finding God in the gaps of our knowledge, rather than recognizing
God as a comprehensive reality pervading the whole of life. We
would be identifying God on our terms rather than really acknowledging God as such. But that is precisely the problem. How can
we acknowledge God as such? Whatever inadequacies there may
be in the secular perspective, it is to a large extent our perspective.
There is no returning behind the turn to this world which has become progressively established through the impact of the Renaissance and the Enlightenment. As Harvey Cox reminded us: "Secularization occurs when man turns his attention away from worlds
beyond and towards this world and this time (*saeculum* = 'this
present age')."22 Whatever the naïveté of secularization as
naturalism, the spirit of "this present age" does not offer much
scope for supernaturalism. The singularity of the world and the
suspicion of any kind of dualistic world view seem to be among
the most established elements of the legacy of secularity, whatever its prospects or inadequacies.

The discomfort with otherworldliness impinges on the understanding of salvation at two crucial points. It challenges the basis
for any kind of interventionist view of salvation. Salvation as deliverance is the least attractive of all versions of salvation because
it implies an external agent coming to our rescue. This is an affront
to our sense of maturity, which we shall consider more directly in
the next section. The other aspect that is subject to immediate
threat is the vision of the object of salvation, which traditionally
has been believed to be another world. The received understanding of salvation regards it as a matter of our individual destiny after
death. In its most consistent variation, this outlook sees this world
as totally preparatory, a training field and a proving ground for the
real life that lies beyond. However, the increasingly positive appreciation of this world, which has characterized the modern period
through the legacy of the Renaissance and the Enlightenment, and
the very substantial improvement in the human condition made
possible through the achievements of modern science and technology have provided stiff competition for any serious otherworldly
understanding of salvation. And yet that connotation clings to this
notion, with the result that Christian believers often experience a

schizophrenic struggle between a recognition of real significance in this world and a feeling of uneasiness with this because of a lingering sense that their real source of meaning should lie beyond.

The duality of worlds has become problematic not only because of the intrinsic interest that this world has acquired in the modern period and the single-minded vision of modern science, but also for theological reasons. A strict otherworldly orientation entails the corollary of a strongly individualistic focus in the basic understanding of what Christian faith involves. If the issue is essentially whether or not we are going to qualify for admission to the next world, or at least to the desirable regions of that world, then the onus is clearly upon each of us to bend our efforts in that direction. However, although such an understanding would probably meet with fairly widespread endorsement as an articulation of the basic thrust of the Christian faith, it is, in fact, luring us in precisely the opposite direction to that which is implied by the central vision of the gospel. Whatever else it may involve, the Christian message of salvation has long been understood as a deliverance from self-centeredness. One of the primary dimensions of sin, implicit in the teachings of Jesus, hinted at by Paul, and spelled out by Augustine is the tendency to place ourselves at the center of life and to revolve around ourselves instead of around the true source and destiny of life, God. The gospel exposes that transposition and reclaims us for God. But if the gospel is taken to be primarily concerned with our individual qualification for a future life, this relocates the self squarely back in the center of the picture.

An important element in the solution to, and a contributing factor in the recognition of, this dilemma, which has gained currency in recent years, involves the recovery of an appreciation of the importance of community for Christian faith. If the gospel is primarily about love, then it is a denial of that pivotal dimension when the Christian faith becomes regarded as a matter of our individual destinies conceived in fundamentally isolationist terms. The matter of the respective significance of, and relations between, individual and social dimensions in the Christian economy of salvation will constitute one of the principal topics when we come to consider the outstanding issues that must be dealt with if a viable vision of salvation is to be achieved for the future. In the present context, this question of the more specific understanding of the nature of salvation is secondary to the more general issue of the destiny and goal of salvation. The tendency of an otherworldly understanding to equate salvation with the destiny of the individual must finally be seen as a total misunderstanding of the deliverance from preoccupation with self which the Christian gospel represents. Whether or not we shall live again beyond this life is subordinate in principle to the recognition that all life is a gift of God. If we have been thus reclaimed by God in Christ, then the question of our personal destiny is surely best left with God. To concentrate on that question is to abandon the very release from self that the deliverance of the gospel proclaims. In this way, the Christian gospel of salvation need not be seriously threatened by the demise of otherworldliness that has characterized modernity. The serious issue is whether it is meaningful and credible to speak of being centered in God in the wake of the immense self-consciousness that lies at the heart of the modern project.

THE MATURITY OF HUMANITY

The cosmological revolution that ejected the earth from the center of the universe had the paradoxical result of propelling our own species into the center of the vacuum thus created. Although Immanuel Kant referred to his critical philosophy as a Copernican revolution in thought, it was really reverse Copericanism. Where Copernicus' heliocentric universe rendered our position somewhat peripheral as occupants of a planet orbiting the sun, Kant's critical stance placed the knower front and center in a way never envisaged by the naive geocentrism of pre-Copernican cosmology. Thus, the modern secular outlook has been characterized by a double paradox. Insofar as the loss of interest in another world is due to the demotion of this world from its assumed position as the center of the universe, we see, in retrospect, that medieval otherworldliness owes some of its credibility precisely to the assumption of the centrality of this world. It was, at least in part, because the people of the Middle Ages assumed that they occupied the center of the universe that they could expect that this world was but a prelude to another world beyond. The demotion entailed by that loss of centrality is an important ingredient in the understanding of this dualistic outlook. It provides the negative background of secularization. The positive development of secularity involves the shift from this loss of a sense of another world beyond to a lively interest in this world in and for itself. In that shift nothing is more pivotal than this reverse Copernican installation of ourselves as the assumed center of reality. Reality is what we say it is for the Enlightenment consciousness; reality is what we make it for the historical consciousness that has become increasingly dominant since the nineteenth century.

In comparison with this self-conscious preoccupation with ourselves, the erosion of otherworldliness is distinctly of secondary significance in the devaluation of salvation in the modern era, in spite of its characteristically high profile. Contrary to Dennis de Rougemont who distinguishes between the two principal aspects of salvation, "the loss of the meaning of the holy, and the loss of the meaning of transcendence,"[23] and contends that it is the latter that is the really serious threat to Christianity, the thesis advanced here is that the opposite is the case. Insofar as transcendence and sacredness can be separated at all, it is the loss of the sense of the sacred that is the more serious blow to Christian faith. A bare acknowledgment of transcendence hardly seems intelligible, much less meaningful. This is what gives the preoccupation with the loss of transcendence an abstract air, because this tends to be treated as the acknowledgment of sheer otherness. The loss of otherness that is significant is of that which makes a claim upon us, and of that which carries for us this connotation of the sacred. Secularization is surely primarily a matter of this loss of the sense of the sacred rather than the sheer loss of the sense of transcendence as such.

It is as the loss of a sense of the sacred that secularization entails the loss of God rather than simply of some transcendent dimension or other. The result is that we are relieved not only of a general sense of wonder about what lies beyond the realm of immediacy, but also of a sense of personal obligation that impinges on us in that immediacy. In *Le Cas Françoise Sagan*, George Hourdin tells of a politician who is unfaithful to his wife, but who strives to help his constituents, and of another who is faithful to his wife but unconcerned about social problems; and it is the former who is judged the more preferable of the two. Charles Moeller comments that this represents a particularly typical portrayal of the modern condition where a recognition of social responsibility has all but displaced any firsthand personal sense of sin.[24] Societal obligations can be readily understood as being of our own devising. As such, they are much more congenial to the anthropocentric perspective of modernity than a sense of personal obligation that is seen to address us from beyond the human.

This assumption that we have "come of age,"[25] to use the phrase of Bonhoeffer, which has figured so prominently in recent paeans to secularity, moves beyond the anthropocentrism that characterizes the Renaissance and Enlightenment to a fundamental sense of human sufficiency which amounts to an inversion of the traditional understanding of the human condition in which Christianity figured prominently.

Christianity was once about human fallibility, about the worthlessness of all earthly expectations. Now it is seemingly preoccupied with human capabilities. It is a very great change.[26]

It may not be particularly deplorable if Christianity has discovered significance in the world. Otherwise, what is the point of creation? And the notion that we are cocreators with God may also be seen as having more positive significance than simply being a concession to modern notions of evolution and technological mastery. But this discovery of the world and of our possibilities in it can also be taken in such absolute terms that it amounts to a total inversion of the traditional Christian understanding of life. This total inversion, so characteristic of much of the theological endorsement of secularity, misses the subtlety of Bonhoeffer's depiction of our "coming of age."

The God who makes us live in this world without using him as a working hypothesis is the God before whom we are ever standing. Before God and with him we live without God.[27]

It is the "before God and with him" that is often omitted in the enthusiasm for the secular contention that "we live without God." When that "without God" is taken *simpliciter*, there is no need for salvation, because there is no possibility of sin.

Without a sense of the sacred, of our ultimate obligation to God, sin can only dwindle to the level of social misdemeanor. For, as the Psalmist knew, sin is finally only against God: "Against thee, and thee only, have I sinned" (Ps. 51:4). Others may well be affected by our sin, and we certainly victimize ourselves, but what makes sin, sin is that it offends the giver of life. Without this dimension, the theological meaning recedes before a moral sense of a failure to realize our true potential or a social sense of having failed to satisfy organizational requirements of efficiency. However, a more radical alternate view of sin emerges among theologians who transfer the theological sense of sin into the context of a total endorsement of self-sufficient humanity. The result, as Don Cupitt acknowledges, is not a loss of the sense of sin but a total inversion in its meaning:

We notice that in the process the meaning of the term sin has reversed. In traditional society the affirmation of one's own radical freedom was the very essence of sin. Sin was discontent, rebellion again the existing divinely-ordered framework of life. But today obedience is sin.

Above all one must not surrender one's inner integrity; and what is integrity?—it is one's *autonomy*.[28]

In the age of autonomy, "obedience is sin." As another contemporary theologian puts it, "sin ultimately is the rejection of one's very personhood and purpose."[29] Where sin used to refer to the rejection of God, today it means the acknowledgment of God. In acknowledging any authority beyond ourselves, we are violating the sacredness of our own absolute independence. The language of sin becomes relevant again because a new sense of the sacred has been located, in ourselves, in the absolute autonomy that is taken to characterize our true reality. Our salvation lies in what used to be considered sin, in absolute self-assertion. We have seen the naivety of this from the social point of view in terms of the implausibility, not to say impossibility, of a full tolerance of pluralism. What remains is to consider the implications of this direction for theological considerations.

Prospects for Salvation in the Wake of Secularism

Secularity may be seen to destroy all sense of appreciation for salvation or to offer its own alternate version, but in either case the understanding of salvation is transformed. Thus, in addition to this external impact of elimination or alternative, secularization has also influenced the way in which salvation is understood theologically.

THEODICY AS ALTERNATIVE TO SALVATION

The tensions between the extremes of a full-bodied endorsement of a traditional understanding of salvation, on the one hand, and either a total abandonment of concern with salvation or the equation of salvation with our own self-interest, on the other, provides the context for a good deal of contemporary theological reflection. The most visible indication of this is the way in which the theodicy issue has tended to displace or modify treatments of the salvation theme. From both sides of the theological spectrum, the concern with our justification before God, which so animated Christian thinkers from Paul to Luther, is qualified by the self-consciousness of modernity that wonders whether God can be justified to us. Thus, Carl E. Braaten qualifies the characteristic Lutheran theme of our justification by divine grace with a depiction of Jesus as

God's apologetic appeal to us. "Jesus is the only answer to the problem of theodicy; he is God's chosen representative to make his case credible in a world of pain and death."[30] From the opposite direction, Rosemary Ruether contends that Jesus answers the theodicy question so completely as to dispense with it.

> When we model our God after emperors and despots who reduce others to dependency, then we have a problem of theodicy. But the cross of Jesus reveals a deeper mystery. The God revealed in Jesus has identified with the victims of history and has abandoned the thrones of the mighty. In Jesus' cross God abandons God's power into the human condition utterly and completely so that we might not abandon each other. God has become a part of the struggle of life against death. This is perhaps why those who struggle for justice do not ask the question of theodicy. They know that the true God does not support the thrones of the mighty, but is one of them.[31]

In the light of modern self-consciousness, Jesus must at least justify God as well as justifying us; for some, the two processes are identical.

The focus on theodicy can be seen as an abandonment, or as a rearticulation of the Christian concern for salvation as this has been represented by the notion of an atonement between God and humanity effected in Christ. Insofar as the loss of the sense of sin that accompanies secularization has penetrated theological consciousness, the relevance of atonement has also receded. This may happen to the point where any sense of our need for justification all but totally disappears behind the question of how we can believe in God in the light of the evil in the world. The problem of how God can be justified to us in the light of evil displaces the traditional concern with how we can be justified before God in the light of our sin. The counterpart to the inversion in the understanding of sin, as advocated by Don Cupitt, is a treatment of theodicy that regards it not as a replacement for the traditional concern with salvation but as a revision of that understanding. Thus, Carl Jung provides his *Answer to Job* in terms of just such a revision "which regards the atonement not as the payment of a human debt to God but as reparation for a wrong done by God to man."[32] With this we move through modern secularity, which assumes human sufficiency and totally dismisses any consideration of God as unintelligible, to an inverted theology in which God reemerges on our terms. Christ represents the theological justification of God to us.

The reversal in the direction of atonement, our reconciling God to ourselves rather than our being reconciled to God, is indicative of the basic shift in the understanding of our predicament. Where in previous ages people considered themselves questionable before God who was assumed to have the answers, we are more apt to find God questionable in the wake of the kinds of answers we have managed for ourselves through the achievements of modern science and technology. This shift in the onus of accountability involves a change in focus from sin to suffering. Where premodern outlooks influenced by the Judeo–Christian tradition assumed that the basic source of our difficulty was sin, from which suffering was often seen to derive directly, the alleviation of suffering through medical and industrial technology shatters this equation and, in so doing, exposes the question of theodicy with a new starkness. The source of our difficulties is perceived to lie in the world rather than in ourselves, in what might be called natural evil rather than moral evil. This provides the context for the theodicy question. But, as such, it represents an intermediary stage rather than a total reversal of traditional Christian concern. The extreme of contrariety is reached when the whole notion of evil is left behind for a perspective that assumes that the root of the problem is suffering itself. Rather than representing a symptom of the more pervasive reality of sin or raising the spectre of divine responsibility for evil, this outlook is absorbed by the fact of suffering as the essence of the challenge confronting us.

The direct concentration on suffering renders not only more traditional concern with salvation, but also the modern interest in theodicy, redundant. If sin and evil are not recognized, approaches designed to deal with these concerns will be deprived of all significance. This need not mean, however, that religious sensibility is totally discarded. It can be seen, on the contrary, as an approximation to the religious vision that has characterized the Far East, in contrast to the morally oriented perspective of traditions emanating from the Middle East.

To the Buddha the supreme problem was the problem of pain. To Christ, on the other hand, this problem and its solution was bound up with that of moral evil. And though to Christ the word "sin" evidently did not mean what St. Augustine and Calvin have since taught Western Christianity to mean by it, it would seem that to him the problem of moral evil was prior to that of pain. In this respect again the outlook of the Buddha is temporally more "modern"—a fact to be noted without prejudice to the question whether this view is the more profound.[33]

In its focus on suffering as the essence of the human predicament, Buddhism strikes a chord with modern Western sensibilities that no longer resound to the suggestion that suffering is secondary to the more personal and moral problem of our orientation and behavior and that ultimately much of the suffering we experience is to be traced to this source in one way or another.

In this curious way, the ultraspiritualistic perspective of the Far East joins forces with the essentially materialistic orientation of the modern Western technological approach, and Christianity, with a foot in both camps, is prevented from playing a mediating role as a result of being squeezed out by this amalgam of opposites. Paradoxical though this may appear at first glance, the common ground between Eastern spiritualism and Western materialism is not far to seek. These fundamental opposites join forces in the conviction that the fundamental challenges of life are not theoretical but practical, not matters for understanding but for action.

> The case of early Buddhism suggests the following general reflection: The less central belief in God is to a religion, the less will the problem of evil take the form of a demand for explanation. It will rather be a matter of correct diagnosis and the recommendation of a practical way out of the human predicament.[34]

The solutions to the human predicament proposed by Buddhism and modern technology are virtually opposites. The pursuit of the immediacy of mastery and control that characterizes the vision of technology cannot be expected to find the Buddhist attempt at detachment from the world particularly attractive. In fact, it is bound to be perceived as fundamentally mistaken. Not withdrawal, but engagement, is the direction of resolution for the technological perspective. Thus, in the long run, Buddhism will not find modern Western technocracy any more sensitive to its distinctive concerns than it has been to the traditional Christian concern with salvation. And yet the appeal of the immediate benefits of technology are perhaps even more attractive in the East than they have been in the West. "The paradox seems to be that the cultures of the West, with their spirit of initiative and enterprise, stand under the judgment of the age-old religious premise, common to East and West, but more consistently sustained among Eastern cultures; yet to assure its people life in a time of unprecedented need, the East must avail itself of this spirit of enterprise, and thereby incur the risk of spiritual regression."[35] It remains to be seen how well Eastern sensibilities will withstand the onslaught of technological management. The greater directness of its spiritual orientation might afford it a defense not so readily available to the more materially oriented stance of Christianity. However, the danger is that the reverse might also happen; that the focus on the common diagnoses of suffering as the central enemy will give the technological spirit a point of entry through which it might effect an even more total takeover than it has achieved in the West.

SECULARIZATION AS CONTEXT FOR SALVATION

The fate of the religious traditions of the Far East in the wake of secularization is an extension of the issue with which we continue to struggle in the West. Whether Eastern traditions ultimately will rebuff or succumb to the secular onslaught, or achieve some workable compromise with it, is the long-range, world-scale issue, of which the struggle for a viable contemporary vision in the West is the immediate focus. Insofar as the Western experience does represent the vanguard of a universal trend, there is reason to think that any form of religious interest in salvation is destined to be superseded either by direct abandonment or by total reinterpretation in conformity to the secular horizon.

There can hardly be any serious doubt that Western culture has taken a massive shift away from any tendency to look to God for solutions of any kind. "We may justly speak of a 'migration' of experiences of sin and of expectations of salvation, apparent also in the 'migration' to seculalized forms and bearers of salvation."[36] Rather than looking to theology for answers to our difficulties, we turn to psychology and sociology; not the priest, but the psychiatrist or the politician represents the agent of salvation for our age, insofar as such designation is not subject to complete dismissal as hopelessly archaic. It will not do to underestimate the gulf between our assumption of self-sufficiency as a species and the traditional reliance on God as solver of problems and source of solace assumed in former times. The situation then was very different.

> There was no sense that humanity could improve its lot through politics, resolve its guilt feelings through psychiatry, or prolong its life indefinitely through the scientific conquest of disease. Such developments have had a profound effect upon our willingness to admit any need for the kinds of salvation looked for in the ancient world. We no longer have the same perception of ourselves and our predicament.[37]

To understand salvation as divine deliverance, effected for us, if not also upon us, is to preserve a ghetto of religious meaning amid an otherwise active sense of our own responsibility for effecting improvement in our lot and legacy. One does not have to subscribe to the total inversion reading whereby previous faithfulness is regarded as contemporary sin, and vice versa, to recognize that the modern technological atmosphere renders every interventionist version of salvation fundamentally suspect. "What the common sense of our culture believes in is salvation by our own human efforts to come to our senses and to recognize our social and political alignments, so as to achieve peace and justice in the world, eliminate poverty, sickness and ignorance, distribute goods and the benefits of health services, education and leisure to all mankind."[38] Any explication of salvation that fails to take this shift of consciousness into account is doomed to languish in the domain of personal attitude and preferences, if it receives any serious attention at all. For a perspective on salvation to enjoy any serious credibility in this atmosphere of confidence in the human capacity to improve life, it must speak directly to that pervasive buoyancy.

One of the most original attempts to articulate such an updated version of salvation is offered by Sallie McFague in *Models of God, Theology for an Ecological, Nuclear Age*.[39] She offers a characterization of God as mother, lover, and friend, as an alternative to traditional divine imagery, not simply because she regards this as more congenial to contemporary sensibilities, but because she finds the traditional triumphalist imagery positively harmful.

> Does it support human responsibility for the fate of the earth, or does it, by looking to either divine power or providence, shift the burden to God? If a case can be made, as I believe it can, that traditional imperialistic imagery for God is opposed to life, its continuation and fulfillment, then we must give serious attention to alternatives.[40]

The alternative McFague proposes understands God: as mother, constantly giving birth to life through intimate associations in which the world is understood as God's body, in contrast to the father God providing redemption from sin from on high; as lover, constantly seeking to promote integration and respect for the divine body, the world, rather than isolating sinners and promoting individual or social reform; and as friend, engaging and eliciting our assistance and enthusiasm in seeking the welfare of the world.

The contemporary tone of this proposal is unmistakable. Indeed, the focus is decidedly secular in the centrality accorded the world as God's body and as the ultimate object of salvation. "The world is our meeting place with God, and this means that God's immanence will be 'universal' and God's transcendence will be 'worldly'."[41] Talk of "worldly transcendence" evokes recollections of the secular theology of the sixties when the worldliness then qualified the transcendence so decisively that it virtually reduced it to a nostalgic recollection of something that used to be meaningful. McFague seeks to avoid this fate by working out a worldly theology that is characterized by substantive alternatives to traditional otherworldly, dualistic, hierarchical visions. To the primary positive vision of the world as God's body, there corresponds a reinterpretation of the negativeness of our condition traditionally designated by the term "sin".

> In contrast to the king-realm model, where sin is against *God*, here it is against the world. To sin is not to refuse loyalty to the Liege Lord but to refuse to take responsibility for nurturing, loving, and befriending the body and all its parts. Sin is the refusal to realize one's radical interdependence with all that lives: it is the desire to set one's self apart from all others as not needing them or being needed by them. Sin is the refusal to be the eyes, the consciousness, of the cosmos.[42]

Where the secular theology of the sixties disclosed a fundamental weakness in its tendency to avoid consideration of sin, its message being characterized by a sense of the positivity of progress reminiscent of the nineteenth century, McFague's "worldly transcendence" not only confronts the issue of sin head-on, but also offers this imaginative reinterpretation of its meaning. Sin is our refusal to play our appropriate part as components in the body of God.

Although this alternative for theology is imaginative and coherent in itself, its adequacy as a vehicle for conveying the full scope of Christian theology is subject to question. One source of misgivings is apparent in the suggestion that sin involves our refusal to be "the consciousness of the cosmos." If we are to be "the consciousness of the cosmos," where does divine consciousness fit in? Since the world is God's body, presumably God is more than the world. This would seem to imply that God must, at the very least, be the consciousness of the world, but there is no indication of this in McFague's exposition. Her position rather seems to be that this is the role of the human species. In fairness she admits that she has concentrated on divine immanence. "Less has been said about how, in our model, one perceives divine transcendence."[43] Her concern has been to offer an alternative to the dualistic, hierarchical understanding of divine transcendence as the omnipotent potentate determining the world from on high. And it must also be acknowledged that process theology, which has been the approach most directly concerned with developing this relational understanding of God and the world in which the world might be seen as God's body, has yet to achieve a convincing articulation of this model that can be seen to do justice to the transcendence as well as to the immanence of God. However, these mitigating circumstances do not remove the problem. The identification of God with the world will lack credibility unless and until this is balanced by a corresponding sense of divine transcendence. This balance will entail an understanding of ourselves that recognizes the danger in our tendency to identify ourselves with God. Instead of seeing sin as a refusal to be "the consciousness of the cosmos," for example, an alternative, which seems to echo the basic concern of McFague, would be: "We refuse to accept ourselves as lovable creatures, who are not and need not be God."[44] This avoids the absolutizing of sin characteristic of neo-orthodox and conservative Protestantism, whereby the elevation of God seems to require the total debasement of humanity, and also the liberal and postsecular reversal that equates sin with the lingering legacy of our animal heritage and our refusal to take charge and assert ourselves. On this view, sin is the very real and constant tendency to forget that we are not, and are not expected to be, God. It is not clear that McFague's proposal for theological reform is sufficiently sensitive to this perennial danger when she chides us for refusing to be "the consciousness of the cosmos."

The source of McFague's definition lies in the fundamental direction of her outlook. The neglect of a convincing articulation of divine transcendence and the corresponding imbalance in the reinterpretation of the Christian understanding of sin are prominent elements in a total approach that evokes reservations because of its fundamental orientation. That orientation might be indicated more accurately by an inversion of the title and subtitle of McFague's book. The *Models of God* that are proposed represent an attempt to construct "Theology for an Ecological, Nuclear Age." McFague sees herself developing theological fictions in line with her previous explanations of the fictive nature of the theological enterprise, but here she is particularly concerned that the models proposed really address the contemporary situation. Again and again she stresses in italics that theology must be appropriate "for our time."[45] This is the criterion for theological models. "The question we must ask is not whether one is true and the other false, but which one is a better portrait of Christian faith *for our day*."[46] What characterizes our day in particular is the total threat to the world posed by the twin dangers of ecological devastation and nuclear holocaust. By this standard, traditional Christian theology is hazardous.

> The monarchical model is dangerous in our time: it encourages a sense of distance from the world; it attends only to the human dimension of the world; and it supports attitudes of either domination of the world or passivity toward it.[47]

The point at issue here is not the adequacy or inadequacy of the monarchical model as a portrait of Christian faith. It is not a matter of whether that model is inconsistent with the "Galilean vision" of Jesus, as Whitehead argued, or whether it is incompatible with the God of grace proclaimed by St. Paul. The central issue is its impact on the contemporary situation. The monarchical model must be opposed because it encourages a diminution of human responsibility for the terrifying circumstances of our time.

It is only possible to appreciate the most serious weakness in McFague's approach when we have fully recognized the basic legitimacy of the concern that prompts her to take that direction. Any vision of life that underwrites the callous environmental exploitation of multinational managers or encourages imperialistic ambitions through self-confirming apocalyptic expectations must be challenged in the name of planetary survival. However, serious and terrifying though this situation is, to accord it the status of ultimacy cannot be warranted theologically. There is something inherently suspect about regarding God as means to the promotion of our responsibility. This is just too much *of our time*. God becomes the ultimate resource to counteract our abuse and possible destruction of the world as a result of regarding it as our resource. Apart from the theological inadequacy of this use of God, it is doubtful whether it is any more promising as an apologetic. Our casual attitude to the world is not likely to be challenged by having it defined as God's body, unless the idea of God has some connotation for us beyond this utilitarian context. The difficulty is the same as that faced by the secular theology of the sixties, and is nowhere more eloquently stated than in the reconsideration of one of the leading exponents of that direction, Paul van Buren:

> It is no service to the world we know in this century to offer it only a reflection of itself. We have better things to say to this world than merely to echo back what it is already saying without us. By this move of secularization, we fail utterly to fulfill our responsibility to the world

for the sake of which we have been called into a Way that is not that of the world.[48]

It would be misleading and unfair to suggest that McFague is simply echoing back what the world is saying on its own. However, without an assurance that the vision she proposes is grounded in a basic sense of the reality of God as such, however provisional the models by which we attempt to articulate that reality, the import of what she has to offer is not likely to be recognized. The Christian message can be significant for our time only in the recognition that our context is much larger than that of our time. Christianity will only be relevant in the wake of secularization insofar as it is seen to be true, and not simply because it is thought to be needed.

SECULARIZATION AS THEME OF SALVATION

The credibility of any Christian understanding of salvation will be contingent upon its handling of the secularization theme. No exposition that neglects that theme will speak to contemporary sensibilities, but, at the same time, any reinterpretation that takes that theme so seriously that it conditions the message in a fundamental way will have nothing to say to those sensibilities. A serious engagement between concern with the traditional religious theme of salvation and the modern atmosphere of secularity will require reconsideration of traditional theological formulations in light of the attractiveness of secularity and also consideration of the adequacy of the secular vision in light of the perspective provided by the reconsideration of the salvation theme. What is called for might be indicated in general terms in Bernard Meland's contrast between traditionalism and historical sensibility:

> Traditionalism is an aging process that resists growth and change. Retaining historical vision and sensibilities in the act of coming to terms with change, and of assimilating its invigorating energy is something else again. It is the simultaneous act of challenging the past to assume its present opportunity for survival, and of summoning the present to be worthy of the legacy of lived experience which history transmits to it.[49]

Whereas we have considered the central challenge secularization poses to the received Christian tradition in terms of its suspicion of transcendence, its abandonment of otherworldliness, and its sense of human sufficiency, which renders even the most immanent forms of divine succor questionable, it remains to balance this by some consideration of the adequacy of the secular vision itself.

Perhaps the most significant aspect that should be noted in any attempt to come to grips with the theological implications of secularization is the fact that secularity itself is a theological theme. The fact that there is room for serious debate about not only the extent and significance, but even the very reality, of secularization, indicates that what we are dealing with is not so much a universally recognized fact as a particular interpretation of diverse phenomena.

> Secularization does not consist solely in the *fact* that man is turning away from God (the Christian God) and from traditional religious forms. It consists as well (and perhaps more importantly) in the reworking of these "facts" by Christians, who pin on them the label of "secularization," and who give them a justification and an extreme interpretation.[50]

This recognition is important first and foremost because it shatters the illusion that secularity represents an unquestionable, neutral fait accompli, in contrast to the always somewhat arbitrary metaphysical and religious visions of previous ages. As such, it calls in question a widely accepted distinction espoused by Harvey Cox, among others, between secularization and secularism:

> Secularization implies a historical process, almost certainly irreversible, in which society and culture are delivered from tutelage to religious control and closed metaphysical world views. We have argued that it is basically a liberating development. Secularism, on the other hand, is the name for an ideology, a new closed world view which functions very much like a new religion.[51]

One can appreciate the motivation for this distinction in the context of the general direction of the modern West. However, a wider perspective makes this distinction questionable. The situation in Iran, in Lebanon, or in the Punjab does not offer support for the inevitability of secularization thesis. Nor is the conflict that characterizes such areas devoid of the benefits of modern technology. If it be suggested that the mentality that goes with this technology has not yet penetrated the consciousness of the people of these areas, that is further confirmation of the Judeo–Christian origin of secularization, a thesis which Cox heartily endorses, but the assumption that such a development is inevitable is undermined by the resurgence of religion to prominence in the contemporary

West. In the American heartland of secularization where Church and state are subject to official constitutional separation, for the first time in history, the presidential primaries include a preacher among the slates of candidates for each of the major political parties. Perhaps we are witnessing the inevitable resurgence of religion, rather than the inevitable onslaught of secularization. At the very least, it renders any blanket endorsement of the secularization thesis problematic, and calls in question any clear distinction between secularization and secularism. A more adequate approach would seem to be to recognize that secularization is a metaphysical perspective, which in retrospect will probably be seen to no more merit the facile acceptance it has been accorded than does the Christian supernaturalism that dominated the Middle Ages. The truth of traditional Christianity and of secularity is undoubtedly more subtle than one-sided endorsements of either can allow.

Beyond exposing the dubiousness of the air of neutrality, which attaches to the idea of secularization, the recognition of the theological sponsorship of the whole idea indicates the context of intelligibility presupposed by it. "We need to bear in mind that the secularized society is an invention of Christians."[52] This means that secularization is really only significant for people who continue to be subject to Christian sensibilities. "Non-Christians do not characterize their society as a secularized society precisely in as much as the 'problem of God' is not their problem and they have turned to positivism."[53] Lived secularity would issue, not in secularism, but in an obliviousness to the whole issue, in a positivistic preoccupation with the immediate that would feel no compulsion to justify itself in terms of some wider perspective. It is only through the lingering influence of that perspective that secularity remains an issue. Thus, secularity represents an unstable midpoint of popular consciousness parallel to the status of theodicy in more overt theological reflection. As the question of whether or not we can accept belief in God in light of the suffering in the world, theodicy constitutes a point of transition between the more traditional concern over salvation as the question of whether God can find it possible to accept us and the total denial of religious interest of any kind. On a wider scale, concern over secularization constitutes a point of transition between overt religious interest of any kind and the total absence of religious sensibilities. Whether this latter state is a realistic possibility, is a matter of dispute. It would seem to require a complete acquiescence in immediacy. Insofar as that is possible, and insofar as it represents a visible characterization of prominent elements of contemporary mass culture to those who make this identification, that acquiescence itself will carry over-tones of religious absorption. Thus, where secularization would appear to be most complete, it may well have passed over into its opposite, a religious devotion to immediacy. Conversely, complete secularization must remain unintelligible to itself.

The result is that far from constituting a neutral base which can provide the foundation for either religious or nonreligious super-structures, secularization represents an intrinsically theological stance. This is the case, not because it overtly says anything about God, but because, as we have known at least since Feuerbach, anthropological positions have theological implications. The optim-ism and sense of autonomy that characterized the secular reading of the human condition are indicative of atheistic rather than of agnostic assumptions, despite the rhetoric about tentativeness and openness. Confirmation of this direction is nowhere more evident than in the naive simplicity with which the secular approach sees only the good in our situation.

> *We still have a rather innocent image of our search for innocence.* We prefer to think of the secular project as a beautiful project run exclu-sively by beautiful people filled with nothing but magnificent feelings.[54]

The contrast between this idyllic image of humanity and the harsh reality that dominates the newscasts exposes the Achilles' heel of the secular perspective. If neutrality entails some reliable reflection of the way things are, this discrepancy dispenses with any boast of secularity to provide a reliable portrayal of the human condition. Traditional theological portrayals of creatures in rebellion against their creator and at enmity with one another would appear to offer a much more realistic assessment of our situation, especially when this is augmented by the awareness of ways in which our structures institutionalize our self-interests. And yet it is not on this abstract level of generalization about the human condition that our basic loyalties in life are decided. Those loyalties themselves help to shape those generalizations. Thus, the sense of innocence that characterizes the secular outlook can continue to prevail, despite the manifold evidence to the contrary, because it depicts the way we would prefer to think of ourselves.

Insofar as this romantic picture of innocence is pierced, the general air of confidence surrounding secularity is quickly reestab-lished through the consideration that any deficiencies represent aberrations from the utopian program which is in the process of being realized. The most serious category of shortcoming that can be recognized is that of problems. This is the negative explanation for lack of interest in salvation in the atmosphere of secularity. Salvation only becomes an issue where there is some recognition of sin. The sense of total orientation that salvation involves is only significant insofar as there is some sense of fundamental malaise, which cannot be addressed by the problem-solving techniques of secularity. From the secular perspective, such talk of sin and salvation is bound to be heard as echoes of an antiquated past. From the sin–salvation perspective, there is a depth of malaise and a height of belonging at stake which one-dimensional secularity cannot know.

> The proclamation of salvation involves not just responding to the needs of which people are conscious, but challenging people to a deeper awareness of their need. Perhaps in this generation we need to be shocked into recognition of the *hubris* in which we are involved, as individuals, as social beings, as members of the human race, even as scholars, pastors and righters of the world's wrongs.[55]

The inadequacy of the secular vision is, finally, a matter of our fundamental self-satisfaction, of the hubris that is endemic to it. But of course this is not experienced in any such direct and bold form. It is always instantiated in particular social forms and personal commitments. Among these, the most prominent and influential is most certainly the culture of consumption. In this way the instability of secularity as a philosophy does not become an issue because its priorities are embodied in the absorbing dedication elicited by the religion of consumerism.

6

Salvation and Consumerism

Secularization is not only a theological term, but also by virtue of that, primarily an academic one. As well as presupposing a theological background to render it intelligible and significant, it also requires some theoretical distance to accommodate its level of generalization. If there is some question about the extent to which some kind of religious orientation is dispensable for human beings, there does not seem to be much doubt that many people find theoretical reflection eminently avoidable. Consequently, while secularization might not be a particularly significant issue beyond the province of theologians and those who continue to be influenced by the mind set with which they function, the reality that this category attempts to articulate may be extremely relevant to the very people who are so disinclined to assess their situation in such abstract terms.

We have seen that, in its most effective form, secularity is a lived reality. It is precisely the encompassing demand of that way of life which seems to bring us full circle and present us with the devotion and ardor that are the typical qualities evoked by religion. In this way the uneasy halfway house represented by secularization gives way to a new religion of immanence and immediacy; more specifically, the myth of secularity is punctured by the reality of the religion of consumerism. "In observing the role of business and related economic matters in contemporary America one might almost suggest that we have moved from a secularized society dominated by religious concerns, through a secularized one in which various major sectors attained considerable autonomy in their own spheres, to a commercialized or an economized culture in which the common denominators which unify and dominate all areas of activity are business-related or business-grounded considerations such as dollar-value, profitability, marketability, efficiency, contribution to the gross national product, etc."[1]

Insofar as such considerations dominate contemporary life, they represent our religion, the ideals and visions to which we really devote ourselves. The extent and tenacity of that devotion suggest that it is simply wrong to regard salvation as an obsolete category made irrelevant by the sophisticated secularity of contemporary society. The reality may rather be that a new variation of salvation has emerged in the form of a religion of consumerism. There is no shortage of signs that such a phenomenon is very real and that it occupies the level of influence exerted by religion in earlier periods. We shall examine this phenomenon by considering the central ingredients in this situation of alternate salvation, by attempting to identify the main sources that account for its appeal, and by assessing the solutions available to us to deal with this situation when it has been recognized and understood in some preliminary way.

The Religion of Consumption

Consumerism is synonymous with citizenship in modern technological civilization. Even back to nature romantics and hermetic isolationists might find it difficult, if not impossible, to avoid the grip of commodity culture completely. For the rest of us who pass our days in the direct embrace of that culture, the impact is so pervasive and routine that we are apt to notice only a very small fraction of the constant reinforcement of the business culture to which we are exposed. Its persistent thrust molds our values, shapes our visions, and monopolizes every area of life, including, as this last expression indicates, our language.

THE MORAL IMPACT OF BUSINESS

The public perception of business does not readily associate it with morality, at least not in any way approaching synonymity. The dramatic development of business ethics courses over the past decade is evidence of the contrary assumption that business needs to be informed and transformed by ethical considerations.

> Until about the middle of the 1960s, surveys indicated that approximately 70% of the American population believed that business "strikes a fair balance between the pursuit of profit and the interests of the public." This figure had declined to 33% by the mid 1970s, and today (1980) it hovers around 15%.[2]

From the point of view of business people themselves, in *The Gamesman*, Michael Maccoby reports that their responses indicate that their motivation is so determined by the pursuit of security, wealth and prestige that "only 7% consider it important to have work that is vital to human welfare."[3] Conversely, there is virtually nothing that they would not do for the right price.

> We asked if there was any project that an individual would not work on for moral reasons. Most could not think of one, or if they did, it was a project outside of their realm; an electronics manager rejected poison gas, and the manager of a chemical company said he wouldn't build an electric chair.[4]

This depressing picture of sheer opportunism cannot be ameliorated by the consideration that "that's just business." At the very least, this promotion of business as an autonomous activity with its own interests and imperatives implies an ethical stance on the part of business itself, contrary to any assumption of an essentially amoral activity. Thus, the most staunch advocates of free market business culture, like Milton Friedman, really endorse business in ethical, and not simply in economic, terms. "Friedman is arguing not that 'good ethics is good business,' but that 'good business is good ethics."[5] This ethical claim, however, is largely implicit. It is an endorsement of the economic calculus and is made explicitly only insofar as it can be expected to promote that calculus. As another defender of the market system, Paul T. Heyne, puts it: "Whatever businessmen may say about ethics, they almost always behave as if good ethics were simply good business."[6] Any independent claims of ethics will not be permitted to intrude on actual business practices. In case there is any inclination to interpret this as a critique of business people, Heyne quickly avers that this is entirely appropriate for business. "With these assertions we are not so much indicting businessmen for hypocrisy as crediting them with the sense to recognize where empty cant must end and responsible decisions begin."[7] The ethics of business is the ethics of responsible decisions. Compared with this, any other ethical claim is empty cant. And, of course, what qualifies decisions as responsible is their adherence to economic criteria. Cost effectiveness is the supreme value, whether this is invested with ethical overtones or not.

The implications of this economic imperative are sobering enough in terms of the operations of the business world itself. "Because of the upside-down morality that pervades the battle for profits (a Wall Street analyst and a Senate investigator independently came up with the phrase in our interviews), honesty is an expensive policy."[8] The incentive to cut corners and to deal in half-truths promoted by the priority afforded profitability locates the source of the widespread cynicism about business integrity at the very heart of the business world itself. And yet, ominous though this may be, it is eclipsed by the impact of this business perspective on the culture at large. The full significance of the ambivalence over ethics in the business world really only begins to emerge when we see this against the background of our whole culture as informed and formed by the values of business.

> Things are in the saddle and ride mankind. Emerson could say more now: He could say they are in the theatre and studio, and entertain mankind; are in the pulpit and preach to mankind. The values of business, in an overwhelmingly successful business society like our own, are reflected in every sphere: values which agree with them are reinforced, values which disagree are cancelled out or have lip-service paid to them. In business what sells is good, and that's the end of it—that is what *good* means.[9]

The nonmorality that provides legitimacy for the dealings of business is generalized through the mammoth reach of business in modern industrial and postindustrial society into the prevailing values of the culture at large. Acquisition and consumption are simply accepted as the parameters of moral vision. Cost replaces worth as the criterion of value. The economic calculus molds the culture at large with the inexorable logic it originally exerted within the confines of the commercial world. How could it be otherwise in modern technologically based nations where we have all become buyers and sellers?

The depth of this commercialization of morality really only begins to be appreciated when we achieve some recognition of the extent to which this outlook shapes our own self-understanding. John Francis Cavanaugh identifies the perspective involved as "the commodity form," in contrast to the long standing conventional understanding of human life that preceded it, which he labels "the personal form," and contends that this shift entails nothing less than a foundational transposition in our fundamental approach to life:

> The pre-eminent values within the Commodity Form of life are marketability and consumption. These two values are the ethical lenses through which we are conditioned to perceive our worth and importance.[10]

Even our genuine and well-founded relief at not living in eras or areas where life has been, or is, characterized by a constant and often losing struggle for survival, has to be tempered somewhat, at least in terms of satisfaction, if not of smugness, when we recognize the extent to which we are implicated in an absorbing struggle for that which is not bread. The implements of ease and the diversions of affluence are not merely external acquisitions. They are extensions of ourselves and, as a result, represent a reshaping of ourselves. The prominence accorded their pursuit and acquisition testify to the status these values have attained for us. Whether it is wise to speak of this as a transition within the sphere of morality, under this nebulous term "value," however, is another question. It might be more accurate to see ourselves as involved in the attempt to abolish morality through a thinly veiled preoccupation with our own determinative self-interest.

THE RELIGION OF BUSINESS

The success with which business has dominated modern developed countries, and through the global reach of multinational corporations is rapidly subduing the whole planet, elevates its influence beyond the range of moral concern as a shaper of a way of life to the level of devotion characteristic of religion. "What we see in our country today is a perfectly good economic process—the mechanisms for producing and consuming goods—made into a religion."[11] The way of consumption does not simply tell us what is good, it takes on the aura of goodness itself. It fills the vacuum, created by the hesitancy of secularization, with visions of security, status and meaning attainable through accumulation and control.

> Material goods have become substitutes for faith. It's not that people literally place their cars on the altar; rather, it is the function of these goods in a consumer society.[12]

People do not place their cars on the altar because the cars themselves displace the altar. The source of this contention, Jim Wallis of Sojourners, a Christian community movement which is attempting to forge an alternative to the competitive isolationism of consumer society, notes how the religious overtones of consumerism are so apparent in the ads for cars: "'Datsun Saves,' 'Buick, Something to believe in.'"[13]

Here too, as with the impact of consumerism on the moral dimension, the depth of penetration of this influence is easily underestimated, precisely because of its ubiquity. We take the pivotal prominence of business so for granted that its massive significance only begins to become apparent when our contemporary business culture is seen in contrast to the dominant features of a different era. Thus, the influence of business sponsorship of the arts, for instance, is set in sharp relief by a consideration of the very different situation that prevailed in the premodern world where the source of sponsorship was more apt to be the Church. "Just as the Church sponsored Michelangelo, Bach, Handel, and other giants of our cultural heritage, so too we find Mobil Oil sponsoring public television, Atlantic Richfield saving a reputable British newspaper and protecting an island against development, and banks, among others, providing a forum for young artists to display their works."[14]

It might be said that in the premodern West, the Church was big business, so that things have not changed that much. And yet while there is some merit in this consideration, it is itself a reflection of the modern self-conscious business perspective. It recognizes that institutional religion is inevitably implicated in the realm of business, and when the institution is as dominant as the Church was in Christendom this will entail a significant commitment to what can only accurately be designated as business matters. But if this is regarded as an exposé of the hidden economic motives of religion, this can only be allowed to stand uncontested through an acquiescence in the religious veneration of business. For although the economic dimension is indisputably part of organized religion, and at times might represent a controlling interest, whether on the part of certain medieval prelates or contemporary electronic evangelists, the horizon of religion is inherently transcendent and inclusive.

From the point of view of religion itself, the identification of this horizon with any more restricted interest represents a basic violation of the religious impulse, idolatry. To find a vindication of the supremacy of commerce in the identification of commercial interests and abuses in organized religion is to attest to the acceptance of the substitute religion that business has become for contemporary culture. A vivid symbol of this displacement is at hand in the way in which in the modern city skyline church spires have been dwarfed by bank towers.

> The medieval cathedral, of course, towered over the squat places of commerce in its town, and even nineteenth-century Wall Street was more or less dominated by the spire of Trinity Church. Admiring the new St. Peter's one can't help thinking how our view of the fitness of things has changed now that it seems natural to see a house of God at the feet of a temple of money.[15]

Prominence on the skyline provides a highly visible indication of the priorities among the people responsible for its shape. The overshadowing of the spire by the tower bespeaks the new Babel project as a shift of allegiance from that comprehensive transcendent reality Christians call God to more immediate sources of salvation.

However, the thoroughness of that shift does not assure its adequacy because, however impressive the accumulation of finite power and possession, the ultimate skyline is measured by infinity. To accord the commercial venture the status of religion is to invest it with this dimension of significance. And yet, absurd though this may appear when stated in these abstract terms, that is what the absolutizing of modern business culture amounts to. It entails the divinizing of the ideals and idols of commerce in defiance of Jesus' warning in the Sermon on the Mount: "No one can serve two masters; for either he will hate the one and love the other, or he will be devoted to the one and despise the other. One cannot serve God and mammon" (Mt. 6:24). The futility of that defiance is captured in the lament of Piers the Plowman as he contemplated the absorbing preoccupation entailed in sending emissaries to the major international market of Bruges or into the domain of Prussia:

> An yf ich sente over see—my servant to Brugges,
> Other in-to Prus my prentys · my profit to a-waite,
> To marchaunde with monye · and maken here exchange,
> Myghte nevere man comforty me · in the meyn tyme,
> Neither matyhs ne mass · ne othere manere syghtes,
> And nevere penaunse performede · ne *paternoster* syede,
> That my mynde he was · more in my goodes
> Than in godes grace · and hos grete myghte.[16]

The pervasive presence of modern business leaves very few of us who would not have to admit that as members of the consumer society our minds are decidedly "more in my goodes/Than in godes grace."

The depth of devotion elicited by this ersatz religion of consumerism is missed unless we recognize that this characterization of it, in religious terms, is itself an acknowledgment of its massive hold over contemporary consciousness. As critics of consumerism, we acknowledge its power and penetration not only in contemporary society but also in ourselves, just as surely as do the most unwary adherents of its captivating faith.

We are witnessing a violent verbal attack against the consumer society, yet, on the other hand, the latter, and everything that goes with it, is the object of a religious exaltation. Consumption, along with the technology that produces it and the advertising that expresses it, is no longer a materialistic fact. It has become the meaning of life, the chief sacred, the point of morality, the criterion of existence, the mystery before which one bows.

Be not deceived, the rejection of consumer society is on the same level. The quarrel is really a religious one. The disputants never leave that world. To the contrary, they serve to reconfirm the religious fact.[17]

As the source of vision and model of aspiration, the dynamic of consumerism constitutes the determinative religion of contemporary Western culture. However inadequate it may be in comparison with the transcendent claims of conventional religion, any critique of it launched under this auspices is bound to appear abstract because of its pervasive influence, and insofar as it defines the terms of the critique, the religion of consumerism is itself implicitly endorsed precisely by such explicit criticism of it. In this way, consumerism may be the most consistent embodiment of the religious extreme of secularity, offering a source of devotion and dedication that is so absorbing that it threatens to eliminate all inclination as well as perspective for dissatisfaction with the prevailing ethos.

THE TOTAL IMPACT OF BUSINESS

Not everyone would accept the picture proposed here of a monolithic business environment, defining the good through the appeal of its promotion of acquisition and consumption with the dedication elicited by these ideals being elevated to the status of the sacred, in an absorption and devotion that require religious terminology to do justice to the depth of dedication involved. For example, Andrew Greeley, the Roman Catholic sociologist, takes issue with this type of characterization as presented by Daniel Bell in *The Cultural Contradictions of Capitalism* and by Alvin Toffler in his warnings regarding *Future Shock*.

Are we really all that different in our sensibility than our predecessors? Or do we merely know a little more, talk a little more, and move about a little more freely?[18]

Greeley shares Bell's suspicion of modern culture, but he wonders if people have really bought into it as fully as analysts like Bell would seem to think, and that would apply as well to the perspective developed here.[19] In this, we encounter a parallel to the caution noted from David Martin regarding the wholesale adoption of the secularization thesis. As with that reservation, the present hesitation constitutes an apposite reminder of the danger of acquiescing in vast generalizations too readily. The prospect of an all-encompassing consumerism is no more credible than that of a uniform and universal process of secularization. We must be wary of the element of arbitrariness in references to modern or contemporary consumer culture. "There is no single point in history before which we were all nature's children, after which we became the sons and daughters of commerce."[20] The reality is more variegated than such expansive designations suggest. And yet, allowing for the inadequacy of such generalizations when taken literally, it is surely undeniable that the modern era has been characterized by the development of pervasive commercial enterprises and that this trend has intensified in recent years.

The only room for debate seems to be with regard to the extent to which people tend to be absorbed by and dedicated to the mode of life promoted by this development. But even this area of questioning seems to be largely self-answering in terms of the massive promotion and pursuit of commercial directions in contemporary culture. The question of the depth of this dedication is less easily discernible, but this is finally the question of the adequacy of this orientation as an object of human devotion. Greeley's reservation may be prompted by such a sense that human beings could not possibly be satisfied to live as consumers with any real degree of seriousness and finality. Yet whereas he calls for evidence for concluding that people do so give themselves to the way of consumption, the predominant impression of this already indicated suggests that the onus is on skeptics like Greeley to provide evidence that people are not so widely and totally absorbed in the consumption game.

A more credible account of the seriousness of consumerism as a captivating orientation is provided by the psychologist, Erich Fromm:

Having fun lies in the satisfaction of consuming and "taking in" commodities, sights, food, drinks, cigarettes, people, lectures, books, movies—all are consumed, swallowed. The world is one great object for our appetite, a big apple, a big bottle, a big breast; we are the sucklers, the eternally expectant ones, the hopeful ones—and the eternally disappointed ones. Our character is geared to exchange and to receive, to barter and to consume; everything, spiritual as well as material objects, becomes an object of exchange and of consumption.[21]

Behind this vivid picture of the consummate consumer there lies the understanding of a fundamental shift in which, for the first time in history, hedonism was embraced as a serious cultural option. Fromm locates the turning point in the seventeenth century and singles out Thomas Hobbes as a prime exponent of the new philosophy.[22] However, this approach to life cannot, by any means, be attributed simply to a change in intellectual perspective. The utilitarian approach advocated by Hobbes attained widespread endorsement because of the impact of the industrial revolution. As Fromm sees it, the central psychological premises of the industrial outlook were the hedonistic endorsement of happiness understood in terms of pleasure as the aim of life and the assumption that the ensuing selfishness and greed that the implementation of the aim entailed would actually issue in overall peace and harmony.[23] This latter assumption is precisely the essence of the modern free enterprise philosophy as articulated most authoritatively by Adam Smith in his contention that it is through each of us looking out for ourselves that the general welfare will be most reliably assured. The net result of that assumption and of the hedonistic orientation which informs it is what Christopher Lasch has called *The Culture of Narcissism*[24] and what Thomas Wolfe terms the "Third Great Awakening in America" wherein the sense of being personally claimed is totally internalized in the uncompromising hedonism of the "me" generation.[25] These assessments indicate a much more monumental development than the reservations of someone like Greeley can recognize, and although we may well dismiss those reservations at our peril, not least because as well as setting forth the query as to whether consumerism can really satisfy human aspirations, they remind us that selfishness is not a modern invention; nevertheless, there is little doubt that in the modern West we have increasingly devoted ourselves to giving that direction a serious try.

In retrospect, there even appears to be a certain inevitability to the hedonistic direction of modern industrial and postindustrial society. The sheer abundance of goods and possibilities it has produced is so dramatic that the quantitative difference itself might be expected to take on qualitative significance. The novelty of the development is graphically conveyed by Alvin Toffler.

> It has been observed . . . that if the last 50,000 years of man's existence were divided into lifetimes of approximately sixty-two years each, there have been about 800 such lifetimes. Of these 800, fully 650 were spent in caves.

Only during the last seventy lifetimes has it been possible to communicate effectively from one lifetime to another—as writing made it possible to do. Only during the last six lifetimes did masses of men ever see a printed word. Only during the last four has it been possible to measure time with any precision. Only in the last two has anyone anywhere used an electric motor. And the overwhelming majority of all the material goods we use in daily life today have been developed within the present, the 800th lifetime.[26]

The exponential nature of the productive process certainly promotes, if it does not assure, the prominence of consumption as a source of interest.

At earlier stages of the process this note of inevitability was not so evident. One of the most perceptive early commentators on the triumph of commercialism in the modern era, R. H. Tawney, for example, distinguished between the industrial process itself and the attitude of industrialism, which he regarded as the according of a prominence to that process which it did not deserve. "The essence of industrialism, in short, is not any particular method of industry, but a particular estimate of the importance of industry, which results in it being thought the only thing that is important at all, so that it is elevated from the subordinate place which it should occupy among human interests into being the standard by which all other interests and activities are judged."[27] In this regard, Tawney might be seen to be espousing an earlier version of the minimization of the significance of commercialization advanced by Greeley in the contemporary context, with the difference in emphasis entailed by Greeley's questioning of the depth of the commercialization of life, whereas Tawney addresses more the issue of the avoidability of the domination. Thus we must wonder if Tawney appreciates the attraction and power of the modern industrial process and the products and preferences it provides, as we have questioned Greeley's apparent underestimation of the grip of consumerism. However, Tawney is undoubtedly on target in his characterization of the mechanics of what he calls industrialism, and what we have come to think of as the consumer society. It entails the elevation of what should be subordinate to the status of standard for everything.

The uniqueness of modern, commercially oriented society, which Tawney saw to lie in its embracing of industrialism, can be seen to reside in this fundamental inversion of means and ends. Where other ages and cultures have at least officially regarded the material base of life as just that, the base which would permit the pursuit of other more inclusive challenges of mind and spirit, modern consumer culture has adopted these means of life as the ultimate goal itself. In this way intrinsic worth is accorded what would otherwise be regarded as possessing only instrumental value. "Economics generally has to do with instrumental and not intrinsic values, and yet we are constantly invited to reverse the order."[28] There is no more graphic indication of the extent of that inversion than the way in which advertising promotes precisely what in the premodern West used to be regarded as the chief forms of evil. "In fact, most advertising appeals directly to one or more of the seven deadly sins: pride, lust, envy, anger, covetousness, gluttony, and sloth."[29] In the absolute dedication to consumption, not only are means turned into ends, instrumental values elevated to the status of intrinsic values, but also the good of consumption is promoted by appealing to the most destructive impulses of humanity. The representation of consumerism as a revived ethic or a new version of religion does not do justice to the magnitude of this movement, which manages to convince the most educated citizenry the world has known that evil is good.

The Consumption of Religion

Designating the massive dedication to consumerism by the label of religion may serve to suggest something of the all-encompassing allegiance it commands, but this must not be permitted to conceal from us the fact that insofar as this label is deserved it is religion itself that is consumed. For as a religion, consumerism can only be idolatrous. It worships the creature rather than the creator. And yet, obvious though this may be, accounting for that misapplication of devotion and appreciating what the difference involves are by no means straightforward. Several explanations of the religious appeal of consumerism might be offered, each of which has some degree of plausibility, but none of which permits a completely satisfactory demarcation between this false religion and the genuine article.

THE RESPECTIVE SIGNIFICANCE OF PERSONS AND THINGS

Probably the most widely advanced diagnosis of the source of, and deficiencies entailed in, the elevation of consumption to the status of a religion is the charge that it treats people as things. It makes things the object of its veneration, and in so doing it reduces persons and the personal to the status of things. This concern for the personal is particularly characteristic of Catholic social thought in its proposed alternative to the emphasis on impersonal structures in Marxism and on the importance of property in capitalism.[30] Thus, one Catholic theologian presents his summation of the problem with consumer society in the following terms: "We no longer see persons, we see *things*. And things, like idols, are dead."[31] The Catholic economist, E. F. Schumacher, subtitles his influential book *Small is Beautiful* with the descriptive phrase "A study of economics as if people mattered."

Of course this diagnosis is not confined to Catholicism. A century ago, Ralph Waldo Emerson complained of Protestant America that "Things are in the saddle, and ride mankind!"[32] This contrast also was prominent in Erich Fromm's characterization of the modern West as fixated on having to the detriment of its appreciation of being.

> The difference between being and having is not essentially that between East and West. The difference is rather between a society centered around persons and one centered around things. The having orientation is characteristic of Western industrial society, in which greed for money, fame, and power has become the dominant theme of life.[33]

The remedy prescribed for this diagnosed ailment consists in an "Up with people! Down with things!" type of revolution in attitude and practice. For some this prescription is directed at the business world in the confidence that the problem is basically that the priorities of business have slipped out of their proper alignment.

> Business is a central activity of society, and a type of human association. Too often it is seen in terms of dollars and cents rather than in terms of people. Although a firm may be established for profit, the profit earned is simply a means to an end and not an end in itself. When this fact is obscured and profit becomes an end, then people are poorly served because they are forgotten and ignored in the business process.[34]

For others, however, this appears to entail a naive view of business, which is seen not as a vehicle for meeting human need but rather, as Adam Smith acknowledged and the progressive triumph of consumerism tends to confirm, as an engine directly fueled by human greed. From this perspective, what is required is not to get business back on the rails, but to challenge the whole direction of business and the culture it promotes as a threat to our existence as human beings through its exultation of commodities over persons. So in these terms, John Francis Kavanaugh develops an elaborate scheme in which what he calls the Commodity Form is contrasted with the Personal Form as two antithetical modes of life. "The Commodity Form sustains and legitimates the entire fabric of dehumanization."[35] It does this by constituting a basis for valuing, knowing, willing, behaving, loving, and perceiving reality that is the contrary of personal versions of these activities.[36] Consequently, the remedy for this is to be found in the promotion of a renewed vision and venture of humanization through the pursuit of the personal mode of these fundamental activities, which have been taken over by the tyranny of the Commodity Form.

The promotion of the personal is an understandable reaction to the determinative position accorded the commodity in consumer society, but that it is an adequate response, even in terms of that society, is another matter. For it can be argued that consumer society is not finally explicable in terms of an obsession with things but rather represents an obsession with ourselves. Things are consumed, not respected. To treat things as commodities is then precisely an expression of our personal tyranny over things rather than of their tyranny over us. Then ironically the Commodity Form is itself an expression of the Personal Form. It is the separation of ourselves from other creatures in what Peter Singer has called "speciesism"[37] that has allowed us to treat other species as commodities. In this sense there is some justification for Lynne White's suggestion that the Judeo–Christian emphasis on human domination over creation must share some of the blame for the ecological crisis.[38] There is a significant difference between the Amerindian hunting, trapping, and fishing for food and clothing, and the mass slaughter of species, and factory farming that have characterized this continent since the arrival of "civilization." The assumption of superiority, which has allowed us to turn other species into commodities has, of course, also sponsored the transformation of plants and minerals into resources available for our exploitation.

The ecological crisis, in both its major forms, the threat to the environment from the massive waste the whole industrial process directly and indirectly spews into air, land, and water, and the prospect of the depletion of nonrenewable resources, gives urgency to the disrespect for things that consumerism entails. Short of the destruction of life on the planet through the impact of atmospheric changes or the poisoning of the food chain, which is not inconceivable, the very personal preoccupation of consumerism might prove to be the Achilles' heel of this whole approach. For besides the environmental limits on consumerism, there are also what Fred Hirsch has called *Social Limits to Growth*.[39] The personal basis of consumerism, residing as it does in the appeal to self-interest, threatens our life together just as surely as it does the wider environment. Social life is finally impossible on the basis of an aggregate of individual greed. Thus, the very personalness at the basis of consumerism appears problematic in itself and not simply because it turns the world into a source of commodities.

The radical nature of the dilemma suggests that a radical solution is called for. The general direction attempted in consumer culture has centered on the imposition of restrictions on the worst excesses of selfishness through the vehicle of some form of social contract. Individuals are seen as the bearers of rights, and thus, their pursuit of self-interest is restrained by this same assumption that authorizes it, in the recognition that other individuals also have the same rights. Some theoreticians who find this general direction satisfactory suggest that it is not only capable of providing enough social coherence to assure our continued existence as a species but also that it can be extended to the environment to provide an antidote to the ecological crisis. Thus, Christopher D. Stone proposes that the doctrine of rights be extended to things, although he acknowledges that a substantial sales job would be required before people would be willing to take this seriously. "There is something of a seamless web involved: There will be resistance to giving the 'thing' rights until it can be seen and valued for itself; yet it is hard to see it and value it for itself until we can bring ourselves to give it 'rights'—which is almost inevitably going to sound inconceivable to a large group of people."[40] The dilemma Stone sketches brings us closer to the problem with consumerism than the contention that it results from having permitted persons to be subordinated to things. There is no doubt that consumer culture does involve an inversion between instrumental and intrinsic goods, but that inversion cannot be aligned directly with the distinction between persons and things. The problem is not that we fail to respect persons in our preoccupation with things, but that we have lost all respect for things as well, and this seems to reflect on our understanding of ourselves as persons. The solution seems to be to treat things as persons, which in the modern context means according them rights, but in view of the utter contempt in which things have come to be held this simply sounds silly.

It is a significant step to recognize that the heart of our difficulty as we struggle under the sway of the consumption imperative is not that we put things ahead of people but that we do not really care about things either. The driving force of consumption is not appreciation but use. The consumer society is the throwaway society. This is what makes it so destructive environmentally and spiritually. Recognition of the environmental devastation is becoming increasingly unavoidable, but as the awareness of the crisis deepens, it also takes on spiritual overtones. As we move from seeing that the problem is not our preoccupation with things, but our contempt for things, we begin to suspect that the source of the difficulty is not any particular facet of life, however broadly based, but in our total orientation. Our rape of the planet and our persistent need to try to outdo one another bespeaks a fundamental disorientation at the very heart of life. The issue is not one of extending the rights we have arrogated to ourselves to other forms of life, including inanimate objects. That is bound to seem silly, unless and until, we come to see our inherent involvement with other forms of life and the whole world of which we are a part. But then it will not be a matter of according to other beings or things rights that we have assigned to ourselves, but of being transformed ourselves. This is why the issue is fundamentally spiritual. What is at stake is not an extension of our largess but a recognition of our own creaturehood. The issue is not the gulf between persons and things but the totally different orientations, which Martin Buber has called I-It and I-Thou.

The modern, industrially based, consumption-oriented direction is the epitome of the I-It approach to life. "The primary connexion of man with the world of I-*It* is comprised in *experiencing* which continually reconstitutes the world, and using, which leads the world to its manifold aim, the sustaining, relieving, and equipping of human life."[41] Experiencing and using have made possible the manifold equipping of human life in the form of the conveniences and enjoyments that so distinguish our age from previous periods. The catch is that "the development of the ability to experience and use comes mostly through the decrease of man's power to enter into relation."[42] That is the difference between consumer culture and more conventional religions. The former is characterized by a fundamental isolationist strain, which is of the very essence of thingness. The extent and depth of this difference is indicated by the way in which it also colors the most sublime spiritual relation as well as applying to the most mundane elements of the natural order.

Life cannot be divided between a real relation with God and an unreal relation of *I* and *It* with the world—you cannot both truly pray to God and profit by the world. He who knows the world as something by which he is to profit knows God also in the same way.[43]

It is not accidental that contemporary theology, under the sway of consumer culture, is increasingly inclined to refer to God as the ultimate resource for the solving of human problems, in pietistic and structural forms. Until this matter of fundamental orientation is squarely faced, such aggravations of the disease of consumerism are inevitable.

THE SPIRITUAL AND THE MATERIAL

Recognition that consumerism is characterized by contempt for things, rather than by obsession with things, confirms the conclusion of W. H. Auden that "the great vice of Americans is not materialism but a lack of respect for matter."[44] A corollary of this recognition is the realization that the change in orientation required is not from materialism to spiritualism. If the way of relation advocated by Buber is taken to imply a spiritualistic alternative to the materialistic orientation of consumer culture, it will only serve to aggravate, rather than to relieve, the dilemma. Because preoccupation with matter and neglect of spirit are only symptoms of the more fundamental issue of total orientation, it is the nature of the relation in which we stand to both these dimensions that is at stake.

The danger of a spiritualistic reaction to consumerism is, perhaps, not high among mainline theologians. The prominence of political and liberation theologies provides a powerful antidote to any temptation to spiritualistic withdrawal from the concrete engagements of life. At least, this would appear to be the case. Concerns with justice, particularly in the face of economic disparity, certainly suggests a very down-to-earth orientation. And yet the fixation on structures and systems, significant though these are, can result in an air of abstraction that would rival the most otiose spiritualism. The plight of the hungry and the exploited can recede before the absorbing captivation of the abstraction called "society." Thus in response to the ecological crisis, Rosemary Ruether contends that this is fundamentally a social problem. The issue only really begins to be taken seriously, according to Ruether, when the environmental and social costs begin to affect middle management. "Social domination is the missing link in the question of domination of nature."[45] The ecological crisis is finally rooted in the systemic crisis of capitalism. As long as those who control the means of production are able to pursue their own goals of power and profit with impunity, the ecological crisis will not be taken seriously. Without in any way denying this social dimension in the ecological crisis, we must question whether the problem can be focused so firmly on the social system. For one thing, whereas conspicuous consumption may be attributed to the privileged, the massive consumption that is the source of the quantitative impact on the environment is due much more to the ordinary consumer who certainly appears to be a very willing victim of this system. On a broader scale, this suggests that structural problems are no more significant than deficiencies of vision and ultimate loyalties. The difference between middle management with their two jet set vacations each year in exotic climes and the working class family with their snowmobiles and secondhand eight cylinder cars is one of degree rather than of kind. Each is pursuing status and enjoyment without regard for the environment. What is needed in both cases is a change of vision, which will enable them to see not only their common involvement with one another but also with the world of which they are apart. If Buber is right, this will not happen unless and until there is a genuine appreciation of the religious dimension. It is only as a person is addressed by the eternal Thou that they are able to transcend the I-It approach of exploitation and enter into genuine relation with God, with one another, and with the rest of creation.

From the perspective of consumer culture, the danger of the direction advocated here resulting in an obscure spiritualism is minimized because of the likelihood of any such proposal being dismissed out of hand as a romantic flight from reality. Whatever the liability of consumerism, it is certainly dealing with concrete realities. The one thing that can be appreciated from this perspective is the concern for material welfare. Although the sense of what constitutes welfare is open to serious questioning, and this in turn, as we have seen, reverberates on the whole understanding of the material order, the importance of the material dimension remains front and center, in spite of the fact that this veneration really constitutes abuse. As a result, insofar as theology addresses the issue of material welfare, it might be accorded a hearing in consumer culture, but then what would be heard would be the material note in abstraction. Concern with the poor takes the shape of the requirement that they be enabled to become consumers. And thus, the gospel mandate is absorbed by the religion of consumption. The alternative to this total preoccupation with the material order as a source of consumption is a segregation of the material from the spiritual so that the spiritual dimension is recognized but precisely in contrast to the material. In this way some of the most ardent devotees of consumerism can also be among the most spiritually concerned. Whether the segregation can be maintained, however, is another matter. For some, the most prominent examples being among the fraternity of electronic evangelists, there is reason to suspect a conscious duplicity in this duality. The contrast between the proclamation of mutual caring and the practice of extravagant self-indulgence is just too glaring to permit any but the most loyal disciples to avoid this impression. On the other hand, there are, no doubt, many who embrace this schizoid spirituality with sincerity, heartily pursuing material consumption and, at the same time, just as fervently embracing a spiritual vision which is not seen to impinge on this other preoccupation in any significant way at all. It is this divorce between the material and the spiritual, in any form, which is at the heart of the devastating appeal of consumerism. By contrast, Buber's distinction between the two orientations of I-It and I-Thou is presented as the means for overcoming this because each of these is seen as a comprehensive vision in itself. The problem is not that we focus on the material to the neglect of the spiritual, in either totalitarian or dualistic terms, but that we take a possessive stance with regard to life as a whole. We "thingify" everything, if we may so put it, including God. The only escape from this is the equally total openness to the living reality, which is making a claim upon us in the immediacy of present relation. But this is only possible insofar as we feel the claim of the eternal Thou, which grounds the whole material-spiritual order.

The diagnosis and alternative represented by Buber's contrast between I-It and I-Thou as a contrast of total orientation in life rather than of two levels or dimensions of reality is as difficult as it is radical. As a total orientation, it can only, finally, be appreciated or remain unintelligible. Fleeting glimpses of its merit and approximations to the relational orientation it endorses leave us caught between the stances of I-It and I-Thou, and so also mired in some variation of the material/spiritual dualism. To live in the I-Thou stance would be to experience the perfect integration of spiritual and material. In one sense we can appreciate this. "It has been said that we are living in two deserts—an exploited planet and a soul in agony—which are in truth one desert."[46] In light of the social self-consciousness achieved in recent years, it is abundantly clear that the devastating poverty of the third world is directly linked to the affluence of the developed world, and we cannot seriously contemplate this situation for long without acknowledging that the fact that we have allowed this to happen, and more incriminatingly, that it is not only allowed to continue but that we actually increasingly benefit from this arrangement, is of much more than economic significance. It is indicative of the fact that the state of the dispossessed is due in significant measure to the fact that we are possessed, both spiritually and materially.[47] This intimate connection between our material wealth and spiritual poverty is equally true on the poverty end of the scale in an inverse way, though not as an assurance of spiritual piety but rather, as Gandhi is reported to have said, "To the millions who have to go without two meals a day the only acceptable form in which God dare appear is food."[48] Northern consumption and southern poverty, and the increasing replication of that world pattern domestically, is a spiritual matter. And yet if that very real and legitimate concern becomes determinative, the results are bound to be spiritually devastating: "'Bread alone' is not enough. 'Bread alone' is even dangerous to the welfare of all human spirituality."[49] The challenge presented by consumer society requires an integrated response that avoids the abstractions of both spiritualism and materialism in a holistic approach that addresses universal material needs while recognizing that the material is not ultimately universal.

BEHAVIOR AND BELIEF

The ambiguity over the respective significance of persons and things not only opens out into the issue of the relation between the material and the spiritual but also runs into the question of the respective significance of believing and behaving. How far is the shift from transcendently oriented approaches to the orientation of modern consumerism a matter of conviction and how far is it a matter of conformity? To a considerable extent, this seems to be what is at stake in Greeley's question of the depth to which people really subscribe to consumerism. He can be seen to be contending that much of consumerism is simply surface conformity and does not touch fundamental convictions.[50] The difficulty is in accepting that a way of life that is pursued on such a scale and with such fervor can be regarded as having superficial impact regardless of how superficial the substance of that way itself might be.

The legacy of human experience suggests that humanity operates with more deliberate conviction than this, so that consumerism would then represent a more substantial commitment than could be attributed to behavioral conformity. In this regard, it could be seen as an instance of a particular *Zeitgeist* such as is described by T. E. Hulme:

> There are certain doctrines which for a particular period seem not doctrines, but inevitable categories of the human mind. Men do not look on them merely as correct opinion, for they have become so much part of the mind and lie so far back that they are never really conscious of them at all. They do not see them, but other things *through* them. It is these abstract ideas at the center, the things which they take for granted, that characterize a period. There are in each period certain doctrines, a denial of which is looked on by the men of that period just as we might look on the assertion that two and two make five. It is these abstract things at the center, these *doctrines* felt as *facts*, which are the source of all the other . . . characteristics of a period.[51]

The doctrines of consumerism are not particularly elusive. We have noticed its dedication to hedonism, to the assumption that, above all else, life is meant to be enjoyed, with the concomitant disposability of objects and associations that this entails, and the perennially elusive prospect of satisfaction, which sustains the whole process. These and other related convictions sustain the drive for consumption as a constellation of doctrines that enjoy the status of fact. They are assumed to describe the way life truly is and is meant to be. As E. F. Schumacher suggests in *Small is Beautiful*, the ethos of consumerism is ultimately metaphysically grounded.

> We are suffering from a metaphysical disease, and the cure must therefore be metaphysical. Education which fails to clarify our central convictions is mere training or indulgence.[52]

Seen in this way, consumerism is indicative of deep-seated beliefs, rather than being subject to characterization as a way of life to which we conform. What is at stake is "not so much what we are doing as the frame of reference within which we are doing it, or, if you like, not so much our way of grabbing at things as our way of looking at things."[53] The foundation of consumerism is in perspective rather than in passion. Its strength is a sustaining vision that it represents the way of getting the most out of life.

This explanation of the convictional grounds of consumerism is characterized by clarity and credibility. It nicely explains the rationale of this dominant orientation of contemporary life. But to stop with this explanation would be to settle for a highly academic reading of the situation. The convictions that underlie consumerism may well operate with something like metaphysical proportions, but it is unrealistic to think that they are embraced in that form with explicit endorsement. Hulme suggested that these pervasive doctrines which dominate an era are "felt as *facts*." He emphasized the impression of factuality with which they are received, but we might also emphasize the *felt* aspect. These foundational convictions are not thought out so much as absorbed by osmosis from the atmosphere of the time. The attractions of affluence and the pursuit of indulgence have an intrinsic appeal that requires neither rationale nor externally enforced incentive. As Dorothee Soelle notes, Pharaoh does not need to use force to maintain control in a time of affluence. "Compulsion and force are unnecessary when persuasion and seduction do the job."[54] Persuasion and seduction exercise their own compulsion, one which is probably much more effective than the externally imposed variety because it is internalized and owned at a visceral level. The seducee is a willing victim. This undoubtedly accounts for the prominence of advertising in consumer culture. Advertising seeks to seduce and it is successful because we have so little inclination to resist. One of the technical sources of that success, however, is the comprehensive nature of the appeal of advertising. It does not work by appealing to our beliefs and attempting to change them, but rather it enfolds us in visions of the good life so that, seeing ourselves in imagination, we are ready to bend our efforts to realize the vision. In this way, contemporary consumer culture can be seen to have left behind not only the transcendent reference of traditional religion but also the vehicle of that reference, belief. "What characterizes the so-called advanced societies is that they today consume images and no longer, like those of the past, beliefs."[55] In these terms, the religion of consumerism operates on the level of behavior, rather than of belief. It represents a comprehensive way of life that commands and challenges loyalties with such authority that there is seldom any felt need to identify, much less to challenge, these loyalties. It is this complete sense of adequacy and the total dedication it evokes that requires that consumerism be seen as a form of religion.

From a more conventional perspective, this of course represents a misapplication of the term *religion*. Beliefs cannot be dispensed with so readily. Any phenomenon which is to warrant consideration in this category must be characterized by certain convictions about the ultimate nature of things. So it can be argued that if the beliefs which underlie consumerism were teased out and made explicit even in the preliminary way we have attempted to do here, the inadequacy of consumerism as a religion would be apparent. And yet, if we are honest, we have to acknowledge that those of us who recognize this inadequacy continue to subscribe to this way of life. This may be taken as further confirmation that beliefs really do not count for much in comparison with the actual commitments and continuities of behavior. A more adequate approach to the situation, however, begins to emerge with the realization that there is ambiguity entailed in this very notion of belief. As academics, we have a predilection to impose our own second-order level of operation on life in general. In this way, it is assumed that belief involves fundamental tenets that are finally subject to explicit endorsement and that the way to ascertain what is truly important in life for an individual or group is to isolate these most fundamental convictions. But this understanding of belief may reflect the deliberate nature of the academic agenda rather than the reality of belief as it functions in the lives of people.

Wilfred Cantwell Smith has argued, with impressive documentation, that what we have referred to as the academic view of belief is a product of the progressive self-consciousness which has become particularly accelerated in the modern West, and that, in contrast to this rather rationalized understanding, the original and long-standing connotation of belief had to do with a total orientation in life, a personal being-claimed rather than with isolated intellectual claims.[56] Ironically, then, consumerism may represent a more robust instance of belief in the contemporary context than many of the more conventional forms of religion. This by no means entails an endorsement of consumerism as a genuine religion. Rather it suggests that recognition of its inadequacy will necessitate the recognition of a more comprehensive sense of belief than the equation of belief with intellectual assent can allow. It seems that modern advertisers share the wisdom of Augustine in their awareness that what we know is ultimately determined by what we love. The religion of consumerism employs this wisdom to foster our love affair with ourselves. If we are to be able to appreciate something of the transcendent love that came to animate Augustine, this will require a holistic appreciation of our condition and of an alternative that avoids the abstraction characteristic of the rationalistic isolation of belief and the complacency inherent in confining attention to the level of behavior.

Religion and Consumerism

The pervasive presence and penetrating grip of consumerism that leads to characterizing it as a religion also indicates the immense difficulty entailed in any attempt to come to grips with it from a serious religious perspective. Because it exercises such a comprehensive influence, we shall draw on some variations of the central categories employed by H. Richard Niebuhr in his consideration of how Christ and culture might be seen to relate, in order to help identify the most prominent directions that lie before us.

RELIGION WITH CONSUMERISM

The most realistic response to consumerism from the point of view of religion might be simply to accept it. This need not entail a wholesale endorsement of its every manifestation, but rather might amount to an acknowledgment of its inevitability. Short of nuclear or environmental holocaust, it seems highly unlikely that technologically based consumption will be seriously threatened in the foreseeable future. The most likely quarter from which opposition might be expected, the impoverished in the Third World and within developed countries, and those who speak for them, tend to challenge the present form of consumerism rather than the orientation as such. Consequently, the sensible approach might be to recognize that consumerism is here to stay, and to make the best of it.

The best that can be made of this direction is illustrated by staunch theological exponents of the market system, such as Michael Novak. Some of the central ingredients in his proposal for a theology of economics are: A recognition of the novelty of the modern world and the corresponding inappropriateness of judging modern capitalist systems by standards drawn from simpler times; acknowledgment of the impracticality of Christian ideals as formative principles for a social system; appreciation of the importance of the individual; the realization that the business corporation has replaced the Church as the contemporary form of community; the need to give productivity priority over distribution in order to ensure the maintenance of human freedom; confidence in the market system as the most effective method for dealing with scarcity.[57] There is no doubt that this approach represents a consistent and coherent position. The challenge is to discover the "theology" in this "theology of economics." The focus on the sufficiency of economics in the form of the so-called free enterprise, market system is so prominent as to exercise not only a determinative but virtually an exhaustive influence. If we are to ask what vision of God is implicit in this proposal it would have to be that God is that power which helps those who help themselves. Thus, in its most ardent forms, the religion with consumerism approach would seem to amount to the absorption of religion by consumerism in further confirmation of the mutual incompatibility of God and mammon as foci of ultimate loyalty.

Yet in spite of this mutual exclusivity, neither is dispensable. We consume to exist just as surely as, from a religious point of view, it is abhorrent to think that we exist to consume. The point at which the encounter is most pressing today is in the area of ecology, not only because of the threat to the environment and even to the survival of life on this planet, but also because the enormity of this danger is once again forcing the issue of total perspective. In this situation, it strains the bounds of credibility to find totally unrepentant advocates of ever expanding consumption, as evidenced in the following statement from a Vice-President of General Foods:

> We differ fundamentally from many other nations in our willingness to accept the new and to discard the old. The extraordinary phenomenon of a whole nation adjusted in its daily life and thought to the principle of obsolescence, ever ready to accept higher standards of material existence, must be attributed partly to the power of advertising to carry into every corner of the land the insistent and attractive news of ideas and inventions that in two generations have revolutionized our standards of life.[58]

The environmental impact of the willingness of the past two generations to accept the new and discard the old is not considered, let alone any projection of the results that might be expected if this promotion of ever expansive consumption does continue in the years ahead. Apparently the inherent appeal of consumption precludes such negative considerations. If they do arise, they are subject to quick resolution through the confidence, voiced by Novak, that the market system is the most effective method for dealing with scarcity. Apologists for the system point out that it deals with shortages by increasing prices, which curtails consumption, whereas the incentive of an unsatisfied demand promotes the search for alternative products and so technological inventiveness and entrepreneurial ingenuity are elicited to develop new channels for consumption.[59] Here again the coherence and consistency of the position is evident, but we begin to see, as well, its own religious dimensions. The confidence in the abundance of alternative resources and in the reliability of technology to effect the requisite correctives in terms of pollution control and energy production amounts to a gigantic venture of faith that is truly of religious proportions.

Although such religion of consumption enjoys widespread endorsement, it is doubtful that many would subscribe to this self-conscious credo attesting to its sufficiency in such explicit and total terms. The religion of consumption is probably more accurately seen as the major version of that conformity of behavior which is not particularly self-conscious about its own believing. Certainly among those who confront the neglected environmental and social costs of consumption, those who are prepared to accept such a reaffirmation of consumption are decidedly in a minority. The more prevalent reaction is to acknowledge something of the inadequacy of consumption as a religion and to move toward some kind of rapprochement between the threat to the environment and the need implicit in this for a more adequate overall vision. Where differences remain is with regard to the extent to which this requisite vision has to be religious. On the one hand, there appears to be a growing recognition of the inadequacy of the exploitative, resource-centered outlook that has permitted and encouraged all manner of harvesting in a preoccupation with immediate advantage and a corresponding disregard of possible long-term consequences. At the same time, this very way of stating the predicament remains within the utilitarian frame of reference, and as a result, it can hardly be expected to offer an alternative to the outlook that has sponsored the massive exploitation that has characterized our way of life. At the most, it can qualify the scale of exploitation by extending the range of concern. It is doubtful, however, whether this is adequate to the magnitude of the problem. The fact that the situation continues to be considered in what amounts to a broadened form of the exploitative approach suggests that it is not. This is further confirmed by the way in which that orientation remains determinative so that its formative power is not recognized. Thus, people think they are promoting a genuine alternative in contending that "a different and indeed, a nonutilitarian rationale is needed to support protectionist policies."[60] The failure to notice the contradiction entailed in this implicit support of a utilitarian rationale, although explicitly rejecting this, suggests that this solution might actually aggravate the disease by offering the promise of an alternative when it is actually endorsing the perspective that underlies the problem.

If the way of consumption is as destructive and disastrous as the prophets of ecological crisis contend, it may well be that there is no adequate response to it short of a total reorientation, a conversion wherein we are turned from exploitation to communion in some terms such as Buber suggests in his contrast between the I-It approach of domination and the I-Thou approach of genuine relation. But this would mean reverting to some kind of inherently religious outlook in reaction against the fundamental confidence in technological control that has distinguished the modern West. Needless to say, resistance to such a fundamental conversion is strong. Some profess to find within ecological consciousness itself a sufficiently comprehensive scope to provide a satisfactory alternative to the murderous dissection of the analytic approach. "Ecology has made it possible to apprehend the same landscape as an articulate unity (without the least hint of mysticism or inevitability)."[61] We have seen how this kind of reservation shapes theology in the example of Sallie McFague's revision of theological models centering on the understanding of the world as God's body so that theology becomes the means by which care for the world is encouraged. In this, we have the total triumph of the utilitarian perspective that lies at the base of the modern exploitative outlook: God becomes the ultimate resource for our proper management of the world. It is difficult to avoid the impression that such thinking represents an aggravation of the dilemma, rather than a source of resolution. If the way of consumption is as destructive and as captivating as it appears to be, it might well require a conversion from it of genuine religious proportions, as suggested, for example, by E. F. Schumacher, "the exclusion of wisdom from economics, science, and technology was something which we could perhaps get away with for a little while, as long as we were relatively unsuccessful; and now that we have become very successful, the problem of spiritual and moral truth moves into the central position."[62] The catch is that if the problem of moral and spiritual truth does really move into the central position, this will mean that it will not be possible to use morality and religion as means of saving the world from ecological catastrophe. Such a result would have to be secondary to a genuine appreciation of a vision of salvation that is of the essence of the religious vision itself. To accept this diagnoses, however, is to be compelled to regard as inadequate any kind of compromise between religion and consumerism.

RELIGION AGAINST CONSUMERISM

If consumerism and religion are inherently incompatible, then the only viable response from a religious point of view is opposition. This direction need not detain us long because we have seen its more prominent elements already. As is evident from what we have noted, such response is, by no means, lacking. Assuming that the depth of that reaction has been amply demonstrated, it remains to notice how this Western malaise has penetrated other traditions and cultures. Speaking out of the Eastern Orthodox tradition, Paulos Gregorios laments: "The affairs of the world are largely in the hands of people who are expert at making money, waging war, and playing politics."[63] In these last two pursuits, the modern era might not be very different from the past, but the underlying motivation provided by the first preoccupation gives the military and political agenda a peculiar cast. The resulting military–industrial complex not only shapes the world economy, but also in the process determines the context of people's lives, consigning some to poverty and inducing others to the pursuit of affluence. The impact is becoming as apparent in the Far East as it is in Eastern Europe and has been in the West. Kosuk Koyama depicts this effect in Southeast Asia.

> Family was sacred. The family has now been invaded by the foreign value called "money." Cash relationship is replacing personal relationship in our society today. *We want* to have money. More money indeed. There are so many attractive things around us! By the power of money we can get them! We belong to money now.[64]

The expansive sweep of the monetarization of life intensifies the concern over the grip by which this orientation claims contemporary allegiance. To hear it said in a Southeast Asian context that "we belong to money now" dispels any illusions that would prevent us from recognizing the universal sway of consumerism.

When the consciousness regarding the threat to the environment is augmented by this realization of the religious range of devotion at stake in the dedication to consumerism, there can be no question about the appropriateness of opposition to what, from the serious religious perspective, can only appear as idolatry. However, the very obviousness of the appropriateness of this reaction conceals its own intrinsic dangers. For one thing, there is nothing easier, and few things more enjoyable, than offering criticism. Compared with the challenges of devising and implementing positive proposals, the negative route of critique is not only far less demanding of original insight and effort, but also likely to expose its promoters to much less strenuous countercriticism. Thus, the temptation is strong to dwell on the critique of consumerism as an end in itself. Insofar as this is resisted and some form of positive alternative is proposed, the advocate of this alternative consequently is rendered more vulnerable to countercriticism, the most frequent direction of which is apt to involve some version of the charge of romanticism. Any rebellion against the monolithic sweep of consumer culture is bound to appear simplistic and naive. "The romantic project of return to nature becomes personalistic and escapist, rather than a real grappling with the interconnections of social and natural domination and an effort to reconstruct these relationships in a new way."[65] The exploitation of nature at the heart of the ecological crisis is an institutionalized operation, promoted and programmed by economic, political, and social structures. Any significant challenge to consumerism will have to address this crucial structural dimension. Because the self-interests that animate consumerism are sustained and fostered by elaborate social structures, the consciousness raising required to expose the shortcomings of this way of life will have to extend to a challenging of these social structures if the opposition to consumerism is not to warrant the charge of romantic escapism.

Recognition of the inadequacy of consumerism and direct confrontation with the structures that support and promote it still represents an inadequate response, however, not least because on their own both of these aspects contain within them the seeds of their own undoing. Insofar as we are convinced that we see a better way or can envisage more adequate structures "we shall be prone to the legalism that always haunts movements away from idolatry and false worship."[66] Not only must the opposition to consumerism as a substitute religion go beyond negative critique to positive alternative, and not only must this alternative confront the structures that sponsor the preoccupation with consumption, but also a credible critique must arise out of a genuinely religious sponsorship so that those who make it are themselves under its judgment and subject to transformation in terms of the distinctiveness of its vision.

RELIGION TRANSFORMING CONSUMERISM

Perhaps the biggest mistake that can be made regarding consumerism is to underestimate its power. This temptation is particularly strong when we think we have seen through its pretensions. Even as astute an observer of the human scene as John Kenneth Galbraith thinks that education can dislodge the grip of consumerism.

> Education . . . is a double-edged sword for the affluent society. It is essential, given the technical and scientific requirements of modern industry. But by widening tastes and also inducing more independent and critical attitudes, it undermines the want-creating power which is indispensable to the modern economy. The effect is enhanced as education enables people to see how they are managed in the interest of the mechanism that is assumed to serve them. The ultimate consequence is that the values of the affluent society, its preoccupation with production as a test of performance in particular, are undermined by the education that is required in those that serve it.[67]

Galbraith may be forgiven this naïveté because he was writing in the early stages of hyperconsumerism, before the emergence of the Yuppie and its ardent imitators. With this phenomenon, we have come to see that far from exposing the manipulation of consumerism, education is rather inclined to refine greed. Still, Galbraith might be expected to have retained more of his own education in Presbyterian respect for the depravity of humanity. Had this not been eroded by the acids of Enlightenment Rationalism, he would have been more suspicious of placing such confidence in education. He emulates Socrates' confidence that clarity of insight will issue in rectitude of action, in disregard of Paul's experience of greater ambivalence: "For I do not do the good I want, but the evil I do not want is what I do" (Rom. 7:19). To see the evils of consumerism is not enough. The attraction runs much deeper. The extension of the range of education beyond the technical and economic skills required to sustain the mechanisms of consumerism to matters of culture and critique only succeeds in refining tastes and elevating consumption. The pervasive power of consumerism requires transformation, rather than simply education, a total reorientation that entails both belief and behavior.

Although the break with the religion of consumerism requires more than a change of perspective, it does entail this element. One of the major sources of dissatisfaction with this very attractive way of life is the suspicion that it is made possible by depletion of resources and accumulation of pollution, which threatens the continuation of life itself. Thus the Club of Rome issues dire warnings about the *Limits to Growth*[68] and although later qualifying the period of grace before the catastrophic point is reached, still insists on the need for massive transformations in attitude and activity. Their second report, *Mankind at the Turning Point*, summarizes the changes needed for survival in the following four requirements: (a) a world consciousness; (b) an ethic for scarcity; (c) an attitude toward nature of harmony rather than conquest; and (d) an identification with future generations.[69] On the other hand, we have seen counterproposals based on the assurance that the alignment between scarcity and price effected by the market and the incentive for technological innovation this entails will assure that resources are not totally depleted and that alternatives will be devised and developed. The result is that there is dispute even about whether or not there is a crisis, as became particularly evident in the contrary positions represented at the first Global Conference on the Future held in Toronto in 1980.[70]

This disagreement over the basic situation is indicative not only of the complexity of the issue but also of the depth at which it operates. The reason that education is inadequate as a source of alternatives to consumerism is that the vision that sustains it is much more than an intellectual one. This is why it represents a total personal claim of religious proportions. As a result, ecologists and technologists confront one another as occupants of two different worlds. Where ecologists warn of the disastrous impact of expansive consumption, technologists offer the promise of technological solutions to technological problems. Each speaks out of the total vision that is only partially susceptible to rational assessment. Ultimately, basic loyalties and investments of self-interest are at stake. Ecologists may challenge technologists as to how they can expect to derive infinite resources from a finite planet. Technologists respond with visions of an infinite universe and the untapped possibilities of space. Technologists charge ecologists with wanting to restrict the benefits of the consumer society to their domain, consigning the poor to continued exclusion from its benefits. Ecologists respond by pointing out that the effect of consumerism has been to widen the gap between rich and poor rather than in narrowing it. And so the debate continues, between two fundamentally different visions of life. Kenneth Bolding characterizes the difference in terms of the contrast between a "cowboy economy," which assumes a limitless frontier to be exploited and a "spaceman economy," which recognizes the finitude of resources.[71] The comprehensive nature of the difference in vision is suggested more clearly, however, in E. F. Schumacher's distinction between the people of the forward stampede and the home-comers. In this he recognizes that the vision is not finally economic but religious.

> The term 'home-comer' has, of course, a religious connotation. For it takes a good deal of courage to say 'no' to the fashions and fascinations of the age and to question the presuppositions of a civilization which appears destined to conquer the whole world; the requisite strength can be derived only from deep convictions.[72]

The pseudoreligion of consumerism can only be seen for what it is, and release from it be effected by the transforming power of genuine religious conviction.

The fundamental deficiency of consumerism is not the threat of ecological crisis it evokes, or even the aggravation of the gap between haves and have-nots that has accompanied its unfolding, but rather its own inherent inadequacy as a way of life grounded in a vision of welfare. Even the perennial dissatisfaction on which consumerism feeds can become stifling through the understanding of the point of life in terms of multiplying diversions and minimizing inconvenience.

> Boredom spreads if the attainment of that for which one hoped no longer drives one on to a newer, greater hope. Swedish socialism, a pragmatic kind of social system without a utopian vision impelling it on, represents a state of built-in freedom from suffering, which nevertheless produces the highest suicide rate in the world.[73]

The attainment of human welfare does not provide an adequate horizon for understanding what life is about. The vision it permits, although captivating and inherently attractive in its immediate appeal to our desire for security and status, courts the despair that Kierkegaard warned awaits all versions of the aesthetic approach to life. Like the stone skipping over the surface of the water, sooner or later, it sinks.

Because of the totality of vision that is at stake, and the institutional imposition by which consumer culture is enforced, for any alternative religious vision to be anything more than a private, pious indulgence, there must be some deliberate pursuit of the vision in the ongoing activities of life. At the very least "this calls for a counterculture of families and groups that cannot be conned or manipulated because they simply do not accept the accepted values or pursue the ambitions that are expected of them."[74] This response stops short of countering the aesthetic with the ascetic. "It is not poverty but balance we are after."[75] This will entail simplifying our way of life, rather than utterly renouncing consumer society. It amounts to an attempt to transform consumer society from within. A more radical approach calls for the establishing of separate communities, formed from people of diverse cultural and religious backgrounds, to live together for five to ten years in an effort to develop a nurturing way of life, which is regarded as impossible in the atmosphere of conquest characterizing consumer culture.[76] If such an alternative way of life could be developed, it could provide a positive alternative to the immediate attractions of the way of consumption.

Candidates for such alternative communities will probably not be numerous. Such a commitment would demand not only massive dissatisfaction with consumer culture but also a sense of religious vision that could sustain such a departure. But then, all that we have seen about the comprehensive nature of consumerism suggests that it may be that only such radical approaches can be expected to offer any hope of matching the captivity it exercises. And yet, although the future may lie with such pioneers, for most of us of less daring, the banning together in mutual support against the incessant demands of the promoters of consumption might provide a much more realistic course of action. In this way we can, at least, give some backing to our sense of dissatisfaction with the religion of consumption. At the very least, as Elie Wiesel suggests, for the sake of our own souls, we are compelled to run the risk of self-righteous superiority by continuing to condemn the consumptive treadmill on which we are all trapped. Wiesel makes the point characteristically in story form.

A teacher, a just man, came to Sodom determined to save its inhabitants from sin and punishment. Night and day he walked the streets and the markets protesting against greed and theft, falsehood and indifference. In the beginning, people listened and smiled ironically; then they stopped listening and he no longer even amused them. The killers went on killing; the wise kept silent, as if there were no just man in their midst. One day a child, moved by compassion for the unfortunate teacher, approached him with these words: "You shout, you scream. Don't you see that it is hopeless?" "Yes, I see," answered the just man. "Then why do you go on?" "I'll tell you why," said the just man. "In the beginning I thought I could change them; today I know that I cannot. If I still shout today, if I still scream, and I scream louder and louder, stronger and stronger, it is to prevent them from ultimately changing me."[77]

7

Salvation and Pluralism

If concern about salvation does not succumb completely to the secular *Zeitgeist*, it still must face the challenge of religious pluralism. Thus, any vestige of significance religion may have retained amid the corrosive acids of secularism is further threatened by the increasing awareness that there are various major religious traditions, each apparently different, and all claiming universal significance in one way or another. This combination of secular horizon and basic religious diversity constitutes an often fatal blow to any residual concern about salvation. Consequently, if salvation is to be intelligible and meaningful in the future, this will only be possible for someone who has come to grips with the challenge of religious pluralism as well as with the inadequacy of secularism.

It might seem strange to speak of the challenge of religious pluralism as though this were something new. After all, Christianity has always been surrounded by other religions from its inception in the womb of Judaism. However, the reality of other religious traditions was kept firmly at bay through the imperial ascendancy of Christendom with the result that it is only with the de-Christianizing of the West and the shrinkage of the world which has transformed the theoretical awareness of other traditions into actual encounter with people of these traditions that religious plurality has become an unavoidable reality. The recentness of this recognition is indicated by the ignorance of, and lack of interest in, other religious traditions on the part of the theological giants of the past generation. From the background of his firsthand encounter with other religions, D. T. Niles recalls the incredulity with which he first heard no less a theological titan than Karl Barth summarily dismiss other religions.

> D. T. Niles recalled that in his first meeting with Karl Barth in 1935, Barth said, "Other religions are just unbelief." Niles asked, "How

many Hindus, Dr. Barth, have you met?" Barth answered, "No one." Niles said, "How then do you know that Hinduism is unbelief?" Barth replied, "A priori." Niles concluded, "I simply shook my head and smiled."[1]

This practical isolation that allowed Christian theologians to avoid direct confrontation with other religious traditions inevitably led to inadequate views regarding these traditions. Thus W. C. Smith reports how Paul Tillich fell victim to a letter in the student paper, *The Harvard Crimson*, which "was able, to show up as superficial in a particular case this eminent theologian's understanding of religious traditions in Asia."[2]

The transformation of our situation, especially during the seventies and eighties, makes the isolation of theologians of the caliber of Tillich and Barth appear astonishing in the nineties. However, if this leaves us with a sense of superiority to these giants of Christian thought, it might be sobering to consider that the future might well produce even more dramatic changes. "The religious history of mankind is taking as monumental a turn in our century as is the political or economic, if only we could see it."[3] The face of this turning that is most evident, at this point, is the fact of religious pluralism. Religious traditions other than Christianity, or even than Christianity's parent, Judaism, and sibling, Islam, are there, and give every indication of being around just as certainly as Christianity itself. This reality must be accounted for in our understanding of the Christian faith.

The Challenge of Religious Pluralism to Christianity as a Religion of Salvation

BROAD SCHEMAS OF WORLD RELIGIONS

A Christocentric perspective such as that held by Barth, and also by Tillich, could assume that religions other than Christianity represented inferior varieties, if they were really even of the same species at all. To be sure, Christian theologians of this era criticized religion as representing the most subtle obstacle to faith, but there was no doubt that insofar as faith was possible it was the faith that found expression through the vehicle of the Christian religion. The idea that other religious traditions might also be vehicles of genuine faith was not seriously entertained. As the attitude of

Barth illustrates, this was largely due to the lack of acquaintance with devotees of other traditions. However, this assurance of Christian superiority was reinforced by generalizations that emphasized the distinctiveness of the Christian tradition.

Thus, as cosmopolitan a theologian as B. F. Streeter, in the first half of this century concluded: there were really only three world religions—Buddhism, Christianity, and Mohammedanism because Hinduism and Judaism were national, closed religions, and contrasted their characterizations of ultimate reality and of the status and value of human beings in the following scheme.

	Buddhism	Christianity	Mohammedanism
Ultimate Being	Peace	Purpose	Power
Human Being			
& Value	Part	Son	Slave[4]

Modern Western sensibilities would have no difficulty noticing the obvious superiority of the personal Christian characterization of God and of ourselves in contrast to the totally impersonal outlook of Buddhism and the authoritarian oppression of Mohammedanism. More recently, the eminent Catholic theologian, Hans Kung, gives voice to a widely recognized contrast between the world-affirming orientation of the religious traditions emanating from the Middle East in contrast to the world-denying perspective of those which derive from the Far East.

> The Jewish–Christian–Islamic tradition sees the *world* (and this life) in principle *positively* as God's good creation, so that man's salvation occurs *in* this world. The Hindu–Buddhist tradition sees the world (and this life) mainly *negatively* as illusion, appearance, *maya*, so that man's salvation is *from* this world.[5]

Such a contrast suggests a categorical difference between these two types of religious tradition. Thus, if we are not ready to write off the Hindu–Buddhist traditions as a mystical otherworldliness that fails to appreciate the world as God's creation, we will at least have to consider that it represents an understanding of life and reality which is so different from the outlook we assume in the West under the influence of the Semitic religious orientation that it has to remain unintelligible to us. Yet if we explore this contrast in more specific terms, the mutual exclusivity of these two forms of religion might not seem so assured.

AMBIGUITIES IN COMPARISONS AMONG RELIGIONS

On the surface, the religions of the Far East seem to assume a cosmic monism in which reality is ultimately one, and the distinction between spiritual and material is a product of illusion, whereas the Semitic traditions accord real significance to the material world. And yet, in the domestic disputes within these Semitic traditions, and especially within Christianity, the Semitic strain appears to endorse an organic unity of spiritual and material in contrast to the Greek dualism between the passing temporal order and the permanent eternal realm to which reason seeks access. When the affinity between this Greek dualism, especially in its more virulent Platonic forms, and the Far Eastern contrast between the material and the spiritual is set against the Semitic predilection for an organic treatment of spiritual and material, we have to wonder where dualism ends and monism begins, or vice versa. This is not to deny the ultimate validity of the contrast between Hindu–Buddhist otherworldliness and Jewish–Christian–Muslim concern for life in this world, but it does suggest that the contrast may not be as absolute and direct as it might appear on the surface.

A similar need for qualification emerges if we consider the basic visions of life that animate the different traditions. The usual contrast between the Far Eastern goal of absorption of self in the world-soul, the Absolute, *Brahman*, or *nirvana* and the Middle Eastern concern to achieve genuine creaturely self-identity in communion with God can also be read the other way around. "There being no overriding concept of a personal Lord to check the mystical tendency towards non-dualism, the devotee in highest truth is, in worshipping, only worshipping the future self."[6] Ironically, the otherworldly orientation of the Buddhist quest for *nirvana*, for example, can also appear as a preoccupation with the human in contrast to which the Semitic interest in personal salvation in one form or another can appear other-centered in focusing on the divine deliverer. Thus of Buddhism, it can be said:

> It is a way in which not God but man and his salvation (or health) are central. For this reason Buddhist devotion is meditation rather than worship or prayer defined as communion with deity.[7]

Thus, although Buddhist meditation is intended to purge the self, it remains focused on the self, whereas the Semitic focus on God, understood in personal terms, gives a transcendent orientation away from self.

These respective methods of meditation and worship lead to a further general contrast in that the contemplative way of the Far East tends to be associated with knowledge and enlightenment, whereas to the worship of God there corresponds the responsive way of faith. The Far Eastern goal of enlightenment in Buddhist *nirvana* and Hindu *moksha* may be seen to entail a kind of *gnosis*, a secret, mystical knowledge, which releases its recipient from the shackles of the illusory existence of self-concern. The Semitic tradition, by contrast, has tended to place a premium on living, on obedience. And yet, it is in these Semitic traditions that orthodoxy, correct belief, true knowledge, has become vital in Judaism's shift from the worship of the temple to become the people of the book worshipping through the synagogue, in Christianity's protracted battles over the formulations that were to become the classical creeds, and in Muslim clashes over whether Sunni or Shi'ite represent the true legacy of the faith. The point is not that there have not been controversies and divisions in Hinduism and Buddhism, but that these do not seem to have focused on the issue of orthodoxy, the concern for correct knowledge, in the way that has been dominant in Semitic traditions despite the general claim that these Ear Eastern religions are fixated on concern for knowledge.

A final contrast, which encompasses some of these already mentioned, is the broad contention that, to use the language of Protestantism, religions of the Far East assume salvation by works whereas the Semitic religions attribute salvation to divine grace. "Eastern religionists save themselves, individually converting from illusory selfhood as separate entities to true selves as divine; Western religionists are saved by God to a blessed, true, redeemed creaturehood of and with, but always under, God."[8] In Buddhism, for example, the devotee achieves enlightenment by subscribing to the four Noble Truths and following the Eightfold Path pioneered by the Buddha. From the perspective of evangelical Christianity, that is, Christianity that centers in the proclamation of a gospel, this appears as a blueprint for a program of moral development that lacks precisely the element that makes a gospel what it is, good news. This evangelical perspective understands the Christian message only secondarily as a challenge to live by certain precepts, being convinced that such living is made possible only by the prior divine acceptance proclaimed in the gospel. But here again, we have to be wary of such a blanket contrast. It may be that these basic directions are implicit in these respective traditions, but it would be precipitous to accede to this without considering the evidence to the contrary in the ways these traditions have actually developed. We can, all too easily, recognize that Christians have not been averse to understanding their religion as a way of exertion not unlike the general Western characterization of Buddhism, and we know too that there is a prominent tradition within Buddhism that endorses an ultimate acceptance that sounds similar to what Christians speak of in terms of divine grace. In short, a genuine encounter between religious traditions must get beyond this stage of abstract comparison to attempt to grapple with the worlds of meaning that underlie these generalizations.

AMBIGUITIES WITHIN RELIGIONS

Viewed from the perspective of the theistic religions of the Middle East, the most distinctive feature of the Far Eastern approaches to religion is their monistic ideal of apparently undifferentiated absorption, which negates any sense of a positive characterization of ultimate reality itself or of ourselves as individuals.

> There is illusion, there is freedom from illusion, but individuals are not freed from illusion. Individuals are the products of illusion. Individuality is itself precisely the illusion from which we seek to be freed.[9]

To people whose vision of life has been molded by the Semitic notion of creation, this outlook appears distressingly negative. It can seem that the position is that the whole point of life is to deny that life has any point. However, if we reflect that millions upon millions of people have found, and continue to find, this outlook positive and meaningful, we might begin to suspect that perhaps it is we who are missing something in our understanding of this Far Eastern orientation. And indeed, further exploration would soon uncover themes that appear more congenial to the Semitic perspective.

Thus, in addition to this veneration of impersonal absoluteness, the complex of visions and practices, which we characterize as Hinduism, also involves acknowledgment of deities and the devotional and moral practices appropriate to such acknowledgment.

> The *Bhagavad Gita*, despite its recognition of the way of mystical knowledge, in fact places the way of devotion (*bhakti*) to the Lord Krishna on a higher plane. This reflects the growth within Hinduism of popular devotional cults in reaction against the abstruse mystical philosophy of the *Upanishads*. Insofar as religion helps the ordinary Hindu to cope with the facts of evil and suffering, it is primarily through the temple cults of the supreme gods Vishnu or Shiva, or the mother

goddess Devi, or the many lesser divinities whose shrines and cere-
monies are a central part of Indian village life.[10]

This further dimension of Hinduism might not provide solace for
the more westernly oriented enquirer. Because of the insistence of
Semitic religions on the cardinal conviction of monotheism, this
plurality of deities might make Hinduism seem even more foreign
than its monistic vision of impersonal absoluteness. However, it
does indicate the complexity of Hindu tradition as one which can
encompass abstract monism and theistic pluralism. At the very
least, this should make us wary about stereotyping Hinduism in
terms of either of these directions on their own.

The idea of salvation (*moksha*) as release from self (*atman*) and
absorption into the All (*Brahman*) implies a devaluation of this
world and of ways of living in it which is not sustained by the cultic
or ethical practices pursued in most versions in Hinduism. We have
already noted how the *Gita*, the most popular of Hindu scriptures,
gives more scope to the theistic and personal dimension of religion
than to the absolute, impersonal perspective. An impressive case
can be made for broadening this base to take in most strands of
Hindu scripture.

> The interpreters who characterize the Hindu view of ultimate reality as
> pure monism or as pantheism appeal to one or two hymns of the *Rg
> veda*, the negative passages of the *Upanishads*, and the acosmism of
> *sankara-Vedanta*. My contention is that a closer study of the *Vedas* and
> the *Upanishads* and the consideration of the *Bhagavad-Gita* (which has
> a much greater influence on most Hindus than the *Vedanta*), indicates
> that the dominant Hindu conception of God has an essentially theistic
> character that is similar in certain respects to that found in Christian
> theism.[11]

In fact, this writer contends that the standard stereotype of the
Hindu idea of salvation in terms of an otherworldly absorption of
self into the impersonal unity of reality is really only indicative of
the *Advaita* doctrine within Hinduism.[12] It may be that the reason
that this tends to be equated with Hinduism, as such, in the West,
is because of the successful promotion of its vision by the *Vedanta*
Societies.[13] This *Advaita* renunciation of the world derives from
the *Vedanta* philosophy, in contrast to which the five other major
forms of Hindu philosophy, are world affirming.[14] Thus rather than
the single-minded pursuit of escape from the illusory entrapments
of this life, much of Hindu tradition in conviction as well as in
practice, pays real attention to life in this world. Ethical serious-

ness is by no means lacking, "for the normal means laid down for the attainment of liberation are largely moral, benevolence to all creatures being almost as important as detachment itself."[15]

It could be held though that the veneration of the abstract Absolute which recedes before the concrete devotions of Hinduism reasserts itself in the program for enlightenment promoted by Buddhism.[16] But here too the popular notion of Gautama as the Enlightened One who bequeathed to his followers the four Noble Truths and the revered Eightfold Path as the infallible means and methods of salvation yields in practice to a variety of practices and accounts of how that enlightenment is finally achieved, so that once again the stereotype represents a deceptive caricature of the diverse reality that we call Buddhism.

Certainly the term Buddhism, by itself, has no identifiable referent that I know of. At one extreme there is the Theravada tradition of the Sangha with its strict adherence to the Pali scriptures, and especially to the Vinaya discipline, such as prevails in Thailand. On the other hand there is the form of tantric religion which, exported from northern India in the early medieval period and blended with elements of the Bon religion, emerged into the modern world as Tibetan Buddhism, with its married monks, its reincarnate bodhisattvas (the Dalai Lamas), who were also supreme temporal rulers, and its acceptance of a vast range of Sanskrit sutras as the word of the eternal Buddha. Again there is the Pure Land Buddhism of Japan, the cult of the savior Amida, who by his grace freely saves all men, even the most sinful, who call upon his name in simple trust, and brings them to his eternal paradise. And again, there is Zen. It is, therefore, very difficult to envisage what single, identifiable, real entity the term 'Buddhism' might refer to.[17]

Some semblance of intelligibility might be imposed on this bewildering variety by noting how the *Hinayana* (the lesser way) or, less derogatorily, *Theravada* (the way of the elders) approach, which understands Buddhism as the program for emulating the way of the Buddha, pointed to in the four Noble Truths and the Eightfold Path, has been supplemented by *Mahayana* (the greater way) Buddhism, which replaces this moral tone by more overtly religious themes of assistance and even deliverance through aids and saviors.

It is tempting to see this variance between moral and spiritual approaches in Buddhism as a parallel to Christian instances such as might be represented by the New Testament contrast between the pragmatism of James and the spiritualism of Paul, or the clash between Jansenists and Jesuits in the seventeenth century or the contrast between recent advocates of a gospel derived directly from the teaching of Jesus and those who insist on a more comprehensive gospel that derives from Jesus' whole activity and being. This temptation is particularly strong when the object of comparison is the Pure Land Buddhism of Japan, which centers in salvation effected through devotion to Amida Buddha. Even Barth was impressed by its similarity to the Christian doctrine of salvation through grace,[18] but not enough to allow for mutual recognition of a common way of salvation. The Christian claim that God accepts humanity through Christ cannot be paralleled by Amida Buddhism because Amida is not a historical figure, and the ultimate goal is not divine acceptance of the believer but the release of the believer from the illusions of existence. Thus, a noted Buddhist scholar warns: "We must also distrust any description of the Buddhist doctrine which, without many qualifications, attributes to the saviors 'grace', 'mercy' or 'forgiveness'."[19] And yet the possibility that there exists in other religious traditions a sense of ultimate grounding which is a true counterpart of what Christians point to by the concept of grace cannot be dismissed without dismissing these traditions as inherently inferior.

Perhaps the most intriguing prospect for a parallel emerges from a distinction within Hinduism between the "monkey holding" and the "cat holding" schools. The former view holds that just as a baby monkey must hold onto its mother when being carried, so the follower must strive to cooperate with God in effecting his or her salvation. From the point of view of the "cat holding" school, however, salvation is provided by God just as a cat carries a kitten by the scruff of the neck so that it plays no part in its own transportation.[20] This certainly sounds like a Hindu variation of a Paulinelike recognition of divine grace. It can seem that deep down such phrasing echoes an experience which is directly parallel to that expressed by the Christian gospel of salvation by divine grace. "Accepting God's acceptance of us, love answering love— this is also the profound theme of Hindu theism."[21] It can even appear that this common sense of divine acceptance takes precedence over the apparently different Far Eastern motivation for acceptance in terms of the escape from the round of rebirth.[22] When we add to this the difficulty we have experienced in Christianity over acknowledgment of divine grace and preservation of the importance of human effort without degenerating into a syncretistic cooperativism, the possibility of parallels in other traditions is all the more impressive. And yet, the basic contrast remains. In the Semitic religions God, understood in personal terms, is primal reality and the goal is somehow to experience and enjoy and live out of the acceptance of God thus understood; whereas in the Far Eastern traditions, however important gods or saviors may be in *Mahayana* versions of Buddhism or theistic cults of Hinduism, primal reality transcends distinctions and the goal is to lose the distinctiveness that constitutes ourselves in the experience of that primal unity. Is it feasible to expect to find parallels across such apparently fundamentally different fields of vision? Can there be genuine encounter between claimants of these respective ways of salvation?

Responses to the Challenge of Religious Pluralism

THE CONTEXT OF ENCOUNTER

The difference between the general isolation of Christian theology up until the last generation and the current unavoidability of other religions impinging on Christian theological reflection may be attributed in large part to the technological shrinkage of our world. The "them" and "us" situation where other religions meant those poor unsophisticates on the other side of the world who have not been favored with the spiritual sensitivity and insight we take for granted has been shattered by the embarrassment of encountering actual devotees of other religious traditions whose moral concern and spiritual devotion often shames our feeble Christian profession. This firsthand experience of the living reality of other religions transforms our preconceptions about their secondary status and puts the relationship between these traditions and our own as Christians on an entirely different footing.

When other religions appear as the ways of foreigners, they are automatically subject to derisive treatment in some form. We have seen that the usual variation on this was to ignore them altogether. Insofar as this was not done, the best acknowledgment that was often accorded was to approach other traditions as subjects of a comparative study. Up until the seventies, this was probably the most characteristic Western approach to non-Christian religions, and, of course, the standard of comparison was the Christian tradition. With the shift from comparison to encounter as the context in which we deal with other religions, this former approach appears embarrassingly provincial. By what authority do we assume that our tradition should be the standard for appreciating other traditions? The most direct answer, the one for which this question would hardly occur, is that it is the obvious standard because it is ours. Christians looked upon other religions in the way in which many Americans look upon the rest of the world, as people encumbered with the misfortune of not being Americans. If this inherent assumption of superiority is pierced, and justification is seen to be required, this is readily available in theological terms. The Christian religion is the obvious standard because it is God-given. However, as we have seen, this, in turn, depends on living as theologically sheltered an existence as the culturally sheltered one that sponsors the assumption of inherent superiority. With the realization that people of other traditions make a directly parallel claim to ultimate endorsement, we are confronted by the inescapable fact of religious pluralism.

The obvious alternative to the unsatisfactoriness of dispensing with other religious traditions because they differ from our own is to try to appreciate those traditions in their own right. Thus, the era of comparative study was succeeded by a sustained attempt to experience life, in some way, as people of other traditions do. Implicit reassurance regarding the superiority of the Christian religion over other world faiths was replaced by multiple temporary conversions to Buddhism, Hinduism, Islam, etc. Theological comparisons of world-affirming Christianity and world-negating Buddhism gave way to attempts to feel something of the Buddhist or Hindu concern for release from the endless round of *maya*. In contrast to the stormy history of Muslim–Christian confrontations which continue into the present in the Middle East, students attempted to appreciate something of the Muslim sense of submission to Allah.

The focus on experience provides an air of realism that is less evident in the more abstract comparative approach. However, this sense of dealing with living experiences rather than with theoretical systems does not necessarily provide a satisfying resolution to the challenge posed by the encounter with other religious traditions because the basis for these experiments in empathy is still our own tradition. Thus, even if we manage some appreciation of the Buddhist quest for enlightenment or the Muslim way of submission, these are being filtered through our own Christian *Weltanschauung* so that our sense of enlightenment or submission is derived in contrast with, or as a variation on, Christian counterparts. The frustrations that emerge from such attempts to replicate pivotal themes of other religious traditions leave us wondering if there really can be any genuine encounter across the barriers represented by these traditions themselves. On what basis can we really encounter Buddhism or Islam?

THE BASIS FOR ENCOUNTER

In one sense, religious traditions have been encountering one another throughout human history. One has only to think of the challenges the faith of the Hebrews encountered from the Baals of Canaan, not to mention the previous influence of Egyptian royal and solar deities or those of their later Mesopotamian hosts, or of the numerous rivals Christianity faced in its formative period before being assured of virtually monopolistic status by Constantine. But in spite of this long history, the encounter of world religions is really a modern development. For it involves the encounter of religious traditions that really do potentially operate on a world scale. Religions in the premodern period defined the worlds of their participants and clashes of participants meant a clash of these worlds. But today religious traditions are seen increasingly as variations or competitors within a single world. It is this sense of a common world permeating the encounter of religious traditions today that gives the encounter its urgency and distinctiveness.

It is not surprising that the initial attempt to come to terms with the plurality of religions in the one world should have been essentially a theoretical one. At this stage the encounter was largely secondhand, through the medium of books and the esoteric reports of sojourners set upon winning souls, expanding commercial ambitions, or tasting exotic foreign delights. This largely secondhand acquaintance with world religions was also acquired under the lingering shadow of Enlightenment rationalism. The prevalence of the assumption that truth has to do fundamentally with ideas, along with the secondhand knowledge of other religions, goes a long way toward accounting for the rationalistic approach to the encounter. The reversal of both these conditions also explains the dissatisfaction with which this intellectual approach to other religions tends to be received today. It is becoming clearer and clearer that far from reflecting a position of neutral rationality, the God's-eye view of religions really represents an absolutizing of our own particular religious perspective. As this is realized, the pretense of any finally valid objective assessment of religions evaporates. "In order to achieve such an enormous assignment, one must not only have a vast knowledge and profound religious experience in relation to these religions, but must also stand at the top of Mount Olympus to make a solemn declaration that one is superior or the *best* one."[23] Those who would claim today to have scaled the heights of Mount Olympus are daring to the point of foolhardiness.

The more congenial approach is to recognize the humanness of all our religious traditions. Thus, Clifford Hospital depicts the major traditions as breakthroughs in which a spiritually sensitive individual achieved new heights of insight and religious experience, inspiring followers who formed communities that resulted eventually in the religious traditions as we know them today. Hospital suggests that this perspective can allow us to benefit from traditions other than our own as part of the richness of human experience. "In the light of such a vision, I also want to suggest that we take a further step and realize that our full humanity can be found in drawing upon the totality of our common human heritage—as demonstrated, initially, in the lives and teachings of our breakthrough figures."[24] The advantages of this humble human approach, which recognizes the limitations of our own particular tradition and looks to other traditions as equally limited, but also equally valid, over the arrogance of Olympian claims of superiority seem too self-evident to require comment. However, we should not let this appearance of humility blind us to the wider implications entailed by this proposal; for, on reflection, it would seem that this wide ranging pluralism is really an expression of a more pervasive monism. The recognition of a plurality of religious traditions is compromised by the terms of that recognition. Each tradition is seen as a reflection of human experience. They are components in "our common human heritage." Thus, what we are offered is not a radical recognition of a genuine plurality of religious traditions, but a unified perspective, not far removed from the Enlightenment rationalism it at first seems to succeed, which assumes a fundamental human horizon in which for pure reason is substituted an appeal to the category of experience.

The attempt to deal with the challenge of religious pluralism by treating different religious traditions as variations on a common spectrum of human experience does not really differ in principle from the comparative approach that sees religions as comparable doctrinal systems. The most basic difference between the two approaches is that where the comparative approach derives its standard of comparison from our own religious tradition, and thus does not really recognize the legitimacy of other traditions, the understanding of religion as reflections of a common range of human experience assumes a standard derived from modern secular humanism, so that even our own religious tradition is excluded from serious consideration in its own right. All religions are expressions of a human essence, which presumably is not dependent on any of them for its own basic integrity. The similarity to the assumption of rationalistic monism underlying the comparative approach is more striking than this difference. In fact, it seems to represent a variation on the common theme. "While motivated by evident good will, the modern dialogue of religions has proceeded at the price of remaking every religion over into a version of philosophical monism or rationalistic humanism."[25]

The inspiration for this variation on the Enlightenment is not far to seek. "This is the method frequently taken by theologians who have been seduced by the psychologists, sociologists, and historians of religion."[26] This is strong language, and certainly not immune to the dangers of overstatement attendant on such generalizations. Yet, the reference to seduction is not to be dismissed out of hand. The modern secular *Zeitgeist*, of which the social sciences constitute the academic flagship, exerts a seductive influence through its sheer pervasiveness. In the contemporary academic atmosphere, it is perfectly natural to think of religion as a variety of the sort of thing psychologists and sociologists study. But from the point of view of these religions themselves, insofar as they have not come under the sway of this secularist perspective, "this solution reduces the transcendent experiences of the various religions to being no more than particular expressions of a common humanity."[27] A genuine recognition of a plurality of world religions must accept these traditions in their own right, and resist reducing them to the status of manifestations of some common essence such as human rationality or human experience.

The conclusion to which we seem to be propelled is that the basis for a serious encounter among world religions must emerge from within those religions themselves. Eric J. Sharpe helpfully identifies four basic forms which religious dialogue may take.[28] He calls what we considered as the rationalistic approach, the discursive form of dialogue, and suggests that this concern with intelligibility represents a necessary but limited initial stage. That stage is transcended in the level of human dialogue, which again reflects the other basic position we just examined, in which the abstractness of discursive interest is superseded by a focus on the reality of living experience. Here too, Sharpe notes the danger of overlooking the importance of the particular religious traditions themselves. In the third form of dialogue, which he calls "secular", representatives of various religious traditions engage in discussions for the immediate practical purposes of learning how to get along in a progressively shrinking world. The fourth form of dialogue is identified as the "interior" type, and is seen to reflect the mystical and contemplative aspects of religious traditions so that representatives of different traditions encounter one another on the basis of a peculiarly religious form of experience.

We need not identify religion with its mystical element in order to appreciate the importance of religious experience and conviction itself as the basis for dialogue. "The meeting of religions is not merely an intellectual endeavor, not a simple practical problem; it is in itself a religious experience and a religious task; it is the meeting of God in my friend who follows another path and perhaps even denies God or at least my conception of God—for though I cannot help having a conception of my own, the living God I worship is not an ideal of my mind, a concept, but transcends all understanding."[29] The temptation for Christians encountering other religious traditions in the wake of Enlightenment rationalism and modern historical consciousness is to assess those religions in terms of the apparent reasonableness, or more likely unreasonableness, of their concepts and doctrines, or to embrace them as variations on a common scale of human experience. Both directions must be resisted because of their failure to take any of these traditions, including Christianity, seriously. What happens in such encounters is that secularists who have abandoned much of the claim of their own tradition seek to forge a new cosmopolitan creed congenial to the antireligious sentiments of modern secularism. Far from offering any hope of resolving the dilemma of pluralism, such approaches do not even recognize the reality.

> The religious question has to be dealt with in the religious perspective. The problem of Christian faith in a religiously plural world cannot be solved by ex-Christians learning to relate to ex-Jews, ex-Buddhists, ex-Muslims, or ex-anything else, in the name of conceptions that do not take these traditions seriously.[30]

Because the encounter of world religions is not primarily a philosophical one, where concepts and doctrinal systems are the issue, nor a pragmatic one, where the future of the world and humankind is the challenge, but finally a religious matter involving the inner meanings and disciplines of these traditions themselves, it will not be resolved by academics of either a theological or a social science bent. The encounter of world religions will be worked out in the long run through the meeting of practitioners of these religious traditions. This significantly reduces the role of the "religious expert" who has been inclined to attempt to dictate the agenda for the encounter, if not actually to anticipate, or even prescribe, its results. However, the theologian is not entirely bereft of function in this situation. There remains the very important role of pointing out the implications of this emerging realization that, if it is to be genuine, the encounter of world religions must itself be fundamentally religious. One of the most vital of these is the fact that this means that the very heart of these traditions is what is at stake.

PROSPECTS FOR THE ENCOUNTER

Even when the inadequacies of rationalistic and humanistic bases for relating religious traditions is recognized, this does not guarantee clear sailing for the encounter. For there are ways of treating the religious base itself in a reductionistic manner so that the distinctiveness of the traditions is glossed over in a leveling process which can be regarded as a further variation on the rational and humanistic approaches. The most evident means of effecting this direction is through the promotion of a too facile pluralism that does not really take the religious traditions seriously in their own right.

The starting point for the advocacy of pluralism is the recognition of the fact of the plurality of religious traditions. This apparently trite truism conceals the two-sided phenomenon of the experience of diversity and its interpretation. Pluralism is a positive endorsement of plurality. As an ideal it represents a widely endorsed position among scholars in theology and religious studies. It amounts to, at least, a temporary "live and let live" recognition that there are other traditions which are just as valid and ultimate for their followers as Christianity is for Christians, and that it might even be possible to learn from these traditions. "True universalism must be able to embrace existing human pluralism, rather than trying to set every people into the mould of religion and culture generated from one historical experience."[31] The rationale for this position is the contention that the divine alone is universal, however conceived within the various traditions, and that these traditions themselves are human and, therefore, relative and partial. It appears from this that we are not far removed from the approach to religious pluralism which is grounded in the assumption that the various traditions represent versions of a common stream of human experience.

It is because of this similarity that the advocate of this form of pluralism, Rosemary Ruether, can be confident that acceptance of such pluralism will not affect the essential significance of Christianity for Christians. "Nor does it seem to me that the power of Jesus' name will become less if we cease to use that name to deny the validity of other people's experience of God through other means."[32] On the surface, this appears to involve a straightforward endorsement of genuine plurality. Christianity represents the means by which Christians have access to the divine and Christians should learn to coexist with followers of other traditions who find access to the holy in other ways; nor should this mutual recognition of diversity of routes affect the devotion of the devotees of any of these traditions. It should not be necessary to deny the validity of any one else's faith in order to assure the validity of our own. As Wilfred Cantwell Smith says: "It will not do, to have a faith that can be undermined by God's saving one's neighbor; or to be afraid lest other men turn out to be closer to God than one had been led to suppose."[33] However, whereas the tendency to depreciate other traditions may be a sign of deficiency in our own faith, on what basis can we be assured that the genuine recognition of other traditions will have no adverse affects on our own? It would seem that the only source of such assurance is the assumption that the different traditions somehow reflect a common universal dimension which is represented no more distinctively in one than in any other. But surely that is not to take the traditions themselves seriously. It is to foreclose the possibility of genuine dialogue that might result in the recognition of the inherent superiority of one tradition. Maybe the Far Eastern sense of the transitoriness of life is fundamental, in which case the Christian contention that God is to be found in the concrete elements of this world will have to be abandoned as mistaken. To be sure that we can have it both ways, that the genuine recognition of other religious traditions will not rebound on our own only seems possible on the basis of a more general assumption about the ultimate nondistinctiveness of these traditions. If they are seen as parallel human windows on the otherness of divinity, each may have its place alongside the others, but if any, or even all of these traditions really do represent the divine in some significant way, then it is difficult to see how any can be indifferent to the existence of the others. A casual pluralism gives an appearance of tolerance, which really amounts to a refusal to take any religious tradition seriously in its own right.

This analysis would seem to suggest that we are back to some variation of the modern secularist perspective that subordinates religion to human categories in one way or another. The fact that these categories are religious is no real improvement on their rational or experiential precedents. However, there is another way of reading this current position. Instead of seeing it as yet another variation on secular reductionism, it could be viewed as a version of the religious base. In this case, the base that would be assumed would be the Far Eastern one, or more particularly, a variation on the Hindu tradition. This is the perspective that depreciates historical particularity and regards the differentiations of this world as finally insignificant. This is why Hinduism can appear to be so tolerant. The kind of toleration is inherent in its basic metaphysics. "The Hindu approach to other religions is to absolutize the relativism implied in the viewpoint that the various religions are simply different manifestations of the one Divine."[34] This generous toleration of other traditions is, in fact, a projection of the Hindu caste mentality whereby religious traditions are subsumed in the Hindu panoply as different castes, each occupying its serial role in the total complex which is Hinduism.[35] In this way what gives the appearance of being a tolerant acceptance of other religious traditions really amounts to an imperialism of absorption where those traditions are embraced as elements within the comprehensive religion of Hinduism.

The hidden agenda of an accommodating tolerance suggests that genuine recognition of religious pluralism may be more difficult than we would like to suppose. Rather than being parallel windows on eternity, religious traditions may represent different, or even contrary, intrusions of the eternal. This is certainly true of the offshoots of the Semitic stream, Christianity and Islam.

> One can't remove the "arrogance" of Christianity without making it something other than Christianity, no more than you could expect Muslims to remain Muslims were their creed to become: "There are many gods beside God, but Mohammed was one of his prophets." Radical monotheism is ultimately intolerant of pluralism.[36]

Insofar as a religious tradition is understood to entail a genuine encounter with God, the distinctive events and symbols of that tradition will take on a significance that derives from participation in the holy rather than merely offering yet another human approach to holiness. Such a perspective seems to reflect much more accurately not only the way that monotheistic religions like Christianity and Islam have understood themselves over the centuries, but also, as the above analysis suggests, the way that even the seemingly most tolerant of religions, Hinduism, also understands itself. Nothing is to be gained by pursuing a form of interreligious dialogue that amounts to an avoidance of the real differences among religious traditions. Any genuine encounter between representatives of different traditions must face the real differences that are present because of the distinctiveness of the traditions themselves. "In other words, one of the most significant things we have in common on which to build our mutual understanding is the experience of having a conviction that by definition precludes the other person's belief, and of being unable to accommodate it with integrity."[37] Real dialogue requires confrontation with real differences. There is no room for the easy assurance that such encounters really will not affect the way any particular faith is perceived by its followers. Such an a priori assurance is a rejection of genuine dialogue rather than the attempt to promote it, it professes to be.

Clearly the acknowledgment of genuine pluralism is a very difficult ideal. A glance at requirements for genuine dialogue laid down in two recent analyses of religious pluralism will indicate just how difficult. Paul F. Knitter, in *No Other Name?*, proposes:

1. Dialogue must be based on personal religious experience and firm truth-claims.
2. Dialogue must be based on the recognition of the possible truth in all religions.
3. Dialogue must be based on openness to the possibility of genuine change/conversion.[38]

The ideal dialogue partner is totally committed and totally open at the same time; believing firmly in the truth of their own religious tradition but ready to attempt to hear representatives of other religions to the point of being subject to conversion to that other tradition.

A hint of how there might be some approximation to this apparently impossible ideal of simultaneous commitment and openness is provided by the conditions for future religious dialogue laid down by Harold Coward, in *PLURALISM*, which include the following:

(1) That in all religions there is experience of a reality that transcends human concepts; (2) that that reality is conceived in a plurality of ways both within each religion and among all religions and the recognition of plurality is necessary both to safeguard religious freedom and to respect human limitations; (3) that the pluralistic forms of religion are instrumental in function; (4) that due to our finite limitations and simultaneous need for commitment to a particular experience of transcendent reality, our particular experience, though limited, will function in an absolute sense as the validating criteria for our own personal religious experience.[39]

The recognition that we are not religious in general, but rather experience the holy through some particular religious tradition, which thereby necessitates that that tradition function in an absolute sense for us (4) is mitigated to some extent by the other recognition that the object of faith, the reality of holiness itself, transcends any particular conceptualization (1). However, unless we are willing to equate the line between divine and human with that between transcendent reality and religious traditions, so that the religions themselves are seen as expressions of human experience and not in themselves as partaking in any direct way of the divine, as some of the leading advocates of dialogue seem willing to do, we will still be faced with the major impediment that the different traditions encounter each other not simply as inadequate reflections of transcendent reality but as different, and perhaps ultimately contrary, expressions of that reality.

There is no doubt that false impediments have been erected against interreligious encounter. When partisans declare the superiority of their own tradition either through the arrogance of isolation or the paranoia of an insecure faith, they are creating what Kosuke Koyama calls "an unnecessary stumbling block." However, it would be equally ill-advised to rush from this realization to an elimination of what Koyama recognizes as "a genuine stumbling block" that is inherent in the faith itself. His own articulation of the genuine variety is the Christian affirmation of "the mercy of the crucified and risen one."[40] The encounter across religious traditions will only be genuine if these central and distinctive affirmations of the various traditions are pursued. This is what makes the prospect so difficult, but also so worthwhile. For the outcome defies prediction, unlike the mere chumminess or assurance of the status quo that might be expected from a humanistic or pragmatic willingness to disavow these distinctive elements in the interests of a superficial tolerance or a compromise in the interests of survival that lacks any profound sense of a rationale for survival.

Religious Pluralism and Salvation

From a Christian point of view, the challenge of religious pluralism is, finally, not a matter of what Christians make of other religions but of the impact of other religions on our understanding of Christianity. If a genuine encounter among religious traditions takes place, the very identity of Christianity will be at stake, its claim that divine salvation is made available through Christ.[41]

For if we manage to leave behind the triumphalist perspective, which automatically assumes the inherent superiority of Christianity to other traditions, and to avoid the secularist alternatives, which pare all religions down to a lowest common denominator, the most distinctive thrust of each tradition will be what is at issue, and for Christianity this has been the proclamation of salvation in Christ.

CHRISTIANITY AS A RELIGION OF SALVATION

It can be held, as it is by no less a student of religion than Gerardus van der Leeuw, that all religions are religions of salvation.[42] Salvation then is seen as the inclusive category instead of human rationality or human experience. The resulting position might be similar to the approach to religious pluralism advocated by John Hick. "We have to present Jesus and the Christian life in a way compatible with our recognition of the validity of the other great world faiths as being also, at their best, ways of salvation."[43]

Hick recognizes that what he is advocating is revolutionary. In fact, he likens it to the Copernican revolution by which the Ptolemaic geocentric universe was abandoned through the recognition that the earth revolves around the sun rather than being itself the center. What is required today in religious sensibility, according to Hick, is a parallel abandonment of the Christianity-centered assumption through the recognition that Christianity is one of several religious traditions.[44] In this way, Hick comes close to epitomizing the common denominator religious alternative to the reduction of religious traditions to expressions of human rationality or human experience. The different major world religions are parallel routes to the common goal of salvation. Because this is the common goal, it must be stated in neutral terms, which do not derive from any one tradition, and yet, in terms that manage to catch the essential thrust of all of them. This neutral statement Hick presents as: "The transformation of human existence from self-centeredness to Reality-centeredness."[45] This is the essence of salvation to which all major religious traditions aspire.

The substitution of a religious for an essentially humanistic foundation for relating the different traditions satisfies the requirement we have seen emerging in the recognition that the encounter between religions must itself ultimately be religious. However, as a neutral common ground, it does not satisfy the further condition that this will only be accomplished to the extent to which the different traditions are taken seriously in their own right. For Hick's

Copernican revolution does not just require a shift from a Christian-centered to a religiously universal perspective, but more generally, a shift from all particular traditions to a comprehensive perspective, which transcends each and every particular tradition. In the new age of world religions, allegiance to particular traditions represents a lingering parochial attachment. Thus, Hick cites Karl Rahner's labeling believers of other faiths as "anonymous Christians" as at best a bridge concept between the parochial era of insular Christianity and the emerging age of the comprehensive world faith.[46] Seen from that world perspective, which Hick is well on the way to attaining, but which Rahner naively fails to recognize, "anonymous Christian" is a patronizing term, which implies an intrinsic absolutizing of Christianity and a corresponding depreciation of other traditions. However, from Rahner's point of view, the danger of presumption is in the other direction. "Non-Christians may regard this as presumptuous but the Christian cannot renounce this presumption which is the source of greatest humility for himself and the Church."[47] Which is more presumptuous: A position that holds that we are capable of forging a new cosmopolitan world that will render the religious experience of past generations parochial and passé, or a position that holds we are sinners saved by grace? Rahner is speaking from within this particularity of Christian experience. "Anonymous Christian" is itself a Christian term, intended for Christians; it is "meant to help *Christians* account for the salvation of others from within their own framework."[48] Thus, rather than constituting a presumptuous absorption of other traditions within the Christian fold, this concept is meant to deal with the reality of other faiths from a Christian perspective. Presumably followers of other faiths will have to do something similar, if they are to take seriously both the reality of other faiths and the distinctiveness of their own religious experience. In this sense, Hick may be right that "anonymous Christian" represents an interim stage. But it is surely presumptuous to proscribe this reading on the basis of an assumed common world religion that will eliminate the most distinctive elements of the long-standing religious traditions it is to supersede.

SALVATION AND WORLD RELIGIONS

Perhaps the most prominent indication of Hick's willingness, and even eagerness, to abandon the most distinctive features of historic Christianity is provided by his editing of the collection of essays published under the title, *The Myth of God Incarnate*. Beyond the helpful warning against taking our religious concepts and vocabulary too literally, so that we become fixated on the notions and words themselves, instead of looking through them to the reality to which they are meant to point, the general thrust of this collection was to shift the focus from Jesus and his significance to the role of believers, whether in the early centuries or the present. Thus, claims that have been made about Jesus, especially the historic claim that somehow he represented the very embodiment of God, are to be seen as reflections of the enthusiasm of believers rather than identifying any distinctiveness in Jesus himself. So Hick, in pursuit of his neutral cosmic religion, can suggest that this traditional understanding of Jesus as God incarnate is essentially a reflection of the Greek culture in which Christian understanding developed. He proposes that "we should never forget that if the Christian gospel had moved east, into India, instead of west, into the Roman Empire, Jesus' religious significance would probably have been expressed by hailing him within Hindu culture as a divine Avatar and within the Mahayana Buddhism, which was then developing in India as a Bodhisattva, one who had attained to oneness with Ultimate Reality but remains in the human world out of compassion for mankind and to show others the way of life."[49] It is nothing short of amazing that a scholar of Hick's caliber can propose a direct parallel verging on identity between the Hindu concept of the Avatar and the Bodhisattva of Mahayana Buddhism, on the one hand, and the Christian claim of incarnation on the other. These may represent the closest parallels there are to the notion of incarnation, but the difference between these two ways of understanding is even more striking.

> The Avatar is a theophany, an appearance of God to men, and herein lies its value as teaching the divine activity in this world to restore righteousness. The Gita says very little else about it, and even in other Hindu legends of Krishna and Rama these visible gods are hardly limited men who really suffer and die. Nevertheless, of all the teachings in the world's religions, the Avatar doctrines are closest to those of the incarnation. They are revelation as event, a visible as well as a spoken word of God.[50]

A more subtle, and, therefore, probably a more accurate and realistic type of comparison was suggested by Hick in an earlier writing where he distinguished three basic elements that are at stake in the conflicting truth claims among world religions. First, there is the difference in modes of experience of the divine reality, for example, he cites the personal view of God in the Semitic religions and in some strands of the Far Eastern religions that appear to be in conflict with the nonpersonal experience of the divine in other strands of Hinduism and Buddhism. These apparently basic differences, he suggests, may turn out to be complementary. Secondly, differences in philosophical and theoretical articulation such as the Far Eastern doctrine of reincarnation and the Christian doctrine of one life may also turn out to be harmonizable in some way. But the third type of difference concerns the formative experiences that shape the whole religious experience and understanding, and these pivotal perspectives, Hick reflects, of which the Christian notion of incarnation is an example, seem to entail an exclusiveness that defies foreseeable resolution. As he puts it: "We must live amid unfinished business . . ."[51] This mundane conclusion lacks the flare of a proposal for a new comprehensive world faith, but what it lacks in dash, it more than makes up for in depth. Far from being a dispensable variant on a common religious theme, the Christian claim of incarnation seems to entail just such a distinctive perspective; the elimination of which would be tantamount to the abandonment of Christianity.

In *The Myth of God Incarnate*, one of the other essayists was constrained to conclude: "There does not seem to be single, exact analogy to the total Christian claim about Jesus in material which is definitely pre-Christian; full scale redeemer-myths are unquestionably found AD but not BC."[52] Never before Christianity, and therefore presumably never apart from Christian influence, has a claim been made that in a real human individual we have to do with the very reality of God. Far from being attributable to cultural circumstances, this claim is integral to the Christian gospel. It is part of the fundamental soteriological claim that in Jesus, God has dealt decisively with the human condition and in so doing provided the basis for renewal and the restoration of humanity to recognition of the divine grace by which life is given and sustained. Far from representing a variation on a common theme, this focus on a particular human being as the organ of divinity must appear not only false but unintelligible to a perspective that thinks of the personal order as ultimately illusory. When this is added to the more specific contention that the point at which God is seen to have acted most decisively in this particular human life is in its ending in death by crucifixion, the total absurdity of this religion must be assured.

The recognition of determinative perspectives reverberates on the other levels of comparison Hick identifies. The sense of an impersonal absolute and of a series of rebirths required to achieve release from the illusions of finite existence are of a piece with the fundamental perspective that finds the notion of incarnation abhorrent, if it is intelligible at all. Conversely, the sense of a personal God and of the singularity of this life provides the necessary context for finding the divine in a particular human being. The difference between these formative perspectives is, perhaps, illustrated most dramatically in their respective approaches to suffering. Although it represents something of an oversimplification, there is merit in the general contrast of their attitudes to suffering, which holds that "whereas the Christian message has involved a transformation of suffering by an immersion into it, the Buddhist message has involved a transcendence of it, and a transformation of it, in the experience of meditation."[53] Where the experience of the cross invites Christians to triumph over suffering by confronting it and passing through it, the enlightenment of the Buddha warns all who would attain enlightenment themselves to rise above suffering by becoming impervious to it and so realizing its ultimate unreality. In practice, this results in the basic difference that Buddhism recognizes and advocates compassion whereas Christianity advocates the practice of love. "Buddhism recognizes compassion but denies love, for compassion may be a way of escaping from the pain of existence while love affirms existence and, consequently, the pain of it."[54] Underlying this practice is the difference in vision according to which for Buddhism suffering is ultimately unreal, whereas for Christianity it is so significant that it elicits nothing less than divine reaction.

From a Christian perspective, the Buddhist denial of the reality of suffering in human experience has as its inverse side an inability to recognize the ultimate instance of suffering, "the pain of God."[55] Because of this very different orientation, the central Christian conviction that God is to be found particularly in the reality of the cross remains foreign to Buddhist sensibilities. A leading Buddhist scholar, Edward Conze, outlines the manner in which Christianity could be understood from a Buddhist point of view. Jesus could be accepted as a Bodhisattva, an enlightened one who remains behind out of compassion to assist others to achieve enlightenment, but the notion of a unique incarnation is not a genuine possibility because it smacks of intolerance and all the conflict that is attendant upon such an attitude. Conze cites the Buddhist best known in the West, D. T. Suzuki, in illustration of how totally alien is the fundamental Christian notion of God being known not only in human particularity, but also in the suffering of the cross: "The crucified Christ is a terrible sight and I cannot help associating it with the sadistic impulse of a psychologically affected brain." He concludes a fundamental elaboration of the familiar contrasts already noted between Buddhism and Christianity with the suggestion that even in Mahayana Buddhism, where there is an appearance of some similarity to Christianity, the saviors are ultimately unreal.[56] Clearly the gap between Buddhism and Christianity is more than one of cultural variety, as Hick's more recent search for a universal world religion would entail. The difference is metaphysical. For one view, suffering is part of the ultimately unreal world of finitude; for the other, suffering is real because the finite world is the divine creation into which the creator has entered directly to the extent of embracing suffering for the redemption of his creatures.

The contrast between these different perspectives is, perhaps, most pronounced in the Hindu attitude to Christianity. In a pamphlet of the Ramakrishna Mission, Swami Ranganathananda outlines what he intends as a sympathetic reading of Christianity, in response to which he invites Christians to be similarly open to Hindu teachings. He regards Jesus as "the man of joy," dismissing "the man of sorrows" portrait as a product of Christian dogma. In commenting on this pamphlet, Robert Lawson Slater notes how this typical Hindu reading of Christianity as a religion centering on one who rose above the misery of life to find the joy that comes with seeing through the illusory attachments of this world of sorrows really misses the heart of the gospel.[57] Behind this Hindu reading there lies not only the disdain of suffering, but also the sense of the futility and unreality of the temporal order. Thus, insofar as a person approaching Christianity from the Hindu tradition would be inclined to consider the cross at all, it would be in some allegorized form, as an instance of the way of release that is the goal for everyone caught in the snare of *maya*. "Jesus signifies Cross, the dying to the self as the way of life."[58]

Perhaps the most striking feature of this Hindu version of Christianity, in light of what we have seen about the attempts to respond to the reality of religious pluralism, is its similarity to Hick's supposedly neutral, universal essence of religion as the release from self to become Reality-centered. It may be that what Hick is really offering is not a new comprehensive cosmopolitan world religion so much as a modern Western version of Hinduism. We have seen how, in spite of its appearance of universal tolerance, Hinduism really only tolerates what it can embrace as an element within its own field of vision. In this way, it is as particular and exclusive as Christianity. This is, finally, what is at stake in the encounter of world religions; their direct encounter of each other in all their idiosyncratic particularity. The notion of release from self-centeredness is very important for Hinduism and Christianity, and perhaps, for every major religious tradition. But no tradition experiences this in this bald, abstract form. What devotees know is enlightenment or salvation. That is something much richer than any common denominator formulation can begin to capture or convey. Whether religious traditions can really encounter each other out of these centers of peculiarity is the most enduring question of religious pluralism.

PROSPECTS FOR MUTUAL APPRECIATION OF WAYS OF SALVATION

The contrast in metaphysical visions between say, Buddhism and Christianity, makes the prospect for genuine communication across that divide anything but promising. In spite of the wide variations within each of these traditions themselves, which leads Frithjof Schuon to suggest that the real divisions among religions are horizontal rather than vertical, that is, that they cut across religions rather than falling at the borders of the traditions themselves,[59] the fundamental perspectives of the major traditions do shape the direction of theological sensibilities. This is so obviously the case that it is tempting simply to concede the mature position of Ernst Troeltsch on the prospects for the encounter between religious traditions: "There can be no conversion or transformation of one into the other, but only a measure of agreement and of mutual understanding."[60] Yet, to accept this would be to foreclose the encounter just as definitely as the lowest common denominator approach. What it does require is the recognition of the formative significance of the particular traditions in terms of which particular convictions and understandings are made possible. Wilfred Cantwell Smith suggests just how formative particular traditions are. "The totality within which it obtains not only confers the meaning upon each term within the statement, and upon the statement as a whole, but determines also 'the meaning of meaning' for such statements."[61] The real question is whether, and to what extent, mutual intelligibility can be achieved across these worlds of meaning.

The inclination toward a negative answer to this question prompted by the recognition of the formative peculiarity of the different traditions is mitigated somewhat by the recognition that the basic meeting ground for religions is not in doctrines or rituals but on the level of experience.[62] It may be that religious experience is more comprehensive than the particular forms in which it is expressed in the major traditions and that, although there is no escaping the significance of these forms in constituting our basic frames of reference, it might be possible to penetrate each others traditions to some extent, insofar as we can recognize common elements of religious experience.

In reference to the art of literature, short story writer and novelist, Flannery O'Connor, has remarked on how little experience a writer really needs in order to enter imaginatively into situations that might seem to be largely foreign territory. Her direct target is those people who complain about the unreal world of the writer.

> The fact is that anybody who had survived his childhood has enough information about life to last him the rest of his days. If you can't make something out of a little experience, you probably won't be able to make it out of a lot. The writer's business is to contemplate experience, not to be merged in it.[63]

If Flannery O'Connor is right, in principle, then there is some hope that our own religious experience may enable us to enter into each other's worlds of meaning with greater empathy than their apparent mutual exclusivity would suggest, and in so doing we might, in fact, discover new depths of meaning in our own tradition. Such is the vision proposed by Paul Knitter under the label, "unitive pluralism."

> The new vision of religious unity is not *syncretism*, which boils away all the historical differences between religions in order to institutionalize their common core; nor is it *imperialism*, which believes that there is one religion that has the power of purifying and then absorbing all the others. Nor is it a form of lazy tolerance that calls upon all religions to recognize each other's validity and then to ignore each other as they go their own self-satisfied ways. Rather, unitive pluralism is a unity in which each religion, though losing some of its individualism (its separate ego), will intensify its personality (its self-awareness through relationship). Each religion will retain its own uniqueness, but this uniqueness will develop and take on new depths by relating to other religions in mutual dependence.[64]

If "unitive pluralism" sounds a little too good to be true, a promise of being able to have our own particular religious cake and eat it too through a genuinely open embracing of other religious traditions, we might at least give this direction an experimental try through attempting to exercise, in a small way, the kind of imaginative capacities O'Connor attributes to literary people.

One of the most basic barriers to interreligious dialogue is the contrast in perspective we have noted between the Buddhist ideal of nirvana, with its attendant implications regarding the ephemeral nature of this life, and the Christian prizing of this life epitomized in the conviction that God is known in the most ungodly elements of this life typified in the cross. We have seen how this results in a dedicated Buddhist like Suzuki, regarding the cross with horror, while Christians lift up this symbol as the epitome of their faith. On this level, there seems to be room for nothing but contrast and head-on collision. But if we are able to hear what Buddhists are saying in this regard on the level of experience, rather than as subscribers to a different ideology, we may find our own profession shaken, not merely negatively but positively, that is, not simply in rejection of the cross but in exposure of new dimensions in the cross of which we have not been aware or which have become obscure. One real possibility here is that we might recover something of the horror that the reality of the cross originally entailed and thereby come to appreciate something of its domestication in Christianity. "To us, the word 'cross' gives little idea of the abominable shame and horror which belonged to it in the view of the ancient world, and belong to it in reality."[65] Or, in light of the materialistic orientation of contemporary Western culture, the orientation of Buddhism might help us to recover a greater appreciation of that transcendent dimension in Christianity that is endangered by the short-term horizon of contemporary sensibilities. For its part, Buddhism might find more enduring significance in the compassion of the Bodhisattva than is presently the case, and there might even be some consideration of the importance of personal identity. All of this, of course, would only be significant insofar as it took place on that level of firsthand experience, and not simply as trade-offs between representatives of contrasting systems.

Because this encounter must take place at the level of experience, not only is it confined to believers of the respective traditions, but also its outcome defies prediction. We have suggested the possibility of modifications in emphases in the respective traditions. However, the results may be far more radical. There is no way of precluding the possibility of total transformations in any or all traditions. John Cobb suggests that this is the next logical step after the stage of dialogue, where members of the different traditions become familiar with each other's points of view.

"*Beyond* dialogue, I suggest, lies the aim of mutual transformation."[66] This may involve Buddhist's appreciating salvation by divine grace so that Amida Buddha actually yields to an acceptance of the historical action of God in Christ, or it might entail Christians finding less significance in the historic particularity that has figured so prominently in Christianity. It may be that Christian and Buddhist will both learn how one of their most obvious points of convergence, the conviction that in some way we are saved by being willing to lose ourselves, discloses new depths of meaning in their own traditions. The one thing that is evident is the most distinctive features of the respective traditions are what is at stake. Consequently, what is involved is nothing less than a gigantic venture of faith.

In light of the possible impugning of the theological reputation of Paul Tillich with which we began, perhaps it is fitting to give him the last word, precisely along these lines.

> Religion cannot come to an end, and a particular religion will be lasting to the degree in which it negates itself as a religion. Thus Christianity will be a bearer of the religious answer as long as it breaks through its own particularity.
>
> The way to achieve this is not to relinquish one's religious tradition for the sake of a universal concept which would be nothing but a concept. The way is to penetrate into the depth of one's own religion, in devotion, thought and action. In the depth of every living religion there is a point at which the religion itself loses its importance, and that to which it points breaks through its particularity, elevating it to spiritual freedom and with it to a vision of the spiritual presence in other expressions of the ultimate meaning of man's existence.
>
> This is what Christianity must see in the present encounter of the world religions.[67]

This statement from the late stages of Tillich's career might redeem his apparent ignorance of the specifics of a particular tradition. For whatever adjustments in the dialectic that he proposes might be required by the actual encounter of followers of different traditions, the basic direction of seeking the universal through the particularity of a given tradition is a shrewd anticipation of what appears to be emerging today as the most promising direction for genuine religious encounter. He might also be right in proposing that this pursuit may well result in a renewed sense of the meaning of our respective traditions. What is clear at this stage is that the encounter must involve these traditions at the point of their most distinctive features, and that for Christianity this means its identity as a religion of salvation. The future of the Christian tradition is thus contingent upon the way in which salvation comes to be regarded through the encounter of world religions.

Part Three
Prospects for Salvation

8

Social Salvation

Amid the buffeting that the whole notion of salvation has sustained in recent years, the one safe harbor that has appeared is represented by the insistence on the importance of the social arrangements by which we live. If we cannot be induced to ponder the condition of our own souls, finding such language archaic in the light of contemporary psychological sophistication, or to become vexed over the ultimate fate of the world, regarding such preoccupation as the property of fanatics, we are not nearly so apt to dismiss contentions that our world is characterized by massive patterns of injustice. The identification of prominent varieties of these patterns and proposals for dealing with them has come to constitute the most dominant focus of theology in the past couple of decades. This could be described as the politicalization of theology, and of Christianity in general.[1] It has taken shape through the political theologies of Europe, the theologies of hope and of revolution, and has gained particular prominence through the theologies of liberation.

In the interests of brevity, we shall focus particularly on liberation theology as a promoter of this social direction for salvation, and within that genre we shall confine our attention largely to the Latin American version. This choice might be dictated by considerations of safety, since it is further removed from our situation than the black and feminist varieties that have strong North American sponsorship. However, the official reason for that focus is the impression that it represents the vanguard of the movement and through its own development and the wider engagement it has elicited provides the clearest source for identifying what is most distinctive and most challenging in this approach.

From a traditional theological perspective, the approach of liberation theology appears to represent an inversion of what Christianity has been taken to involve. "The modern insistence within the Church for establishing what is regarded as a just society has shifted the whole center of Christianity, so that it is now becoming defined in terms of precise political morality."[2] The social emphasis seems to entail the placing of ethics, in the form of social ethics, front and center, with a consequent demotion of more strictly theological considerations to some kind of secondary status. But from the perspective of liberation theologians themselves, what is at stake is not a promotion of ethics and a demotion of theology proper, but a fundamental change in the understanding of the nature of theology itself. The generally acknowledged pioneer of Latin American liberation theology, Gustavo Gutierrez, contends that what is at stake is not a change in focus or subject matter but the emergence of a new way of doing theology as such.[3] Because this is the case, the way to appreciate what is involved in liberation theology is not to identify any of its central themes, but to examine its fundamental procedure. "The real novelty of the theology of liberation lies in its methodological approach."[4] This will entail an attempt to get some sense of what is involved in its claim to arrive at theological reflection only on the basis of direct involvement in the pursuit of liberation; its insistence on the primacy of praxis.

The Concreteness of Salvation

The initial obstacle identified in traditional theology by the liberation approach centers on its abstractness. It talks in universal categories and never gets down to the concrete realities actually faced by people in their day-to-day lives.

> Redemption theologians have talked about death in itself, sin in itself, suffering in itself. They can, therefore, express views about a radical liberation from each of the aforementioned terms concerning the universal human condition. But in this way, the real situation in which Jesus announces the Kingdom of God has vanished.[5]

The most evident distinguishing feature of liberation theology is this concern for the concrete situation. In order to be real, theology must not only address particular situations, but also it must emerge out of a direct involvement in such concrete conditions. In the terminology of liberation theology itself, rather than being a matter of academic, theoretical reflection, theology must be sponsored and sustained by "praxis."

THE PRIMACY OF PRAXIS

On the surface, this shift from orthodoxy to orthopraxis as a crite-rion for theology[6] represents a challenge to Christians to practice what they preach. Abstract theology, which has no impact on the ongoing commitments and relations of life, is simply hypocrisy. However, embarrassing though such an insistence on the import-ance of practice might be for many Christians, the thrust of libera-tion theology is more pointed still. For praxis is not to be equated with practice. It is not a matter of putting into effect something that is otherwise believed. Praxis is itself the source and ground of belief. Rather than being a counterpart to theoretical reflection, it is a comprehensive reality that includes both active involvement in a given situation and the thought and reflection prompted by that involvement. Praxis entails the claim that our thinking is ultimately grounded in our living. Thus, the opposite of praxis is not theory in the sense of reflection, but any outlook that accords theory prima-cy, assuming that we can take reality in from some height of spe-culative detachment and then apply the insights derived in a secon-dary act of practice. The reality is that any insight we do have is a product of praxis, and its confirmation and continuing validity will depend on the continuation of that praxis, of that combination of involvement and insight that is available only in this combined form.

Behind this insistence on the primacy of praxis there lies the emer-gence of historical consciousness, the awareness that our under-standing is conditioned by our location. The most direct version of this is represented by the Hegelian legacy, especially as it is medi-ated by the most famous left-wing Hegelian, Karl Marx. The praxis orientation is heavily indebted to Marx's insistence that under-standing is shaped by the concrete circumstances of life. "Con-sciousness can never be anything else than conscious existence, and the existence of men is their actual life-process."[7] From this back-ground, praxis is invested with epistemological, and not simply with moral significance. Rather than representing merely the put-ting into practice of what is otherwise known, praxis refers to the privileged perspective through which understanding becomes possi-ble. The point is made succinctly by the dean of liberation theo-logians, Gutierrez: "Historical reality thus ceases to be the field for the application of abstract truths and idealistic interpretations; in-stead it becomes the privileged locale from which the process of knowledge starts and to which it eventually returns."[8] Implicit in this change of locus for theology is a shift in the notion of truth.

Every academic understanding of truth as some kind of consistency or correspondence effected in abstraction is displaced by an act of understanding whereby truth is verbal rather than substantive. It is primarily something done rather than something possessed.

From this perspective, the truth of Christianity is not primarily a matter of a metaphysical viewpoint, but of a life of charity.[9] The generally accepted view of truth as a matter of abstract insight, which then awaits application in practice, is seen as a Greek legacy that stands in sharp contrast to the outlook of the Bible that it was used to expound. "In the Bible . . . words have meaning only as the expression of a deed, and theory has meaning only as the expression of practice."[10] Thus, in the Old Testament, the Word is a creative agent, rather than a conceptual communication, and in the New Testament, John speaks of "doing the truth." "It seems clear enough that the classical conception can claim no biblical basis for its conceptual understanding of truth or for its distinction between a theoretical knowledge of truth and a practical application of it."[11] That dualistic approach to truth is of Greek origin, and its impact on the biblical heritage has been disastrous. "Greek theism . . . created a whole ideological sphere of truth totally separated from the world of man."[12] Through the praxis orientation, liberation theology sees itself recovering the biblical approach to truth, as a matter of living, in contrast to the Greek inspired evisceration of this living reality through the concentration on the anemic shadows of theological abstractions.

The indebtedness of liberation theology to Marx extends beyond this epistemological reconsideration of the nature of truth to embrace the activist orientation of Marx's own position. The emphasis on praxis in Marx himself is focused in his call to revolution, the most succinct, and probably best known statement of which is to be found in his eleventh thesis on Feuerbach: "The philosophers have only *interpreted* the world in various ways; the point is to *change* it."[13] Doing is the route to knowing because the doing is self-authenticating. In the struggle for the revolution, the rightness of that cause will be seen. Some liberation theologians stick fairly closely to this Marxian program; others employ the "knowing through doing" approach along more conventional Christian lines, such as in the following application by Jon Sobrino:

> We will know Jesus as the Son in the measure in which our own life is a life of sonship. Latin American Christology tries to reflect on Christ from within the praxis of becoming historically like him; it tries to reflect on his sonship from within the becoming real of the sonship of all people.[14]

Whether in direct promotion of political, or even military revolution, or in a more circumscribed focus on more conventional Christian themes, liberation theologians are distinguished by their concern to pursue theology from within the peculiarities of their own local conditions. To accept theological positions formulated elsewhere is, as they see it, to acquiesce in, and to assist in the perpetuation of, the foreign domination of Latin American peoples, where this is precisely the reality that Christian theology should be addressing, as they understand the gospel. "We are faced with the challenge of being able to talk about God, not to a world come of age but to a world of diminished and belittled human beings, not to non-believers but to people rendered less than human."[15] If Jesus were in Latin America today, would he not be with these little ones who are consigned to the margins of life? Some of the most prominent exponents of liberation theology contend that the reality seen in Jesus is in Latin America today through the agency of the risen Christ and the pervasiveness of the Holy Spirit, and that if there is to be any genuine theologizing in that situation, it will have to be done through identification with these little ones. Christian theology in Latin America can only be reflection prompted and pruned through such praxis.

THE LIMITATIONS OF PRAXIS

The distinction between praxis and practice allows scope for the acknowledgement of a theoretical dimension in praxis that is excluded by definition from the immediacy of practice. However, this scope within the understanding of praxis is a two-edged sword. For as well as allowing for reflection and for some distancing of the persons involved from total captivation by their involvement, this element can constitute the thin edge of the wedge, to vary the metaphor, which can serve to readmit speculative interests and thus compromise the primacy of praxis. Even Marxist scholars have been baffled by this dilemma in the master himself.

> Absolute knowledge, speculative thought, and the (metaphysical) logos of the being-becoming of the totality of the world must be one and all superceded in and by total praxis, multilateral activity, real action. But total praxis even in the form of an offered vision, remains nevertheless quite problematic. Will it be an activity that is only practical? Will it leave no place at all for any theoretical thought? Does it encompass thought *and* action, that nevertheless remains separated from each other? Or will it, precisely as praxis that is material, real, sensible, actual, effective, and objective, dominate and determine all thought, consciousness and knowing?[16]

In spite of the aphoristic force of Marx's eleventh thesis on Feuerbach, and the significant influence it has exerted on praxis-oriented approaches to theology, a moment's reflection on its stark contrast between the philosophical attempts to understand the world, which it dismisses, and the admonition to change the world, which it asserts, will show that this thesis is plagued by an intrinsic contradiction. For how can there be any program to change the world, without some prior awareness of what needs to be changed?[17] Even as ardent an advocate of liberation theology as Hugo Assmann concedes that "there is a danger of unreflective action, just as there is of inactive reflection."[18] And the chief proponent of the pedagogy of praxis, Paulo Freire, admits that without critical reflection "action is pure activism."[19] The significance of theoretical perspective would appear to be too great to allow for any easy acquiescence to the primacy of praxis where that is taken to entail some kind of primacy of practice. If the two sided nature of praxis, in contrast to straightforward practice, is taken seriously, this would seem to require rather a sense of an ongoing dialectic in which practical involvement and theoretical perspective mutually inform each other so that it is impossible to say which of these elements is primary. The most that can be assured is that neither is dispensable, and that if one is neglected, the other will thereby be impaired.

One of the most striking concessions to the significance of theoretical perspective in Marx himself is in his doctrine of the vanguard, whereby in *The Manifesto of the Communist Party*, he acknowledges the need for intellectuals to stimulate the revolt of the proletariat.[20] That concession, however, is vastly overshadowed by the emphasis on the determinative significance of the particular circumstances, for Marx especially the economic circumstances, from which one looks out at the world. The official position is that consciousness is molded by circumstances; the tactical position is that provocateurs who can see beyond present circumstances are needed to act as catalytic agents for changing these circumstances. The significance of this concession for the praxis orientation is particularly crucial for the central position of liberation theology.

The requirement for the vanguard can be seen to compromise the populist orientation that is supposed to characterize liberation theology. Because of the need for this leadership, the whole approach can be seen as an imposition from outside intellectuals, rather than a grass roots movement to which theologians commit themselves. One critic of liberation theology, Edward Norman, goes so far as to say: "Western Christians who listen in to the Latin American church, in the belief that this is the authentic word of the Third World, hear only the echoes of their own voice."[21] He notes how Sheila Cassidy, the British doctor imprisoned in Chile for treating fugitives without filing the required reports, has remarked that the revolutionaries she encountered were "not desperate, oppressed peasants, but university students or young professionals from middle class families."[22] Cassidy mentions Camilo Torres, the son of a wealthy Columbian pediatrician, himself a professor of sociology and a Roman Catholic priest, who joined guerrilla revolutionaries; and Nestor Paz, a medical student who also gave his life in the cause of revolution. She also cites doctors Miguel Enriques of Chile and Bautista van Schauwen, suggesting that these references are "enough to show that a high proportion of revolutionaries of Latin America are seeking to change a system which is unjust, not to themselves or to the class from which they come, but to the dispossessed of the land: The underfed, poorly housed, undereducated majority of their fellow countrymen."[23] One might ask how far the base communities in Latin America, the most proletarian form of the liberation movement, could have progressed without middle class, externally educated leadership. The need for this extra contextual agency not only constitutes an embarrassment for any strict adherence to Marx's prophecy of the proletarian revolution, but also it could be seen to represent a serious threat to the praxis orientation by according the theoretical element more scope than that orientation can readily permit.

This dilemma for praxis is illustrated directly in Paulo Freire's, *Pedagogy of the Oppressed*. Freire's delineation of the contours of praxis acknowledges the necessity of what Marx had called the vanguard, to counter the formative influence of the status quo.

> The oppressor elaborates his theory of action without the people, for he stands against them. Nor can the people—as long as they are crushed and oppressed, internalising the image of the oppressor—construct by themselves the theory of their liberating action. Only in the encounter of the people with the revolutionary leaders—in their communion, in their praxis—can this theory be built.[24]

And yet Freire insists that the revolutionary leaders do not bring any particular message to the people. They merely act as a catalyst. This is how they differ from the preservers of the status quo. Rather than imposing their views on the people, they seek to help the people come to appreciate their own situation. "This task

implies that revolutionary leaders do not go to the people in order
to bring them a message of 'salvation,' but in order to come to
know through dialogue with them both the *objective situation* and
their awareness of that situation."[25] This necessity that there be
leaders to apprise the people of their true situation, and the claim
that these leaders really do not bring anything to the situation that
is extrinsic to it, focuses the dilemma inherent in the praxis
orientation. Are these leaders really as neutral, or as empty, as this
portrayal would suggest? Freire contends that, ideally, the only
values that will be passed on to the people will center on a critical
attitude to the world, and he is confident that such an outlook must
be freely embraced so that by its very nature it defies external
imposition.[26] However, students of modern Western thought have
learned that the claim to represent a critical stance is likely to be
anything but neutral. Criticism is only possible on the basis of
some other tacitly embraced convictions. The claim is that the
leader from outside merely represents a method or procedure. It is
the people themselves who come to understand their situation.
"The task of the dialogue teacher in an interdisciplinary team working on the thematic universe revealed by the investigation is to
're-present' that universe to the people from whom he first received it—and 're-present' it not as a lecture, but as a problem."[27]
The innovation represented by the external agent, then, amounts
to a problematizing of what the people recognize for themselves.
Elsewhere, however, Freire betrays expectations that are more
substantive than this procedural neutrality can allow. In acknowledging the duality of focus characteristic of the external leader,
identification with the people on the one hand, and on the other,
the raising of wider problems that otherwise would not occur to the
people on their own, he states that the leaders must see that the
workers must become owners of their own labor.[28] This phrasing
leaves no doubt about what Freire himself brings to the situation,
and what he expects other external leaders to bring.

The tension between the indispensability of external leaders and
the equally mandatory denial of their representing anything of substantive significance in themselves erupts into contradiction by
rendering these leaders exceptions to the fundamental praxis
orientation. The embarrassment of this requirement for external
leadership can be accommodated in the praxis orientation through
the recognition that praxis involves something of the detachment
of theoretical perspective. Its defining characteristic is not an insistence on the sufficiency of practice, but on the interconnection of
theory and practice. Now, this alignment is ascribed to the masses.

"We must realize that their view of the world, manifested variously in their action, reflects their *situation* in the world."[29] Their understanding of life is molded by their circumstances. The outside elite, however, who help them see their situation as it really is, are not so molded. In fact, they apparently have no perspective at all. They are purely neutral critics who serve only to elicit critical consciousness in people whose consciousness is otherwise molded by their circumstances.

Yet, perhaps even this difficulty can be accommodated by the praxis approach through the explanation that although the masses typify praxis through their view of life being shaped by their circumstances, the external leaders are equally representative of this approach because of their recognition that that view of life can only be changed through changing those formative circumstances. But this vindication of the praxis orientation is confined to the masses. We do not hear about the circumstances of these leaders themselves. All that we are told about them tends to imply that they are circumstance free. They are permanent revolutionaries. helping people to become revolutionary, and so free to change their circumstances, and themselves.

> For the truly humanist educator and the authentic revolutionary, the object of action is the reality to be transformed by them with other men—not other men themselves. The oppressors are the ones who act upon men to indoctrinate them and adjust them to a reality which must remain untouched.[30]

This humanistic concern to enable people to transform their world, in contrast to the approach that preserves the shape of the world by requiring people to conform to it, can appear neutral only in the context of modern Western anthropocentrism. Feminists, of course, will detect a very definite bias in the phrasing employed, but we must also wonder how far the educator portrayed here really is "truly humanist." For the refusal to manipulate human beings is immediately compromised by the aim of encouraging human beings to manipulate the world. The unacknowledged vision that appears to be informing this supposedly neutral proceduralism would seem to be not one of humanism but of modern technology. Strong confirmation of this is provided by Freire's misreading of Martin Buber's contrast between I-Thou and I-It approaches to life as though this corresponded to a contrast between persons and things. Persons are invited to engage in mutual dialogue as subjects to "name" the world in order to transform it.[31] Freire completely misses the holistic range of Buber's contrast, whereby the division is not between persons and things but between two fundamentally different approaches to the whole of reality, from God to the most mundane object. As a result, seen from the holistic perspective provided by Buber, Freire can be seen not only to be advocating a very definite perspective, but also one that is dubious by his own terms. For it is surely optimistic to the point of naivety to think that human beings can freely conspire to manipulate the world, without having that manipulation rebound upon themselves. But is that not precisely the insight of the praxis orientation? Ironically, it could appear that this pioneer of the pedagogical implications of the praxis approach really betrays that approach by exempting its own leading practitioners from its own insights and demands.

THE PRAXIS OF PRAXIS

As a comprehensive approach seeking to encompass the otherwise disparate directions of theory and practice, praxis is inevitably exposed to these opposing forces. The result is a variety of understandings of praxis ranging from virtually total immersion in practical activity to an essentially theoretical stance that accords only slight recognition to the need for application. Matthew Lamb identifies five possible models, which he somewhat carelessly designates as models of the theory–praxis relation. If we modify this so that we think instead of models of the theory–practice relation within praxis, the main stages he identifies can indicate something of the range of the praxis orientation: (a) A primacy of theoretical perspective sees practice as the application of independently discovered theoretical insight; (b) a primacy of practice, on the other hand, sees theory as a secondary approximation to an encompassing reality that is only disclosed through our involvement in it; (c) a middle-of-the-road combination of theoretical and practical dimensions represented by what Lamb calls the primacy of faith–love, as in the revelational approach of Karl Barth; (d) a critical theoretical correlation attempts to combine theoretical concerns and practical involvements largely from the theoretical perspective; and (e) a critical practice correlation attempts to develop a unified approach largely from the situation of practical involvement.[32] Even if some variation on the third model was available, and we might wonder how theology of any kind could be possible without according some kind of primacy to faith and love, from the self-consciousness elicited by the notion of praxis, we must wonder whether it too would be subject to the inexorable tug-of-war between the theoretical and the practical poles. If so, and assuming that the first two models represent unsatisfactory extremes, the heart of the praxis issue lies with models four and five. Of these the fifth represents the most satisfactory understanding of praxis. What is at stake is not a straightforward concentration on practice to the neglect of reflection, but an insistence on the primacy of practice, so that reflection is seen to emerge out of life, rather than in abstraction from it.

In its suspicion of abstraction, however, the praxis orientation does not significantly move beyond the parallel concern in liberal theology to deal with moral imperatives rather than simply with spiritual indicatives. Indeed, the emergence of kingdom building proposals under liberal auspices can be heard echoing in some quarters of liberation theology. What makes this latter development different and interesting is the critique of ideology, which it adds to the critique of abstraction. The problem is not just that theology indulges in imaginary constructs that do not come to grips with the real world, but, on the contrary, that these constructs serve to sanctify the way the world is arranged. Theological affirmations are not simply and directly about absolute reality. They also reflect social and political arrangements. Their influence in this respect is particularly inimical when it is least noticed. Those who think they are doing pure theology, with no social or political overtones, are the unwitting proponents of the social and political status quo.

Peter Hinchliff identifies three basic ways of failing to confront the political dimensions of theology. The most direct way is to assume that our own politics is not politics at all; to so take it for granted that its political nature is not recognized. A second popular approach is to make an absolute division between God and Caesar such as in the medieval natural/supernatural division or the Lutheran two realms doctrine or some modern variation of these. Finally, there is the avoidance of confrontation with the political dimension because of the inevitable partisanship of politics.[33] None of these offers any adequate reason for avoiding the political dimension, and in fact, the dubious aspects of all three further substantiate the plea for political sophistication on the part of advocates of praxis. If our own political position is so ingrained as to be unnoticed, this certainly provides ample testimony to the inescapability of the political. To accept an absolute gulf between God and Caesar is tantamount to according divine status to Caesar. And the partisan nature of politics, although disturbing from the point of view of the Christian premium on peace and reconciliation, may not only be inevitable, given the divisions and conflicts in society, but insofar as in these divisions and conflicts right and truth are seen to be found more on one side than on the other, the failure to enter into this partisan area would be tantamount to sanctioning the imbalance and those who profit from it.

This last insight is the most characteristic legacy of Marx's own insistence on praxis. The strict practice reading would see him insisting that all understanding is a product of economic arrangements. The more comprehensive primacy-of-practice reading would allow scope for insights such as those of the Vanguard or Freire's revolutionary leaders, or even of religious believers; not that Marx himself would have given much credence to this latter category. What would be required of all such insights is that their rootage in the actual arrangements of life be recognized and appreciated. This would entail an identification of both the practical advantages enjoyed by the advocate of a given position and a theoretical recognition that a position is involved. In this way the glossing of both political realities and of substantive theoretical affirmations should be avoided. A practitioner of praxis will be a maker of affirmations and not simply a neutral catalyst. At the same time, those affirmations will be seen against the background of that person's real life situation.

Although the ideal balance of practice and theory is much more easily admired than attained, the adequacy of the praxis orientation depends on its being maintained. A monopolistic tendency in the direction of either practice or theory undermines the credibility of praxis. Because it is the practical side that tends to be given priority, and because the very term tends to invite this association, the most evident danger to praxis lies in this direction. Paul van Buren offers a cogent comment on the inadequacy of the valuable recovery of the realization that Christian faith represents a way of walking when this neglects the importance of the conversation that takes place along the way.

> The relationship between our conversation and our walking, however, is more complex than can be captured by the pattern of theory and praxis, for we have matters to speak of which cannot be put into practice. Much of what we must discuss concerns others than ourselves, and even more has to do with one quite other than ourselves. One might stretch the terms and say that respect or even sheer wonder is the praxis of the former and prayer or silent adoration the praxis for the latter. Rather than force the model, it seems simpler to use another: Theology is related to Christian life as conversation is to walking.[34]

With the by now familiar caveat about the importance of distinguishing between praxis and practice, we may endorse this broader view of praxis that not only allows for, but insists on, taking into account the conversation that arises on the way. This acknowledges the importance of practice, the fact that our conversations are rooted in and provide endorsement for certain political and social arrangements, and also encourages a contrary suspicion that prevents this recognition from exercising monopolistic sway so that wider dimensions are lost in an absolutizing of the practical. This latter course would compromise the recovery of the living reality of faith made possible through the comprehensive approach of praxis.

The Context of Salvation

The insistence on the integration of theory and practice, and in particular the contention that right theory only emerges out of right practice, is not a new insight. It is as old as the platonic–biblical amalgam represented in Augustine's awareness that what is finally important in life is not what we know, but what we love, and that in the end what we know will be determined by what we love. What is new in the emphasis on praxis is the recognition of the way in which our loyalties and interests take definite shape in terms of particular social and political arrangements. It is not accidental that Latin American liberation theology reflects its liberal and neo-orthodox antecedents. Its originality is not theological, in the conventional sense. As we have seen, its claim is to represent a completely new way of doing theology. The novelty centers particularly on the factor of social awareness. This is the common thread that links theologians who endorse a relatively conservative theological stance and others whose orientation is liberal to the point of agnostic or even atheistic inclinations. The praxis approach to theology, thus, involves not only an emphasis on the importance of practical involvement but also an understanding of that involvement as being significantly shaped by social circumstances.

THE RECOGNITION OF THE SOCIAL

For all its insistence on reflecting the particular conditions of Latin America, the most distinctive feature of liberation theology is probably derived from outside sources in the form of sociological self-consciousness. The impact of social awareness has rendered traditional private versions of Christian faith suspect. Approaches that tend to think of Christian faith as a matter for the individual soul have become problematic in the wake of the awareness of our mutual involvement with one another, which has accompanied the rise of the social sciences.[35] The resulting social imperative, to employ Gregory Baum's term, entails the requirement to deprivatize the Christian message, to hear it in primarily public, rather than private terms. Its focus then is not what God has done for me but what God is doing in the world; not the assurance of my eternal destiny, but the proclaiming of liberty to the captives and good news to the poor.

What gives this social consciousness shape and force is the understanding that what is involved is not simply the fact that we are all mutually implicated with each other as individuals, but the more strictly social insight that this involvement takes on very definite structural form. Earlier theologians can be found advocating the importance of the social for Christian faith. Thus, John Wesley wrote: "When I say, [Christianity] is essentially a social religion, I mean not only that it cannot subsist so well, but that it cannot subsist at all, without society—without living and conversing with other men."[36] However, what Wesley means by society is very different from the connotations that have become associated with that term in recent times. "A careful exegesis of the contexts in which these expressions occur will show, I believe, that for Wesley, society is not an anthropological concept, but simply a convenient arrangement for the growth of the individual."[37] What is distinctive about the social consciousness that informs liberation theology is the contention that the inexorable social nature of our lives as human beings is contoured and compacted into particular political configurations that are equally unavoidable. "Every human act, even the most private, possesses not only a social content (because it transcends the individual) but a political content (because that transcending of the individual is always related to change or stability in society)."[38] This is why attempts to avoid political involvement in theology are illusory. To regard theology as apolitical, or above the confrontations of political interests, is tantamount to endorsing the prevailing political interests. "Dualism, in short, is a political ideology of 'law and order' and the status quo."[39] Far from representing a neutral position above the partisan interest of politics, any such attempt to avoid political involvement through some kind of separation tactic really amounts to a tacit endorsement of the prevailing political arrangements and a covert blessing of those who benefit most from those arrangements.

If we compare this situation to the kind of social analysis pursued in North American universities, it will soon become apparent that we are not dealing here simply with an application of social self-consciousness to theology. The social analysis involved is of a very definite kind. Where the dominant trend in social studies in most North American universities reflects an attempt to emulate the nineteenth century ideal for the natural sciences, so that different societies and different groups within society are analyzed in a supposedly detached and objective manner, the type of analysis assumed by liberation theology insists on the unavoidability of involvement. The difference is, of course, due to the fact that the model that is emulated by liberation theologians is not the model of the more academically inclined pioneers of sociology, but of the passionate revolutionary, Karl Marx, "The Latin American theologians have opted for a conflictual sociology model, making use of a Marxist-style class analysis, which brings to light not the stability but the contradictions present in the social order and orients the imagination toward the transformation of the present society."[40] Without Marx, there could be no liberation theology.

The claim of most liberation theologians is that they draw on Marx as a social analyst, and not for strictly theological, or even philosophical insights. Dom Helder Camara spoke for many when he said: "I think we can avail ourselves of the Marxist method of analysis, which is still valid, leaving aside the materialist conception of life."[41] It is not his atheism, or his materialism, which is admired, but his recognition of the importance of social arrangements, and particularly of economic arrangements, for the shaping of human life. In particular, the doctrine that is found to be most significant is his insistence on the fundamental importance of divisions of class. There are oppressors and oppressed, rich and poor, owners and workers, and these groups are not distinguished by degrees but by a fundamental gulf.[42] This is what makes structures so significant.

> There is no evidence that the Pharaoh was not a "good man" with streaks of compassion. But he was the Pharaoh responsible for an economy that would collapse without slave labour.[43]

As liberation theologians see it that is also profoundly true of the situation in Latin America. This is what makes Marx's analysis so relevant. Life is shaped by the unrelenting and ever widening chasm between the multinational corporations and the local elites who manage and supply their operations, on the one hand, and the masses of landless peasants and marginalized workers, on the other. What Marx shows is that in continuing to proclaim what it regards as an apolitical gospel of salvation in this situation, the Church is really condoning that arrangement, and thus, in effect, assuring its perpetuation. This means that the Church is siding with those who benefit from this arrangement, the local elites and the foreign commercial interests. Once this illusion of neutrality has been pierced, the Church must decide whether it will continue to bless this inequity, or to shift its allegiance to the victims of the system. For liberation theologians, the Bible leaves no room for ambiguity about the course mandated for the Church in both its Old Testament background and in the basic thrust of the gospel. Through Israel and in Christ, God demonstrates particular concern for the poor and oppressed. This bias for the poor sets the mandate for the Church today in Latin America.

This adoption of Marxist analysis results in giving Christian faith and theology a very different orientation from its more traditional formats. The enthusiasm for this new direction sometimes encourages condescending caricature of the more traditional ways. "One does not directly announce salvation to a person whose only need to find fulfillment is a little bit of the 'holy'."[44] Yet, whereas it would not be easy to find seekers of salvation who would be satisfied with the conviction that they had come to possess "a little bit of the 'holy'," the concern with holiness can never again neglect the context of its seeking, once the importance of that context has been identified as it is by liberation theology. "Today the announcement of salvation passes through the class struggle."[45] The material context of faith and theology is of theological import: "Theologians must eat before they do theology. They see the world through the eyes of those who guarantee them their daily bread."[46] This awareness of the importance of the ways in which our society is arranged for our fundamental understanding of life has been described as "the basic sociological insight."[47] Because liberation theology generally follows the Marxist analysis of social arrangements, centering on the view that society is constituted fundamentally by class structures, it follows, as Jose Miguez Bonino says, that the only way really to be for the poor is to identify them and seek their welfare as a class.[48] Otherwise, concern for the poor is merely sentimentality. The pivotal importance of class structures means that a gospel that proclaims good news to the poor and deliverance to the captives must challenge these structures that are seen to underlie poverty and oppression. It is in such terms that the social context has come to dominate the liberation theology of Latin America.

THE TRIUMPH OF THE SOCIAL

The recognition of the importance of social circumstances, which animates liberation theology, renders any future isolationist pursuit of theology impossible. Theological affirmations have social origins and implications, the neglect of which leaves theology performing the function of unwitting endorsement of particular social arrangements. This recognition, however, is inclined to elicit even stronger claims regarding the significance of the social dimension whereby it is seen to represent not only an inescapable element in any human perspective, but also itself to constitute the horizon and substance of any and every perspective. The realization that our social situation is a constant factor in our living and understanding becomes so absorbing for some that rather than representing one of the indispensible lenses through which we reach out to the world around us society itself comes to be equated with that world. Social reality is reality.

The progression is evident, for instance, in the writings of Leonardo Boff. At times he simply requires acknowledgement of the importance of their social circumstances on the part of theologians. "Unless it is to evaporate in metaphors and euphemisms, a theology of liberation requires of theologians a clear definition and consciousness of their social locus."[49] But within the same writing, he can also promote what appears to be a much stronger endorsement of the determinative significance of the social. "The critical point seems to me to reside mostly in the first moment, that of the socio–analytic interpretation of historico–social reality, and less in the second and third (theology and pastoral action)."[50] Not only is consideration of the social situation important, but also theology and pastoral action take second and third place in relation to such consideration. This order of priorlties is stipulated even more bluntly by Hugo Assmann:

> The theology of liberation sees itself as critical reflection on present historical practice in all its intensity and complexity. Its "text" is our situation, and our situation is our primary and basic reference point. The others—the Bible, tradition, the magisterium or teaching authority of the Church, history of dogma, and so on—even though they need to be worked out in contemporary practice, do not constitute a primary source of "truth in itself" unconnected with the historical "now" of truth-in-action.[51]

This, too, is subject to a weaker or stronger reading. It can be taken to be advocating a praxis approach to Christian faith along the lines of the inclusive understanding of praxis as an on-going dialectic of practice and theoretical reflection. Such a reading is suggested by Luis G. del Valle:

> Theology, then, is to be fully included under the historical sciences and subordinated to the social sciences that analyze the facts of collective human life . . . It will be an "evangelical" rereading of politics as a liberation praxis, and a "political" rereading of the gospel.[52]

Here, the shock of the contention that theology is to be subordinated to the social sciences is mitigated somewhat by the explanation that this means that the social sciences are to be used to facilitate an evangelical reading of politics so that the political significance of the gospel is recognized. This can be regarded as a comprehensive praxis approach to Christian faith. But Assmann's recourse to the social sciences does not seem to be subject to any such qualification. His intention seems to be to endorse the stronger reading regarding the role of the social sciences for theology.

> The theology of liberation takes a decisive step in the direction of the secular sciences by admitting that the fact of human experience, on which the secular sciences have the first word to say, is its basic point of reference, its contextual starting-point. One might say that, by defining itself as critical reflection based on the inner meaning of the process of liberation, the theology of liberation can be seen not only as the "second act" after the "first act" of action, but the "second word" after the "first word" of the secular sciences—which is not to be understood as presuming to be the "last word".[53]

It is not just that the social sciences provide the means for recognizing the social implications of the gospel in the contemporary situation; they provide the fundamental basis for defining reality itself. Reality is what the social sciences say it is, including theological reality. Bonino sums up the situation when he avers that "the sciences dealing with historical life—sociology, politics, the sciences of culture—have more and more provided the categories and articulations for theology."[54] It is one thing to be told that theology does not operate in a vacuum, that it develops in particular social and political circumstances, and that consequently these circumstances must be taken into account as an element of theology; it is another matter to be told that theology is about social and political circumstances. But that is the contention of prominent strands of liberation theology, and this is so much the case that one can understand how Michael Novak can conclude "liberation theologians have an old-fashioned dogmatic faith in social science, rather than in theology."[55]

We have seen something of the sources of this faith in social science. It stems particularly from the insistence on the ubiquity of social structures that entails, as its corollary, the recognition that in terms of social arrangements there is no neutral stance. We all occupy some social position and this affects our whole outlook on life. This leaves no room for compromise with any approach that does not take the social context with absolute seriousness. Thus, Jean Guichard criticizes the French bishops for exhibiting only a half-hearted acceptance of this in the text from Lourdes, "Pour une pratique chrétienne de la politique."[56] He complains that the bishops claim to be following Marx in seeing class struggle as the central dynamic of human life, but that they really lose the force of this by treating it as a structural, economic issue, failing to realize that this ongoing struggle also shapes the people involved. In this approach, they are really preserving a dualism of "heart" and "structures" so that there is assumed to be a space for private freedom, which is untouched by the structural situation, with the result that the structures themselves are not subject to total challenge. Inclinations of the heart seek to reform the structures, rather than recognizing their total formative power and the consequent need for their total transformation. The recourse to social science on the part of liberation theology is prompted by this abhorrence of dualism. Theology that deals with spiritual and private concerns is illusory. The spiritual and material concerns and the private and public concerns are inseparable. Approaches that think they are confining themselves to spiritual and/or private matters are unwittingly endorsing particular material conditions and public structures.

The unitary approach of liberation theology is clearly indicated by its prime mover, Gustavo Gutierrez, as interpreted by Rosemary Radford Ruether.

> Gustavo Gutierrez constantly reminds Christians of the First World that the subject of liberation theology is not theology, but liberation. Christ calls us to be about the task of liberation, not about the task of theology, unless that theology is a servant of liberation. There is no neutral theology, any more than there is a neutral sociology or psychology. Theology is either on the side of all by being on the side of the poor, or else it is on the side of the oppressors by using theology as a tool of alienation and oppression. This is why theology in Latin America is a serious matter, a life and death matter, and not simply an affair of academe.[57]

The tools of social science are used to pursue the unified course of praxis. Theology, then, is reflection on the process of liberation as the divine plan for creation. But here again we run into the difficulty encountered in considering the meaning of praxis. From within the process, how do we know what liberation means? Just as praxis was seen to require the direction provided by people who could transcend the immediate situation, so the vision attained by such people will determine what liberation is taken to entail. For some, like Gutierrez, this will involve the mysterious connotations familiar to Christian tradition, along with the attempt to work out the import of these connotations in the total circumstances of life. For others, the understanding of liberation tends to suggest a less holistic horizon. Thus, for example, while Bonino pays passing tribute to accepted Christian notions of salvation, he interprets this in such a way that he can be seen to be advocating a new dualism rather than offering support for the unified approach that liberation theology is supposed to be pursuing. "The church is itself when it witnesses to God's saving activity in Jesus Christ, that is, when it makes clear God's renewed authorization, commandment, and liberation to man to be human, to create his own history and culture, to love and to transform the world, to claim and exercise the glorious freedom of the children of God."[58] Such statements raise the question as to whether the unity of the spiritual and the material, the private and the public, which constitutes one of the main motivating factors for liberation theology, is not here being compromised by the reintroduction of dualism in the contrast between God's reclaiming of humanity in Christ and an assumption that humanity is characterized by a fundamental autonomy. Bonino seems to equate the two, seeing modern secular autonomy as the substance of God's endorsement of humanity in Christ. "We move totally and solely in the area of human rationality—in the realm where God has invited man to be *on his own*."[59] The problem is that if there is a realm "where God has invited man to be *on his own*," we are back into dualism. The holistic approach for which spiritual sensitivity is materially incarnate, and private concerns arise out of and find expression in public structures, is seriously compromised, if there is a realm where God is not involved. From the point of view of liberation theology, which places such a premium on human history, this is particularly devastating because that is precisely the area in question.

The reason for dualism slipping in through the back door, when it has been ejected out of the front, may lie in the nature of that ejection. For the most ardent advocates of the socialization of theology reject not only dualism, but duality, not just the divorce between spiritual and material but any distinction between them, not just the separation of public and private but any acknowledgement of difference. Material circumstances and public structures are accorded such determinative significance that spiritual reality and private interests are regarded as totally derivative, if not completely inconsequential. It should not be surprising that any tendency toward such a monolithic perspective would result in fostering a surreptitious dualism necessitated by the complexity of life that such artificial uniformity suppresses. As André Dumas notes, it is always dubious to baptize structures instead of persons.[60] But that is what is involved in much of the socialization of theology. One of the leading advocates of the social direction in Canada, Gregory Baum, notes, for example, how Catholic social teaching has come to recognize that the problem with capitalism is not that the people who operate the system are greedy, but rather that the system itself produces the gulf between haves and have-nots. The evil results are due to the social arrangements of capitalism and not to the persons involved in its operations. "They occur whether the men who run these institutions be saints or sinners: the ill effects are built into the system."[61] Similarly, when the Canadian Catholic bishops in their Labour Day statement of 1975 criticized the way in which the north was being developed without consultation with its native population, contending that "the maximization of consumption, profit and power has become the operating principle of this society," Baum assures us that this critique is meant strictly in structural terms. "This is not a reference to the attitudes of the men in charge of these institutions; it refers rather to the operational logic associated with them."[62]

When the self-consciousness that leads us to recognize the formative significance of the social arrangements by which we live is absolutized to the point where those arrangements absolve the persons within them of all responsibility for their own commitments and actions, we must wonder about the accomplishment of the exposure of the naive acceptance of dualism. Although that acceptance might entail our unwitting endorsement of formative social structures, if the recognition of the significance of those structures results in the demise of the personal, both in terms of spiritual sensitivity and of our own significance as individuals, we must wonder about the benefits of this development. We would seem to be embarked on a sociological equivalent of the technological pursuit of cybernation.

Mechanical systems sufficiently elaborate and autonomous to be called robot-like have already been made with any number of "fail- safe" devices built into them. But it should not be necessary to point out that the most elaborate system of such safeguards merely underlines the fact that men are trying to resign choice to a machine.[63]

In terms of social arrangements themselves, the goal would seem to be the one T. S. Eliot warned of when he pictured people "dreaming of systems so perfect that no one would need to be good."[64] From the spiritual point of view, the fascination with social systems merits Tennyson's reminder:

> Our little systems have their day;
> They have their day and cease to be;
> They are but broken lights of thee,
> And thou, O Lord, art more than they.[65]

Insofar as the more of God is compromised in the fascination with the significance of social arrangements, then rather than simply reflecting a medium of divinity, "broken lights of thee," these arrangements themselves take on the aura of divinity.

The result of this enthusiasm over social self-consciousness thus reaches beyond the requirement for the qualification of theological affirmations by consideration of social circumstances to a displacement of theology as such by sociology. Of course, advocates of this direction are not so blunt about their proposals. When they deal with the issue explicitly, they are much more inclined to portray the sociological enterprise in modest terms. Thus Robin Gill suggests that the sociology of religion really only operates on an "as if" basis:

> The sociologist is committed to an "as if" methodology: in the specific instance of religion he is committed to the methodological assumption that there are sociological determinants of all religious phenomena, even if he is at present unable to specify all of these determinants with accuracy. This is not an imperialistic claim for the sociological perspective: it is guarded against positivism or social determinism precisely because it is an "as if" methodology. It is the sociologist's role to apply social explanations to religious phenomena quite relentlessly— and *not* psychological, or even theological, explanations. This method does not deny, though, that the latter may still be relevant to religion.[66]

On this reading, the largess of sociologists makes them willing to allow that there might be some relevance to theological explanations of religious phenomena, but for their own part they must operate "as if" these phenomena were completely determined by social circumstances. There are at least two fundamental deficiencies in this account of how sociology treats religion. In the first place, it fails to recognize the inherent duplicity of the "as if" approach. Michael Polanyi has identified this duplicity with regard to the approach's most famous modern exponent, Immanual Kant. Polanyi argues that the professed tentativeness really masks a tacit assumption of the truth of the operational premises at stake. In evidence, he notes that we would never used hypotheses we believed to be false or a policy we believed to be wrong.[67] The "as if" approach is simply a way of deception, perhaps usually self-deception, so that its exponents should be suspected of naïveté rather than of deliberate deviousness. They are fooling themselves in thinking that they do not really believe the position they are embracing for academic purposes.

The second deficiency in this account of how sociology treats religion confirms the truth of this first one, which is that as a matter of fact the pioneers of sociology did not simply approach religion "as if" it were subject to sociological explanation; they really believed this to be the case. "It is notable that the best minds in the social sciences by the third decade of the twentieth century were deeply alienated from the Western religious tradition."[68] This should not be surprising, given the negative attitude to any theological explanation of religion that characterized sociology from its inception. What is surprising is that people of theological sensitivity, such as Gregory Baum, do not find this particularly significant. "While Durkheim was an atheist and Weber an agnostic, their method, even though scientific, led to an appreciation of the role of religion in the making of society that was remarkable indeed and remains to this day the starting point of any sociology of religion."[69] We are being directed to find insight into the significance of religion from a discipline that traces its origins to an atheist and an agnostic. Our amazement at this is not due to any prejudice against atheists and agnostics as possible sources of wisdom, but to the equanimity with which a discipline with this pedigree can be presented as virtually eclipsing the established disciplines of theology. This amazement may be mitigated somewhat, however, if we notice that the point of focus is not really religion but society. What is at stake is "the role of religion in the making of society." Religion exists to serve society, rather than society being regarded as an expression of religion.

This inversion of society and religion testifies to the triumph of the social in the whole *Weltanschauung* of recent years, and not simply in theology, much less simply in liberation theology and its immediate counterparts. Social self-consciousness has attained such proportions that it readily slips from the position of qualifying factor where we are prompted to take our social circumstances into account to a focal point of attention until it ultimately arrives at a status of obviousness from which it reigns with the anonymity of the assumed. Insofar as this point has been reached, sociology displaces theology, society becomes the new name for God. Failure to recognize this is only possible because of deceptive devices of the "as if" variety. On the illusion that sociology is engaged in exploring only the immediate sphere of social arrangements, merely treating these "as if" they were exhaustive of truth and reality, it can appear that the big questions are left open. The reality, however, is, as Baum acknowledges, that sociology "presupposes the possibility of universal human communication and hence inevitably edges towards metaphysics."[70] Indeed, the sociological insight that there is no social or political neutrality, that we always see life from some particular vantage point where our own loyalties and interests are at stake, has its theological counterpart. There is no theological neutrality either, because we always have some sense of the whole, which sustains and guides our living and probing. This is the reason why the "as if" approach is illusory. We never merely deal with an immediate area only, or treat any approach seriously in merely an "as if" fashion. For the moment at least, we take that approach as true and final. But once this is recognized, it is difficult to see how there can be any stopping, short of a renewed acknowledgement of the significance of religion in its own right, an abandonment of what Robert Bellah has called the "symbolic reductionism" that tries to explain religion in other terms, such as those of sociology, and an embracing of what he calls "symbolic realism," an approach to religion that acknowledges its own integrity and in which the investigator is prepared to find her or himself significantly challenged and affected.[71] Signs of the need for treating religion with such respect are at hand, but they still represent a minority report in the atmosphere of the triumph of the social.

THE TYRANNY OF THE SOCIAL

The triumph of the social has obvious repercussions for academics in that practitioners of the social sciences and those in other fields who are willing to acknowledge their hegemony can expect to enjoy more favorable professional treatment in this prevailing atmosphere than those who are constrained to question this conventional wisdom. Beyond the walls of academia, the dominance of the social perspective translates into according particular attention to the pursuit of justice.

> Society raises questions of culture, methodology, politics, but its deepest issue is justice. So, as sociology has had impact, justice has come more to the theological fore.[72]

As a depiction of the main direction taken by liberation theology, this description could hardly be improved on. The most characteristic contention of the liberation approach in this regard is that the standard Christian emphasis on the love of God and its availability to all regardless of status or circumstances has served to deflect attention from situations that really represent conditions of injustice. Hugo Assmann states the central thesis with uncharacteristic mildness:

> Love tends toward reconciliation, dialogue, unity: this is basic to the Christian viewpoint. But can "love" be the idea of peace at any price? Has this in fact been the Christian position in practice? In many ways it would seem that it has.[73]

The demand for justice cuts through the "peace at any price" masquerade, which follows from the blanket embrace of the message of universal love.

What gives this focus on justice particular poignancy is the claim that it is an articulation of the cries of the victims of injustice themselves. "Liberation theologies are theologies *of* the oppressed, *by* the oppressed, and *for* the oppressed."[74] We have seen reason to question the accuracy of the middle preposition. Marx needed his vanguard to incite the proletariat, Friere acknowledges the importance of revolutionary leaders, the leaders of Latin American liberation movements are middle-class intellectuals rather than oppressed peasants, and feminists recognize the need for consciousness-raising to convince women of their true situation. Thus, liberation movements can hardly be regarded as popular mass eruptions of the oppressed. They require the stimulus of self-consciousness available to the detached perspective of intellectuals. The aim, however, is to enable the oppressed to speak for themselves. This is one of the pivotal differences between liberation theology and its recent ancestor, the social gospel movement. That earlier movement was essentially a middle-class attempt to help those in need. Its motivation and rationale centered in charity. The liberation approach, by contrast, in spite of its middle-class leadership, intends to animate the disadvantaged to assert their own claims. Its motivation and rationale centers in justice. In some cases, the demand for the justice it promotes is strident to the point of belligerence: "As the Reverend Canaan Banana, of the Zimbabwe African National Council has put it, in his version of the Lord's Prayer, 'Teach us to demand Our share of the gold, Forgive us our docility, As we demand our share of justice.'"[75] The aim of liberation movements—to enable people to recognize their own oppression and to empower them to seek to transform the social structures that institutionalize their condition—is understood primarily as the cultivation of a demand for justice. The oppressed are not in need of charity from their oppressors. They are entitled to some of the wealth, status, and power that the oppressors have arrogated to themselves. They are owed justice.

In its espousal of justice, liberation theology elicits an automatic empathy, which casts anyone who would presume to question this approach in the role of champion of injustice. However, this uninvited appellation must be risked, unless liberation theology is to be treated with a reverence that most of its practitioners insist no theology deserves. If we take this risk and subject the liberation approach to critical scrutiny, certain fundamental questions arise with regard to this emphasis on justice. One immediate problem is an apparent contradiction over what is the determinative feature of human history.

> On the one hand, it says that history is class struggle. On the other hand, it says that justice ought to prevail. But if the last is true, then the main interpretative key to history is not oppression but justice, not struggle but reconciliation.[76]

One solution to this dilemma is to distinguish between the situation that prevails and the situation that is desired, between what is and what ought to be. We live in a world characterized by division between oppressors and oppressed, but this is not the ideal situation; ideally there should be justice for all. The difficulty with this obvious solution is that it would not be obvious from the strict liberation perspective itself. That perspective is very impressed with Marx's claim to be operating "scientifically." It adopts his social analysis because this is regarded as the most accurate description of the way things are. However, the more confidence is invested in this description, the less scope there is for acknowledging any genuine alternative. If the division between oppressor and oppressed is the principal fact of life, then justice will involve the elimination of that division. Some such negative understanding of justice is all that can be attained on this descriptive base. If justice is seen to have a more positive meaning, this will only be possible on the basis of some wider vision about what life could or should be. In this, we are confronted once again with the difficulty in the approach of praxis. The tendency to equate praxis with practice corresponds to the claim to be operating essentially, if not exclusively, in terms of the reality at hand, whereas the more comprehensive sense of praxis that allows scope for some element of detachment and the alternative vision that that makes possible has its counterpart in the openness to some moral, or even religious, vision of what might or ought to be. The difference is that here we are dealing more directly with the substance of the liberation vision, whereas in considering praxis the focus was essentially confined to more fundamentally epistemological questions. In this regard, what we seem to be coming to is the recognition that if liberation theology is seriously concerned with justice, it will have to develop its positive vision rather than relying on a negative characterization of justice as referring to what is not the case in the division between oppressor and oppressed.

This requirement for a more substantial account of justice represents one of the points of greatest vulnerability for the critic of liberation theology. For it is almost guaranteed to evoke a liberation equivalent of Marx's eleventh thesis on Feuerbach in the form of a charge that this interest in the meaning of justice is a middle-class academic way of avoiding engagement with the reality of injustice, which is only too apparent all around us. What makes this charge particularly difficult is that in one sense it is unanswerable. To ponder the nature of justice is not to do justly. But then liberation theology is itself, at best, an advocate of doing justly and not the action itself either. Gustavo Gutierrez has stated in the concluding words of his seminal *A Theology of Liberation*, that all political and liberation theologies "are not worth one act of faith, love, and hope, committed—in one way or another—in active participation to liberate man from everything that dehumanizes him and prevents him from living according to the will of the Father."[77]

This recognition that liberation theology itself is involved in seeking to understand the need and possibility for promoting justice, rather than directly practicing justice itself, can help alleviate some of the intimidation entailed in contending that the nature of justice itself must be clarified. However, the main justification for this concern lies in the conviction that not only is a merely negative view of justice inadequate but also that any view of justice that does not entail the acknowledgement of a wider context by which justice is defined and motivated is bound to be inadequate. If liberation theology amounts to a program for animating the dispossessed to demand their just deserts, this is understandable in light of the injustice of this dispossession, but what shape justice would take and why it is theological are not so clear. Liberation theologians tend to be evasive when it comes to positive proposals as to what a just society might look like. One of the leading North American critics of liberation theology charges that "it refuses to describe the institutions of human rights, economic development, and personal liberties that will be put in place *after* the revolution."[78]

This reticence on the part of liberation theologians may be more indicative of wisdom than of culpability, for the delineation of structures of justice is no simple operation.

> Since the time that a mature agriculture made city life possible, human beings have shown themselves unable to manage society. Their signal failure has been to create a politically effective religious vision of justice.[79]

Yet, if liberation theologians cannot be expected to devise blueprints for the just society, they surely can be expected to account for the elevation of justice to the zenith of theological virtues. This is especially so because in the Judeo–Christian tradition, justice, though important, is only one of the central concerns of God. It is particularly prominent in the prophets, and it is not accidental that liberation theology finds particular affinity with the tradition of the prophets. However, even in the prophets the demand for justice is not usually far removed from the proclamation of the divine *chesed*, mercy. "The prophets, Hosea the first of them and next to him Jeremiah, knew that if it had not been for God's *chesed*, the story of God's people would have ceased before it had begun."[80]

On its own, the passion for justice is as dangerous as it is understandable. As the central or sole preoccupation, the drive for justice is virtually destined to degenerate into moralism, if not full blown self-righteousness, and when it is focused on the demand for fundamental structural change the net result can be a tyranny, which is even worse than the injustice from which deliverance was sought. Peter Hinchliff notes the danger posed by people who become so absorbed by the rightness of their cause that they forget their own limitations, suggesting that it "makes me suspicious of anyone—of the left, right, or center—who is absolutely certain that there is only one political goal and only one way to reach it."[81] Without a broader base, justice is a very precarious ideal.

The precariousness of justice on its own is both motivational and theological. Even where justice functions as an absorbing obsession, it derives from some wider source. This source might reside in the appalling conditions that are recognized as manifestly unjust. This would seem to be the case with Marx himself. However, this is also the reason why Marx can provide no rationale for his position. The injustice is obvious. Concern with rationale is culpable. The only adequate response is revolt. It would be understandable if theologians in Latin America should take a similar approach in their circumstances. Their impatience with the preoccupation with rationale on the part of mainline theology is also understandable. However, the wisdom of the Judeo–Christian tradition suggests that unless there is a wider basis for the pursuit of justice the result is apt to be, as the history of Marxism shows, renewed tyranny, or as recent expressions of idealism in Western society indicate, a dissipation of dedication in the face of discouragement. Long term dedication to justice is feasible and realistic only when it is sustained by a broader base such as the Judeo–Christian tradition has affirmed in its proclamation of the unmerited graciousness of God.

> Our idea of justice may be the achievement of equity, like treatment for everyone, fairness in all things. This is good as far as it goes, but God goes beyond this. In his strange mercy he loves and saves the undeserving as well as those who come closer to the mark.[82]

Such universalism is particularly suspect to the liberation perspective. Talk of divine care for all, particularly the undeserving, is so easily glossed into an endorsement of the status quo with all its injustice. And yet, to react to this by giving the demand for justice priority is open to the difficulty just considered. "Liberation theology can learn from the wisdom of Augustine, who saw that without justice there can be no society but that without piety there can be no justice."[83] One of the central challenges for liberation theology is undoubtedly this requirement to integrate the centrality of the demand for justice into a framework of piety, which, to this point, tends to occupy a somewhat random and disconnected domain in most liberation writings. Unless and until this is more firmly effected, liberation theology runs the risk of compromising its theological roots in what would amount to not only an acquiescence in the triumph of the social but also to a tyranny of the social.

The Content of Salvation

The long range prospects for the new way of doing theology represented by the liberation approach will depend on its development of praxis as a comprehensive union of practice and theory that does justice to each dimension and on its articulation of a politically challenging understanding of the Christian faith that does not surrender theological affirmation to the horizon of social self-consciousness. No aspect of this articulation will be more central than its understanding of salvation. Liberation is generally used as a synonym for salvation. The issue is whether the social and political focus of liberation manages to preserve the transcendent scope of salvation so that the terms are essentially synonymous, or whether the gain of structural reference is achieved at the expense of something vital to the older term.

THE DIRECTION OF SOCIAL SALVATION

For liberation theologians, there is a naturalness involved in substituting the term *liberation* for the more traditional *salvation*. Thus Bonino affirms: "Using 'liberation' as a transcription of the biblical concepts, which the theological tradition has usually rendered by 'salvation' or 'redemption,' is not new and should not be startling."[84] Emphasis on the normalcy of this substitution can prove counterproductive, however, because the other side of such emphasis is the implication that liberation theology then does not represent any particular originality in its approach to Christian faith. Liberationists themselves, of course, would not accede to this. Bonino himself goes on to identify what he finds lacking in conventional approaches. "Traditional Protestant theology—and much Roman Catholic post-Vatican II thought, which forms a parallel line—is so concerned with the prevention of any 'sacrilizing of human projects and ideologies' that it seems to some of us to result in emptying human action of all theological meaning."[85] The shift from salvation to liberation is meant to signal a restoration of theological meaning to human action. But this distinctive emphasis of liberation is precisely what leads some to question the equation of liberation with salvation. "The kind of salvation liberation theol-

ogy lifts up generally is something Athens could in principle discover without the help of Jerusalem, something Marx in fact called
for without reference to Jesus, something which will come about
through human praxis without any necessary dependence on God's
act in Christ."[86] The human relevance of liberation, it is claimed,
displaces the divine dimension of salvation so that the theological
meaning recedes before the preoccupation with the human action
in and of itself.

One of the most vivid aspects of the difference represented by
the liberation approach concerns the way in which the mission of
the Church is understood. For the liberation perspective, the
Church compromised its mandate as a sign of salvation by setting
itself apart as an institution of salvation. "Instead of being a sign
pointing to salvation, the Church became a place where salvation
was to be sought, where it was guaranteed, from where it was dispensed: 'outside the Church there is no salvation'."[87] This custo-
dianship of salvation transforms the self-understanding and role of
the Church from that of servant to master, from vehicle of the gospel to definer and imposer of the gospel. This insight is not peculiar to liberation theologians. Thus, Leonard Hodgeson proposes
that the lesson that God is attempting to get through to the Church
in the twentieth century is that "it is redeemed in order that it may
give itself to the service of mankind in the name of God."[88] There
are differences over how and why the Church failed to recognize
this mandate and pursue it. Hodgeson identifies the failure with
the missed opportunity of the establishment status toward which
the Church was destined through the embrace of Constantine. As
he sees it, the Edict of Milan "was God's call to the Church to realize its vocation to be instrument as well as object."[89] For Douglas
Hall, on the other hand, the Constantinian settlement marks the
point of embarkation on the full scale abandonment of the
Church's mandate to serve.[90] This scope for difference to the point
of contradiction over the source of the Church's deviance from its
appointed path is not paralleled when it comes to understanding
what the Church's mandate should be. Hodgeson and Hall are in
basic agreement that that mandate is essentially one of service. In
this, they are in line with the fundamental direction of liberation
ecclesiology, as testified to in Gutierrez's admonition that the
Church must stop regarding itself as the exclusive place of salvation and instead come to see its mission in terms of a radical service of people.[91] In promoting itself, the Church is taking exactly
the opposite direction to that of its lord. The only way in which it
can be true to him is to follow him in service to those in need.

The apparent unassailability of the logic of this parallelism is breached somewhat with the recognition that Jesus worshipped as well as served. Although he identified with the poor and the outcast, he also withdrew from "society" and made it a practice to be in attendance at the temple. This recognition of the dimension of worship discloses complexities in this insistence that the Church's mandate is to serve humanity, which make a straightforward equation of the Church's *raison d'être* with human service problematic at least for some. "There are, of course, many nuances among these new soteriological theories, ranging from a balanced integration of love of God and love of one's neighbour to an undialectical identification in which 'God' seems to be no more than a cipher for the claims made on one's conscience by one's neighbour."[92] Thus, Hugo Assmann challenges even the distinction between verticalism and horizontalism.[93] Acknowledgement of God and service of others are one and the same. It is in the immersion in history, particularly in the attempt to transform history toward liberation that we encounter the mystery of God.[94] As we have seen, one of the most characteristic features of liberation theology is such abhorrence of dualism and insistence on unity. Once again, Gutierrez captures the essence of the matter:

> It seems clear today that the purpose of the Church is not to save in the sense of "guaranteeing heaven." The work of salvation is a reality which occurs in history. This work gives to the historical becoming of mankind its profound unity and its deepest meaning. It is only by starting from this unity and meaning that we can establish the distinctions and clarifications which can lead us to a new understanding of the mission of the church.[95]

These requisite distinctions and clarifications center on the relation between vertical and horizontal dimensions. It is simply too strong to suggest that the liberation approach amounts to a rejection of the distinction between vertical and horizontal dimensions.[96] The suspicion that this is the case is what leads critics to complain: "The unitary view of history which most liberation theologians espouse is too one-dimensional."[97] The emphasis on history and the human project can, thus, be seen to displace all real theological points of reference. Consequently, if the unified approach that liberation theology advocates is to avoid this counter-charge of achieving unity at the expense of the divine dimension, it will have to develop this insistence on unity in such a way that the divine as well as the human element is seen to be acknowledged. Just as the unity of praxis must encompass practice and theory, so the unified understanding of salvation must involve engagement in the promotion of liberation, which not only sees this as engagement with God but, at the same time, recognizes that God also transcends this engagement. To articulate a unified understanding of salvation that acknowledges the duality of God and ourselves without allowing this to dissolve into a dualism where salvation again becomes spiritualized and privatized is a tall order. But the alternative is to press the concern with unity to the detriment of all recognition of diversity, and then there would not seem to be much point in continuing to talk of salvation at all.

THE MEANS OF SOCIAL SALVATION

Insofar as Christian faith has had a praxis orientation in preliberation theology, one of the traditional foci of action–reflection, which appears to be threatened by the liberation approach, is the insistence on the divine initiative in salvation. The most direct instance of this is probably the version articulated by Paul, developed by Augustine, and recovered by Luther, in the doctrine of justification by grace through faith. The core of this doctrine is the contention that our salvation, like our creation, is a gift of God rather than anything we can accomplish by our own efforts. Dennis McCann contends that the question of how liberation, which is "a gift of God" can also be said to be "won in a struggle," is "the major difficulty in correlating the themes of 'salvation' and 'liberation.'"[98] The blatant emphasis on what must be done, on the necessity for engaging in the struggle for liberation, tends to convey an impression of the abandonment of the whole notion of grace and a straightforward advocacy of salvation by our own works, tempered, to be sure, by the refinements of modern social consciousness. "'Liberation', their word for 'salvation', is certainly the work of God active in history; but we, in an almost Pelagian way, bring it into effect by our deeds and sacrifices."[99] This impression is virtually the inevitable one for most Protestants and post-Vatican II Catholics who look at liberation theology from the outside.

From the vantage point of first world theologians, it is possible to appreciate something of the frustrations that lead liberation theologians in this direction. The traditional emphasis on divine initiative and on our complete reliance on divine grace can produce a quietism that depreciates human effort in either a *Deus ex machina* view of God or a mystical separation of spiritual salvation from the

ongoing involvements of life. As we have seen, liberation theologians insist on the unity of life. Salvation is a concrete reality,
pervading the structures and commitments by which we live. If
this does not happen deliberately, it will happen by default. A
purely spiritual salvation is an unwitting endorsement of the material status quo. Thus, although salvation is by grace through faith,
it does not happen without our deliberate efforts. Salvation is not
a divine seal of approval, guaranteeing our personal acceptability
to God. Salvation is God's encouragement of the acceptance of the
least accepted, the poor, the oppressed, those who are marginalized in any way. Thus, as Clodovis Boff contends, salvation is the
means of liberation.[100] The emergence of liberation is a barometer
of the reality of salvation.

The presentation of liberation as the manifestation of salvation
could be seen as an updating, from the point of view of modern
social consciousness, of the contention of the letter of James that
faith without works is dead. This is perhaps the most fruitful way
of reading the summation of Ch. Duquoc:

> Christian salvation does not offer a myth of liberation. It offers a fu-
> ture, provides a meeting place with the Absolute, yet leaves to man the
> discovery of the definition of the means for freeing himself.[101]

Rather than a story of something God did in the past, such as rescuing the Hebrews from slavery in Egypt or vindicating Jesus after
the defeat of the cross, liberation consists in the awareness that
God is doing similar things today. It is up to us to detect this and
to find ways of implementing that divine program. But just as
James' assumption that there could be faith without works paves
the way for the promotion of works without faith, so the emphasis
on the effecting of liberation can become detached from the base
in salvation. When Boff suggests that salvation is the means of
liberation, this can mean that liberation is the manifestation of
salvation, as we suggested, or it can mean that liberation is what
salvation is all about. For there is a world of difference between
these two understandings. As a manifestation of an ongoing divine
claim upon us, we may feel constrained to attempt the "discovery
of the definition of the means for freeing [ourselves]." However,
any tendency to isolate this attempt from the wider context of
divine claim and sponsorship leaves us with a contemporary social
version of the dilemma of James in its tendency to accord priority
to works and thereby compromise the faith context.

The danger of imbalance in the faith–works dialectic is a coun-

terpart on the practice side of praxis to the inadequacy of justice
from the theoretical side. Just as justice requires the broader sponsorship of caring and concern, so works must occur in the context
of faith in the divine embrace and directive, and continue to be renewed from that context. As a quid pro quo arrangement designed
to effect justice cannot produce the comprehensive concern, which
transcends such an arrangement, so attempts to effect human liberation cannot be expected to issue in divine salvation. As Clodovis
Boff has the priest say in the dialogue he constructs involving a
priest, an activist, and a theologian about liberation theology,
"Means have to be homogeneous with ends."[102] If liberation is a
political project that we are expected to devise on our own, there
will not be much point in talking of salvation as some wider horizon involving God. Indeed, insofar as liberation itself becomes
synonymous with salvation, any inclination even to recognize any
wider horizon tends to recede. This disappearance of any transcendent reference for salvation also renders any need for a savior redundant. As the activist in Boff's dialogue puts it: "The people, the
organized people, is its own liberator."[103] With this, Christian faith
has been significantly transformed, so much so that there must be
some question as to whether we are really any longer dealing with
Christian faith. The central concerns of people like Paul and
Augustine and Luther seem to be totally abandoned. It is not surprising that someone sympathetic to those concerns should conclude: "The emphasis is on the sanctification of the socially involved,
not the justification of the ungodly."[104]

If it would not appear condescending, the emphasis on the
effecting of liberation as the focus of salvation might be regarded
as a corrective to the quietism that has too often characterized
more traditional forms of Christian faith. But such a reading is
bound to strike that note for liberation theologians because it does
not allow for the total transformation of theology that this
approach professes to represent. Its concern is not to balance a
spiritualistic aspect of faith with a political emphasis on works, but
rather to revolutionize the understanding of faith itself so that it is
seen to entail works and to be entailed by them. At least in its
more substantial variations, such as in the writings of Gutierrez
himself, this holistic ideal is evident. Contrary to a direct and narrow promotion of some kind of pursuit of justice, he recognizes
that only gratuitous love provides an adequate basis for genuine
liberation. In this, he goes so far as to endorse Bonhoeffer's claim
that the only credible God is the God of the mystics.[105] The spiritualistic direction indicated by this reference is confirmed by his

book on spirituality, *We Drink From Our Own Wells: The Spiritual Journey of a People*,[106] and yet, this endorsement of spirituality is accompanied by an uncompromising insistence on the necessity that spirituality, if it is to claim the name Christian, must be incarnate. Clearly, it is not part of Gutierrez's intention to promote a program of works to balance a quietist faith. His aim and that of liberation theology at its best, is much more ambitious. It amounts to the effecting of a revolution in faith and theology so that a genuinely comprehensive praxis is developed in which the spiritual and the material constantly encounter one another in an ongoing process of salvation through which concrete liberation is effected for those most in need and through them for us all. The success of this attempted revolution remains to be seen. Its prospects may be surmised in terms of its alignment of liberation and salvation.

THE MEANING OF SOCIAL SALVATION

The comprehensive nature of the agenda for liberation theology was set by Gutierrez's designation of the three levels on which it was to be understood, in terms of: (a) the freeing of oppressed peoples and social classes; (b) an understanding of history as the self-conscious acceptance of responsibility for our own destiny on the part of human beings; and (c) the theological meaning deriving from the understanding of Christ as liberator.[107] The subtlety of Gutierrez's position has to do not only with the recognition of this scope in the meaning of liberation but also in particular with the way in which these three dimensions are seen to relate. They are seen to be mutually implicative, but distinct; different levels of the one salvation process.[108] Salvation is a comprehensive reality with political, historical and theological dimensions. It is distorted when any of these elements is neglected or overemphasized. Of course, such a comprehensive and balanced approach is much more easily stated as an ideal than pursued in practice.

In light of the particular interest of liberation theology in social and political arrangements, it is no surprise to find that Gutierrez is criticized himself for neglecting the last named dimension, theological liberation from sin.

It is true that Gutierrez emphasizes the deep-rooted and objectively-structured nature of sin, salvation from which is a *sine qua non* of any kind of liberation. Therefore we must accept, at least at the level of intention, the desire to integrate liberation from sin with political and other human liberations. Nevertheless, in his exposition of liberation

Gutierrez very rarely goes beyond the external liberation, summed up in the reconciliation of man with man through a new and just ordering of society's structures.[109]

One answer to this charge is that the paucity of explicit reference to the forgiveness of sin is due to the fact that it is taken for granted because it has been so dominant in Christian tradition. This is the defense offered by Robert McAfee Brown. "If the third level receives less quantitative treatment than the others, this is for the good reason that it has always been the central if not exclusive message of the institutional Church, hardly in need of new champions, whereas levels one and two have only infrequently been acknowledged as part of the Christian agenda."[110] This is further confirmed by the conservative theological tone of much liberation theology. It has been noted that Gutierrez himself assumes a basically orthodox Christology,[111] and also that liberation theologians generally tend to be conservative in biblical exegesis.[112] That the forgiveness of sin understanding of liberation was presupposed by liberation theologians from the start, rather than abandoned, is affirmed from within by Leonardo Boff.

Liberation from sin, from deviant interior attitudes, and the like, was simply presupposed as already belonging to the solid, sure treasury of Christian faith. It was not discussed. But silence was not denial. What was already known and received was not discussed. What was discussed, was this new vision: God's liberation is present within the historical liberation of human beings.[113]

We may take it as established then that in its origins liberation theology's attempt to revolutionize theology did not involve an abandonment of traditional understandings of salvation in the name of political liberation. The point rather was to try to understand and participate in the reality of that salvation in terms of the actual political situation in Latin America, which cried out for liberation. Failure to confront this reality was seen to render salvation as conventionally understood, abstract, and ideological.

The difficulty with this project is that it is dealing with a tension that is so basic that it seems inevitably to lead to dichotomy. The universal reference of theology and the particularity of historical circumstances represent such antithetical forces that one tends to dominate to the point of trivializing the other. Liberation theology complains that traditional treatments of salvation have failed to appreciate the importance of particular circumstances and the ways in which theological affirmations reflect those circumstances whether this is recognized or not. For its part, liberation theology is charged with becoming so fixated on historical circumstances that it ends up according them universal significance in an idolatrous foreclosure on the genuine universal scope of theology. The attempt to avoid this dilemma by endorsing a comprehensive approach, as advocated for example by Gutierrez, only illustrates and aggravates the dilemma, because insofar as the comprehensive nature of salvation is the focus, this deflects attention from the concrete requirements of liberation. This inherent pitfall in the comprehensive approach is highlighted by Leonardo Boff in his warning about the limitation of what he calls "integral liberation," his term for the comprehensive approach:

> It runs the risk of "dehistoricizing"—of evaporating in pure phraseology, in words without substance. Indeed it is easily susceptible of ideological utilization, precisely in virtue of its universalizing, vague nature. Whenever anyone points to historical liberations on the economic and political level, we hear at once: "Be careful; liberation is integral and involves spiritual liberation from sin."[114]

This concern with theological propriety remains one of the chief obstacles for liberation theology, even though some of its leading proponents recognize the legitimacy of that concern and also endorse it themselves. At the same time, frustration over the way in which that preoccupation can detract from confrontation with particular historic circumstances can result in a concentration on those circumstances, which renders recognition of integral liberation a token endorsement.

This inherent tension is implicit in Gutierrez's comprehensive portrayal of the scope of liberation. We have focused here on the first ingredient, the liberation of oppressed peoples and classes, because that is the most characteristic focus of Latin American liberation theology. However, promotion of that political and economic liberation is sustained by convictions deriving from the second and/or third dimensions of liberation. Which of these, or what combination of them, provides that motivation and rationale can result in very different understandings of what liberation really involves. At its starkest, the second and third levels of liberation can constitute antitheses rather than elements in a comprehensive whole. This happens when integral or comprehensive liberation is identified with the third level, the theological, and this is seen to be, in some way, complete in itself. This may be the main source of the frustration with integral liberation noted by Boff. On the other hand, whether in reaction against this frustration or via some more direct route, the second level of the historical project of liberation can also take on this comprehensive role. Indeed, it would seem that even in more balanced treatments, one or the other of these perspectives must ultimately prevail. Either there is an ultimate power before whom we are finally answerable or else life is ours to make of what we will. The contrast has been presented by Dennis P. McCann in terms of Gutierrez's more traditional endorsement of the former assumption and Freire's more secularized promotion of a Marxist making of history. "The tension between Gutierrez's epiphanic vision and Freire's dialectical vision is based on the fact that an orthodox understanding of the Incarnation simply cannot be reconciled with a dialectical interpretation of history."[115] Although the divine-human matrix is complex and difficult to articulate, if the divine is recognized, then, whatever the range and role of human freedom, it cannot have the last word.

This fundamental difference in basic perspective is illustrated by the contrast between Gutierrez and Freire, but it is also present in Gutierrez himself in a basic unresolved tension over the priorities intended between the second and third levels of liberation. J. Andrew Kirk is on target when he suggests that one of the fundamental difficulties in Gutierrez's position is "that he has not yet seen clearly the dilemma inherent in the championing of man as the free agent of his history."[116] His comprehensive account of liberation is pulled in opposite directions by a traditional theocentric perspective, which assumes that we live by the grace of God, and a contrary endorsement of the modern anthropocentric assumption that life is finally of our own making.

The incompatibility of these directions comes out more clearly in more direct endorsements of the making of history direction. Thus, Jon Sobrino suggests, from this point of view, that the traditional ways of understanding salvation must be abandoned, "not because of Christology's incomprehensibility, but because it is irrelevant to the transformation of a sinful world into a world according to the Kingdom of God."[117] We might venture to paraphrase this in line with Marx's eleventh thesis on Feuerbach in some such terms as the following: "Enough of this talk of our sinfulness, let's get on with building the kingdom." The most straightforward endorsements of the making of history approach are provided, of course, by exponents of versions of Marxism untainted by theological overtones.

> When the system has been overthrown and the means of production
> have been socialized, anarchy in social production is replaced by plan-
> ned and conscious organization. The struggle for individual existence
> disappears. For the first time, man in a certain sense, is finally marked
> off from the rest of the animal kingdom and emerges from animal to
> really human conditions of existence. The whole of life which condi-
> tions man, and which hitherto has ruled man, now comes under the
> domination and control of man. For the first time he becomes the real
> and conscious lord of nature because he has become master of his own
> social organization.[118]

The absolutization of humanity obviously leaves no room for acknowledgement of divine absoluteness. That is the problem faced
by any theology that embraces the making of history approach.

Put in these abstract terms, expression of concern about the absolute invites the charges of abstraction and ideological neglect of
historical circumstances. However, it should be clear from counter-
considerations of praxis and of the implications of the adoption
of the social horizon that the issue is not between abstraction and
practicality but between different versions of abstraction and practicality. A view that regards humanity as the pinnacle of reality is
no less abstract than one that acknowledges God, and each reflects
practical commitments and implications. This is where the directions endorsed by liberation theology become particularly acute.
The uncompromising anthropocentric vision of a human domination of nature must strike terror in the heart of anyone familiar
with the ecological crisis. The precarious state of the environment
is due especially to the domination of nature that we have
achieved. Thus, rather than the prospect of our control of society
foreshadowing our control of nature, the devastation of nature we
have effected carries ominous overtones for any prospect of our
controlling ourselves. For all its claims to be scientific and practical, the making of history approach must appear naive in light of
the realities of human history. Yet, perhaps this naivety is only
apparent from the perspective of a theological understanding of
salvation. The reemergence in recent years of strains of optimism
that enjoyed such prominence in the nineteenth century, despite
the disastrous history of the twentieth century, and the calamitous
prospects of the present, suggests that there is a particularly virulent strain of optimism resident in the human species. It may be
that we are inclined to challenge this only because of the influence
of a theological understanding of salvation, which sees the cross as
indicative of the reality of God. The corollary of this is the anthropological implication; that far from being competent builders of

utopia, we are so perverse that we attempt to slay the very source of life itself. This perspective renders purely anthropocentric visions of our making of history not only suspect but terrifying. Without the exposure to judgment and grace involved in the theological dimension of salvation, historical liberation holds the prospect of becoming total bondage, the self-absolutizing of self-assured fanatics. Kosuke Koyama indicates the qualification that must always accompany any Christian promotion of liberation. "I believe that the crusading mind is a Christian mind if it is guided by the crucified mind."[119] Without the theological discipline of the cross, the making of history is a frightening prospect.

Insofar as liberation theology entails a direct endorsement of anthropocentric history making, it sets itself on a collision course with theological understandings of salvation. But this must be counterbalanced by what we saw to be the legitimate concern of liberation theologians that theological understandings become abstract and ideological when they neglect the historical situation. The demands of these conflicting concerns are addressed by Schillebeeckx's two principles for aligning faith and politics. According to the "eschatological proviso" no political project is to be absolutized because it will always fall short of God's eschatological salvation. However, the "anthropological constants" of Christian faith require the overcoming of whatever enslaves humanity. "Christian faith contributes, then, both a critical impulse toward overcoming whatever enslaves people and the eschatological proviso which refuses to absolutize any movement to create a better world."[120] Another way of taking account of a concern for liberation without allowing it to displace the full scope of salvation is suggested by Leonardo Boff's proposals for relating salvation and liberation on the model of Chalcedon.

> Salvation and liberation are distinct; but they are united, without confusion and without separation. It is monophysitic to assert that there can be salvation without historical liberation; it is Nestorian to assert that there can be historical liberation without an openness to salvation.[121]

The challenge of liberation theology to the understanding of salvation centers in this recognition of the necessity for affirming both unity and duality in salvation. Salvation is one unified process. Difficulties emerge when separations are made between thought and practice, faith and works, spiritual and material. Salvation entails the organic interrelation of all these elements.

Yet at the same time, these elements must also be distinguished from one another, because when they are not, the fundamental difference between God and ourselves disappears and salvation becomes a social project. At this point, we have abandoned concern with the absolute and are on the way to absolutizing our own cause. Thus, social consciousness creates the requirement for salvation to take account of the way our lives are shaped and lived, but the novelty of this demand can exert a fascination in which the transcendent focus of salvation is lost in preoccupation with the social.

9

Personal Salvation

If some social variant is the one form of salvation that remains generally viable in the contemporary situation, it is equally clear that the understanding that is most suspect is the one that has come to dominate popular consciousness, the equation of salvation with the personal. Not only does this life offer prospects and challenges, which relegate speculation about a future life to the realm of obscurity, but also the idea that we should be concerned about our own personal destiny smacks of selfishness in light of the social awareness that has been achieved in recent years. Over a decade and a half ago, an astute observer of the theological scene was warning: "The Church will have to reckon with the probability that the salvation of his soul is no urgent issue for contemporary man."[1] In spite of the right wing revival in North American Christianity, both in terms of sheer numbers and also in terms of depth of interest among the committed themselves, it would seem that there is more rather than less reason to endorse that warning today. By and large, people are not interested in the salvation of their souls, principally, perhaps, because they have no idea what that would involve.

Although secularization and social self-consciousness go a long way toward explaining the decline in interest in personal salvation, to this there must be added a theological motivation derived from the awareness of the importance of community for Christian faith. If the fundamental truth in life is that God is love, rooted in the conviction that God has reached out to us in love to the extent of the cross, and if the corollary and goal of this divine condescension is to elicit a responsive love in us, then it follows that the point of all this is not to isolate us as individuals, each seeking our own welfare, but to draw us together in mutual caring and concern for one another. The centrality of love requires that salvation be understood in communal rather than private terms. Thus, even from a theological point of view, the contemporary suspicion about personal salvation need not, by any means, be totally unwelcome. And yet, the disappearance of concern with personal salvation can hardly be met with equanimity. For without something of this dimension, it is difficult to see how more socially oriented understandings of salvation can be either appreciated or sustained. Thus, it is necessary to consider what would be lost through an abandonment of the personal dimension of salvation. This will involve something of a defense of the personal, just as the current dominance of the social perspective necessitated more of a critique in considering what was involved in the essentially social understanding of salvation.

Personal Salvation as Private

Contemporary social consciousness does allow scope for the personal, but it tends to do so by subsuming the personal under the social. What we are as persons is a result of our social relations. Thus, the most basic contrast with the social is not the personal, but the private. This is what is threatened, if not directly eliminated, by the hegemony of the social. Consequently, the most distinctive significance of the personal is to be found in direct confrontation with this issue of privacy. Is there a private domain, an aspect of life centering on the individual, which cannot be acceded to the imperialism of the social?

THE INESCAPABILITY OF PERSONAL RESPONSIBILITY

We have seen that social consciousness has encouraged the transference of responsibility from people to structures. Economic disparity is due not to personal greed but to the institutional arrangements of capitalism. It is undoubtedly true that the free enterprise system, as endorsed originally by Adam Smith, gives organizational authority to individual initiative on the assumption that as each person pursues their own interests the welfare of all will be advanced. The inclination of social consciousness is to question this structural legitimation of private interests. From the point of view of Smith, however, who, after all was a moralist, this was not meant as a structural legitimation of any and every private interest, but rather presupposed a basic personal integrity on the part of the entrepreneur. The system would only be as good as the people operating it; the direct contrary of the contemporary assumption that the personal morality of the people involved is irrelevant because of the determinative significance of the system as such. In addressing this stalemate, we must recognize that Adam Smith lacked the awareness of the importance of social arrangements such as we have come to take for granted. At the same time, however, we must question whether this social awareness has not served to obscure the significance of the individual element.

At the very least, it must be recognized that the free enterprise system is based on a vision of the individual, a vision that not only accords the individual fundamental importance but also assumes a utopian-constructing capacity for the isolated self, a utopia of, as well as by, the self. Structures that promote self-seeking ultimately rest on a view of life that regards the self as ideally independent and self-sufficient.

> In recent years, they (such views of the self) have led to a politics not based on the needs of the commonwealth or even on the best interests of certain groups within the commonwealth, but a politics based on the fulfillment of *idealized selves*. Any understanding of American politics merely in terms of corporate greed, the profit motive, the maintenance of comforts for the middle class at the expense of the Third World or anything of this sort, is bound to fall short of the truth. For the real question before recent governments in the United States has not been the pragmatic one—how best to get the job done, whether it be concerning national health, the economy, unemployment, crime—but rather the spiritual one—what best allows me (all the me's) to keep the ideal image alive? What social policy best promotes my image of myself as an autonomous unit, not dependent on man or God, living in a world of autonomous units?[2]

Challenging social, political, and economic structures, essential as this is, will be inadequate unless and until this vision that sustains those structures is also identified and confronted. But to do that requires acknowledging personal responsibility. We are not simply victims of the system. At the very least, we are willing victims, if not accomplices or even promoters of the very vices we officially deplore.

If it is true that much of the injustice and poverty in the world can be traced to a defining vision of ourselves as inherently competitive beings forever seeking to outdo one another in acquisition and status, then the personal dimension figures prominently in the diagnosis of our situation. But if this is the case, it is not unreasonable to expect that this dimension should also play a role in any satisfactory resolution. This has been affirmed in Christianity, at

least until the triumph of social consciousness led some to so concentrate on the changing of structures that the personal dimension
was neglected or even rejected. If we return to the teaching of
Jesus, as portrayed in the gospels, we find not only the focus on
the kingdom emphasized by the social approach to theology but
also the implicit assumption that the way of the kingdom is something that must concern individuals. Although it is an overstatement in itself, it is understandable in the wake of the submergence
of the personal in much recent theology to find the suggestion that
"in the Gospels the teachings of the Saviour clearly describe a personal rather than a social morality."[3] This is certainly true in that
Jesus did not address the problem of institutional structures, which
has become so significant for us. It is not so adequate when a less
rigorous understanding of the social is assumed, for the personal
address of the way advocated by Jesus has very definite social overtones in its requirement for care and concern for others, especially
those in need.

Thus, although the substance of the morality taught by Jesus was
essentially social, the motivation and source was seen to be fundamentally individual.

> It cannot be denied that the Jesus of the gospels is represented as being
> concerned to interiorize morality. Inevitably this interiorization also
> has the effect of individualizing morality.[4]

An impersonal form of morality, represented by established codes
or structured social expectations, presupposes a relatively simple
and settled situation. This hardly describes contemporary conditions. Thus, the personal nature of motivation and the complexity
of the field of application conspire to assure the requirement that
morality must ultimately be personally grounded in the responsibility and concern of the individual. Problems emerge when this personal nature of motivation slips over into a substantive mode so
that the self is also seen to be the goal as well as the agent of
morality. This results in what Gustavo Gutierrez calls *arribismo*,
which Harvey Cox renders as "getting- ahead-ism".[5] On this view,
motivation is identified with the individual to the point of virtually
total isolationism. The importance of personal motivation for responsibility takes on the tone of total culpability for one's situation. This represents the failure to recognize the formative influence of structures and circumstances, which evokes the reaction
against the personal. Neither of these strictly social nor strictly personal, strictly structural nor strictly private, approaches is adequate

to the realities of the human condition. We all function within structural arrangements that are beyond our control and that exert influences beneath our threshold of recognition. To call for the overthrow of these structures presupposes personal insight that transcends these influences and control. Whatever the merit of this call in any given situation, if it is issued with the demand for blind obedience and with the assurance that it represents a panacea for present and future ills, such shortcircuiting of the personal dimension must be rejected not simply as naive but as positively wrong. Recognition of inadequacies and anticipation of utopian possibilities in social structures are activities of persons. Without going to the other extreme of so minimizing the significance of circumstances that persons are held individually responsible for their total situation, the inescapability of the personal as motivation and goal of moral responsibility must be acknowledged.

THE INDISPENSABILITY OF PERSONAL APPRECIATION AND APPROPRIATION

The inescapability of the personal dimension in morality is due, in part, to the impossibility of someone else understanding and acting for me. In the final analysis, each one of us must take our own stand in life, if not deliberately. then by default. Nor is this simply the wisdom of existentialists. No less an advocate of social consciousness than Paulo Freire makes the same point: "I cannot think *for others* or *without others*, nor can others think *for me*."[6] The ubiquity of the social is acknowledged in the reference to the impossibility of thinking "without others," but the distinctly personal note is acknowledged in the contention that we cannot think for others, nor others for us. Ultimately, we all have to do our own thinking, thinking not just in the discursive sense but in the organic, imaginative sense of fundamental visions concerning what life is all about. Of course, we can conform to the conventions of a culture, of a particular group or influential individual, but genuine conviction requires confession rather than conformity. And that is something that each of us must do for ourselves. "'Confessing,' like martyrdom, has to be an act of personal decision."[7] In ultimate matters, we must look and see and settle things for ourselves.

It is not accidental that the most intense religious experiences have been of a mystical nature, available only to the recipient of the experience, and that some of the most prominent accounts of religion in the twentieth century, the most analytic of centuries, have emphasized this note of solitariness. Perhaps, the best known of these definitions is Whitehead's: "Religion is what the individual does with his own solitariness."[8] However, the same focus was proposed by William James in his influential *Varieties of Religious Experience*, where he defined religion as *"the feelings, acts and experiences of individual men in their solitude, so far as they apprehend themselves to stand in relation to whatever they may consider the divine."*[9] That this equation of religion with solitariness is rooted in the very nature of religious experience itself is attested more recently by Gordon Allport.

> From its early beginnings to the end of the road the religious quest of the individual is solitary. Though he is socially interdependent with others in a thousand ways, yet no one else is able to provide him with the faith he evolves, nor prescribe for him his pact with the cosmos.[10]

Because of the intense preoccupation with the social dimension in contemporary thought, to the point where religion has often come to be regarded as a function of society rather than representing a transhuman engagement, which has social repercussions, it is particularly important to recognize this indispensable personal core at the heart of religion. In the wake of the pervasive tendency to equate the relation with God with our treatment of one another, so that our visions and images become absorbed by social projects, it is salutary to hear Whitehead's warning: "If you are never solitary, you are never religious."[11]

The identification of religion with social projects is prompted not only by the positive merit of these projects themselves but also by a suspicion of solitariness, which sees it as a religious means of avoiding engagement with the real needs of others. That religion can and does serve this ideological function is undeniable, and once that has been recognized, it must remain as a constant criterion of genuine religion. However, this does not mean that it is either a universal or a sufficient criterion. To regard it as universal would amount to expelling the most ardent mystics from the sphere of genuine religion. The singularity of focus and tenacity of dedication demanded by the way of the mystic requires the allowance for an exception to the rule that contemplation of God must issue in service of humanity, at least, insofar as that service is defined independently of that way of spiritual discipline itself. Unless we are willing to endorse a basic welfare understanding of human life where the meeting of immediate needs is regarded as totally adequate, suspicion of ideological avoidance must be qualified by a recognition of the legitimacy of spiritual discipline, which is so intense that it requires withdrawal from, rather than engagement with, fellow mortals. Indeed, that very withdrawal can be the contemplative's service of others, as Thomas Merton suggests. "The hermit's ability to live alone is his gift to the community and his witness to the grace of Christ in his own life."[12] The illegitimacy of a universal identification of genuine religion with social dedication implies the requirement for a further qualification of this criterion, in terms of its sufficiency, even for less mystically absorbed individuals. The interconnection of the spiritual and the material, attested by the divine endorsement of the goodness of creation, and confirmed by the incarnation, forbids the separation of the two tables of the law. Recognition and reciprocation of the love of God must entail participation in that love for all creatures and for all of creation. But just as the variety of talents and vocations among human beings and the utterly demanding nature of serious appreciation of the divine require that some people be so absorbed in spiritual pursuits that they disdain the material, so dedication to material welfare, no matter how egalitarian and altruistic, is, in itself, no guarantee of spiritual sensitivity. The danger of divorcing the spiritual and the material is not adequately met by ricocheting to the opposite extreme of identification. Religious appreciation involves more than a dedication to our fellow beings, and without that more such dedication as does emerge is almost certain to be very precarious.

Many of the flower children of the sixties who embraced the message of universal peace and love for all are at the core of the way of life that has evoked the designation YUPPIE in the eighties, the young urban professionals who are dedicated to their own pleasure, comfort, security, and status. If the current vogue of social consciousness is not to suffer a similar fate it will only be prevented because of the presence of some more substantial base. But that base will not be provided by social awareness. Egalitarian visions are no more substantial than ideals of universal peace and harmony, no matter how profusely they are sprinkled with sociological jargon. The only assurance of long-term social commitment resides in a personal sense of security, which frees one genuinely to seek the good of others. Henri Nouwen refers to this as paying attention without intention. "Anyone who wants to pay attention without intention has to be at home in his own house—that is, he has to discover the centre of his life in his own heart."[13] To pay attention without intention is to encounter people on their own terms, without the constant appeal of self-interest prompting us to wonder how we can profit from the encounter. The promotion of peace is possible only for people who are at peace with themselves.

The ideal of taking others seriously for their own sakes is, of course, widely endorsed. It is central, for example, to Paulo Freire's *Pedagogy of the Oppressed*.[14] However, as we have seen, Freire's approach to the oppressed is not as neutral and open as he would have us believe. He arrives with an analysis of the situation of the oppressed and a prescription for their deliverance. The encounter with the oppressed themselves provides the mechanics for effecting their recognition of that analysis and their embracing of the means of deliverance. Thus, Freire compromises his own intention through his prior commitment to the Marxist ideology. When this happens with someone who puts such a premium on operating with what Nouwen calls "attention without intention," it suggests that there is a certain inevitability about the compromising of this other-centered approach. This is not surprising from a religious point of view because it involves the recognition that how we function with each other is conditioned by our own ultimate orientation. In Christian terms, our difficulty in dealing with others in terms of their interests rather than in terms of our own, or of our own perception of their interests, is exactly what we should expect because of the understanding of our situation as one characterized fundamentally by the self-centeredness of sin. From this vantage point, it is only through the personal salvation entailed by the experiential acceptance of that diagnosis and the release from self-preoccupation which is the positive side of that acceptance, that we find the security to accept ourselves and one another. The difficulty in this is that, as we have seen, diagnosis and cure are two sides of the same phenomenon. To recognize ourselves in these terms is to have been delivered from that predicament, at least in a preliminary manner, and, conversely, we cannot recognize ourselves in these terms so long as we experience neither the reality of, nor the need for, deliverance.

Like many of us, William James had an amateur appreciation of the religious sensitivity involved. "There is a state of mind, known to religious men, but to no others, in which the will to assert ourselves and hold our own has been displaced by a willingness to close our mouths and be as nothing in the floods and waterspouts of God."[15] Although that kind of religious experience is, by no means, automatic or obvious, it is difficult to the point of impossibility to imagine any understanding of salvation worthy of the name without it. The realities of hunger and poverty might elicit sympathetic identification which becomes as absorbing for some as the mystical experience is for others. It would reflect a substantial endowment of academic arrogance to veto either of these extremes for some individuals. But what must be said from the remove of reflection is that the norm can be expected to include both a sense of divine acceptance and demand and an identification with the neighbor, and that the two should be neither separated nor identified. In the present climate of social consciousness, it is necessary to emphasize the nonidentification in terms of the indispensible role of personal appreciation and appropriation.

THE INSUFFICIENCY OF PERSONAL AS PRIVATE

The personal dimension is instrumentally indispensable because motivation for social improvement ultimately rests on personal insight and inspiration. However, the personal is indispensable in its own right because it represents the highest level of reality known to us. Salvation itself must ultimately be personal in some comprehensive sense, or else it is bound to remain partial and incomplete. But this means that the personal must encompass the social rather than either reacting against it or merely serving it in instrumental fashion. This is what makes the private understanding of the personal particularly problematic.

The direct equation of personal with private is responsible for a caricaturing of the whole personal dimension. Thomas Merton offers a particularly vivid depiction of this caricature, which he confesses to having evoked himself. "Due to a book I wrote thirty years ago, I have myself become a sort of stereotype of the world-denying contemplative—the man who spurned New York, spat on Chicago, and tromped on Louisville, heading for the woods with Thoreau in one pocket, John of the Cross in another, and holding the Bible open at the Apocalypse."[16] Whether in this guise of monastic asceticism or the currently more prominent evangelical piety promoted in the popular media, this ultraindividualistic understanding of the personal has been counterproductive. It is probably the case that nothing has contributed more to the wholesale adoption of the social horizon than the inadequacy of this privatistic reading of the personal. It is equally true that this reading is not endemic to either monastic or evangelical traditions. For its dispensability in the monastic tradition, we need look no further than Merton himself. His insistence on the importance of normal human intercourse would make it difficult for him to acknowledge even the legitimacy of the monastic extreme for individuals, such as we have proposed here. "The basic requirement of the contemplative and cloistered life today is this: Before all else, before we indulge in asceticism or go on to quiet contemplative absorption in God, we must recognize the need to maintain a healthy human atmosphere and a normal human relationship to one another and to reality in our communities."[17] The evangelical ideal is authoritatively articulated by P. T. Forsyth: "Salvation is personal, but it is not individual. It is personal in its appropriation but collective in its nature."[18] Again the claim is more modest than the one being advanced here, although the difference may be partly a matter of definition. The present contention is that salvation must be personal not only in the appropriation of the individual but also in its ultimate realization. Forsyth's reluctance to employ the personal, in this sense, is probably due to his identification of it with the private, as his contrast with "collective" suggests. In any event, it is clear that he does not regard personal in the sense of private as an adequate designation of the evangelical understanding of salvation. Salvation requires the appreciation and appropriation of the individual person but its goal is communal.

The ambiguity over the role of the personal for religion is illustrated by the two prominent advocates of solitariness as the primary religious requisite. William James represents a fairly typical understanding of the personal as essentially synonymous with private.

> By being religious we establish ourselves in possession of ultimate reality at the only point at which reality is given us to guard. Our responsible concern is with our private destiny, after all.
>
> You see now why I have been so individualistic throughout these lectures, and why I have seemed so bent on rehabilitating the element of feeling in religion and subordinating its intellectual part. Individuality is founded in feeling.[19]

Genuine religion comes down to the experience of the individual. This is not simply because only the individual can really experience and appreciate what is really at stake but because what is at stake is the destiny of the individual. "Our responsible concern is with our private destiny, after all." By contrast, Whitehead is equally insistent on the importance of individual appreciation and appropriation of religious experience in his insistence on the importance of solitariness, but this is understood as an element in a wider picture that encompasses the individual. Indeed, for anyone familiar with Whitehead's philosophical position, the insistence on the importance of solitariness for religion is shocking. For nothing is more fundamental for his outlook than the insistence on the interconnectedness of all things. In fact, this language of things is precisely what is challenged in the interests of an organic understanding of reality, for which every instant of existence stands in relation to every other instant. Consequently, for Whitehead, there is no such thing as absolute solitariness.[20] The solitariness of the individual in religious experience entails the recognition of the interconnectedness of life. It is precisely this wider connection, rather than any self-sufficient isolation, which requires the note of solitariness. "The reason of this connection between universality and solitariness is that universality is a disconnection from immediate surroundings."[21] Paradoxically, the solitary and the universal meet in distinction from partial preoccupations with more immediate ranges of interest.

Whitehead's organic perspective permits an understanding of the personal, which recognizes the importance of the individual and private dimension without segregating this in some kind of abstract isolation. He shares the basic experience of life articulated by the psychologist Carl Rogers who was driven to conclude: "What is most personal is more general."[22]

There have been times when in talking with students or staff, or in my writing, I have expressed myself in ways so personal that I have felt I was expressing an attitude which it was probable no one else could understand, because it was so uniquely my own. . . . In these instances I have almost invariably found that the very feeling which has seemed to me most private, most personal, and hence most incomprehensible by others, has turned out to be an expression for which there is a resonance in many other people. It has led me to believe that what is most personal and unique in each one of us is probably the very element which would, if it were shared or expressed, speak most deeply to others.[23]

James does not share this experience. For him, personal is much more intrinsically bound up with connotations of the private. It concerns the dimension of feeling, which leaves us essentially isolated in our little worlds of experience. "To redeem religion from unwholesome privacy, and to give public status and universal right of way to its deliverances, has been reason's task."[24] The difference between the organic Whiteheadian approach, which understands reality in terms of fundamental interconnections and ourselves as unified beings whose thinking and feeling dimensions of experience interpenetrate and mutually influence one another, and the more analytic approach of James, which divides reality into what we as humans can master and the "more" that evokes religious interest and thinks of ourselves in terms of a kind of faculty psychology, which separates the private domain of feeling from the public realm of rationality, is illustrative of what is at stake in the understanding of the personal. The Jamesian outlook, which until quite recently was, by far, the more dominant perspective, undermines the credibility of the personal by its almost total identification with the private.

Surveying the American scene just three years after James' death, Josiah Strong in 1913 noted a fundamental division in American Protestantism between two basic approaches that were:

> not to be distinguished by any of the old lines of doctrinal or denominational cleavage. Their difference is one of spirit, aim, point of view, comprehensiveness. The one is individualistic; the other is social.[25]

What is particularly interesting about Strong's diagnosis is his contention that the individualistic strain is, in fact, an innovation, in spite of its widespread endorsement as the accepted norm for what Christian faith is intended to be.

> There are two types of Christianity, the old and the older. The one is traditional, familiar, and dominant. The other though as old as the Gospel of Christ, is so rare that it is suspected of being new, or is overlooked altogether.[26]

Strong's thesis would find much more ready acceptance today in the wake of the virtual reversal in outlook, which has resulted from the development of social consciousness. Under the influence of that development, we are apt to do less than justice to the originality of his insight and the radical nature of the thesis he is advancing. Our awareness of the inevitably social nature of human life leads us to take for granted the social nature of early Christianity, even apart from its own insistence on the primacy of love and the correlative requirement for a mutual concern and community. To regard the individual emphasis as a later imposition on what, in its essence, was inherently social is not particularly startling for people influenced by the social perspective. However, that very casualness with which this thesis, which appeared so offensive when it was broached in the early part of the twentieth century,[27] can be accepted today should give us pause. Is the difference simply due to the fact that we have come to appreciate the primacy and sufficiency of the social, where previous generations had not attained this level of awareness, or is it possible that we might be missing something precisely in this enthusiasm for the social?

There is no doubt that the emphasis on the individual acquired a gigantic boost with the Protestant Reformation and that this was augmented and intensified by the rationalistic thrust of the Enlightenment, both of which figured prominently in the background of the American experience on which Strong is reflecting. However, the importance of the individual was not a discovery of modernity, nor of Protestantism. As we have seen, the direction is apparent in medieval monasticism. "'Go to God yourself' is an admonition from the fourteenth century that contains a pointed attack against ecclesiastical regimentation and sacramentalism."[28] Nor is this sense of the need for the individual pursuit of a depth of meaning, which can only be embraced by the person directly, an invention of the monastic movement. We have seen that the gospel itself assumes a mode of direct address, which implies a premium on the person, that is precluded by any stark contrast between the individual and the social such as Strong proposes. The reality of the gospel and our general experience of life would seem to require something more subtle than either the twentieth century enthusiasm for the social or the assumption of the independence of the personal, as encountered by Strong and endorsed by James, are able to provide. The most promising route would seem to be indicated in the direction pointed to by Whitehead of an understanding of the personal, which insists on the indispensability of individual wrestling with the mystery of life ("If you are never solitary, you are never religious."),[29] but which also recognizes that this most personal struggle entails the most universal matters.

Personal Salvation as Social

The comprehensive understanding of the personal implicit in Whitehead's insistence on the indispensability of both solitariness and interconnectedness would seem to receive its most promising articulation in the social understanding of the personal. Consideration of that approach should help to clarify what is at stake in a well-rounded understanding of the personal.

THE SOCIAL NATURE OF THE PERSONAL

The social understanding of the personal can be regarded as an expression of the wider emergence of social consciousness that has increasingly characterized the twentieth century. However, as the conjunction of the social and the personal, it represents a particular climactic point of this whole trend. Perhaps the best known exponent of the social composition of the personal was George Herbert Mead in his concept of the "generalized other" as the necessary medium by which an individual internalized the impact of the social environment.

> So the self reaches its full development by organizing these individual attitudes of others into the organized social or group attitudes, and those becoming an individual reflection of the general systematic pattern of social or group behavior in which it and the others are all involved— a pattern which enters as a whole into the individual's experience in terms of these organized group attitudes which, through the mechanism of his central nervous system, he takes toward himself, just as he takes the individual attitudes of others.[30]

This determinative significance of the social for personal development advocated by Mead is mirrored in the field of psychiatry by Henry Stack Sullivan's definition of personality as "the relatively enduring pattern of recurrent interpersonal situations which characterize a human life."[31] Another version of this direction is represented by the field theory approach, of which Kurt Lewin is the principal exponent. "In essence the field theory maintains that behavior is to be understood as due not so much to the nature of the individual as to his relationship to the physical and social environment acting upon him and in which his behavior occurs."[32]

The common denominator among these otherwise diverse approaches is the underlying conviction that our being, as persons, is constituted first and foremost by the social environment of which we are a part. Indeed, it is only possible to think of ourselves as "we" or "I" because of the differentiation that social relations make possible. Mead articulates the sustaining assumption of this perspective. "The individual enters as such into his own experience only as an object, not as a subject; and he can enter as an object only on the basis of social relations and interactions, only by means of his experiential interactions with other individuals in an organized social environment."[33] Recognition of the formative significance of social interaction provides the basis for recognizing ourselves as objects, but what happens to our being as subjects? This is the dilemma posed for psychologists who are concerned with the living person. "Society and culture thus become the sovereign organizers of human behavior and human life, and the personality psychologist is left with nothing to do."[34] Perhaps, the most blatant form of this displacement is represented by the field theory where the elements of the objective environment are much easier to identify than aspects of the person so that they tend to become the subject of the investigation. "In field theory, it is the field that is organized—and if the field is comprised overwhelmingly of environmental forces, what place is left for a psychology of personality?"[35] Recognition of the importance of social circumstances for our development as persons has provided an unavoidable ingredient for any future self-understanding we may attempt. Yet fascination with that dimension can result in losing the person amid the web of interconnections that make up the social matrix. It is one thing to acknowledge that there is no person apart from social relations; it is another to say that the person is nothing other than the sum of social relations.

Acknowledgement of the social nature of the personal is made, for example, in the recognition that the fruits of the spirit Paul lists in Galatians 5 ("Love, joy, peace, patience, kindness, goodness, fidelity, gentleness, and self-control") presupposes social relations.[36] Although some of these virtues might appear to be primarily private dispositions, such as joy and peace and patience, a moment's reflection will confirm that these only make sense in relation to others. Even such an apparently private virtue as self-control is required and facilitated only because of our involvement with other selves. At the same time, however, this acknowledgement of the social dimension does not warrant a complete capitulation to that dimension so that any and every shade of individual initiative and sensitivity is absorbed by the social horizon, as often seems to be the case in contemporary academic writing influenced by social consciousness. Having concentrated on Latin American liberation theology in considering this social dimension, we may now draw on James Cone, the leading advocate of black theology, in illustration of this tendency.

> God's act of reconciliation is not mystical communion with the divine, nor is it a pietistic state of inwardness bestowed upon the believer. God's reconciliation is a new relationship with *people* created by his concrete involvement in the political affairs of the world, taking sides with the weak and the helpless.[37]

Although this may be regarded as a typical statement of the social direction embraced by much recent theology, Cone's brother, Cecil Wayne Cone, contends that it is not representative of black religion.

> While the striving for freedom and equality is an element in black religion, it nonetheless is not identical with its essence. The essence of black religion is the *encounter* with an Almighty Sovereign God. Therefore, any view of black religion that does not make divine encounter the beginning and the end of its essence encounters difficulty.[38]

More specifically, he charges his brother with succumbing to the humanistic horizon of Black Power. "Cone must make up his mind concerning his confessional commitment: is it to the black religious experience or to the Black Power motif of liberation with a sidelong glance at the black religious experience?"[39] As with Latin American liberation theology, it is easy to understand the impatience with injustice and social and racial degradation that would make the social horizon an attractive focus. But the equation of the social project with the experience of the divine constitutes the theological counterpart to the psychological loss of the person resulting from an identification of the person with the social matrix.

The focus on the social as the source of our being, psychologically and/or theologically, entails a leveling process, which threatens both human and divine distinctiveness. The loss of individuality is reflected in fictional portrayals of life in literature and the visual media, in terms of what William H. Whyte, Jr., has called, *The Organization Man.* "Society is no longer merely an agreeable setting in which they place their subjects; it is becoming almost the central subject itself."[40] It displaces both ourselves as living subjects and God. "Society itself becomes the *deus ex machina.*"[41] Whyte notes that it is, no doubt, to our credit that we never really lived by the rugged individualism of the official American credo. "But in searching for that elusive middle of the road, we have gone very far afield, and in our attention to making organization work we have come close to deifying it."[42] The total dedication to social projects, so enthusiastically embraced by much contemporary theology, is a striking example of this capitulation.

From this social perspective in which the divine is to be encountered exclusively in the neighbor, any suggestion of a more personal relation with God is subject to the kind of derision implied by James Cone. The direction of a spiritual classic like Thomas à Kempis' *Of the Imitation of Christ* would be anathema to this sophisticated social consciousness. "The greatest Saints," Thomas avers, "shunned the company of men when they could, and chose rather to live to God in secret."[43] This historical observation is endorsed in an admonition of imitation. "For who so withdraws himself from his acquaintances and friends, to him will God draw near with His holy Angels."[44] It is difficult to imagine more antithetical positions than this medieval advocacy of solitary meditation and the contemporary predilection for collective engagement. For this contemporary perspective, such talk of withdrawal from human engagement to commune with God smacks of escapism. To withdraw from people is to withdraw from the God who embraces people. However, the crucial question centers on the nature of that embrace. If that embrace is essentially social, is it an embrace of people? It is an embrace of people on the social understanding of personality, but we have seen that this understanding threatens the distinctiveness of the person.

One of the principal reasons for this social account of persons and for the appeal of this account for theology has to do with its egalitarian nature. The change in the shape of society in the modern period from hereditary, vertical monarchianism to popularly elected democratic government entails a metaphysical shift for anyone who regards society with the awe that endows it with formative significance for understanding ourselves and even as a synonym or surrogate for God. It is, perhaps, only the obviousness of this connection, which generally prevents its explicit acknowledgement. If society constitutes our horizon of vision then we ourselves and any viable vision of God will be determined by that horizon. Since modern society is constituted by, at least, the ideal of democracy, our own being and even the being of God must be realized through some form of mutuality. Conversely, any notion either of ourselves as distinct individuals or of God understood vertically, rather than simply in horizontal terms, merely represent an archaic legacy from the hierarchical orientation of the past. Matthew Fox is forthright and uncompromising in his embracing of social horizontalism. His most vivid rebuke to the residue of the vertical orientation is to be found in his disdain for what he calls worsh*up*. "We celebrate the end of up-spirituality, of climbing, of worsh*up*, of pedestal piety, of God as Judge instead of God as justice, of mercy as buffer instead of compassion as justice-making."[45] The sophisticated look around, rather than up. God is to be found in our relations with one another rather than in any depth of our own being and experience. The difficulty is in knowing what God means other than the social matrix itself, just as psychologists wonder what person means when personality is equated with the social process. In both cases, it would seem that either we are standing on the verge of a massive revolution in thought that is destined to transform our most fundamental assumptions about ourselves and the nature of reality as such, or else we are the victims of the most colossal detour in rationality that the human species has yet concocted.

THE IMPERSONAL NATURE OF THE SOCIAL

It is not accidental or insignificant that attempts to construe the personal in social terms seem invariably to result in a threatened dissolution of the person as such. That outcome is due to more than the tendency to diffusion in the social matrix. It is also encouraged by an intrinsically impersonal bias attaching to considerations of the social as such. The fact that the study of the social has developed as the social sciences is indicative of a preference for the ideal of impersonal objectivity such as was assumed to characterize the natural sciences in the early modern period. In fact, it would probably not entail any serious distortion to suggest that the ideal of objective neutrality, which the natural sciences were constrained to abandon in this century through such developments as the recognition of relativity and indeterminacy, has been assumed by the social sciences in their attempt to manage human life conceived as social reality.

The reason that this development amounts either to a dramatic revolution in human thought and conviction or else a horrendous detour in human sense and sensibilities is due to the total nature of the vision involved. The acceptance of the social horizon constitutes a whole way of appearing to retain control in a world where people have ceased to count. Personal sensibility and responsibility is superceded by a problematizing of life. So pervasive has this mentality become that it can only be recognized, much less questioned, from some other vantage point. One of the most striking vantage points is provided by a way of life that is particularly marginalized by the pursuit of social management, the way of contemplation. In reflecting on the obstacles encountered by novice monks, Thomas Merton is constrained to identify the problematizing mentality as particularly hazardous.

> Basically our trouble remains the same: An obsession with questions and answers, with problems and solutions, with momentous decisions, and even with "identity" raised to the level of a kind of absolute. The traditional wisdom of monasticism and of the Gospel ought to help us

see through this mystification and bring us back into contact with reality. Our life does not consist in magic answers to impossible questions, but in the acceptance of ordinary realities which are, for the most part, beyond analysis and therefore do not need to be analyzed.[46]

In the era of social engineering, nothing is beyond analysis. Everything is grist for the analytic mill to the point where the abstraction takes over. The reality of people and things and even of God are subsumed under the great abstraction, "society."

Elsewhere, Merton depicts the background for his diagnosis of the contemporary situation in an endorsement of a question posed by Simone Weil:

"How will the soul be saved" she asked her philosophy students in the Lyceé "after the great beast has acquired an opinion about everything?"

The void underlying the symbols and the myths of nationalism, of capitalism, communism, fascism, racism, totalism is in fact filled entirely by the presence of the beast—the urge to collective power. We might say, developing her image, that the void thus becomes an insatiable demand for power: it sucks all life and all being into itself.[47]

That the heart of this dilemma resides in a loss of individuality under the impact of the structural fixation of the social perspective is confirmed by Victor Kramer's commentary on Merton's summation.

As long as real, individual, human values are plunged into nothingness in order that collectivity may attain to some ideal, the soul is in danger of being lost. This is what happens with all blind acceptance of institutions.[48]

Social self-consciousness seems to be impelled beyond the awareness of our mutual influence on one another, which makes the equation of personal with private appear naive and abstract, to develop its own abstract fascinations with structures and arrangements in which not only persons but all sense of living reality is sacrificed to the mentality of management and control.

This direction, which we are suggesting is implicit in the ambitions of the social sciences, has been given its most explicit articulation not in the direct social focus of sociologists but in an area that might have been expected to retain more of the personal dimension, that of psychology. The behaviorist approach of psychology where human beings are seen as stimulus–response mechanisms *Beyond Freedom and Dignity*,[49] to employ the title phrase of the best known exponent of this position, B F. Skinner, concedes personal distinctiveness to the impersonal inducements of the environment.

> The sum and substance of Skinnerian psychology is that rewards, threats, and punishments shape the patterns of behavior that make up human personalities. And the most important fact is that a person's own behavior brings consequences that change his action. In addition, consequences arise in the environment; the environment influences or controls changes in behavior.[50]

In his outspoken endorsement of the behaviorist approach, Skinner presents a particularly bold picture of the agenda that has come to be assumed by the most dominant forms of social science. On the one hand, he cheerfully sacrifices the person to the deterstminative influences of the impersonal environment. Yet, at the same time, he sees himself as the pioneer of a new breed of savants who will transform the human condition by changing the environment. As a species, we are completely subject to our surroundings; as a profession, the behavioral scientist is doubly competent, able to reshape humanity by restructuring the environment.

From a humanistic point of view, it is easy to identify with Carl Rogers' assessment of Skinnerian social engineering. "To me this is a pseudo-form of the good life which includes everything save that which makes it good."[51] However, it is not so easy to be so sanguine about his confidence that the indispensability of the personal will prevail even through such apparent annihilation.

> In conclusion then, it is my contention that science cannot come into being without a personal choice of the values we wish to achieve. And these values we choose to implement will forever lie outside of the science which implements them; the goals we select, the purposes we wish to follow, must always be outside of the science which achieves them. To me this has the encouraging meaning that the human person, with his capacity of subjective choice, can and will always exist, separate from and prior to any of his scientific undertakings.[52]

It does seem clear that behaviorists regard themselves as exceptions to the impersonal determinism they endorse generally. But that would seem to be a typical human reaction rather than simply a particular behaviorist inconsistency. In spite of our awareness of the massive influence of social conditioning, or even an endorsement of a deterministic understanding of the human condition, we assume deep down that this does not finally apply to us. If it is that willingness to make ourselves an exception that Rogers is appealing to as his source of confidence in the persistence of the personal, that must be regarded as a fragile base at best. But this does seem to represent the direction implicit in the conclusion he draws from his distinction between scientific approaches and the antecedent decisions they presuppose. "Unless as individuals and groups we choose to relinquish our capacity of subjective choice, we will always remain free persons, not simply pawns of a self-created behavioral science."[53] Probably even the most dedicated behaviorist would endorse this image for themselves, however far removed it might be required to remain from the official position they would articulate. But this is precisely what makes the status of the personal so precarious. Has it been reduced to the dimension of private whim in an atmosphere where the important issues of life are seen to be decided by structural manipulation? The pursuit of the perfect society can allow for personal choice because the nature of the choice is seen to be determined by the planners. In this way, the egalitarian goal issues in a new hierarchy of planners and plannees, of behavers and behavior modifiers. What constitutes the difference between the two? Is there really any difference? Are the planners any more free than the plannees?

THE TRANSCENDENCE OF THE PERSONAL

The precariousness of our present existence, as signaled by the constant nuclear threat necessitated by the way we have organized ourselves, and the massive onslaught on the environment constituted by our conquest of nature leave us wondering whether our predicament is principally due to our lack of control or to the excess of control we have exercised. The obvious solution is to conclude that the source of our difficulties can be traced to an excess of control over our environment and a lack of control over ourselves. "As we become civilized, we grow in power over everything but ourselves, we grow in everything but power to control our power over everything."[54] The catch, of course, is in the implication that we should control ourselves, which is really to say that we should impose on ourselves the kind of dominance we have exercised over nature; precisely what the social engineering movement is attempting.

In spite of the prominence of this direction in political, military, and business bureaucracies, and in the alliances forged between these and the academic experts who dispense their wisdom through the mass media and, in the name of scientific neutrality, have the audacity to try to plan the planners, there are signs of an alternative to this 1984 kind of world. It can even be suggested that the underlying dynamic, the absolute veneration of the autonomous and self-sufficient scientific method, is itself in the process of being transformed from within.

> The significance of our era is that science has been forced by its own development to recognize its limitations, and thus to make room again for the other way of knowing, whose place it usurped for almost three centuries. The quantitative method is approaching perfection and with it saturation; its aggressiveness is beginning to change into the modesty of achievement. The flat, two-dimensional plane of nineteenth-century mechanism is gaining depth and height by the eruption of the new hierarchy of levels, and the validity of the "vertical" approach is beginning to be recognized again.[55]

In addition to the recognition of relativity and indeterminacy, already mentioned, which have served to shatter the understanding of science as the externally effected determination of absolute cause and effect connections, the accounts of such philosophers of science as Thomas Kuhn[56] and Michael Polanyi[57] have exposed the humanness of the scientific enterprise so that the myth of the omnipotent and omniscient march of scientific progress should be laid to rest once and for all. Although this revised understanding of science has yet to filter through the popular consciousness, it has reached the level of an anticipatory kind of awareness through the challenges posed by ecological imbalance. Although there might not be widespread recognition of the gigantic venture of faith we are involved in through the scientific enterprise, there is a growing awareness of the precariousness of the way of life we have developed.

The most sobering source of awareness of this precariousness is probably to be found in the dire assessment of the Club of Rome and the radical nature of the transformation required for survival, which it proposes in its second report, *Mankind at the Turning Point*: including the development of a world consciousness on the part of every individual; an ethic of conservation for scarce resources; an attitude toward nature of harmony rather than of conquest; and a sense of identification with future generations.[58] The fact that these requirements represent the direct antitheses of the features most prized in the way we have developed suggests the magnitude of the transformation that is proposed. It is not surprising that this diagnosis and prescription has aroused opposition. In challenging the way of life we have fashioned, this assessment is challenging us. Beneath the debate about the seriousness of the ecological crisis in depletion of resources and destruction of the environment, there lies the issue of our fundamental vision of ourselves and of the whole point of the life we are living. Thus, what is at stake is not finally amenable to determination by resource predictions or environmental forecasts. Apart from the margin for error with issues of this scale, the vested interest of our own visions and priorities make this, finally, a very personal issue. The changes that the Club of Rome report prescribes are all possible only through a personal transformation on the part of the individual. The magnitude of the change proposed might seem more feasible on a Skinnerian basis, where incentives to conserve and deterrents to indulgence would be devised in order to structure a sustainable society. However, in spite of the realism of this direction, unless we are willing to entrust ourselves to the wisdom of the planners, we will probably find the personalistic approach proposed by the more humanistic direction in psychology represented by Erich Fromm more congenial. "A new society is possible *only if* in the process of developing it a new human being also develops, or in more modest terms, if a fundamental change occurs in contemporary man's character structure."[59] This more radical assessment of our situation is called for, unless we are willing to consign our fate to the same sources that have fashioned the present predicament, the "experts." To take this latter course, however, is tantamount to denying the seriousness of our condition and to renouncing our own responsibility for it.

The silver lining in this threat to survival resulting from the very success of our conquest of nature might be precisely this challenge to think for ourselves and pose again questions regarding the fundamental meaning of life that have widely come to be regarded as a throwback to the socially naive era of existentialism. However, the recovery of this personal dimension is not without its dangers, and not only because of the temptation to use such questioning for the ideological purposes identified by the social perspective. Even apart from that danger, the search for personal meaning has its own inherent liability in that the direct pursuit of self-fulfillment is just as naive and self-defeating as the direct attempt to construct the perfect society. The liability is eloquently identified by Viktor Frankl, the founder of what has been called the "Third Viennese School of Psychiatry," because, in contrast to Freud's assumption that human life is characterized fundamentally by the pursuit of pleasure and Adler's counterclaim that the basic drive is the will to power, Frankl held that the distinguishing characteristic of human life is the will to meaning.[60] In elucidating what that need for meaning involves, Frankl has no illusions about the elusiveness of the goal.

> Human existence is essentially self-transcendence rather than self-actualization. Self-actualization is not a possible aim at all, for the simple reason that the more a man would strive for it, the more he would miss it. For only to the extent to which man commits himself to the fulfillment of his life's meaning, to this extent he also actualizes himself. In other words, self-actualization cannot be attained if it is made an end in itself, but only as a side effect of self-transcendence.[61]

To switch from social engineering to the pursuit of self-fulfillment would amount to a change of focus within the same fundamental horizon, the assumption of finite sources of meaning and fulfillment. The recovery of the personal will only be significant if its inescapably transcendent implication is recognized. What is at stake is not self-actualization, but self-transcendence, or at least, self-actualization that occurs only through the process of self-transcendence. But this carries with it the further implication of our unavoidable involvement in transcendence as such.

It is not accidental that the most ardent personalists also tend to be sensitive to the religious dimension, whereas the advocates of impersonal structures and behaviorist approaches tend to be characterized by religious insensitivity. This inherent interconnection of the religious and the personal is almost certainly the most serious casualty of the present fascination with the social. The gains achieved through the recognition of the role and significance of social structures have been realized at the price of a loss in depth accessible only to personal sensitivity. The seriousness of the loss is itself a matter for that very sensitivity. From a perspective that gives priority to the arrangements of impersonal structures, the personal represents, at best, a private diversion or, at worst, an ideological deflection from the real interests and benefits of prevailing social structures. To endorse the personal as the legitimacy of the private dimension in contrast to this preoccupation with structures is, at best, preliminary and very likely will convey the impression of special pleading. Genuine appreciation of the personal is possible only in the dimension of depth that is itself accessible only through personal appreciation and appropriation. The difference may be illustrated by the contrast Henri Nouwen borrows from Gabriel Marcel between wishing and hoping. Marcel's point was that much of what passes for hope is really the process of wish-fulfillment. The difference is that wish-fulfillment fixes its gaze on particular desires and projects, whereas hope is inherently transcendent. As a result, wishing is subject to frustration and disappointment, where hope represents the buoyancy of the long-term. "Only through hope is a man able to overcome this concretionary attitude, for hope is not directed to the gift but to Him who is the giver of all good."[62] In the personal we ourselves are at stake. There is no abiding security in anything we may fashion or receive. Our fundamental grounding is in "the giver of all good." There is no denying the lesson that this can function as a means of justifying social privilege. But the price of allowing that risk to determine our basic direction is a loss of the depth of life only accessible to personal sensitivity and without which the most blissful social structures would seem to retain a vital deficiency.

Personal Salvation as Theological

The one central conviction that emerges from a consideration of the prospects for serious concern with salvation in the future is that the recognition of the importance of social structures and circumstances represent a mixed blessing because, in addition to alerting us to possibilities for the practice of bad faith, it can also become such an absorbing concern that social causes can become displacements rather than vehicles for salvation. We now find ourselves impelled toward a correlative conclusion, namely, that the retention or recovery of the personal, in the wake of the massive impact of social consciousness, is intimately connected with the awareness of the divine as inclusive and transcendent reality beneath and beyond the social horizon. Thus, a serious interest in salvation in the future will depend on the presence of an awareness of the divine as other than, though not separated from, the arrangements and projects of life that we have come to call "social."

THE IMPORTANCE OF PERSONAL EXPERIENCE

One of the principal influences behind the emergence of political theology over the past couple of decades and of the transition stage of secular theology in the 1960s was the prison musings of Dietrich Bonhoeffer, especially his concepts of "religionless Christianity" and "man come of age." It is probably not an exaggeration to suggest that he was a principal source of a new spirituality involving the shift from the classical sin/salvation perspective to the notion of being caught up in the messianic activity that is establishing the Kingdom of God.[63] As a prisoner of war in Nazi Germany, Bonhoeffer detected stirrings of the spirit and perceived signs of the times, which proved to be of prophetic significance. The directions he anticipated have largely been adopted in mainstream postwar Western Christianity. However, the enthusiasm of this adoption has been inclined to miss important elements in Bonhoeffer himself. The advocate of religionless Christianity had, by no means, abandoned religion himself, as demonstrated by the references in his letters to his own devotional practices. The reality is rather, as Thomas Merton suggests, that Bonhoeffer himself even retained something of the monastic ideal. "So too Bonhoeffer, regarded as an opponent of all that monasticism stands for, himself realized the need for certain 'monastic' conditions in order to maintain a true perspective in and on the world."[64] In the light of this sensitivity, it is doubtful that Bonhoeffer himself would be able to endorse the socialization of faith and theology which has so readily claimed him as a benefactor. Were he to appear on the scene today he might well find more congenial the warning issued by Henri Nouwen. "I am afraid that in a few decades the Church will be accused of having failed in its most basic task: to offer men creative ways to communicate with the source of human life."[65] The focus on the building of the kingdom has a centripetal tendency to absorb energies and visions so that communication with the source of life is rendered redundant.

The identification of salvation with social engineering not only serves to demote the personal dimension to peripheral status but also enforces this trivialization by the connotation that any concern with self such as the personal is bound to involve constitutes the antithesis of salvation. Concern with self is indicative of the failure to appreciate the profoundly social nature of life wherein our true identity is to be found in collectivity rather than in isolation. In this way, the social horizon subsumes the individual quest for meaning and thirst for transcendent orientations in the perfecting of the social matrix. We have questioned the strategy of promoting collective or systemic solutions, which solicit conformity rather than challenging the convictions of individuals. What has to be recognized at this point is the legitimacy and indeed the necessity for each of us as individuals to "find ourselves." This requirement for coming to terms with ourselves has been implicit in all that we have said about the instrumental significance of personal dedication for the long-term success of any social measures as well as because of its intrinsic significance entailed by the fact that the supreme form of reality known to us is the personal. The upshot of such considerations is the realization that concern with self cannot simply be dismissed as selfishness.

> What human beings seem to hunger for at all costs is a sense of self possession that is the same thing as the good taste of self. Nor is this a selfish phrase; for it also includes the good taste of otherness. Nor is it merely a pious phrase; rather it is one that gives substance and actuality to the evangelical ideas of redemption and salvation.[66]

Because religious faith has been used for selfish purposes in terms of what contemporary social consciousness calls "ideology," this is no reason to jump to the opposite extreme and directly equate any and every concern about self with selfishness. The stability of society and the personal nature of reality dictate otherwise, as major religions, even those that might seem to be devoted to the elimination of the self, testify. "So both Christianity and Buddhism traditionally have correctly insisted that one's first concern must be for one's own salvation."[67] This is bound to sound paradoxical to Western ears because of the popular impression that Buddhism entails the elimination of self. The reality, however, is much more subtle.

> The coming of wisdom gives the seeker the understanding that release from painfulness is achieved through the proper cultivation of ethics, intention, and meditation. Through them one knows how to "change the current of desire" and how at last to dissolve that current altogether. This is *nirvana*. Taken in this conative and ethical sense, the term can be translated as extinction.[68]

This is clearly an extinction of fulfillment, rather than of destruction. As the source of this analysis, Bruce Matthews, goes on to point out, it in no way justifies the inversion which would simply regard annihilation as nirvana. If that were the case, the obvious method of salvation, from the Buddhism perspective, would be suicide. That such a reading represents an outsider's misreading of what Buddhism involves, is due to the fact that Buddhist salvation is a much more positive one than a straightforward notion of the extinction of self would suggest, and consequently, concern with self is more significant in Buddhist soteriology than our remote generalizations are inclined to suggest. But if this is true of Buddhism, how much more significant must concern with self be for Christian faith where such a premium is placed on the personal?

If one is inclined to dismiss the focus on personal experience as self-indulgent avoidance of the challenge of social involvement, a reading of the accounts of such experiences collected in *Conversion, the Christian Experience*,[69] ranging from the experience of the apostle Paul to that of Charles Colson, might be salutary. After all, St. Ignatius, the founder of the Jesuit order, was converted through reading the lives of the saints while convalescing from war wounds at his family castle.[70] Even if, with William James, we are inclined to regard the experience pointed to in such personal accounts as foreign ("my own constitution shuts me out from their enjoyment almost entirely, and I can speak of them only at second hand"[71]), a secondhand appreciation that there are such personal experiences could represent an important recognition. To counter the stereotypical image of such experiences as self-centered world-denying fanaticism, we might consider the sober account of one who exerted great influence in the part of the world where this is being written, Henry Alline, described in an addition by a relative to his North Hampton, New Hampshire gravestone as "a burning and a shining light and justly esteemed the Apostle of Nova Scotia."[72]

> At that instant of time when I gave up all to him, to do with me, as he pleased, and was willing that God should reign in me and rule over me at his pleasure: redeeming love broke into my soul with repeated scriptures with such power, that my whole soul seemed to be melted down with love; the burden of guilt and condemnation was gone, darkness was expelled, my heart humbled and filled with gratitude, and my will turned of choice after the infinite God, whom I saw I had rebelled against, and had been deserting from all my days. Attracted by the love and beauty I saw in his divine perfections, my whole soul was inexpressibly ravished with the blessed Redeemer; not with what I expected to enjoy after death or in heaven, but with what I now enjoyed in my soul: for my whole soul seemed filled with the divine being. My whole soul, that was a few minutes ago groaning under mountains of death, wading through storms of sorrow, racked with distressing fears, and crying to an unknown God for help, was now filled with immortal love, soaring on the wings of faith, freed from the chains of death and darkness, and crying out my Lord and my God; thou art my rock and my fortress, my shield and my high tower, my life, my joy, my present and my everlasting portion.[73]

Those who would regard this experience as a pious escape from social involvement or attempt to account for it in purely psychological or social terms must reckon with the resulting itinerant ministry in which Alline was propelled through the summer flies and winter snows of what is now the Maritime provinces of Canada and into New England in tireless proclamation of the gospel by which he was so gripped. It is not insignificant that the once-born William James sighted Alline as a classic example of the twice-born Christian.[74] What remains open for discussion is the question as to whether Alline had enjoyed a depth of spiritual experience that James could not finally appreciate.

There is room between the first hand experience of the twice-born and the inclination of the resolutely once-born to attribute the difference to psychological makeup or environmental influences for a realistic openness to the genuine spiritual dimension entailed in that kind of experience. Without discounting the drama of such an experience, the suggestion of an absolute contrast between those who are thus favored and the masses of ordinary mortals who have been deprived of such peculiar experiences might be mitigated somewhat by a recognition of different types and levels of spiritual experience. Besides the dramatic personal encounter, which is generally assumed to characterize this kind of experience, there are also less dramatic and more reflective varieties, which are, nevertheless, extremely powerful for those involved. Paul Tournier tells of how his wife was overcome by an intense awareness of the infinite grandeur of God as the bells pealed on New Year's Eve, marking our finite designation of the march of time: "I have suddenly realized for the first time the greatness of God!"[75] Without something of this personal sense of the divine, and a readiness to recognize that there are others who almost certainly have enjoyed a more intimate experience of God than we have, it is difficult to understand why there should be any interest in religious matters at all.

THE PERSONAL-IMPERSONAL DIALECTIC

The distaste for personal salvation is due not only to the suspicion of selfishness induced by social consciousness but also to the shift in eschatological vision entailed in the transition from the two-story focus on a world beyond for which this life was regarded as the preparatory stage to the unified interest in this life. Even as conservative a scholar as the orthodox Lutheran, Carl Braaten espouses this latter perspective:

The criterion for the presence of salvation is not spiritual ecstasy but somatic wholeness. Many Christians still suffer from a gnostic hangover, thinking of Christianity as a religion which wings souls into an otherworldly communion with God.[76]

This is a far cry from the warning of Thomas à Kempis: "Alas that you do not make better use of your time, when you might be meriting life eternal!"[77] Thomas' characteristic admonition to look to the welfare of our own souls has found an echo in this century.

It was well expressed in Moody's statement, "I look upon this world as a wrecked vessel. God has given me a lifeboat and said to me, 'Moody, save all you can.'"[78]

This understanding of salvation, as a rescuing of doomed individuals from a sinking ship, animates much of the conservative revival in North American Christianity, but in so doing it has tended either to foster an otherworldliness which permits or even condones materialistic indulgence, perhaps because the official position is that the material does not really matter, or else to forge political alliances with the most imperialistic and self-righteous tendencies in national politics. The most visible representatives of the conservative boom, the electronic evangelists, illustrate both tendencies.

Given the resilience of this ultraspiritualized and privatized understanding of personal salvation, it is not surprising that the social emphasis should have captured the liberal imagination, as it has, and, as a result, transformed the understanding of salvation. "We are invited from a preoccupation with redemption of an introverted and caged soul to the redemption of the world *which is itself a soul*."[79] We have argued that this type of inclusive alternative, which totally dismisses the individual locus of personality, represents a reactionary rebounding to the opposite extreme from isolationist spirituality. It demands not only self-denial, but self-annihilation on the part of the individual, with no promise of personal fulfillment.

The unsatisfactoriness of these stark alternatives, individualistic personal salvation or impersonal social salvation, is matched by the widely endorsed academic expedient of advocating an amalgam of the two. From a more traditional perspective, P. T. Forsyth insists: "that salvation of ours comes to us in the salvation of a world, and not of our own soul single and alone."[80] Of course, the world Forsyth refers to is not the socially self-conscious world of structures but the world redeemed by God in contrast to our own individual achievement; but the mutual importance of individual and context is clear. Dorothee Soelle does speak out of social self-consciousness in insisting that personal transformation and change of social circumstances are both required for the rehabilitation of prostitutes in Viet Nam.

> Personal change can have enduring results only in a changed environment. And only where people with such seriousness aim at restoring the dignity of every last lady of pleasure can one speak of socialism.[81]

Soelle's advocacy of a *modus vivendi* from her perspective on the social structure side can be matched by parallels from the opposite direction, of which we may take Henri Nouwen as typical.

> For a Christian, Jesus is the man in whom it has indeed become manifest that revolution and conversion cannot be separated in man's search for experiential transcendence. His appearance in our midst has made it undeniably clear that changing the human heart and changing human society are not separate tasks, but are as interconnected as the two beams of the cross.[82]

The obviousness of this amalgam is only exceeded by its uselessness. For the obviousness appears on the theoretical level. When we stand back, there is no question that both personal growth and structural change are requisites to any real fullness of life. But the theoretical ideal and the requirements of real life are by no means necessarily synonymous. "And it appears that it is always precisely at this practical level of what one ought to do, here and now, in this particular moment in the history of this particular society, that the application of Christian morality to politics breaks down."[83] In spite of their theoretical agreement on a comprehensive ideal, Soelle and Nouwen would probably react quite differently to any given situation, such as Soelle's example of the Viet Nam prostitutes. Where she would be inclined to give priority to the social structures that encourage prostitution, he would almost certainly be struck by the plight of the individuals involved, and, whereas each might well recognize the other dimension, their priorities would dictate different responses to the situation.

The practical divergence, in spite of theoretical agreement on the need for a comprehensive, balanced approach, suggests that the difficulty lies on the practical level. If agreement could be reached regarding a plan of action, then the theoretical harmony could be realized in practice. However, our earlier discussion of praxis should have alerted us to regard with suspicion any such neat division between practice and theory. The theoretical advocacy of balance and the practical divergence of emphasis both arise out of different fundamental visions concerning what is finally significant, what is wrong in life, and how that wrong is to be overcome and what is finally significant to be realized. The theoretical recognition that we ourselves are at stake in this and that the circumstances that structure our common existence are also important is an academic amalgam, which dissolves in the realities of engagement. This latter situation precludes what Arthur Koestler calls "the synthesis between saint and revolutionary,"[84] and allows, at most, for some form of compromise. In that compromise, one or the other perspectives remains dominant. Koestler designates these perspectives as the orientations of the Yogi and the Commissar, and in this way dramatizes their mutual exclusivity.

> The Commissar's emotional energies are fixed on the relation between individual and society, the Yogi's on the relation between the individual and the absolute. Again it is easy to say that all that is wanted is a little mutual effort. One might as well ask a fish to make a little effort towards becoming a bird and vice versa.[85]

Somber though this stark contrast is, it undoubtedly represents a more realistic appraisal of the situation than pleas for comprehensiveness. Though such pleas are right ideally, the history of Christianity since Koestler's essay was written in 1944 confirms the prophetic acumen of his characterizations of the two antagonistic perspectives. There is no more pervaslve division within Christianity today than that between Christians who understand the faith as having to do with the relation of the individual to the absolute and those who understand it as having to do with the relation between the individual and society. In his descriptions, Koestler even anticipated the way in which that division has come to focus on the contrast between the personal and the structural. Nothing is to be gained by ignoring or minimizing this gulf. If theoretical recognition of the need for both personal and social dimensions is to have any credibility beyond the elevated climes of academic insight, this will only be made possible through a blunt recognition of the reality of this fundamental division. Some of us are fish; some of us are fowl.

The serious acknowledgement of this gulf requires more than the simultaneous recognition that we stand on one side of the divide at the same time as we advocate comprehensive balance. It also requires that we confront one another precisely in our different understandings. This is where the fish and fowl analogy begins to break down. For, in spite of the deep seated difference between personal and social perspectives, which justify the comparison to breathing in air as opposed to breathing in water, we are not members of different species; we are all human. At the risk of indulging in the easy academic balancing act, it could be suggested that our goal should be to become amphibian. This suggestion will reach beyond the level of academic solution and deserve to be taken seriously only insofar as it engages the genuine differences of people who hold personalist and socialist perspectives. It will involve facing the fact that from the social perspective, personalists are avoiding the only encounter with God there is, the one that comes through the neighbor. Because today we recognize not only that the neighbor is the one abandoned by the roadside but that that abandonment has a lot to do with the nature of those roads and the traffic they make possible, this entails the correlative realization that we are called not simply to be ambulance drivers and attendants but to address the more fundamental problem of road safety and access so that the casualties by the roadside will be reduced, if not eliminated. Once the importance of this structural dimension has been identified, it can never again be ignored with impunity. Structures are beneficial to some and detrimental to others, and the difference between beneficiary and victim may be due to native ability, disposition, geography, history, race, sex, or some other factor beyond the control of any individual. A gospel rooted in divine love must address this level of structural arrangements and its promoters must be vigilant in guarding against using it for personal benefit through ignoring and thereby tacitly blessing such injustices.

From the personal perspective, however, this social emphasis is fatally flawed in its rightness. For this recognition of the importance of social structures has a tendency to become so absorbing that it dominates the whole field of vision: the impersonal ousts the personal; society displaces God. In the concern to manipulate the environment to the best advantage of all, we inevitably become manipulators. We become behavers rather than believers, response mechanisms rather than interacting persons. The way we see the world and what we become ourselves are mutually reinforcing. "Thus everything with which we come in contact takes on the tone-quality of thing or of person, according as to whether we are ourselves a thing or a person in respect to it."[86] There is no doubt that we live in a very impersonal world. The temptation to succumb to that impersonal tone, especially with high motives of forcing that world into more human shapes, is very strong. But the personalist worries that this humane end will succumb to the impersonal means employed to achieve it.

> "We live," wrote Saint Exupéry, "not on things, but on the meaning of things." The meaning of things is of the order of the person. When our eyes are opened to the world of persons, things themselves become personal.[87]

The concern with unjust structures arose through the direct encounter with suffering persons for Karl Marx and for liberation theologians in Latin America. This initial encounter was then traced to economic and political arrangements that were seen to be the source of the suffering. At this point, the parting of the ways is reached. One direction fastens on this impersonal world of organization and institution, confident that if these are overthrown or changed, people will then be free to find their own way. The other direction identifies with the sufferers themselves and seeks total transformation not just of the structures but of the people involved. The attack on structures is much more modern, direct, and immediately promising, not to mention much more understandable in light of the frustrations of the exploited. However, its prospects also appear to be short term and ambivalent. The structural approach tends to regard structures as means for independent personal growth, but this contradicts the fundamental, holistic perspective, which abhors dualisms of spiritual and material, which, presumably, would also embrace personal and impersonal. But the insistence on the spiritual import of the material should also entail recognition of the inevitable personal implications of the impersonal. This would serve not only to expose the danger of assuming that we can deal with impersonal structures without having this rebound on our life together as persons but also to keep before us the fundamentally personal motivation and goal of life itself. Such recognition, however, would seem to be only possible for, and required by, a view of life that regarded the personal as characterizing ultimate reality. In other words, the source and assurance of the genuineness of personal life is rooted in the belief in the personalness of God.

THE DIVINE BASIS OF THE PERSONAL

The absorption of the personal by the social horizon has been facilitated by the loss of transcendence that has characterized the modern Western outlook. Social consciousness was preceded by self-consciousness, through which we became aware of ourselves as centers of meaning. Whereas in previous ages people assumed that they were sponsored in life from beyond themselves, modern self-consciousness has constrained us to assume that we can and need only look to ourselves as guarantors of hope and sources of meaning. This shift in sensibilities had to do with the revolution in cosmology broached by Copernicus and with the ensuing success of the scientific method in effecting the mastery of nature, but its extent was of theological proportions. Indeed, the overall effect of this revolution, in perspective, has been the displacement of the theological horizon by an anthropological one. Even in spiritual matters, the mandate of modernism dictates the displacement of God by our own devices and devisings.

> As we progress in the religious life God must steadily withdraw. Spiritual maturity requires a gradual relinquishing of the consolations of religion as God becomes less a person, more a principle.[88]

The striking thing about this principlizing of God is that it is assumed not only that this still allows us to thrive as persons, but even that it is positively required in order to provide scope for our personal development.

> So the relation to the religious requirement is personal, in that it generates a highly dramatic religious life in the believer. But I do not anthropomorphically project the personal characteristics into the requirement itself, for to do so would be to fall into the pathetic fallacy. So far as we can tell, there is no objective personal God. The old language is still used, but the modern believer should use it expressively rather than descriptively.[89]

The anthropocentric perspective is so taken for granted that our species is assumed to constitute the personal with the result that any other form of personalness can only be a projection initiated by us. Why this is so we are not told. Apparently anthropocentrism is too obvious to require defense. However, in spite of its paradigmatic status, it is not universally endorsed. The suggestion that "so far as we can tell, there is no objective personal God" must dismiss the evidence of those who claim to have encountered, or rather to have been encountered by, the objective personal God, such as Henry Alline or his predecessors and successors whose experiences are documented by Kerr and Mulder. If such claims are to be dismissed, what is the point of continuing to use that language "expressively rather than descriptively"? What is being expressed? If this language now refers to our subjective wish that there were a personal God, even though there is not, then the total humanism of Freud would seem to be preferable to this duplicitous retention of obsolete religious language.

There is one sense in which concern over references to an "objective personal God" can be shared without absolutizing the anthropocentric outlook, as seems to be the case here. That source of concern is the tendency to domesticate God so that there is some justification for regarding the resulting understanding as a human projection. However, the source of this concern is not anthropocentric but theocentric, prompted not by the assumption of our own exhausting of the category of the personal, but by the threat of idolatry, which hangs over all our theological affirmations. There is no question that any "description" of God we may propose is bound to be inadequate. But it does not follow that this inadequacy must be total so that our descriptions can only amount to reflections of our own psyches. To enter into the recent debate over traditional theism and its neoclassical and panentheistic alternatives would take us too far afield here. Our present concern is not to advocate any particular theological conceptuality. The point at issue is that, however God is conceived, Christian faith is contingent upon the conviction that God is objectively real and personal. To assume that such conviction can only be a projection of ourselves toward the absolute is a reflection of modern prejudice, which runs counter to the experience of persons who have been claimed by God and whose lives testify to the genuineness of that claim.

The modern assumption that talk of a personal God can only be a projection of ourselves out into the cosmos is, of course, the direct inversion of the classical Judeo–Christian understanding according to which our identity as persons was seen to derive from God. Rather than fashioning God in our image, the understanding was that we were made in the image of God, or, as Douglas Hall has put it in verbal form, which is at once more contemporary and more biblical, our being consists in our imaging of God.[90] What makes the modern reversal particularly disturbing is the very real possibility that in arrogating the personal to ourselves we are actually engaged in its destruction. The language of projection we have been following so far derives essentially from Freud. If we go behind Freud to the similar, but theologically more sensitive perspective articulated by Feuerbach, we learn of the intimate connection between theology and anthropology. Although Feuerbach himself was not about to allow any independent integrity for theology, any more than Freud was to later on, in developing his anthropological interpretation of theology, he serves to suggest the intimate relation between the two for anyone who does take theology seriously in its own right. Having read Feuerbach, it is forever impossible to think of theology functioning without anthropological implications. Thus, our understanding of God rebounds on our understanding of ourselves, and vice versa. In contrast to both, naive theism, which assumes a direct vision of God that could be accused of projection, and a naive anthropocentrism, which assumes that all talk of God in personal terms is a projection on our part, the legacy of Feuerbach could take the form of a theological personalism for which our understanding of ourselves and our understanding of God are two sides of a single sensibility. If this is true, then the proposal that we regard God as an impersonal principle can be expected to rebound on our understanding of ourselves. Instead of allowing scope for our development as persons, to regard the ultimate in impersonal terms would then be tantamount to asserting the transitoriness of our own personalness.

The plight of the individual who would presume to possess personalness although denying its ultimate validity is depicted by Martin Buber as confinement to the past. "The *I* of the primary word *I-It*, that is, the *I* faced by no *Thou*, but surrounded by a multitude of 'contents,' has no present, only the past."[91] To accord principle the status of ultimacy is to attempt this possession that excludes personalness. "The present arises only in virtue of the fact that the *Thou* becomes present."[92] This is also the source of the person. "Through the *Thou* a man becomes *I*."[93] This encounter with the other Thou in turn is a reflection of the eternal Thou. "Every particular *Thou* is a glimpse through to the eternal *Thou*; by means of every particular *Thou* the primary word addresses the eternal *Thou*."[94] To be sure, this eternal *Thou* is no object; but neither is the finite *Thou*. The central point of Buber's personalism is that the reality of the personal subsists only in relation. In this sense, God is not an object, but in a very real sense is objectively personal; "God is the Being that is directly, most nearly, and lastingly, over against us, that may properly only be addressed, not expressed."[95] With this inevitable note of mysticism, which we have seen to be characteristic of religious sensibility, Buber gives voice to an outlook that is the antithesis of the modern anthropocentric perspective.

Only in one, all embracing relation is potential still actual being. Only one *Thou* never ceases by its nature to be *Thou* for us. He who knows God knows also very well remoteness from God, and the anguish of barrenness in the tormented heart; but he does not know the absence of God; it is we only who are not always there.[96]

Far from our conferring our personalness on God through projection, God alone is truly personal. We are persons only fitfully insofar as we participate in genuine relations with others and grow from that, a participation that, in turn, is grounded and sustained by the only truly enduring presence.

In his articulation of a fundamentally religious view of reality according to which we derive from God rather than God simply being our invention, Buber is not unaware of the human dimension that preoccupies modern self-consciousness. Far from allowing the human to become absorbed in the eternal Thou, he not only acknowledges our own reality as I's, but also sees that reality as involving an essential and continual struggle and conflict. "Man's religious situation, his *being there*, in the Presence, is characterized by its essential and indissoluble antinomy."[97] Where Kant resolves his antinomy between necessity and freedom by assigning the former to the world of appearances and the latter to the world of being, this reflective expedient is not available from the religious point of view. For "if I consider necessity and freedom not in worlds of thought but in the reality of my standing before God, if I know that 'I am given over for disposal' and know at the same time that 'It depends on myself,' then I cannot try to escape the paradox that has to be lived"[98] It is in the living that my total dependence on God, on the ever present eternal Thou, and my own distinct reality and responsibility are both affirmed and realized together. The process has been likened to our being conductors, directing the orchestra of our lives, which is really playing the score composed by God. And, of course, to avoid overtones of deistic absenteeism, it must be realized that the composer is present for the performance, available for consultation if we are sensitive enough to seek guidance and direction for our own directing.[99] Undoubtedly, all such analogies and metaphors run the risk of trivializing the divine. Insofar as the objection to an "objective personal God" is addressing that danger, it is salutary and can be ignored only at our peril. But when the intent is total, an absolute dismissal of every kind of personal understanding of God, then from the point of view of the Judeo–Christian perspective, this must be regarded as an abandonment of the faith.

It is doubtful even whether religious traditions, which from our point of view, do not think in terms of "a personal God," like Theravada Buddhism, would find this modern objection to divine personalness congenial. Although proponents of this modern Western view sometimes claim this alliance, in one essential respect the two positions are virtually antithetical. For where the central Buddhist aim is to transcend the attachments of selfhood, the fundamental assumption of this modern Western perspective is that we ourselves are the one reality that can be taken for granted. Whatever the difference is between Far Eastern traditions, which to our way of understanding represent impersonal notions of the ultimate, and the personal understanding of God which dominates the Middle Eastern traditions that form our religious sensibilities, they are in fundamental agreement, over against modern anthropocentrism, that the center of life is beyond us. It may well be that no other single factor compares with that shift in sensibility in accounting for the lack of interest in salvation in the modern West.

Thomas Merton has proposed a prescription for the renewal of monasticism, which has much to commend it as a directive for our general contemporary spiritual plight. Lest it be thought that this amounts to a personalistic absorption of social concern, we should perhaps first note his diagnosis of the predicament within monasticism.

When everything is centered on liturgy and on the harmonious, aesthetic decorum of traditional monasticism, then poverty and work may suffer. When everything is centered on poverty and labour, then the community may be overworked and lose interest in reading, prayer and contemplation.[100]

No effort is required to generalize from this analysis of monastic life to the wider spiritual environment. Insofar as interest in salvation does persist, it is characterized by a debilitating division between personal pietists and social activists. Merton's prescription for monastic renewal advises transcending both of these forms of preoccupation in a radical reconsideration of the point of the whole thing.

Actually, the renewal of monasticism cannot have any real meaning until it is seen as a renewal of the *wholeness* of monasticism in its *charismatic* authenticity. Instead of concentrating on this or that means, we need first of all to look more attentively to the end.[101]

If that end is perceived, the forms will follow. But if the forms themselves are allowed to dominate, the question of the "real meaning" of monasticism is not confronted. In the wider context of modern secular loss of interest in salvation or religious preoccupation with partial foci of personal or social approaches to salvation, the only possible source of any renewal of the "real meaning" of salvation lies in a rekindling of the sense of our divine sponsorship and destiny. Our view of salvation is ultimately a reflection of our view of God.

10

Eschatological Salvation

Although social and personal approaches to salvation are inadequate in themselves, advocates of each approach might acquire some tolerance for that of the other, and each approach might be more legitimate in itself, if these advocates are ultimately grounded in a sense of the eschatological basis of salvation. For finally, salvation is not a matter of the structures by which we live or of the personal sensitivity of which we are capable, but of the nature and activity of God. Any salvation that entails more just social arrangements that will endure or assurance of our own personal significance that is more than projections of our own wishes depends ultimately upon confidence in the metaphysical reality of a just and loving God. Perhaps the most promising note in this otherwise gloomy picture of the dissipation and dissolution in concern with salvation is the emergence in recent years of a new vision of the nature and activity of God that offers some prospect for a more truly eschatological understanding of salvation than has been available at any time in the past. This new vision amounts to a virtual reversal in the understanding of God from the assumption that divinity is constituted fundamentally by total self-sufficiency and imperviousness to a view that acknowledges the reality of sympathy and vulnerability in God. The radical nature of this reversal is indicative of the new opportunity to develop an understanding of salvation that is genuinely theologically grounded, but it also sounds a note of warning lest that reversal obscure something vital in the long-standing tradition against which it is reacting.

The Reversal on Divine Passibility

THE CLASSICAL ASSUMPTION OF DIVINE IMPASSIBILITY

In the controversies through which Christian orthodoxy was fashioned nothing was so assured as the assumption that God was characterized fundamentally by self-sufficient imperviousness. Whatever the differences between the two sides in the major controversies, Trinitarian and Christological, the protagonists on both sides tended to be equally convinced about the divine aseity. Thus, the leading combatants in the first round of the Trinitarian Controversy promoted their divergent conceptions of the Son within the context of a primary agreement on the basic nature of God. Arius assures Alexander: "We know one God . . . immutable and unchangeable . . . "[1] Athanasius differs from this affirmation only because he insisted that these qualities must also be attributed to the Son: "But the Son being from the Father and peculiar to his substance is unchangeable and immutable as the Father himself."[2]

We might expect that the triumph of the *homoousion* identification of the Son with the Father, and the identification of the Son with Jesus, would have occasioned a reconsideration of the divine imperviousness in the Christological Controversy, but, as Athanasius' position indicates, the effect was the reverse. Instead of finding the claim of incarnation indicative of divine sensitivity, the Christological Controversy transposed the assumption of divine immutability into the understanding of the person of Christ, and here again the pervasiveness of the assumption transcends the differences between Antiochene and Alexandrian positions. In the shot that launched the Christological Controversy, his sermon against the *theotokos*, Nestorius emphasizes the humanity of him who was born of Mary:

> That which was formed in the womb is not in itself God. . . . But since God is within the one who was assumed, the one who was assumed is styled God because of the one who assumed him. That is why the demons shudder at the mention of the crucified flesh; they know that God has been joined to the crucified flesh, even though he has not shared its suffering.[3]

This Antiochene insistence on the distinction between the divine and human natures in the person of Christ is countered by the Alexandrian emphasis on the unity of the person of Christ as the Word made flesh. Yet this insistence on the genuineness of incarnation does not prevent the champions of the Alexandrian position from invoking a distinction between the natures, which would rival anything in the Antiochene corpus, in the interest of preserving the divine Logos from human vulnerability. Thus Cyril of Alexandria writes to Nestorius:

We assert that this is the way in which he suffered and rose from the dead. It is not that the Logos of God suffered in his own nature, being overcome by stripes or nail–piercing or any of the other injuries; for the divine, since it is incorporeal, is impassible. Since, however, the body that had become his own underwent suffering, he is—once again—said to have suffered these things for our sakes, for the impassible One was within the suffering body.[4]

THE DEPTH OF THE ASSUMPTION

The conviction regarding the immutability and the impassibility of God was so fundamental that it was assumed rather than argued. The debates centered on the question of how the impassible God could be associated with passible humanity. Those who deviated from this view were very much in the minority, and tended to recede before the emerging consensus. Hippolytus records the heresy of one Noetus who held that God is both invisible and visible, unbegotten and begotten, immortal and mortal. This led him to say the following things: "When indeed, then, the Father had not been born, He [yet] was justly styled Father; and yet it pleased him to undergo generation, having been begotten, He himself became His own Son, not another's."[5]This allowed Noetus to predicate suffering of God. "That this person suffered by being fastened to the [accursed] tree, and that He commended His Spirit unto [the keeping of] Himself, having died [to all appearance] and not being [in reality] dead. And He raised Himself up the third day, after having been interred in a sepulchre."[6]

A more famous exponent of patripassianism was the target of Tertullian's ire, Praxeas. The latter's concession that the Father suffered only with the Son did not impress Tertullian.

> [Our heretics] indeed, fearing to incur direct blasphemy against the Father, hope to diminish it by this expedient: they grant us so far that the Father and the Son are two; adding that, since it is the Son indeed who suffers, the Father is only his fellow-sufferer. But how absurd are they even in this conceit! For what is the meaning of "fellow-suffering," but the endurance of suffering along with another? Now if the Father is incapable of suffering, he is incapable of suffering in company with another; otherwise, if He can suffer with another, He is of course capable of suffering.[7]

The classical consensus in theology was concerned with preserving God from the reality of suffering. In retrospect, it is amazing that a gospel which centered on the proclamation of the crucified as the very embodiment of God should have inspired such dedication to the goal of achieving formulations that would assure that God was not really identified with this reality. So the Trinitarian Controversy distinguished the comprehensive Father from the incarnate Son, and, although it was not the official position, for many this amounted to the assurance that it was the Father who really constituted the godhead so that the most that had to be conceded in the direction of divine passibility is that it was the Son who was associated with the way of the cross. Tertullian's rebuke of this tendency is prophetic for the ensuing Christological development which provided the means for preserving the Son from such contamination as well by confining the suffering to the human nature of Jesus. People like Noetus and Praxeas who had the temerity to suggest that God might actually be implicated in the sufferings of Jesus found themselves very definitely on the wrong side of the emerging consensus.

THE RECENT REVERSAL

The pervasiveness of the assumption of divine immutability and impassibility that underlays the consensus of classical Christian orthodoxy is matched today by an equally impressive emerging consensus to the opposite effect. Richard Bauckham credits English theologians with the initiation of this development.

> For once, English theology can claim to have pioneered a major theological development: from about 1890 onwards, a steady stream of English theologians, whose theological approaches differ considerably in other respects, have agreed in advocating, with more or less emphasis, a doctrine of divine suffering.[8]

But Bauckham acknowledges that the same direction has emerged in different quarters, apparently largely independently. No less a champion of traditional theological themes than Karl Barth endorses the reversal.

> In Jesus Christ God Himself, the God who is the one true God, the Father with the Son in the unity of the Spirit, has suffered what it befell this man to suffer to the bitter end. It was first and supremely in Himself that the conflict between Himself and this man, and the affliction which threatened this man, were experienced and borne. What are all the sufferings in the world, even those of Job, compared with this fellow-suffering of God Himself which is the meaning of the event of Gethsemane and Golgotha?[9]

The legacy of this admission is evident in Bonhoeffer's prison musings to the effect that God has allowed himself to be edged out of the world and onto the cross, and that only as the suffering God is God available to help us,[10] as well as in Moltmann's trinitarian theology of the cross, articulated under the telling title, *The Crucified God*.[11] A Lutheran version of this direction has emerged in Japan in Kazoh Kitamori's *Theology of the Pain of God*.[12] In America, the tendency is evident in Geddes MacGregor's *He Who Lets Us Be: A Theology of Love*,[13] and in process theology. Tertullian's dissatisfaction with Praxeas' concession that "the Father is only [the Son's] fellow-sufferer" suggests that he would be no more impressed by the Whiteheadian characterization of God as "the fellow-sufferer who understands."[14] The process version of divine passibility has been developed particularly by Charles Hartshorne.[15] The extent of this development combined with the fact that it constitutes a reversal of classical orthodoxy lends credence to Daniel Day William's description of it as a "structural shift in the Christian mind."[16]

If there is anything more striking than the magnitude of this transformation, it is the apparent naturalness with which it has unfolded.

> What is particularly remarkable about the theopaschite mind-set has been its development as a kind of open secret. . . . Indeed, this doctrinal revolution occurred without a widespread awareness that it was happening.[17]

From the long-standing unquestionableness of the impassibility of God, the perspective of large segments of contemporary theology has changed to the point where a recent book on this subject can begin with the words: "The concept of divine suffering is not only the core of our faith but the uniqueness of Christianity."[18] Noetus and Praxeas would enjoy a very different reception if they lived in the late twentieth century.

The Explanation for the Reversal

THE "IMPASSIBILITY" MISTAKE

How does heresy become orthodoxy? One approach is to recognize that the heretical designation was itself a misunderstanding. But in order for this claim to be convincing, some explanation for the misunderstanding must be provided. In this case, the explanation offered is that the view that God is essentially immutable and impassible arose from extraneous circumstances attendant on the formation of early Christian belief. Two features in particular are singled out as especially significant, the Greek philosophical influence under which early Christian doctrine was formulated and the impact of Roman political and military power that constituted the civic environment of early Christianity.

The term "theology" betrays its Greek origin. Thinking about God takes place on a more abstract plane than the experiential immediacy in which the Hebrews knew the deliverance of God in their own history and heard the divine demands through the prophetic prescriptions of the law and prophets. Christian theology emerges from this dual background. The situation is not quite so simple as to permit a direct parallel to be drawn between the austere God of Greek speculation and the involved God of Hebrew experience. For the Hebrews, God is the elevated *Elohim* of the first creation account as well as the intimate *Yahweh* of the second. That tension continues in the New Testament, but the balance was tipped decisively in the *Elohim* direction through the doctrinal debates of the early centuries of the common era as Christology developed under the influence of Greek philosophical inspiration. The Stoic ideal of imperviousness, the perfection of the absolute Good of Plato and the Prime Mover of Aristotle exerted their influence on the classical formulations of Christian theology.

Greek thought represents one prominent strand of a perspective that understands ultimate reality in contrast to the apparent reality of the world around us. "To Greek philosophy, as to Indian, it was axiomatic that divinity is intrinsically incapable of pain, and the classical Christian theology inherited this axiom of the 'impassibility' of God."[19] The Eastern perspective, in both Greek and Indian forms, is characterized by an immediate dualism, which conceals an ultimate monism. The Indian outlook, for example, in Hindu and Buddhist variations, advocates discipline designed to effect release from the confinement of egoistic desire. Those who are able to achieve this realize their oneness with true reality, which transcends this transitory realm. Greek philosophy gives this distinction an intellectual twist as the spiritual enlightenment sought in the Far East becomes the insight of wisdom achieved through disciplined reflection. But here too, the point is to rise above the instability of this passing world of change and decay to participate in the unchanging transcendent order. Even when Aristotle pulls this order down to earth, it is the form that gives shape to otherwise chaotic matter. The perennial theme is the primacy of permanence. The true is the eternal, the unchanging, in contrast to the undependability of the transitory.

For this outlook, God is characterized essentially by *autarkeia*, independence and sufficiency. What makes God, God is the totality and completeness of perfection, which allows no hint of any kind of need or lack that would suggest some kind of dependence on an external source. Whatever else might need to be affirmed, at the very least, God is exclusive actuality, autonomous and complete in the uniqueness of divine sufficiency. It is an indispensible corollary of this view that divine perfection entails a corresponding immunity to external forces. The primacy of permanence is accompanied by an equally primal imperviousness. To *autarkeia* is added *apatheia*.

The metaphysical contrast between the unchanging eternal realm and the transitory temporal realm has an epistemological counterpart in the contrast between the trustworthiness of reason and the deceptiveness of the experience of the senses. In Greek philosophy, reason is the route to reality, whereas reliance on experience and feeling is the surest way to court deception. As supreme reality, God, therefore, must be pure rationality. Any semblance of feeling would compromise the divine sufficiency, suggesting that God was somehow implicated in the realm of change, and consequently, less than totally sufficient and holy. To allow for divine passion would be to return to the mythic stage of the Homeric deities from which rational reflection had delivered Greek culture. It would also imply an element of passibility in God, which was excluded by the notion of God as pure act. As supreme rationality God must be beyond feeling and impervious to external influence, totally active without any element of receptivity. In order to be truly *autarkeia*, that is, in order to be truly divine, God must also be *apatheia*.

This apathetic understanding of God was reinforced by the perennial might and majesty of Roman political power. Through the immediacy of the Empire, the model of Roman authority was adopted for Christian organization and its veneration of power and control influenced its theology in decisive ways. Perhaps no one has called attention to this impact more suggestively than Whitehead in his contention that the understanding of God promoted by Jesus, which Whitehead calls the Galilean vision, was surrendered by Christians at an early stage as they began to render unto God attributes that belonged to Caesar.[20] The God of love whom Jesus addressed as Father became the imperial deity, ruling the universe from deistic heights of almost callous disregard. Somehow the two visions of God coexisted through the centuries of Roman founded Christendom. Personal piety looked to the God of Jesus, whereas theological reflection undermined this conviction through its insistence on primary attributes, which relegated divine compassion to the status of transitory concession. The pervasive presence of the Constantinian establishment encouraged and endorsed this whole direction so that the contradiction, when noticed, was tolerated as a paradox expressive of divine mystery.

THE RECOVERY OF THE BIBLICAL GOD

If for now we accept the explanation that the austere understanding of God, which made patripassianism seem heretical, is to be attributed to the influence of Greek philosophy and Roman politics, it remains to be shown how this came to be recognized and, thus, how Christian theologians came to countenance, and even insist on, the acknowledgement of divine suffering. There is one obvious source of this conversion, which in turn broadens into two progressively wider perspectives that together helped to normalize belief in divine pathos.

The obvious source of the change of heart on divine passibility is the renewal of interest in the Bible in the twentieth century. Examination of the Bible itself exposed the inadequacy of the immutable and impassible model for God. Thus, in his study of *The Prophets*, Abraham Heschel is constrained to develop a theology of divine pathos, which contends that for the prophets God is seen to be characterized most basically by concern rather than by power or wisdom, as the conventional view assumed.[21] Kazoh Kitamori suggests that "Jeremiah was surely the first man to see the pain of God."[22] But he concedes that this was a late insight, Jeremiah's more characteristic preoccupation being the wrath of God. The opening for the recognition of divine pain occurs in Jeremiah's poignant thirty-first chapter with its picture of the divine agonizing over Israel's fate and the promise of a new covenant in which Israel will experience God in the profound depth of its own life.

Recipients of the new covenant testify to the wisdom of Jeremiah's hope, claiming to find God in the unlikely experience of one condemned to death as a criminal. It is not surprising that Jews found this scandalous and Greeks regarded it as foolish. What is amazing is that Christians have been able to accept it so casually. The shocking implications are only now receiving widespread attention in terms of a recognition that if the way of the cross really points to God, then God is characterized in some fundamental way by that direction. It is neither accidental nor insignificant that this conclusion has been reached, especially by Protestant theologians, because theirs is a tradition centered on the authority and preeminence of the Bible. Luther's return to scripture impelled him in the direction of a *theologia crucis*, and the insistence on the necessity of recognizing divine suffering occurs today among theologians who are heirs of the return to the reformers and to their reverence for scripture which characterized the neoorthodox theology of the first half of the twentieth century.

THE INSPIRATION OF HISTORICAL CONSCIOUSNESS

The focus on the Bible as the authoritative source of knowledge of God encourages the disentangling of the God and Father of our Lord Jesus Christ from the impassible God modeled on Greek metaphysics and Roman imperialism by affirming the primacy of history over the longstanding assumption of the foundational status of nature. Luther's sympathy with Ockhamistic nominalism, liberal Protestantism's disavowal of metaphysics (as in Ritschl's neo-Kantianism), and neoorthodox emphasis on the novelty of God's action in Israel and in the Christ event (as in Barth's opposition to natural theology), all indicate how Protestant interest in scripture has been accompanied by a veneration for history and a corresponding depreciation of the natural and metaphysical orientation of traditional Christian thought. This development entails a progressively comprehensive understanding of the significance of history. From a recognition of the authoritative significance of the particular events attendant on the foundation and fortunes of ancient Israel and the early Christian community, through a concern for the authenticity and reliability of the records of these events, to the conviction that the reality to which the events and the records testify is itself essentially historical, the understanding of history becomes increasingly more prominent and inclusive.

Insofar as the Thomistic "grace perfects nature" may be taken as typical of the pre-Reformation Christian perspective, the events to which scripture testifies appear as restoration of an impaired innocence. Even the more holistic Augustinian perspective, preferred by the Reformers, assumes a transcendent metaphysical stability of which the historic events reflected in scripture are themselves testimonies. The historical consciousness that led to attributing particular significance to the events themselves reaches a climax in Barth's

Christocentrism. Here the development by which creation, however conceived, is subordinated to what happened in the Christ event accords an authoritative primacy to history. If God has come to humanity in the person of Christ, this must constitute the exclusive basis for our understanding of God. The ontological primacy of creation over redemption is displaced by the epistemological primacy of the saving Word through which creation becomes intelligible. Thus, in answer to what he characterizes as the Cartesian demand for some kind of general designation of God posed in the following terms: "Israel apart, what do we mean by God?" Barth's former student, Paul van Buren, suggests:

> The way out of this trap is to reject the question. Apart from Israel, God can be anything or nothing—an abstraction, an idea, an hallucination, what you will.[23]

Barth's Christocentrism is here broadened into an Israaeocentrism, but the confinement to the historical horizon and, indeed, to *Heilsgeschichte* is not compromised. In spite of having articulated an answer that would have been perfectly intelligible, if not also acceptable to Descartes, a few pages earlier—"*The Daily Prayer Book* of the Jews, which certainly addresses God as the God of Israel, also addresses Him innumerable times as King of the Universe: melek ha-olam."[24]—Van Buren's historical orientation cannot allow that this designation can be intelligible apart from the esoteric insight of heirs, genetic or spiritual, of this historic tradition.

The pervasiveness of historical consciousness is evident in the variety of its forms. It emerges as the identification of religious sensibility with the confessional particularity of esoteric religious traditions, as hermeneutic emphasis on the importance of the finitude of location, and as the social science insistence on the significance of social circumstances. These varieties of historical consciousness suggest that the historical orientation is symptomatic of a more pervasive outlook. Because history is in the first instance the story of the human drama, it is natural to locate this wider perspective in the anthropocentric outlook, which has increasingly displaced the traditional theocentric perspective in the modern era. Then ironically, Van Buren and Descartes share a common standpoint. The self-consciousness that led Descartes to focus on himself as a rational ego reaches Van Buren through the refinement of nineteenth century historical consciousness. The early modern awareness of our finitude characteristic of the most influential thinkers of the seventeenth and eighteenth centuries is qualified by the nineteenth century recognition of the importance of our particularity. The common denominator is that the finitude and particularity are both ours. The preoccupation with history is an expression of the more pivotal, pervasive, modern assumption of the anthropocentric perspective. When we refer to the Bible as being concerned particularly with history and even with being the source of historical awareness, in representing lineal development in contrast, for example, to the Greek cyclical assumption of unoriginal repetition, we must recognize that this characterization itself comes from the modern anthropocentric perspective, as does the concept of history itself. Thus, although the Bible might sustain such a reading, and there might be antecedents for the modern historical perspective in someone like Augustine, the self-conscious articulation of an explicit sense of history is a variation on the modern anthropocentric outlook. It is not insignificant that even Barth, who came to prominence as a theologian through his endorsement of Kierkegaard's affirmation of the infinite qualitative distinction between God and humanity, should have come to focus toward the end of his career on "the humanity of God."

The Import of the Reversal

THE LEGITIMACY OF THE REVERSAL

The recognition of a human dimension of God that not only allows for but also requires the acknowledgement of genuine suffering in God has an intuitive rightness as a reading of the gospel in contrast to which the classical reading appears highly problematic. How a gospel that centers in the claim that God is characterized essentially by caring, and which is seen particularly in one whose life was characterized by an altruism so offensive that it resulted in the cross, can be squared with an assumption of divine imperviousness is very far from evident. The most that can be allowed on this premise is that God makes some concession to creation, and even in creation, which in light of the divine aseity, is essentially a matter of indifference.

Much more credible is the view that understands God to be characterized by an inherent *kenosis*. "It is not *kenosis* in the sense of self-limitation, but it is kenosis as the superabundant and inevitable outpouring of the Divine Nature—God giving himself up to us completely in Creation, Providence, Redemption, and Regeneration."[25] Such affirmation of the essential graciousness of

God is not possible without recognizing a real and fundamental vulnerability that is the antithesis of imperviousness. It requires attributing real suffering to God. This violation of the traditional impassibility requirement is potentially as illuminating for one who gives it serious consideration as it is offensive for one who rejects it out of hand. It can be seen to plumb new depths of the gospel. "The pain of God is part of his essence! This is really the wonder."[26]

THE ILLUMINATION OF THE REVERSAL

The contrast with the imperial ruler could not be more pronounced. Whereas we accuse each other of playing God by trespassing in our respective spheres of freedom, the implication of this understanding of divine passibility is that God does not play God. This vision defies prosaic description. It is suggested more adequately in poetry, in the closing stanzas of the poem that reflects the title of W. H. Vanstone's book, *Love's Endeavour, Love's Expense*:

> Therefore He Who Thee reveals
> Hangs, O Father, on that Tree
> Helpless; and the nails and thorns
> Tell of what Thy love must be.
>
> Thou art God; no monarch Thou
> Thron'd in easy state to reign;
> Thou art God, whose arms of love
> Aching, spent, the world sustain.[27]

The prosaic reality entailed in this vision is the difference between power and worth. In contrast to the conventional wisdom, which equates these, the gospel of divine love necessitates their differentiation in the recognition that the supremacy of God consists not in pure power but in a security, which far from requiring the assurance of assertion, rather allows for the self-depreciation that gives scope for creation and the creatures who compose it. This understanding is captured in Geddes MacGregor's title, *He Who Lets Us Be: A Theology of Love*[28] If we feel uneasy about this characterization, fearing that it somehow compromises the ultimacy of God, MacGregor assures us that this understanding does not dispense with divine omnipotence; it only requires that this be regarded as the omnipotence of love according to which the meaning is not that God possesses some totality of power, whatever that would be, but rather it "can only mean that nothing diminishes his love."[29]

If we get past the sense that this somehow diminishes God, we might still wonder if this does not free God too easily from responsibility for the misery of life. The contrast between power and love is sometimes developed as a theodicy in which the appeal to love dissolves the troublesome question of how power, goodness, and evil are to be reconciled. Without entering into the complexities of this issue, we should note that whatever its merits or defects as a direction for theodicy, this understanding does not let God off the hook. On the contrary, if God really is characterized by love, this may well represent the most demanding course, from the divine perspective. Sheila Cassidy, the English doctor who suffered with and for the people she had come to care for following the coup in Chile that overthrew Allende in 1973, reflects on the price of fellow suffering. "I think it must be one of the hardest things in the world to do nothing when someone you care for is in trouble."[30] She tells of visiting two nuns in the *población*, who shared life with the residents of that area, the *pobladores*.

> They had shared the terror of the *pobladores* when the *población* had been surrounded and the tanks had driven between the little houses and over some of them, and they had stood numbly by as armed men searched their clothes for arms and their bookshelf for Marxist literature. Now, in the days of steadily increasing hardship, they shared their bread and more important, for it is easy to give what you have, they shared the desperate impotence of watching children die because they had no more to give. It is this standing by helpless that is so difficult and yet so important, the simple being there to share in the suffering of birth, of living and of death. It is when we have nothing left to give that we are forced to open our hearts to share in the grief of the other. What can you tell a woman whose son has just been shot or whose baby has died of malnutrition, or a woman with no bread in her house when you have none either? It would be so much easier to go away and do something constructive which would make one feel warm inside, but it is in the silent sharing of pain that love is shown.[31]

If we read this with parabolic rather than allegorical intent, we may see in it an indication of how difficult it must be for God who is intrinsically characterized by caring to endure the sufferings of the world. How much easier to send a legion of angels to deliver the faithful Jesus from the cross, but this is not God's way, for "it is in the silent sharing of pain that love is shown." Here we reach the real depth of the contrast between the classical and contemporary approaches to divine suffering. Where the classical consensus found it necessary to understand God in trinitarian terms in order to preserve God from the compromise that could be implied in incarnation, the contemporary understanding is reflected in Moltmann's contention that it is precisely the cross that requires that God be viewed in trinitarian terms, because the cross only makes sense theologically when it is seen as the Father sacrificing the Son in the Spirit.[32]

Moltmann's theological reflection and Shiela Cassidy's direct experience come together in the theological reflection prompted by the experience of Nathan Söderblom, who was consecrated Archbishop of Uppsala on 8 November, 1914 and found himself with friends and colleagues on both sides in the war that raged in the succeeding years. He was Swedish Chaplain in Paris from 1894 to 1910, and he had many friends in England and Scotland, especially as a result of the reproachment between Anglican and Swedish churches that began in 1908 when he was professor at Uppsala, and he was professor at Leipzig when war broke out. His efforts to bridge the gulfs of war helped pave the way for the Stockholm Life and Work Conference of 1925, but during the war he was a helpless bystander.

> The Archbishop of a neutral nation could only look on helpless, without the distraction of endless practical duties and the excitement of the conflict, which in large measure mitigated the suffering of the war for citizens of the belligerent nations. Then it was that he was driven back to ceaseless pondering on the Mystery of the Cross. It was his part to long to do something, yet to be helpless, and suffering is essentially helplessness, passivity. But Christian suffering, as in the Head of the Body, so also in the members, is at the same time activity, the activity of long-enduring love, which in the midst of sin and its awful consequences still goes on believing in God and trusting God.[33]

God endures the sufferings of the world with a depth of anguish that our glimpse of the cross can only begin to imagine.

THE IMPLICATION OF THE REVERSAL

Recognition of genuine suffering in God has an intuitive rightness as a reading of the basic thrust of the gospel. But this very rightness is subject to distortion unless it is handled very carefully. If it is taken in any sense to involve divine endorsement of suffering this renders us ultimately hopeless and God ultimately masochistic, if not sadistic.

The God who can meet our deepest needs will not be one who is himself entangled in its contingencies—not merely "the great companion—the fellow sufferer who understands"—-but one who, while his loving care extends to the least of his creatures and while he knows them in their weakness and need better than they know themselves, is himself unchanged and unchangeable, the strength and stay upholding all creation who ever doth himself unmoved abide. A God in whom compassion and impassibility are reconciled in the union of omnipotence and love.[34]

This more traditional affirmation from E. L. Mascall constitutes a reminder that MacGregor's "omnipotence of love" is subject to distortion if the love is sentimentalized so that the omnipotence amounts to an endless supply of sympathy. If possibility shades over into passivity, the corrective itself then stands in need of correction. For God, understood in passive terms, cannot be regarded as redeemer, and then, ironically, we should have to wonder whether it really makes sense to say that God is characterized fundamentally by love.[35] The sympathetic human identification Doctor Cassidy found inspiring in Chile points to a source of ultimate hope in the divine sympathy only if that identification has an active dimension such as Archbishop Söderblom finds in the cross.

Whitehead's characterization of God as the "fellow sufferer who understands" provides assurance only if the understanding exceeds the suffering. If we can be confident that God regards the suffering of life as worth the price for achieving the way of the Kingdom, then we may find consolation in the acknowledgement of divine passibility. Otherwise this alternative tradition may simply reflect the modern anthropocentric perspective. Sally McFague draws on Ruth Page's explication of God as friend[36] as an expression of the contemporary maturity of humanity that can only appreciate God in the horizontal terms of the mutuality of friendship and not in the more traditional vertical notions of salvation from above. However, in spite of her appreciation of the contemporary relevance of this approach, McFague also recognizes that the friendship model is inadequate for recognizing guidance, leadership, protection, governance, pre-eminence, in God and it is unable to express experiences of awe, ecstasy, fear, and silence in relating to God.[37] If these qualities are excluded, God may well be acceptable to sophisticated moderns, but the price of this relevance is finally irrelevance, because God so conceived adds nothing distinctive to the human sphere. The result will be a liberal humanism the epitome of which is expressed by Peter de Vries' Reverend Andrew Mackerel of People's Liberal Church.

People's Liberal is a Church designed to meet the needs of today, and to serve the whole man. This includes the worship of a God free of out-moded theological definitions and palatable to a mind come of age in the era of Relativity. "It is the final proof of God's omnipotence that he need not exist in order to save us," Mackerel had preached.[38]

The Christian understanding of God as characterized essentially by self-giving love bears very different meanings when it is under-stood as self-giving that constitutes the being of God and as self-giving that dissolves the being of God. The deicidal deity of Reverend Mackelel is the inevitable result of a sentimentalized understanding of divine love that is really nothing more than the reverse side of modern anthropocentrism. The God who is there to bless us and affirm us totally is finally indistinguishable from ourselves. What makes the love of God significant is the fact that it is the love of *God*. That is to say God is not to be equated with pure identification but is to be characterized by a divine integrity that makes the identification significant. Without this integrity that characterizes God as God, talk of divine love is too coincidentally compatible with our own self-interest to allow God to escape sus-picion and ultimately irrelevance.

Short of countering this complete loss of God, recognition of divine otherness is also essential for anything approaching an ade-quate understanding of the love of God as such, and of divine suf-fering. Acknowledgement of the divine integrity prevents a senti-mental understanding of divine love by providing a sense of the cost of that love to God. It then appears that far from representing an anthropocentrism, divine suffering represents a peculiar depth of suffering such as we mortals call only vaguely and tangentially grasp.

Ironically, such an appreciation of divine suffering depends on a recognition of that element, which has appeared to be the most formidable obstacle to its recognition. The assumption of divine immutability and impassibility promoted by Greek culture and sanctioned by Roman authority also reflects the theological aware-ness of divine otherness, which the Bible refers to as the holiness of God. Whereas the preoccupation with immutability and impassi-bility obscured the gospel of divine love, the present recovery of that proclamation is in danger of perpetrating a similar overreac-tion in the other cdirection by failing to recognize the divine in-tegrity which gives the divine identification with humanity poignan-cy and depth. The fundamental development of this renewed appreciation of the God who suffers with us and for us must address this recognition that it is God who suffers so that the genuineness of the suffering is recognized as the impossible possibility of divine passibility. Only such a truly eschatological understanding of salvation can overcome the inadequacies of social and personal approaches and, at the same time, provide the basis and rationale for affirming the legitimate concerns that animate each of these directions.

Conclusion

11

The Bottom Line for Salvation

Our survey of the checkered course that the Christian understanding of salvation has taken over the centuries and, in particular, the
buffeting it has received from the challenges of modern secularity
and contemporary religious pluralism suggests that any conclusion
about the prospects for an appreciation of salvation in the days
ahead is a precarious undertaking at best. And yet no professed
audit, no matter how metaphorically the term is used, can avoid
positing some overall summation. In light of what we have seen
about the ways salvation has been appreciated and the challenges
these have faced, it is possible to draw some general conclusions
regarding elements in the received understandings that now appear
especially problematic, other elements that appear equally indispensible and, on the basis of this, to venture some suggestions as
to the main ingredients that are likely to characterize any vital
sense of the significance of salvation in the future.

Redundant Dimensions in Salvation

If we think of salvation in terms of the prevalent stereotype of the
assurance of our own individual destiny in another world beyond
this life, the prospects for widespread interest in the subject do not
seem to be great, despite the recent revival experienced by conservative segments of Christianity. Our basic sensibility and understanding of life is simply too different to allow this stereotype to
retain credibility in the world as we have come to know it. We may
identify three elements in this understanding that have become
especially problematic.

THE OTHERWORLDY CONTEXT

For most people who have imbibed the contemporary consciousness developed in the modern West, far from representing a locus

of meaning, the idea of finding supreme reality in another world is bound to appear illusory and escapist. The legacy of the Renaissance and the Reformation, mediated by the accomplishments of modern technology, discloses too much complexity and challenge in this world to allow attention to be deflected to a hypothetical world beyond. "One life at a time," might be the most positive concession to otherworldliness that can be expected in the present.

We have seen that this can represent a threat to religious faith, to the point of constituting an *ersatz* religion in its own right, the principal extant version of which is the contemporary devotion to consumerism. But this possessive interest in the world is not the only form that this direction may take. In fact, it can take an almost directly contrary route in terms of a positive appreciation of this world for its own sake. This interest may be assumed to be inherent in the world itself, as demonstrated by the many who are dedicated to the ecological movement and by those who are simply fascinated by the complexities of nature in either a scientific capacity or an involvement that is more direct and personal. While for many this fascination with the intricacies of the world constitutes an absorbing interest in its own right, others are impelled to wonder about the origins of this intricacy. Through this wonder emerges a chastened form of natural theology; less imperialistic in pretentions to rational coercion than the seventeenth and eighteenth century variety, but equally convinced that the world is not intelligible in itself precisely because of the fascination it elicits.

From the other direction, that of a positive theological sensibility, which affirms belief in God apart from any natural base, a similar theological evaluation of the world may be forthcoming in the form of the insistence that neglect of this world in the interests of a concentration on a world beyond amounts to an insult to the creator of this world. To understand salvation in such otherworldly terms that this world is relegated to the status of dispensable launching pad for the real world beyond empties the doctrine of creation of all real significance. And although we are apt to ascribe this mistake to our medieval forebearers, the most thoroughgoing version of this development was problably that devised in the modern period. Under the medieval penitential system, this life served as the proving ground for the true life beyond. Thus far, this life was significant. Indeed, this life was invested with eternal significance because what we did with this life determined our eternal destiny, with due allowance for further purgatorial adjustments. But later Protestant preoccupation with divine grace fostered a suspicion of moral exertion that resulted in the contracting of the preparatory life into the dramatic moment of decision. And even if that decision has to be renewed, it still reflects instantaneous points with no more than tangential connections with everyday life. In this regard, extreme otherworldliness may be more a post-Reformation development than a medieval one, with the result that it is modern Christians rather than their medieval progenitors who have been most inclined to disparage creation.

When this is recognized, the loss of interest in otherworldliness, which has progressively characterized the modern outlook, does not appear quite so threatening because the extreme preoccupation with otherworldliness is itself largely a modern phenomenon. This is not to say that Christian faith can readily embrace a purely secular worldliness, as was widely advocated in the 1960s. The point is rather that it can and must welcome the lively interest in this world that has come to be taken for granted in the modern era. A faith that regards this world as God's creation cannot do otherwise. Where a cause for protest does arise is when this interest becomes dogmatically secularist, constituting an abstract foreclosure on the vitality of life no less stifling than an arid otherworldliness. At this point, Christian concern for the gospel of salvation must insist that its readiness to abandon the preoccupation with otherworldliness does not entail an abandonment of otherness, of the sense of being surrounded by a reality that far exceeds any horizon we can perceive or imagine. It is on this type of distinction between otherworldliness and otherness that the credibility of the Christian gospel of salvation largely depends.

Although, in theory, Christian faith might be able to abandon the fixation on otherworldliness to its actual benefit, because its real concern is with otherness, in practice, this shift in focus might not be so easily achieved because the other-worldly focus has become so identified with the substance of the faith. This brings us to the more serious challenge to otherworldliness that has emerged in recent years. According to this challenge, the problem with otherworldliness is not simply that it represents a deflection of interest from this world to a nebulous otherworld about which we can only speculate, but, on the contrary, this deflection really represents a subterfuge, because this otherworldly preoccupation has very definite implications for the way we actually live in this world. The primary source of this critique is, of course, Karl Marx, in his charge that precisely through its promise of a better life beyond, Christianity defused the discontent of those whose lot in this life was most miserable and, at the same time, protected the privileged position of those who benefited from the status quo. The Marxist solution, sometimes enthusiastically endorsed by Christians, is to apprise the proletariat of its condition and aid its revolt against the injustice of it. We have seen that in their embracing of this direction, Christians may tend to become so absorbed in the social revolution that they do not pursue the more radically theological implications of the Marxist critique. These implications reach beyond the critique of otherworldliness to challenge the Christian claim about being grounded in otherness. For if the central focus of Christianity concerns my eternal destiny, then the primary interest is not in otherness but in myself. Christian faith has somehow become inverted from an experience of release from self through recovery of our grounding in divine grace to a preoccupation with self to the extent of making my ultimate significance the focal point of the faith. If otherworldliness does entail such a foreclosure on otherness, then it is not only dispensable as an impediment to a wholesome appreciation of God's creation and of the inherent significance of this life, but also representational of an actual perversion of the faith itself. The preoccupation with otherworldliness then, must be challenged precisely in the interests of a genuine grounding in otherness.

THE DETERMINISTIC TONE

After the suspicion of otherworldliness, the aspect of the proclamation of salvation that is probably most offensive to contemporary sensibilities is the suggestion of determination from beyond. The notion of salvation carries the connotation of acquiescence in some kind of cosmic fate. This impression may owe a great deal to such prominent molders of Christian thought as Augustine and Calvin. In his insistence on the primacy of divine grace, Augustine was led to imply, if not actually to advocate, a doctrine of predestination. Our dependence on divine grace is so thorough that the logic of this dependence seems to entail the conclusion that our direction in life is fundamentally determined by divine fiat. Followers of Calvin left no doubt as to the implications of this Augustinian insistence on grace, which had been renewed by their mentor. For if justice were to be done to the inescapability of divine sovereignty, the determination would have to extend to nonbelievers as well as to believers. Just as the "saved" must attribute their salvation to God, so too, they can recognize that ultimately the "damned" cannot be credited with sealing their own fate through rejection of divine grace, but rather their fate must also be traced to divine determination. This terrible doctrine of double predestination, whereby some are destined for salvation and others for damnation, represents the zenith in deterministic understandings of salvation. As such, it provides the context for appreciating most clearly the objections to the deterministic tone.

The note of determinism is the practical point of eruption for what might otherwise appear as theoretical reservations about interest in another world. As we have seen, far from entailing an intrinsic depreciation of this world, belief in another world, when seen as the culmination of what we have done in this world, actually heightens the significance of this world. The depreciation of this world really becomes significant when concern with how we live here is contracted to a moment, or moments of decision, which in themselves are fundamentally unconnected with the ongoing involvements of life. In this abandonment of the world, opposites meet; the supposedly supremely free decision of the individual and the sense of inevitability by which the believer is constrained to attribute that decision to divine grace. It is this sense of predetermination that most effectively drains this life of significance. When even the moment of decision is attributed to God, one must wonder what scope remains for human activity. It is this sense of the divine determination of life that appears to modern consciousness to entail the corollary of the futility of creation.

This sense of futility may be nowhere more pronounced than in the reaction to the accounts of atonement by which Christian theologians have attempted most directly to articulate the Christian understanding of salvation. We have seen how these accounts have indulged in crude imagery, portraying divine deception and, perhaps, even implying sadistic tendencies on the part of God, and how, even at their best, these accounts leave the sense of a remote transaction, effected totally apart from us. In what might be dismissed as utter caricature, were it not for the fact that it does seem to reflect what a significant number of Christians seem to have believed, and in some cases continue to believe, Dorothy Sayers presents a vivid portrait of the God who requires atonement:

> God wanted to damn everybody, but his vindictive sadism was sated by the crucifixion of his own Son, who was quite innocent, and, therefore, a particularly attractive victim. He now only damns people who don't follow Christ or who have never heard of him.[1]

All that needs to be added to complete the picture is to make explicit the corollary of divine sovereignty, which states that the saving and the damning are ultimately attributable to God.

In spite of the predilection to understand the doctrine of atonement in ways that lent some credence to this grim portrait of a sadistic God, we have seen that they are susceptible to different treatment. The God who satisfies his sadistic impulses through the sacrifice of "his own Son" takes on a different appearance when the implications of "his own Son" are recognized. For although it is true that there is something in God's nature that demands payment for sin—the basis for the sadistic reading—the other side of the picture is that it is also God who provides that payment because the Son is no less God than the Father. We have seen Jurgen Moltmann's contention that this is the real basis for the doctrine of the Trinity; the requirement that to make sense of the cross we must understand it as the Father sacrificing the Son through the Spirit. However, although this answers the charge of sadism, it only serves to aggravate the sense of determinism implicit in the impression of an alien transaction carried out entirely by God on our behalf.

The modern, subjective understanding of atonement, the moral influence theory, proposed initially by Abelard, but only adopted on a broad scale since the emergence of the liberal approach to theology in the nineteenth century, can be understood as an attempt to counter this sense of an alien transaction that does not really involve us. On the moral influence view, atonement is not something effected by God on the cross, but rather entails the relation into which we are invited through the cross. Atonement is effected through our recognition of the extent to which God reaches out to us in the cross, and the resultant reciprocation on our part. But as we have also seen, this gives us a significant role in the transaction that constitutes atonement only at the price of minimizing the seriousness of sin to the point where it is no longer clear that atonement is really required. Far from providing recompense for sin, all that is needed is the recognition that God does not require such recompense. A solution to a problem that amounts to eliminating the whole subject that constitutes the problem in the first place is, to say the least, a drastic one. It certainly undermines the claim of Rudolf Otto that Christianity excels in its appreciation of atonement. "No religion has brought the mystery of the need for atonement or expiation to so complete, so profound, or so powerful expression as Christianity."[2] As we have seen, the factor that, above all, accounts for Otto's characterization of Christianity as the religion of atonement and for the virtual disappearance of the whole subject in the modern subjective reading, is that of the holiness of God. The divine acceptance, which the moral influence view takes to be so evident and so immediately available, is for Otto marvelous to the point of being unbelievable precisely because of the holiness of God. "To take this paradox out of Christianity is to make it shallow and superficial beyond recognition."[3] That this has been so largely accomplished in our day may well be due in considerable measure to the development Otto deplores. A religion of atonement will not present a vital and engaging demeanor when it itself is portrayed in such a way as to negate any sense of need for atonement.

Seen in these terms, proponents of Christian faith must bear a sizeable share of responsibility for the fate of the gospel of salvation in the contemporary context. And yet that diminution in concern with atonement also reflects an element of modern sensibility that cannot be ignored. The idea of a determination of our condition effected from beyond ourselves and without our participation strikes directly at the sense of responsibility that is so fundamental to our contemporary understanding. Nor is the situation greatly relieved by the Barthian expedient of emphasizing the representative humanity of Jesus so that the atonement effected in him is seen to involve a genuine struggle between God and humanity. For if the divine/human struggle is encapsulated in Jesus, this does touch our own species, but this contact remains remote and fundamentally unreal to us. Events in first century Palestine are not much nearer than decisions in the heavenly councils. It might be that the single most significant failure of the Church has been its inability to effect a credible sense of connection between what is supposed to have been accomplished in Jesus and the realities of life as we experience it today. Where that was accomplished throughout Christendom, primarily by means of the Eucharist, the process of secularization has left that central sacrament isolated as a liturgical island in a sea that sustains voyages with many different destinations and itineraries. The Protestant shift of focus to the individual affords a means of retaining some sense of meaning for the gospel, but at the price of an even more drastic isolation of it from the ongoing engagements of life. Luther's two realms repeatedly accelerated into the identification of faith with the inner feelings of the pious, which in turn issued in the modern evangelical isolation of the moment of decision for Christ. When this decision appears, in retrospect, to have been prompted by divine grace, we have the total irony of a fundamentally deterministic understanding of life, which does not really affect life as it is lived day by day. Thus, to the apparent futility of a life that is supposedly determined from beyond, through its divine origin and reclamation is added the insult apparently to both God and ourselves of a spiritual determinism that does not significantly determine the most fundamental commitments and preoccupations of the present. It is not surprising that the modern anthropocentric turn should have taken such a decidedly secularist direction in characterizing humanity in terms of the assumption of a virtually absolute freedom of self-determination, or that this self-consciousness should have been succeeded by the social consciousness that attempts to effect a determination of life in purely immanent terms. The viability of salvation today depends on an understanding of it that avoids the sense of being determined by decisions and transactions from beyond, as in the traditional views of atonement and, at the same time, provides a more definite direction that the modern subjective version of atonement seems to allow.

THE NOTE OF FINALITY

In addition to the unwitting or culpable deflection of attention from the realities of this world perceived in otherworldliness, and the apparent futility implicit in the acceptance of an externally imposed determination of life, the other particularly offensive element in the prevailing understanding of salvation is the connotation of finality. Indeed, this objection to finality can be regarded as the frustration with determinism perceived from the other end. Where determinism bears the connotation of life being programmed in advance, the sense of finality reflects this futility seen as a foreclosure of future possibilities. As some grand solution to the enigmas of life, salvation appears simplistic and naive, a short-circuiting of the complexities and challenges that make up the ongoing substance of life.

This suspicion of finality owes its origins particularly to the historical consciousness that has come to dominate the Western outlook, especially since the mid-point of the nineteenth century. Although the age of optimism was shattered by the disastrous events of the first half of twentieth century, two world wars bracketing a massive economic depression, the sense of expectancy of better days ahead has been so buoyed by the innovations of modern technological mastery that not even the colossal environmental threat that is now seen to be the accompaniment of this innovation has been able to puncture this fundamental sense of the inevitability of infinite progress. Insofar as this threat is taken seriously, the only finality that is contemplated is the finality of destruction, not of salvation. The world might end as a smoldering greenhouse or a wintry nuclear wasteland, but if this fate is to be prevented, this will be accomplished only through the painful and prolonged adjustments of the inhabitants of the planet. To look for a single, final solution is precisely to embrace the apocalyptic visions that would welcome just such annihilation.

The positive appreciation of this world and the sense that what we do in it must be significant, which makes otherworldliness and determinism so offensive to contemporary sensibilities, entails the further requirement that what that significance is must itself somehow emerge in living rather than being subject to any definite kind of anticipation. The notion of "the final solution" immediately conjures up recollections of the tyrannical fanaticism that underlay and the atrocities that accompanied the second World War. The tyranny and torture of any such grandiose visions of finality must be precluded by the recognition of the open-ended nature of life, of the impossibility of our possessing any conclusive knowledge of its ultimate destiny.

Where the objection to determinism represents a defense of human freedom and a demand for scope for human initiative, the opposition to finality can be seen to reflect a more humble vision of the human condition. Rather than placing ourselves front and center, the questioning of finality amounts to a confession of the limitations of human wisdom. We do not have a firm grip on a master plan for the universe. We are finite creatures, whose horizon of vision cannot help but reflect that finitude. And yet, significant thought this concession is, in a broader sense, the opposition to finality is even stronger than the objection to determinism in its promotion of our own species. For the renunciation of a controlling vision also amounts to the rejection of any sense of direction that is not entirely of our own devising. It is not just that the destiny of life must come to be appreciated through the living of it, but that any notion of destiny must itself be fashioned by us. The depth of historical consciousness reaches beneath the level of our own finitude and locatedness to embrace even the foundations of life. Those foundations themselves must be subject to development, emerging out of the ongoing historical processes of life itself. Thus it is not just our own understanding, but reality itself, that lacks any clearly identifiable final consummation.

This totalitarian thrust of historical consciousness renders the concern with claims to finality the most significant challenge faced by proponents of an appreciation of salvation that would aspire to contemporary credibility. The otherworldly focus, though deeply imbedded in Christian consciousness, might be amenable to relegation to secondary status, and the concern over determinism can be shared by all but the most ardent predestinarians. However, when the scope for human initiative is seen to encompass the very foundations of life, this entails a threat to the theological sensibility itself, which would eliminate any basis for an appreciation of salvation. It is one thing to admit the tentativeness of our grasp of the final point of life, but to hold that there is none, other than the approximations we ourselves develop, is to abandon the context that makes salvation intelligible. On such a basis, it is doubtful whether there can be a sense of common meaning, beyond our own individual hopes and wishes. The intelligibility of salvation depends on the recognized need for ever more comprehensive-sources of sustenance and direction, as indicated by James William McClendon's sense of the requirements of Christian ethics.

> Two essential Christian convictions must round out the account. One is the conviction (call it the doctrine of the church, if you please) that my own story is inadequate, taken alone, and is hungry for another to complete it. That gives us the communitarian element in Christian ethics: My story must be linked with the story of a people. The other is the conviction (call it the doctrine of salvation) that *our* story is inadequate as well: The story of each and all is itself hungry for a greater story that overcomes our persistent self-deceit, redeems our common life, and provides a way for us to be a people among all earth's peoples without subtracting from the significance of others peoplehood, their own stories, their lives.[4]

While the scope of this requirement must leave a lot of room for the limitations of our vision, the exclusion of this sense of overall significance is probably the single most important obstacle facing any attempt to appreciate salvation in contemporary terms.

Required Dimensions in Salvation

With the advantages of hindsight, it is possible to see some of the challenges posed by the modern post-Enlightenment outlook as agents of purification, rather than simply as sources of annihilation, for Christian concern with salvation. Some of the chastened convictions that emerge from these refining fires can be anticipated from what has been said about the chief sources of dissatisfaction with the notion of salvation. However, because such a procedure can give the appearance of retroactively baptising modern secularity, in Christian terms, it is necessary to indicate more precisely what it is about the Christian understanding of salvation that finally remains untouched by these challenges of modern sensibilities.

OTHERNESS RATHER THAN OTHERWORLDLINESS

The cardinal and indispensable context of the Christian gospel of salvation is not the assumption that there is another world in contrast to this present world, but that this world is embedded in a surrounding and sustaining dimension of otherness. There is not much room for controversy regarding the lack of otherworldly interests in the Old Testament. While the psalmist gives voice to the prospect of descent into Sheol, this very definitely refers to a present option rather than an otherworldly destiny, whatever it might imply about the cosmological assumptions of the day. At the same time, it is clear that the references to heaven are to the canopy of the earth rather than to another world seen in contrast to this world. Heaven is the essential dwelling place of God, but the God who is to be found most immediately in the ongoing drama of the people who were rescued from Egypt. Old Testament concern with salvation reaches from that deliverance as the formative saving event to the day of Yahweh, when that drama will reach its climax. What that climax will involve is subject to different understandings, particularly among the prophets, but that it does not refer to another world, in distinction from this world, is quite clear.

The Old Testament focus on the people gave the Old Testament notions of salvation a fundamentally communal form. This orientation is continued in the New Testament in the centrality of the kingdom in the teachings of Jesus. The kingdom is life lived as God intended it to be; it is where the will of God is done on earth as in Heaven. This communal orientation constitutes an object of concern, which appears in retrospect to be quite different from the stereotype of Christian faith as being fundamentally preoccupied with the destiny of the individual in another world. Indeed, this whole development can be regarded as a deviation from the primitive interest and intent of the gospel as reflected in the message of Jesus. This is the crux of the charge that the Christian theology of salvation obscured and abandoned the original gospel of Jesus, a charge that, as we have seen, has been particularly leveled at St. Paul. However, the lack of basis for this charge is even more evident here than in the more general considerations concerning Paul's emphasis on Christology and atonement. For the reality is that, from the New Testament accounts, references to another world are more characteristic of Jesus himself than of Paul. Aside from the use of "heaven" with the general designation of firmament or as standing for the otherness of God, which we take to be the indispensable reference, when the term is used to indicate the personal destiny of the individual in another world, sayings attributed to Jesus are more susceptible of this reading than are citations from Paul's letters. Thus, the beatitudes promise great reward in heaven (Mt. 5:12; Lk. 6:23); we are admonished to "lay up treasure in heaven" (Mt. 6:20) (an admonition that was certainly not lost on medieval Christianity and later protestant evangelicalism); and the so-called rich young ruler is promised "treasure in heaven" in recompense for the renunciation of his preoccupation with his present treasure. To find anything comparable in Paul we have to turn to his assurance of the reality of resurrection and the explanation regarding the spiritual body in I Corinthians 15, but we easily overlook the fact that the climax of that familiar passage, employed so regularly as a source of consolation in funeral services, is not the promise of individual reward in another world, but the assurance that "in the Lord your labour is not in vain" (I Cor. 15:58). The only references to heaven that could be taken to endorse a promise of reward in another world are those of Philippians 3:20–21 ("But our commonwealth is in heaven, and from it we await a Saviour, the Lord Jesus Christ, who will change our lowly body to be like his glorious body, by the power which enables him even to subject all things to himself.") and the introductory allusion in Colossians 1:5 to "the hope laid up for us in heaven."

At the very least, this suggests that the recollections of Jesus' message are every bit as interested in our qualification for life in another world as is Paul, if not more so. If it be held that the accounts of Jesus' message as we have them might bear traces of Pauline influence, such concern can be dissipated by noting the total absence in Paul of any threat regarding the negative possibility of another world. According to the synoptics, Jesus warned of the dangers of "hell fire" (Mt. 5:22), of the body being cast into hell (5:30; 18:9; Mk. 9:47), or of the destruction of "both soul and body in hell" (10:28; Lk. 12:5). According to Matthew's portrayal, Jesus wondered how the Pharisees could possibly "escape being sentenced to hell" (23:33). By contrast, Paul, who supposedly is preoccupied with sin and damnation, never mentions hell. Although he does look to a life to come, his focus is very largely on the quality of life that is available to, and expected of, the Christian now.

A full consideration of this issue would involve careful analysis of the way in which the early Church came to terms with the delay of the parousia, but without entering into this complex subject, what is clear is that the main source of the otherworldly orientation in Christianity is not the apostle of salvation. If the future of Christianity lies in a return to Jesus and his message, then we shall have to reckon with the apocalyptic warnings of the rewards and punishments in the world to come, and not arbitrarily confine our attention to pronouncements on the ways of the kingdom, which are so amenable to interpretations contiguous with contemporary social consciousness. The main alternative and the one advocated here is to regard an understanding of Christianity dominated by these apocalyptic references as no less a distortion of the basic thrust of the faith than the anachronistic reading of the references to the kingdom as though these were meant to promote projects in social engineering. The central focus of the gospel may then be seen to reside not in an emphasis on the importance of our ultimate individual destiny or on the importance of how we organize our institutions but on the restoration of life by, in, and through its creator, our restoration as creatures of God rather than as individuals who must be concerned with our own destiny or as engineers of social utopias. If that central thrust is appreciated, concern over our individual destiny should recede, because we find our security in God rather than in ourselves, and the communal and social repercussions of this reorientation should follow as a matter of course, because our restoration to God entails our restoration to one another. At their best, approaches to theology that focus on issues of meaning for individuals and on the perfecting of social arrangements recognize their rootedness in the otherness of God by which we are claimed and cleansed. It is this otherness as constant source of challenge and transformation that lies at the heart of the gospel, rather than belief in another world or reaction against such belief in attempts to transform this world without facing the transformation of our basic condition proclaimed in the gospel.

DIRECTIVE RATHER THAN DETERMINISM

Just as the central focus of Christian faith concerns the otherness of God present to us in Christ, rather than the insistence that there is another world in contrast to this world, so too, in spite of equally prominent examples to the contrary, its fundamental affirmation is not that life is finally predetermined but that it comes with a built-in directive. It is difficult to imagine a more futile exercise than the world as understood in the Christian doctrine of creation, if that is taken to entail a total preprogramming by the creator. Such an undertaking not only renders our existence pointless; it is also insulting to the creator. Only an extremely insecure and unimaginative creator would bother to create such a world. This is the ironic note that is missed by people who end up insisting on some form of determinism because this seems to be required by a due appreciation of the sovereignty and majesty of God.

The trend in recent theology to recognize passibility in God, a trend, which would be abhorrent to this sensibility, that results in affirmations of determinism, then actually appears more flattering to God than this insistence on total divine control. For the greatness of God is then seen to consist not in self-sufficient imperviousness, from which it could follow that everything must be traceable to divine stipulation, because God bothered to make the concession of creating the world in the first place, but rather divine greatness is manifest in the far superior ability to take the risk of a genuinely free creation. Then God is not bound even by the need to maintain control. In fact, according to the Christian revelation, God is so committed to creaturely freedom that the divine response to the effrontery of a rebellious creation still eschews the expedient of coercion, identifying rather with the victims of this rebelliousness and seeking to quell the disturbance by persuasion rather than by power.

We have seen, however, that, in spite of the attractiveness of this portrait of divinity as a depiction of the theological implications of the gospel, this understanding can also represent a reflection of the tendency of modern anthropocentrism to fashion a vision of God congenial to our own interests. Because of this inclination, we must be wary of any depiction that would rebound to the opposite extreme from the deterministic stance, to affirm a total indeterminism, a complete freedom for us mortals to do what we will. That extreme is approached, for example, by some process philosophers and theologians, the most prominent of whom is probably Charles Hartshorne. On his interpretation of the two sides of God identified by the process thought following Alfred North Whitehead, the primordial side which provides ever new possibilities for life and the consequent side that receives from the world what has been done with those possibilities, Hartshorne goes so far as to accord priority to the consequent side.[5] This allows him to affirm that God, too, is genuinely subject to process, actually developing through time, but more importantly, from his point of view, it allows genuine scope for the reality of human history. What we do with life is significant, so significant that God is shaped by it through the necessity of receiving our contributions via the consequent side. However, whereas this concern with a genuine dialectic wherein the world does make God in a sense, just as in another sense, God makes the world, also characterized Whitehead's original organic philosophy, he was more circumspect in preserving the divine distinctiveness. "There remain the inescapable realm of abstract forms, and creativity, with its shifting character ever determined afresh by its own creatures, and God, upon whose wisdom all forms of order depend."[6] In his own terms, Whitehead accords a primacy to the primordial side in God, as the eternal source of novelty, whereas Hartshorne broadens this base to take in the whole process, God and world together. In so doing, there can be no doubt that Hartshorne speaks for contemporary sensibilities more adequately than Whitehead. Freedom, understood as the antithesis of determinism, is for many the *sine qua non* of any adequate contemporary vision of life. Whether this can be true theologically, however, is another matter. From this point of view, Whitehead's reservation might be more sagacious.

The problem with the modern tendency to elevate freedom to absolute status is that this essentially obliterates the distinction between God and humanity in principle. If we are characterized fundamentally by freedom, then we have life entirely at our disposal. What we do will have consequences, and so, in that sense, there will be restrictions, but these are seen as clashes of freedom. The standard liberal political philosophy, which is essentially the philosophy of total freedom, is that we must agree to restrictions on our freedom in the recognition of the freedom of others. The anthropocentrism of modern liberalism has been exposed in recent years through the environmental crisis, which suggests that there are limits on human activity inherent in nature, and not simply in the presence of other human beings. We have seen that one prominent response to this amounts to an attempt to broaden the base of liberality to take in nonhuman species, to attribute rights to animals and plants as an extension of the claims made by, and on behalf of, human beings in the modern West. We also suggested that the artificiality of this expedient could be avoided by reconsidering the adequacy of this assumption regarding the primacy of freedom itself rather than by attempting to extend it even further. Perhaps the lesson and challenge of the ecological crisis is not that we should come to treat nature as we treat ourselves, but that we should rethink our understanding of ourselves. Perhaps the fundamental difficulty is not that we have failed to respect the freedom of other species, but that freedom itself is not the basic category. The ecological crisis might really entail the reemergence of the importance of the whole, of the basic connectedness of reality. Where we have prized independence and autonomy, we now see that the impact of isolated tampering with elements of the environment has been anything but isolated. This recognition of the interrelatedness of life suggests that the modern advocacy of freedom in a total sense might represent an aberration that has temporarily deflected attention from something that was generally accepted in premodern cultures, the assumption of a basic givenness and even directedness at the heart of life.

It is such a sense of directedness that the gospel suggests and requires, rather than either a rigid determinism or an essentially random, if not chaotic, freedom. The paradigmatic biblical stance is articulated in the account of the reaffirmation of the covenant effected through Moses: "I call heaven and earth to witness against you this day, that I have set before you life and death, blessing and cursing; therefore choose life, that you and your descendants may live" (Deut. 30:19). To modern sensibilities, assuming the primacy of freedom, this is bound to appear contradictory. How can there be a genuine choice, when one of the options is promoted in the very offer? If the choice is to be genuine, then the options must be presented in completely neutral terms. There must be an equal possibility of going in either direction. But this is not what the God of Israel provides. The choice is offered with directions: "Choose life." On the biblical understanding, we do not exist on our own, making absolute choices as totally self-determining beings. The freedom we possess is exercised within certain parameters, so that that exercise is supported or negated by the wider order of reality. Our choices lead to life or to death, and we are encouraged to choose life. Encouraged, but not compelled. There is real choice, although it is not absolute, neutral choice.

In fact, in the New Testament there emerges the contention that we are subject to strong influences in the negative direction, which offset the divine predilection for the life affirming option. This negative inducement is what came to be articulated in the Christian doctrine of original sin, the notion that human history has developed a cumulative legacy of sin, which constitutes a negative bias for each of us. While the Augustinian biological version of this doctrine sounds the deterministic note, which is so offensive to contemporary sensibilities, this wider historical reading can be seen to be pointing to the importance of social circumstances and thus to represent a very contemporary illustration of one of the cardinal assumptions of the social sciences.

The negative bias of original sin and the divine promotion of life then provide the context for human choice. Rather than existing as executors of absolute choice in some kind of antiseptic neutrality above the involvements of real life, the reality is that we are torn between the legacy of self-assertion, which sets us against one another, against the rest of creation, and against God and the original divine intention for life renewed through those instances where individuals and societies rise above the betrayals of that negative inheritance and predilection and reaffirm the positive possibilities of life. For Christians the supreme instance of that renewal is the accomplishment of Jesus, which is understood as nothing less than the renewal of life by God. Characteristically, the God who sets before Israel the option for life or death and advocates life, restores the option for life in Jesus, but does so without compulsion. This is what the gospel proclaims and requires; the recognition that life comes with a directive, and one that we ignore at our peril and at the peril of our world, but one that we can ignore because it would be the antithesis of God's nature to compel compliance through a deterministic imposition of divine will.

DESTINY RATHER THAN FINALITY

Just as the Christian gospel centers on otherness rather than on otherworldliness, and assumes a basic directive in life rather than a rigid determinism, so too its ultimate goal is more a matter of a destiny than of finality. It may be that the note of finality is due particularly to the portrayal of the destiny envisaged by the gospel in otherworldly terms. The notion of another world bears connotations of fixity and permanence, which imply finality. There is more than caricature in anticipations of heaven as a state of spiritual rigor mortis, so released from tensions and stress that nothing remains but totally insipid lethargy. This negative understanding of peace is a far cry from the Hebrew ideal of *shalom*, which carries the positive connotation of satisfying fulfillment. The difference suggests that here too there has been a serious distortion of the fundamental intent of the gospel.

The principal contemporary source of suspicion of finality is, as we have seen, that sensibility that we call "historical consciousness." The awareness of development cannot abide the thought of any kind of closure. The sense that significance is being produced by the events of history entails the conviction that there is always more to come. Even the rude awakening suffered by the age of progress through the disastrous events of the first half of the twentieth century and the question mark placed against our whole industrial way of life by the present ecological crisis have not done more than to qualify the confidence in development by calling its straightforward inevitability into question. There will be ups and downs, obstacles to be overcome, but on the whole, faith in progress remains intact. In the long run, things are bound to improve, and in principle, there can be no limit set on that improvement. What lies ahead, we cannot say; what we do know is that there will always be "more."

That this sense of openness to the future should be seen to constitute a fundamental challenge to Christian faith is particularly ironic, when we consider that the historical sense itself is so largely attributable to the Judeo–Christian tradition. It is the Greek outlook that assigns primacy to the fixity that implies finality. Plato's world of forms is the classic instance of this. This level of human events that we call history only acquires significance for Plato insofar as we reach above its ephemeral attachments to some appreciation of the eternal realm in which the forms abide eternal and unchanging. The upshot of this outlook is that history at its best is imitative rather than original. It is significant when it approximates the eternal verities. As a result, history is understood fundamentally in cyclical terms. It consists in the repetition of attempts to appreciate eternal truths and insofar as these attempts are successful what will be realized is only what was there all along.

From the point of view of modern historical consciousness, this does not really count as history at all. Far from cyclical repetition of eternal patterns, history is seen to involve the emergence of new developments. Rather than implementing a fixed pattern, it is creating meaning itself. This notion that what happens in this world is important in itself may be traced to the Enlightenment and the Renaissance, but the wider context that undergirds this perspective is the Judeo–Christian conviction that this world is God's creation and that God cares about what happens in it to the point of rescuing slaves from foreign captivity and identifying particularly with an artisan from an obscure village and confirming his faithful martyrdom. It is because these events were seen to have ultimate significance, to be in some way indicative of the reality and care of God, that history came to be seen to be significant. Truth is then not identified with the eternal realm beyond, but rather emerges in the temporal sphere. History is not a secondary repetition of the abiding truth of eternity in repetitive cyclic patterns, but a genuine emergence of new developments on a linear path reaching into the future. Indications of this historical consciousness can be detected in such influential Christian thinkers as Augustine and Luther, although its full development had to await the self- consciousness of the modern period.

How has it come about that this historical consciousness, which owes so much to the biblical tradition, should have become one of the main obstacles to an appreciation of salvation? Part of the answer has to do with the note of fixity and finality that came to characterize the Christian understanding of salvation. This appears, from the historical perspective, as a foreclosure on genuine historical possibility. But the other source of difficulty lies in the opposite extreme in which historical consciousness issues in historicism. This extreme puts such a premium on novelty and openness that it is not only visions of finality that are suspect, but also any sense of destiny at all. But this is what the gospel proclaims and requires, a controlling vision of the destiny of life rather than a conviction regarding some terminal consummation. The central Christian conviction is that God is characterized fundamentally by caring and that the destiny of life is meant to entail a community of caring that embraces all. That vision does not seem to be exposed to any serious danger of imminent realization, but even if it were to be realized, even if the kingdom were to be established, this way of caring hardly implies a moribund foreclosure of scope for interest and creativity. On the contrary, it suggests the most promising context for truly constructive creativity, where negative distractions and deflections have been eliminated. Thus, contrary to the rigidity of finalist versions of Christian faith and to the vacuous requirements of historicism, what the gospel offers and requires is a vision of a destiny, which, even in its realization, remains vital and challenging, a living salvation rather than a sterile final solution.

Resilient Dimensions in Salvation

The biblical proclamation of salvation and the antithetical atmosphere of the modern West are the intersecting vectors that constitute the position from which we must attempt to arrive at a credible contemporary understanding of salvation. The issue only arises for us because of our inheritance of the Judeo–Christian tradition. But it is a problematic issue because that tradition has been subjected to such intense opposition from modern secularity, not to mention the more recent awareness of religious pluralism. Our surveys of the central sources of hesitation about salvation and of the indispensable elements in the gospel proclamation suggest that, although there are inevitable tensions, and, at times, direct conflicts between the biblical stance and the priorities of the modern outlook, it is not impossible to live in the intersection of these two vectors. The side of us that remains captivated by the biblical legacy and the other side that breathes the air of modernity encounter and challenge each other at certain key points. It is at these points that the forging of a contemporary appreciation of salvation will either be achieved or abandoned.

THE INDISPENSABILITY OF VISION

The Christian gospel and the modern *Zeitgeist* encounter one another as basic visions of life. This is not so apparent in terms of the modern Zeitgeist as it is with the gospel. For while the gospel obviously entails an overall vision of the meaning and purpose of life, the modern Zeitgeist makes the more modest claim of attempting to deal with immediate concerns. The implication of this procedure is that the focus is entirely on the immediate, with wider questions being left in abeyance until the range of competence is expanded so that they can be addressed adequately. The appeal of this outlook is understandable in light of the revolutionary mastery exerted by the technological transformations of modern scientific know-how. Its plausibility, however, depends on not noticing that this approach really entails an overall vision. If it is meant seriously, this confidence in a piece by piece extension of a secure foundation of knowledge assumes that reality is composed of disconnected bits, which can be dealt with in isolation. At the very least, this vision of reality as a collection of discreet particulars is implicit in the positivistic stance that characterizes the modern outlook. However, as the ecological crisis suggests, there is good reason to question the adequacy of this perspective.

A major source of the current ecological malaise can be attributed to the assumption that a particular species can be "controlled" without concern about any wider ramifications or the confidence that that particular effluent will be absorbed by the wider environment. The disappearance of songbirds after trees are sprayed to "control" insects and the growing awareness of the finitude and vulnerability of the oceans and even of the atmosphere proclaimed the connectedness of life more eloquently and unanswerably than many explicit systematic attempts to articulate a philosophical or theological understanding of this connectedness. The difficulties in articulation, then are, by no means, indicative of a lack of sponsorship for the articulation. It is becoming increasingly apparent that the whole cannot be neglected, no matter how difficult it may be to envisage what that involves. Whether deliberately or by default, we shall have some guiding vision behind our primitive confidence in the fundamental reliability and constancy of the universe.

That the Christian gospel provides the best source of that vision is by no means a foregone conclusion, even in the West, today. On the contrary, its assurance of God's love for us can be seen to foster an arrogance and superiority to the rest of creation, which may be more indicative of our present crisis than a source of promise for creative measures. Although it is probably too extreme to attribute the ecological crisis to the Judeo–Christian understanding of creation with its mandate to take dominion over the earth and subdue it, as argued by Lynn White, Jr., it would be no less questionable to ignore the warnings of more moderate critics, like John Cobb, who contend that as the Christian tradition has developed, it has taken a decidedly anthropocentric turn, so that our own species has been elevated above the natural order in a disastrous, if not pernicious, manner. Any significant recognition of the Christian vision as an adequate articulation of the sense of wholeness for which we feel the need will have to take seriously our implication in the whole natural order and allow a prominent place for a serious repentance regarding our failure to appreciate and conform to that involvement. Only through such recognition of our finitude and vulnerability can we hope to recover any real appreciation of the otherness that leads us beyond the sense of wholeness to the awareness of holiness, which lies at the heart of the Christian vision. In this way, coming to grips with our planetary crisis might offer scope for a chastened revitalization of the basic vision that has all the time informed our higher sensibilities and rationalized our follies. To reach the state of repentance that can recognize the difference and to appreciate the central thrust of the Christian vision may be very close, if not identical operations.

THE INEVITABILITY OF VALUE

The modern secularist assumption of the dispensability of vision has its counterpart in a relegation of matters of value to the domain of private preference. The positivistic perspective derives its confidence in the progressive establishment of a secure foundation of solid knowledge from the conviction that we are thus involved in erecting an ever expanding edifice of assured facts. This is so firm and definite that it can only be accepted with recognition and resignation. If there is any room for debate or reflection, this is a clear indication that we are dealing with something that has not yet been incorporated into this inelastic web of factuality. It can only be left to the basically arbitrary preferences of personal valuation. Public facts and private values represent the controlling ideology of modern Western culture.

Considered in its own terms, this fact/value dichotomy can be regarded as an overly enthusiastic dedication to the pursuit of positive certainty on the part of philosophers enamored of the early scientific ideal. Philippa Foot pointed out how the distinction has been imposed, particularly by moral philosophers, rather than discovered, as its promoters would tend to suggest.

> Now it was said that words with emotive or commendatory force, such as "good," were not to be defined by the use of words whose meaning was merely "descriptive." This discovery tended to appear greater than it was, because it looked as if the two categories of fact and value had been identified separately and found never to coincide, whereas actually the factual or descriptive was defined by exclusion from the realm of value. In the ordinary sense of "descriptive" the word "good" is a descriptive word and in the ordinary sense of "fact" we say it is a fact about so and so that he is a good man, so that the words must be used in a special sense in moral philosophy. But a special philosopher's sense of these words has never, so far as I know, been explained except by contrasting value and fact. A word or sentence seems to be called "descriptive" on account of the fact that it is *not* emotive, does *not* commend, does *not* entail an imperative, and so on according to the theory involve.[7]

To separate off the firmly established as a realm of hard facts, consigning everything else to the discretionary domain of values, seems to represent a promising way of consolidating the march of scientific progress. When that consolidation is effected by what amounts to an arbitrary division, however, this procedure itself is seen to be anything but scientific. When what is involved is not the cataloging of bare facts, which have been shown to be independent of value considerations, but the stipulation of an area where considerations of value are not allowed to intrude, the legitimacy of the division is seriously called into question.

In spite of the dubious academic credentials of the fact/value dichotomy, there can be little doubt that it does give articulation to a fundamental aspect of modern Western sensibility. Science is seen to be engaged in amassing an ever expanding area of solid facts, with the area left over remaining susceptible to our choice of values. But even on this popular level, there is evident ambiguity. It is not clear, for example, whether the dimension of values represents a truly valuable preserve of human dignity and freedom, or whether it is rather a dimension of arbitrariness, which is in process of being subsumed under the progressive onslaught of factuality. Conversely, it is equally unclear whether facts are characterized by the total exclusion of elements of value or whether facts are ultimately the only true values. It is difficult to imagine how facts could be interesting at all, if they are seen to be characterized by a total exclusion of value. Yet, any concession to their value compromises the strictness of the division and invites the apparently equally desperate expedient of regarding facts as finally the only genuine values.

The fact/value dichotomy is particularly insidious from a religious point of view because it provides a means for actually undermining religious integrity at the very point where the intention is to affirm it. This point has been made most insistently by George Grant. "What is comic about the present use of 'values' and the distinction of them from 'facts,' is not that it is employed by modern men who know what is entailed in so doing; but that it is also used by 'religious' believers who are unaware that in its employment they are contradicting the very possibility of the reverence they believe they are espousing in its use."[8] By adopting the fact/value perspective, religious people think they are defending religious sensibilities as values, but what they are really doing is implicitly endorsing the destruction of all basis for religious conviction, because the values language assumes that the only significance in life is what we ourselves create. Grant notes that the founder of the values orientation was Friedrich Nietzsche. His central conviction was that what distinguished our modern situation was the displacement of God through our own assumption of control over questions of meaning and value. This is the basic logic of "values" language. The world we confront is a world of brute fact, simply there; any considerations of value are left for our devising. But, as Nietzsche recognized, such a world is possible only after the death of God.

If we are willing to play God ourselves, to live as though we were our own creators, to regard ourselves as the sole originators of meaning and significance, then either we will not be concerned with salvation at all, or conversely, we will think of ourselves as our own saviors. From a Christian perspective, that can only be seen as the antithesis of salvation, the epitome of the self-sufficiency that constitutes the condition that makes salvation necessary, the condition of sin. Neitzsche's dismissal of Christianity as a morality for slaves, and his contrary advocacy of the self-assertion of the superman, is seen, in Christian terms, as a failure to appreciate the communal ideal of servanthood and the corresponding exposure of the deleterious effects of self-interest and aggression that this entails. Insofar as Neitzsche's focus on values has come to prevail, then, interest in salvation in anything other than the self-sponsored form is bound to be negligible. To insist on the importance of values only intensifies this relegation, no matter how positive the intention behind this insistence may be. A vital interest in salvation can only be expected to thrive on the other side of the exposure of the endemic inversion implicit in this values perspective. This will involve exposing the precariousness of this fact/value dichotomy and some kind of recovery of an organic sense of the inherent value of life. One direction in which this might be attempted would be to abandon the language of value entirely and return to the more substantial language of worth. This would carry the connotation of an intrinsic connection between reality and worth, which alone could sustain a sense of worship through the understanding of God as characterized by both reality and worth. On the modern fact/value dichotomy, this combination is impossible; which is to say, God is impossible.

THE UNAVOIDABILITY OF VERACITY

Even if we were to acknowledge the indispensability of vision, and actually find the Christian vision attractive, and to recognize the inevitability of value and the necessity for its grounding in reality, contrary to the modern insistence on the intrinsic gap between facts and values, it would be premature to interpret such acknowledgement and recognition as the harbinger of a recovery of an appreciation of salvation. At most, such acknowledgement and recognition could legitimately be seen as a necessary, but not a sufficient, condition for this kind of appreciation. The additional ingredient required to assure the recovery is a firm conviction of the truth of the proclamation of salvation itself. The sense of the dispensability of vision and the arbitrariness of value are obstacles that stand in the way of any vital interest in salvation in the present. The reduction, or even the elimination of these obstacles represents an important negative preparation for the hearing of the gospel of salvation. For that hearing to issue in acceptance, what is heard must itself elicit assent and endorsement. And this will only happen if that proclamation is seen to be true and vital in itself.

We have seen that the modern inversion by which we have taken charge of life ourselves not only tends to render the gospel of salvation redundant because of the assumption of our own self-sufficiency, but also that the interest in salvation which does remain tends to be tailored to this inverted perspective. Thus, insofar as it is dealt with at all beyond the echoing of tired cliches, salvation tends to be promoted in fundamentally pragmatic terms, as being essential to our survival as a species or to the survival of the planet. We have considered at some length Sallie McFague's attempt to fashion "Theology for an Ecological, Nuclear Age." A similar direction is advocated by Gordon Kaufman with the elevation of this project from subtitle to title in his *Theology for a Nuclear Age*.[9] This direction yields an understanding of salvation that is inclusive and altruistic. "All movements toward reconciliation and healing and liberation, toward overcoming oppression and alienation and deterioration, are to be understood as the activity of the salvific divine spirit—the spirit of Christ—at work in the world."[10] It is the activity and not the sponsorship that is important:, "Those who are engaged in activities of actual reconciliation and healing, not those who are fastidious about identifying themselves with Christ or the church, are the ones through whom the divine salvific activity is at work."[11] Kaufman anticipates the obvious question as to the motivation for such an understanding of salvation, and replies that that motivation is not to be found in any kind of self-interest either in terms of success in this life or rewards in the next. The motive is to be found in the realization of our fundamentally social nature and the knowledge that through our sacrifice we are helping to enhance the quality of life for others.[12] This monolithic insistence on what is unquestionably a central theme in Christianity begs the further question raised by a child in Sunday school who was the object of a similar ultra-altruistic vision: "What are the others here for?" Once that question is broached, however, the genuineness of the altruism becomes suspect. To insist that our role is to effect salvation through concern for others could be taken to assume that we ourselves are fundamentally sound, if not entirely self-sufficient. Insofar as this is involved in this orientation, the position is, of course, implicitly self-centered, rather than altruistic. A viable altruism, which really takes our interdependence seriously, will have to be concerned about our own vulnerability, and be interested in what we may gain from the others who might

otherwise remain the objects of our condescension. This latter possibility would clearly be unacceptable to Kaufman, but the irony of
his position is that it could result in just such an inversion of what
he really intends.

A primary source of Kaufman's difficulty would seem to lie in the
fundamental inversion in theological sensibility such as we saw to
be characteristic of the similar project adopted by Sallie McFague.
When the focus of theology is regarded as a means to some more
immediate end, it should not be surprising that that end will distort the theological sensibility itself. If the dominant concern is
that we find some way to avoid blowing ourselves up, or otherwise
destroying the world through our boundless avarice, then it should
not be surprising if salvation comes to be equated with survival and
God becomes a resource for our attempt at species preservation.
When this is advanced in the name of humility, and in opposition
to the imperialism and self-interest of more traditional versions of
Christian faith, however, the naïveté of this inversion has to be
challenged. Kaufman denounces dogmatists who think they see
some direction in our present confusions as the most dangerous
kinds of persons; and to avoid succumbing to their solutions he
demands that we "work together toward the common goal and the
common good, drawing upon whatever resources—religious or
secular, philosophic or poetic, mythic or scientific—are available
to us, and offering them to each other as we grope toward an unknown future."[13] The innocuousness of this demand for tolerant
cooperativism belies the positive vision that motivates and sustains
Kaufman's concern. He has some idea of what the common good
entails; it involves our learning to care about one another, even
though this might be costly to ourselves. And he knows whence he
has derived this vision; it is based ultimately on the way of Jesus.
But why is the way of Jesus particularly significant? Kaufman's fear
of dogmatism prevents him from subscribing to any of the conventional answers to this question. In elliptical fashion, he indirectly
acknowledges that the way of Jesus is significant because in it is
to be seen "the very structure or activity which Christians call
God."[14] Presumably Kaufman uses this oblique form of reference
because of his suspicion of labels and the dogmatism they seem to
evoke. But the net result of this avoidance of the particularity of
the Christian confession is not the humane openness he seeks to
espouse, but the loss of the distinctive insights of the Christian vision that give it depth and credibility. Each of us individually disappears as expendable resources for the nebulous others; and the
Holy Other who was taken to be the supreme, inclusive individual

of traditional Christian conviction equally disappears as expendable resource for the survival of our species and our planet. This result raises a very serious question as to whether the salvation thus promoted really has much more to commend it than the lack of interest in salvation that it seeks to address.

In one sense, of course, this kind of reservation is irresponsible. The threat of nuclear holocaust or ecological disaster is all too real and urgent. Any quibbling over doctrinal concerns that would detract from the seriousness of this threat and the urgent need to address it expeditiously and constructively can be regarded as an aggravation of that danger. And yet, this reservation must be voiced, because behind it there lies the sense of an even greater risk implicit in this insistence on a direct concentration on this immediate threat to our survival. That risk concerns the possibility of missing the real source of our dilemma in a preoccupation with its symptoms. On a widely endorsed reading of the Christian gospel, its characterization of our situation does not consist in an appeal to self-sacrifice in defiance of a predilection to pursue our own self-interest, but rather in an identification of the source of that predilection. That source is seen to reside in our failure to receive life as the divine gift that it is; a failure that is expressed in our grasping at life rather that receiving it. If this is what is at stake in our competing and conflicting with one another as individuals, races, classes, genders, nations and international blocks, and in our careless and callous attitude toward the natural order, then there is not much prospect for alleviating these conflicts and this callousness, unless this source of alienation is addressed. But that is not going to happen when the symptoms of this alienation are allowed to become the issue.

If the modern anthropocentric outlook is going to be adopted, and the crucial issue is seen to be the question of our surviving, then the honourable course would seem to be to leave God behind completely. A God who exists to cater to our interest collectively is hardly a challenge to our self-interest. The proposal that self-interest can be transcended by collectivization finds its God in the great collectivity, society. The proclamation of salvation in the Christian gospel is not primarily social, or private, but eschatological. It is first and foremost a revelation that "God so loves," and only as such does it address "whosoever believes"and affirm the significant of "the world." It is an assurance of our own security, not in the sense that including ourselves among the "whosoever believes"will guarantee admission to heaven, but in the sense that "our life is hid with Christ in God" (Col. 3:3). It is an affirmation of the world, not in an uncritical endorsement of the world as it is or as we would have it be, but in an endorsement that includes the warning to "not be conformed to this world but be transformed by the renewal of your mind, that you may prove what is the will of God, what is good and acceptable and perfect" (Rom. 12:3).

Like happiness, salvation is a goal that is so elusive as to be self-defeating. The surest way to undermine the reality of salvation is to attempt to grasp it directly. To claim our own salvation is to admit to not really participating in its reality. To equate salvation with particular expressions, social or ecological, is to have abandoned the eschatological scope that characterizes salvation most distinctively. The greatest obstacle to a vital sense of the veracity of salvation today may well be the very reality itself, its scope and challenge; for its implications for ourselves and our world are so radical, in comparison to life as we live it, that we resist it even as we recognize that it rings true as the most fulfilling direction for ourselves and the most hopeful course for our world.

Notes

Chapter 1. The Dilemma of Salvation

1. E. M. B. Green, *The Meaning of Salvation* (London: Hodder & Stoughton, 1965), p. 12.
2. T. S. Eliot, "The Cocktail Party," in *The Complete Poems and Plays 1909–1950* (New York: Harcourt, Brace & Co., 1952), p. 362.
3. Lee E. Snook, *The Anonymous Christ, Jesus as Saviour in Modern Theology* (Minneapolis: Augsburg Publishing House, 1986), p. 161.
4. W. H. Vanstone, *Love's Endeavour, Love's Expense* (London: Darton, Longman & Todd, 1977), p. 79.
5. C. J. Bleeker, "Isis as Saviour Goddess," in S. G. F. Brandon, ed., *The Saviour God* (New York: Barnes & Noble, 1963), p. 2.
6. Carl E. Braaten, "The Christian Doctrine of Salvation," *Interpretation* 35 (1981): 123.
7. Dietrich Wiederkehr, *Belief in Redemption*, trans. Jeremy Moiser (Atlanta: John Knox Press, 1979), "Preface."
8. Walter Rauschenbusch, *A Theology for the Social Gospel* (New York: Abingdon Press, 1945), pp. 75f.
9. Frances M. Young, "Salvation Proclaimed," *Expository Times* 94 (1983): 103.
10. Ibid.
11. Paul Jersild, *Invitation to Faith* (Minneapolis: Augsburg Publishing House, 1978), pp. 106f.
12. Peddi Victor Premasagar, "Crisis for Salvation Theology!" in *The International Review of Missions* 61 (1972): 66.
13. Ibid., p. 62.
14. Claus Westermann, *BLESSING, In the Bible and the Life of the Church*, trans. Keith Crim (Philadelphia: Fortress Press, 1978), p. 3.
15. Ibid., p. 8.
16. Ibid., p. 10.
17. Walter Brueggemann and John R. Donahue, "Series Forward," in Claus Westermann, *BLESSING*, xi.
18. Ibid., p. 49.
19. Ibid., p. 90.
20. Carl E. Braaten, "Christian Doctrine," p. 119.
21. Claus Westermann, *BLESSING*, p. 3.
22. David Jenkins, "What does Salvation Mean to Christians Today?" in S. J. Samartha, ed., *Living Faiths and Ultimate Goals* (Geneva: World Council of Churches, 1974), p. 41.
23. Norman Pittenger, *The Meaning of Being Human* (New York: Pilgrim Press, 1982), p. 91.

24. D. J. Davies, *Meaning and Salvation in Religious Studies* (Leiden: E. J. Brill, 1984), pp. 32f.

25. Ibid., p. 33.

26. Donald W. Schriver, Jr., "What Business Managers Need to Know About the Clergy," in Donald G. Jones, ed., *Business, Religion, and Ethics* (Cambridge, Mass.: Oelgeschlager, Gunn & Hain, 1982), p. 127.

27. John B. Cobb, "God and Buddhism," in *Talking About God*, with David Tracy (New York: Seabury Press, 1983), p. 60.

28. David Ray Griffin, "Griffin's Response to Critiques," in Stephen T. Davis, ed., *Encountering Evil* (Atlanta: John Knox Press, 1981), p. 132.

29. Jan Milic Lockman, *Reconciliation and Liberation*, trans. David Lewis (Philadelphia: Fortress Press, 1980), p. 16.

30. Dermot A. Lane, *Foundations for a Social Theology: Praxis, Process and Salvation* (New York: Paulist Press, 1984), p. 24.

31. Lockman, *Reconciliation*, p. 15.

32. Sallie McFague, *Metaphorical Theology* (London: SCM Press, 1983), pp. 185f.

33. Ibid., p. 186.

34. John A. Hutchison, *Paths of Faith*, Second Edition (New York: McGraw-Hill, 1975), p. 20.

35. Dietrich Wiederkehr, *Belief in Redempton*, "Preface."

36. Thomas Oden, *Agenda for Theology* (San Francisco: Harper & Row, 1979), p. 121.

37. Don Cupitt, *Taking Leave of God* (London: SCM Press, 1980), pp. 42f.

38. Ward J. Fellows, *Religions East and West* (New York: Holt, Rinehart and Winston, 1979), p. 361.

39. See note 11 above.

40. Robert S. Paul, *The Atonement and the Sacraments* (London: Hodder & Stoughton, 1961), p. 217.

41. E. M. B. Green, *The Meaning of Salvation*, p. 240.

42. George M. Newlands, *Theology of the Love of God* (London: Collins, 1980), p. 59.

43. John Fischer, "Survival U: Prospects for a Really Relevant University," in Garrett DeBell, ed., *The Environmental Handbook* (New York: Ballantine Books, 1970), pp. 138f.

44. Keith Davis, "An Expanded View of the Social Responsibility of Business," in *Business Horizons*, 18/3 (June 1975).

45. Ibid.

46. Paulos Gregarios, *The Human Presence. An Orthodox View of Nature* (Geneva: World Council of Churches, 1978), p. 86.

47. George Newlands, *Theology of the Love of God*, p. 166.

48. Paul van Buren, *Discerning the Way* (New York: Seabury Press, 1980), p. 159.

49. John Updike, *Roger's Version* (New York: Alfred A. Knopf, 1986), p. 6.

Chapter 2. Salvation and the Bible

1. E. M. B. Green, *The Meaning of Salvation* (London: Hodder & Stoughton, 1965), p. 143.

2. Frances Young, "Two Roots or a Tangled Mass?" in John Hick, ed., *The Myth of God Incarnate* (London: SCM Press, 1977), p. 118.

3. Hugh Anderson, *Jesus and Christian Origins* (New York: Oxford University Press, 1964), pp. 40f.

4. William Wrede, *PAUL*, trans. Edward Lummis (Lexington, Kentucky: American Theological Library Association, 1962), p. 179.

5. Ibid., p. 180.

6. Ibid., p. 178.

7. Ibid., p. 167.

8. Ibid., p. 179.

9. Ibid., pp. 164f.

10. Ibid., p. 163.

11. Ibid.

12. Ibid., p. 165.

13. Ibid., p. 179.

14. Ibid., p. 178.

15. Ibid., p. 180.

16. Ibid., p. 152.

17. Ibid., p. 181.

18. Adolf von Harnack, *What is Christianity?* trans. Thomas Bailey Saunders (New York: G. P. Putnam's Sons, 1904; reprint, Philadelphia: Fortress Press, 1986), p. 52.

19. Adolf von Harnack, *History of Dogma*, vol. 1, trans. Neil Buchanan (New York: Dover Publications, 1961), p. 58.

20. Harnack, *What is Christianity?* p. 57.

21. Ibid., p. 11.

22. Harnack, *History of Dogma*, vol. 1, p. 71.

23. Ibid., p. 73.

24. Harnack, *What is Christianity?*, p. 179.

25. Ibid., p. 183.

26. Harnack, *History of Dogma*, vol. 1, p. 18.

27. Ibid., p. 21.

28. Ibid., p. 71.

29. Harnack, *What is Christianity?*, pp. 187f.

30. Harnack, *History of Dogma*, vol. 1, pp. 50ff.

31. Ibid., p. 48, n.l.

32. Ibid., pp. 133f.

33. Ibid., pp. 56f.

34. Ibid., p. 17.

35. Harnack, *What is Christianity?*, p. 186.

36. Ibid., pp. 186f.

37. Ibid., p. 146.

38. Ibid., p. 131.

39. J. Andrew Kirk, *Liberation Theology: An Evangelical View from the Third World* (Atlanta: John Knox Press, 1979), p. 123.

40. Ibid.

41. Jon Sobrino, *Christology at the Crossroads: A Latin American Approach* (Maryknoll, New York: Orbis Books, 1978).

42. Kirk, *Liberation Theology*, p. 220, n.2.

43. Leonardo Boff, "Christ's Liberation via Oppression: An Attempt at Theological Construction from the Standpoint of Latin America," in Rosino

Gibellini, ed., *Frontiers of Theology in Latin America* (Maryknoll, New York: Orbis Books, 1979), p. 108.

44. Gustavo Gutierrez, *A Theology of Liberation*, trans. Sister Carided Inda and John Eagleson (Maryknoll, New York: Orbis Books, 1973).

45. Ibid., p. 262.

46. Boff, "Christ's Liberation," pp. 116ff.

47. Albert Schweitzer, *The Quest of the Historical Jesus*, trans. W. Montgomery (London: A & C Black, 1931).

48. Ibid., p. 396.

49. Ibid.

50. Ibid., p. 397.

51. Ibid., p. 401.

52. Ibid.

53. Martin Kähler, *The So-called Historical Jesus and the Historic, Biblical Christ*, trans. Carl E. Braaten (Philadelphia: Fortress, 1964).

54. Ibid., p. 46.

55. Ibid., p. 48.

56. Ibid.

57. Ibid., p. 126.

58. Ibid., p. 81.

59. Ibid., p. 65.

60. Ibid., p. 68.

61. Ibid., p. 66.

62. Hugh Anderson, *Jesus and Christian Origins*, p. 96.

63. Kähler, *The So-called Historical Jesus*, p. 66.

64. Ibid., p. 139.

65. Ibid., p. 96.

66. Carl E. Braaten, "Revelation, History and Faith" in Martin Kähler, *The So-Called Historical Jesus and the Historic, Biblical Christ*, p. 28.

67. Rudolf Bultmann, *Theology of the New Testament*, vol. 1, trans. Kendrick Grobel (London: SCM Press, 1952), p. 299.

68. Rudolf Bultmann, "New Testament and Mythology," in Hans Werner Bartsch and Reginald H. Fuller, eds., *Kerygma and Myth*, vol. 1 (London: Society for Promotion Christian Knowledge, 1964), p. 41.

69. Ibid.

70. Ibid., p. 42.

71. Ibid., p. 43.

72. Ibid., p. 44.

73. Rudolf Bultmann, "Jesus and Paul," in *Existence and Faith*, trans. Schubert M. Ogden (London: Collins, The Fontana Library, 1964), pp. 238f.

74. See above, note 56.

75. Joachim Jeremias, *The Problem of the Historical Jesus*, trans. Norman Perrin (Philadelphia: Fortress Press, 1964), p. 12.

76. Ernst Fuchs, *Studies of the Historical Jesus* (Naperville, Illinois: Alec R. Allenson, 1964), p. 49.

77. James M. Robinson, *A New Quest of the Historical Jesus* (London: SCM Press, 1970), p. 94.

78. Ibid., p. 95.

79. Ibid., p. 111. The internal quotation is from Rudolf Bultmann, *Theology of the New Testament*, vol. 1, p. 43.

80. P. Josepll Cahill, "Rudolf Bultmann and Post-Bultmann Tendencies," in Martin E. Marty and Dean G. Peerman, eds., *New Theology*, no. 2 (New York: Macmillan, 1965), p. 235.

81. Hugh Anderson, *Jesus and Christian Origins*, p. 106.

82. Paul Ricoeur, "Biblical Hermeneutics," *Semia* 4 (1975): 138.

83. E. M. B. Green, *The Meaning of Salvation*, p. 111.

84. Lloyd Gaston, "Paul and Jerusalem," in Peter Richardson and John C. Hurd, eds., *From Jesus to Paul* (Waterloo, Ontario: Wilfred Laurier University. Press, 1984), p. 72.

85. Johannes Munck, *PAUL and the Salvation of Mankind* (Richmond, Virginia: John Knox Press, 1959), p. 72.

86. P. T. Forsyth, *The Work of Christ* (London: Collins, The Fontana Library, 1965), p. 106.

87. Kazoh Kitamori, *Theology of the Pain of God* (London: SCM Press, 1966), p. 40.

88. Martin Hengel, *The Atonement, The Origins of the Doctrine in the New Testament*, trans. John Bowden (Philadelphia: Fortress Press, 1981), p. 73.

89. J. A. Ziesler, *Pauline Christianity* (Oxford: Oxford University Press, 1983), p. 140.

90. Frances M. Young, "Salvation Proclaimed," *Expository Times* 94(1983): 100.

91. F. F. Bruce, "'Our God and Saviour'—A Recurring Biblical Pattern," in S. G. F. Brandon, ed., *The Saviour God* (New York: Barnes & Noble, 1963), p. 52.

92. E. M. B. Green, *The Meaning of Salvation*, pp. 136f.

93. Martin Hengel, *The Atonement*, p. 54.

94. Frances M. Young, *Sacrifice and the Death of Christ* (London: Society for Promoting Christian Knowledge, 1975), pp. 47f.

95. Kazoh Kitamori, *Theology of the Pain of God*, p. 36.

96. Maurice Wiles, *Faith and the Mystery of God* (London: SCM Press, 1982), p. 65.

Chapter 3. Salvation and Theology

1. Thomas C. Oden, *Agenda for Theology* (San Francisco: Harper and Row, 1979), pp. 103f.

2. Hastings Rashdall, *The Idea of the Atonement in Christian Theology* (London: Macmillan, 1919), p. 454.

3. Robert S. Paul, *The Atonement and the Sacraments* (London: Hodder and Stoughton, 1961), p. 158.

4. Elizabeth R. Moberly, *Suffering, Innocent and Guilty* (London: Society for Promoting Christian Knowledge, 1978), pp. 23ff; Robert S. Franks, *The Work of Christ* (London: Thomas Nelson & Sons, 1962), pp. 145ff.

5. Friedrich Schleiermacher, *The Christian Faith*, ed. H. R. Mackintosh and J. S. Stewart (Edinburgh: T & T Clark, 1928), p. 425.

6. Ibid., p. 55.

7. Ibid.

8. Martin Redeker, *Schleiermacher: Life and Thought*, trans. John Wallhausser (Philadelphia: Fortress Press, 1973), p. 143.

9. Albrecht Ritschl, *The Christian Doctrine of Justification and Reconciliation*, trans. H. R. Mackintosh and A. B. MacAulay (Edinburgh: T & T Clark, 1900), pp. 448ff.

10. James Richmond, *Ritschl: A Reappraisal* (London: Collins, 1978), p. 176.

11. Albrecht Ritschl, *The Christian Doctrine of Justification and Reconciliation*, p. 451.

12. Adolf Harnack, *What is Christianity?*, p. 147.

13. Ibid., p. 162.

14. John McConnachie, *The Significance of Karl Barth* (London: Hodder and Stoughton, 1931), p. 157; see *CD* IV.1, pp. 252f., and II.1, pp. 152f.

15. Donald G. Bloesch, "Soteriology in Contemporary Christian Thought," *Interpretation* 35 (1981): 143.

16. *The Myth of God Incarnate*, ed. John Hick (London: SCM Press, 1977); *The Truth of God Incarnate*, ed. Michael Green (London: Hodder and Stoughton, 1977); *Incarnation and Myth: The Debate Continued* (London: SCM Press, 1979).

17. *Incarnation and Myth*, 4.A. "Incarnation and Atonement," pp. 77–103.

18. Schubert Ogden, *Faith and Freedom* (Belfast: Christian Journals, 1979).

19. Lonnie Kliever, *The Shattered Spectrum: A Survey of Contemporary Theology* (Atlanta: John Knox Press, 1981), pp. 173f.

20. George M. Newlands, *Theology of the Love of God* (London: Collins, 1980), p. 33.

21. John Francis Kavanaugh, *Following Christ in a Consumer Society* (Maryknoll, New York: Orbis Books, 1982), p. 94.

22. Robert S. Paul, *The Atonement and the Sacraments*, p. 28; J.K. Mozley, *The Doctrine of the Atonement* (London: Gerald Duckworth & Co. Ltd. 1962), p. 11, n.1; F. W. Dillistone, "Atonement," in *A New Dictionary of Christian Theology*, ed. Alan Richardson and John Bowden (London: SCM Press, 1983), p. 50; K. F. Dougherty, "Atonement," in *New Catholic Encyclopedia*, vol. 1 (Washington: The Catholic University of America, 1967), p. 1024.

23. F. W. Dillistone, *The Christian Understanding of Atonement* (Philadelphia: The Westminster Press, 1968), p. 242.

24. Gustaf Aulen, *Christus Victor* (London: Society for Promoting Christian Knowledge, 1970), pp. 141f.

25. Faustus Socinus, *De Jesu Christo Servatore*, I.1 in Robert S. Franks, *The Work of Christ*, p. 365.

26. J. K. Mozley, *The Doctrine of Atonement*, p. 148.

27. St. Anselm, *Cur Deus Homo* (Edinburgh: John Grant, 1909), 2, 6, p. 66.

28. St. Thomas Aquinas, *Summa Theologia* (London: Eyre and Spottiswoode, 1965), 3a, qu. 46, art. 2.

29. J.K. Mozley, *The Doctrine of Atonement*, p. 210.

30. Paul Tillich, *Systematic Theology*, vol. 1 in combined volume (Digswell Place: James Nisbet & Co., 1968), pp. 319f.

31. Jung Young Lee, *God Suffers for Us* (The Hague: Martinus Nijhoff, 1974), P. 9.

32. Peter Hinchliff, *Holiness and Politics* (Grand Rapids, Michigan: William B. Eerdmans, 1983), p. 65.

33. Donald G. Miller, "Expository Article on Jh. 3:1–21," *Interpretation*, 35 (1981): 177.

34. Kazoh Kitamori, *Theology of the Pain of God* (London: SCM Press, 1966), p. 24.

35. D. M. MacKinnon, "Subjective and Objective Conceptions of Atonement," in *Prospects for Theology: Essays in Honour of H. H. Farmer*, ed. F. G. Healey (London: Nisbet, 1966), p. 172.

36. Maurice Wiles, *Faith and the Mystery of God* (London: SCM Press, 1982), p. 66.

37. Michael Goulder, "Jesus, The Man of Universal Destiny," in *The Myth of God Incarnate*, p. 58.

38. Paul van Buren, *Discerning the Way, A Theology of the Jewish Christian Reality* (New York: Seabury Press, 1980), p. 116.

39. Gustaf Aulen, *Christus Victor*, p. 56.

40. Kazoh Kitamori, *Theology of the Pain of God*, pp. 111f.

41. B. H. Streeter, *The Buddha and the Christ* (London: Macmillan, 1932), p. 216.

42. Emil Brunner, *The Mediator*, trans. Olive Wyon (London: Lutterworth Press, 1934), p. 506; *The Christian Doctrine of the Church, Faith, and the Consummation, Dogmatics*, vol. 3, trans,. David Cairns (London: Lutterworth, 1962), p. 369.

43. Horace Bushnell, *The Vicarious Sacrifice*, p. 241, in Robert S. Paul, *The Atonement and the Sacraments*, p. 152.

44. Jürgen Moltmann, *The Crucified God*, trans. R. A. Wilson and John Bowden (London: SCM Press, 1974), pp. 235ff.

45. Dorothee Soelle, *Suffering*, trans. Everett R. Kalin (London: Darton, Longman & Todd, 1975), p. 28.

46. Ibid., p. 25.

47. Ibid., p. 163.

48. Dorothee Soelle, "Brief," in *Christian Theology: A Case Method Approach* ed. Robert A. Evans & Thomas D. Parker (London: Society Promoting Christian Knowledge, 1977), p. 127.

49. Dorothee Soelle, *Suffering*, p. 32.

50. Robert S. Franks, *The Work of Christ*, pp. 614f.

51. Maurice Wiles, *Faith and the Mystery of God*, pp. 66ff.

52. Carl E. Braaten, "The Christian Doctrine of Salvation," *Interpretation* 35 (1981): 121.

53. Thomas Kuhn, *The Structure of Scientific Revolutions* (Chicago: University of Chicago Press, 1962); "Second Thoughts on Paradigms," in *The Structure of Scientific Theories*, ed. Frederick Suppe (Urbana: University of Illinois Press, 1977), pp 459-482.

54. Jim Garrison, *The Darkness of God: Theology after Hiroshima* (London: SCM Press, 1982), p. 11.

55. Robert S. Paul, *The Atonement and the Sacraments*, pp. 290f.

56. P. T. Forsyth, *The Justification of God* (London: Independent Press Ltd., 1948), p. 169.

57. Ibid.

58. Ibid., p. 40.

59. Rudolf Otto, *The Idea of the Holy* (New York: Oxford University Press, A Galaxy Book, 1958), p. 56.

60. Ibid., p. 57.

Chapter 4. Salvation and the Church

1. Alexander MacMillan, *Hymns of the Church, A Companion to the Hymnary of the United Church of Canada* (Toronto: The United Church Publishing House, 1965), p. 111.

2. Ibid., p. 11.

3. Erik Routley, *Hymns Today and Tomorrow* (London: Darton Longman & Todd, A Libra Book, 1964), pp. 68f.

4. Alexander MacMillan, *Hymns of the Church*, p. 131.

5. Lionel Adley, *Hymns and the Christian "Myth,"* (Vancouver: University of British Columbia, 1986), p. 125.

6. Susan S. Tamke, *Make a Joyful Noise unto the Lord: Hymns as a Reflection of Victorian Social Attitudes* (Athens: Ohio University Press, 1978), p. 140.

7. Lionel Adley, *Hymns and Myth*, p. 126.

8. Susan S. Tamke, *Make a Joyful Noise*, p. 141.

9. Lionel Adley, *Hymns and Myth*, pp. 4–5.

10. Ibid., p. 126.

11. Alexander MacMillan, *Hymns of the Church*, p. 14.

12. Ibid., pp. 30f.

13. Ibid., p. 8.

14. Ibid., p. 31.

15. Nathan Söderblom, *The Mystery of the Cross, Thoughts for Holy Week and Other Weeks*, trans. A. G. Herbert (London: SCM Press, 1933), p. 56.

16. Susan S. Tamke, *Make a Joyful Noise*, p. 6.

17. Lionel Adley, *Hymns and Myth*, p. 198.

18. Carl A Volz *Faith and Practice in the Early Church* (Minneapolis: Augsburg, 1983), p. 89.

19. R. M. French, "Introduction" to Nicholas Cabasilas, *A Commentary on the Divine Liturgy*, trans. J. M. Hussey and P. A. McNulty (London: Society for Promoting Christian Knowledge, 1983), pp. 3f.

20. Ibid., p. 21, n.l.

21. Ibid., p.9.

22. Nicholas Cabasilas, *A Commentary on the Divine Liturgy*, p. 34.

23. Ibid., p. 81.

24. P. Benoit, O. P., "The Accounts of the Institution and what they Imply," in J. Delorme et al., *The Eucharist in the New Testament, A Symposium* (Baltimore & Dublin: Helicon Press, 1964), p. 98.

25. Ibid.

26. Ibid., p. 99.

27. Theodor Klauser, *A Short History of the Western Liturgy*, trans. John Halliburton (Oxford: Oxford University Press, 1979), p. 98.

28. Ibid., p.99.

29. Ibid., p. 101.

30. Ibid., p. 105.

31. Ibid., p. 120.

32. Ibid.

33. Ibid., pp. 136f.

34. Maurice Wiles, *Faith and the Mystery of God* (London: SCM Press, 1982), pp. 91f.

35. Michael Gough, *The Origins of Christian Art* (New York: Praeger Publishers, 1973), p. 39.

36. Ibid., p. 18.
37. Ibid., p. 31.
38. Ibid., pp. 26ff.
39. Ibid., pp. 22f.
40. A. J. B. Higgins, *The Lord's Supper in the New Testament* (London: SCM Press, 1972), pp. 57f.
41. C. F. D. Moule, *Worship in the New Testament* (Richmond, Virginia: John Knox Press, 1961), p. 21.
42. Oscar Cullmann, "The Meaning of the Lord's Supper in Primitive Christianity," in Oscar Cullmann and F. J. Leenhardt, *Essays on the Lord's Supper* (Richmond, Virginia: John Knox Press, 1958), p. 18.
43. Ibid., pp. 14f.
44. Ibid., pp. 6ff.
45. Ibid., pp. 14f.
46. Joachim Jeremias, *The Eucharistic Words of Jesus* (London: SCM Press, 1966), p. 30f.
47. Ralph P. Martin, *Worship in the Early Church* (Grand Rapids, Michigan: Wm. B. Eerdmans, 1964), p.122.
48. A. J. B. Higgins, *The Lord's Supper*, p. 63.
49. C. F. D. Moule, *Worship in New Testament*, p. 21.
50. Joachim Jeremias, *The Eucharistic Words*, p. 82.
51. A. J. B. Higgins, *The Lord's Supper*, pp. 22f.
52. Joachim Jeremias, *The Eucharistic Words*, pp. 44ff.
53. Ibid., pp. 48f.
54. Ibid., pp. 49f.
55. Ibid., pp. 50ff.
56. Ibid., pp. 54f.
57. Ibid., pp. 55ff.
58. A. J. B. Higgins, *The Lord's Supper*, p. 59.
59. Ibid., pp. 27f.
60. Oscar Cullmann, "The Meaning of the Lord's Supper," p. 18.
61. C. F. D. Moule, *Worship in New Testament*, pp. 32f.
62. Ibid., p. 25.
63. Ibid., p. 22.
64. Ibid., p. 34.
65. Ferdinand Hahn, *The Worship of the Early Church*, trans. David E. Green (Philadelphia: Fortress Press, 1973), p. 103.
66. *The Didache*, 14, in *Early Christian Writings, The Apostolic Fathers*, trans. Maxwell Staniforth (Harmondsworth, Middlesex: Penguin Books, 1968), p. 234.
67. Ignatius, *The Epistle to the Philadelphians*, 4, in *Early Christian Writings*, see note 66, p. 112.
68. Ignatius, *The Epistle to the Smyrnaeans*, 8, in *Early Christian Writings*, see note 66, p. 121.
69. Ibid.
70. Geoffrey Wainwright, *Eucharist and Eschatology* (New York: Oxford University Press, 1981), p. 125.
71. Ramsay MacMullen, *Christianizing the Roman Empire* (A.D. 100–400) (New Haven & London: Yale University Press, 1984), p. 101.
72. Alistair Kee, *Constantine versus Christ, The Triumph of Ideology* (London: SCM Press, 1982), p. 165.

73. Reinhold Niebuhr, *An Interpretation of Christian Ethics* (Cleveland & New York: World Publishing Co., Meridian Books, 1963), p. 36.

74. Geoffrey Wainwright, *Eucharist*, p. 123.

75. E. M. B. Green, *The Meaning of Salvation* (London: Hodder & Stoughton, 1965), pp. 60f.

76. Ferdinand Hahn, *Worship Early Church*, p. 107.

77. Ibid., p. 37.

78. Ibid., pp. 38f.

79. Ibid., p. 108.

80. J. K. Mozley, *The Doctrine of the Atonement* (London: Gerald Duckworth & Co. Ltd., 1962), p. 25.

81. Leonard Hodgson, *The Doctrine of the Atonement* (London: Nisbet & Co. Ltd., 1955), p. 27.

82. Ferdinand Hahn, *Worship Early Church*, p. 86.

83. Ibid., p. 60.

84. Ibid., p. 50.

85. Ibid., p. 60.

86. Ibid., pp. 84ff.

87. Frances M. Young, *Sacrifice and the Death of Christ* (London: Society for Promoting Christian Knowledge, 1975), p. 11.

88. Ibid., p. 12.

89. Ibid.

90. Leonard Hodgson, *Doctrine of Atonement*, p. 148.

91. Frances M. Young, *Sacrifice and Death of Christ*, pp. 96f.

92. Ibid., p. 138.

93. Philip J. Lee, *Against the Protestant Gnostics* (New York: Oxford University Press, 1987), p. 80.

94. Ibid., p. 208.

95. Daniel Day Williams, *The Spirit and the Forms of Love* (New York: Harper & Row, 1968), pp. 187f.

96. Robert S. Paul, The *Atonement and the Sacraments* (London: Hodder & Stoughton, 1961), p. 308.

Chapter 5. Salvation and Secularization

1. Jacques Ellul, *The New Demons*, trans. C. Edward Hopkin (New York: Seabury Press, A Crossroad Book, 1975), "Preface," vii.

2. John Cagley, *Religion in a Secular Age* (New York: New American Library, A Mentor Book, 1968), p. 133.

3. David Martin, *The Religious and the Secular, Studies in Secularization* (London: Routledge and Kegan Paul, 1969), p. 16.

4. Ibid., p. 154.

5. Ibid., p. 55.

6. Owen Chadwick, *The Secularization of the European Mind in the Nineteenth Century* (Cambridge: Cambridge University Press, 1975), pp. 265f.

7. Ibid., p. 264.

8. William F. Lynch, S. J., *Christ and Prometheus, A New Image of the Secular* (Notre Dame, Indiana: University of Notre Dame Press, 1970), p. 8.

9. Denys Munby, *The Idea of a Secular Society* (Oxford: Oxford University Press, 1963), chap. 1.

10. Bernard Eugene Meland, *The Secularization of Modern Cultures* (New York: Oxford University Press, 1966), p. 33.

11. Ibid., p. 27.

12. John A. T. Robinson, *Honest to God* (London: SCM Press, 1963).

13. Ibid., p. 27.

14. Paul van Buren, *The Secular Meaning of the Gospel* (Harmondsworth, Middlesex: Penguin Books, 1963).

15. William Hamilton, "The Death of God Theologies Today," in *Radical Theology and the Death of God*, Thomas J. J. Altizer and William Hamilton (New York: Bobbs-Merrill, 1966), p. 28.

16. Thomas J. J. Altizer, "America and the Future of Theology," in *Radical Theology and the Death of God*, p. 11.

17. Van Buren, *Secular Meaning*, p. 109.

18. Harmon R. Holcomb, "Christology Without God: A Critical Review of *The Secular Meaning of the Gospel*" in Jackson Lee Ice and John J. Carey, eds., *The Death of God Debate* (Philadelphia: Westminster Press, 1967), pp. 74ff.

19. John A. T. Robinson, *Exploration into God* (London: SCM Press, 1967), Title of Chapter 4, p. 73.

20. Dietrich Bonhoeffer, *Letters and Papers from Prison* (London: Collins, Fontana Books, 1959) pp. 103f.; see also pp. 93, 115, 122.

21. See, note 5 above.

22. Harvey Cox, *The Secular City* (New York: Macmillan, 1965), p. 2.

23. Denis de Rougemont, *The Christian Opportunity* (New York: Holt, Rinehart and Winston, 1963), pp. 10ff.

24. Charles Moeller, *Man and Salvation in Literature*, trans. Charles Underhill Quinn (Notre Dame, Indiana: University of Notre Dame Press, 1970), pp. 48f.

25. Bonhoeffer, *Letters and Papers from Prison*, pp. 122, 164.

26. Edward Norman, *Christianity and the World Order* (Oxford: Oxford University Press, 1979), p. 14.

27. Bonhoeffer, *Letters and Papers from Prison*, p. 122.

28. Don Cupitt, *Taking Leave of God* (London: SCM Press, 1980), p. 4.

29. John Francis Kavanaugh, *Following Christ in a Consumer Society* (Maryknoll, New York: Orbis Books, 1982), p. 85.

30. Carl E. Braaten, "The Christian Doctrine of Salvation," *Interpretation* 35 (1981): 126.

31. Rosemary Radford Ruether, *To Change the World* (London: SCM Press, 1981), p. 29.

32. Carl A. Jung, *Answer to Job*, trans. R. F. C. Hull (London: Hodder and Stoughton, 1965), p. 91.

33. B. H. Streeter, *The Buddha and the Christ* (London: Macmillan, 1932), p. 59.

34. Brian Hebblethwaite, *Evil, Suffering and Religion* (London: Sheldon Press, 1976), p.8.

35. Meland, *The Secularization*, p. 130.

36. Dietrich Wiederkehr, *Belief in Redemption*, trans. Jeremy Moiser (Atlanta: John Knox Press, 1979), p. 48.

37. Frances M. Young, "Salvation Proclaimed," *The Expository Times*, 94 (1983): 102.

38. Ibid., p. 103.

39. Sallie McFague, *Models of God, Theology for an Ecological, Nuclear Age* (Philadelpha: Fortress Press, 1987).

40. Ibid., "Preface," ix.

41. Ibid., p. 185.

42. Ibid., p. 77.

43. Ibid., p. 185.

44. Kavanaugh, *Following Christ*, p. 55.

45. McFague, *Models of God*, pp. x, xiii, 3, 6, 7, 13, 19, 30, 41, 62.

46. Ibid., xiii.

47. Ibid., p. 69.

48. Paul van Buren, *Discerning the Way, A Theology of the Jewish–Christian Reality* (New York: Seabury Press, A Crossroad Book, 1980), pp. 58f.

49. Meland, *The Secularization*, p. 115.

50. Ellul, *The New Demons*, p. 38.

51. Cox, *The Secular City*, p. 18.

52. Ellul, *The New Demons*, p. 38.

53. Ibid.

54. Lynch, *Christ and Prometheus*, p. 108.

55. Young, "Salvation Proclaimed," 103.

Chapter 6. Salvation and Consumerism

1. Paul F. Camenisch, "Business Ethics: On Getting to the Heart of the Matter," in Donald C. Jones, ed., *Business, Religion, and Ethics* (Cambridge, Mass.: Oelgeschlager, Gunn and Hain, 1982), p. 202.

2. *Report of the Task Force on Corporate Social Performance*, Dept. of Commerce, Dec. 1980, p. 47, in Andrew B. Gollner, *Social Change and Corporate Strategy: The Expanding Role of Public Affairs* (Stamford, Connecticut: Issue Action Publications, 1983), p. 83.

3. Michael Maccoby, *The Gamesman* (New York: Bantam Books, 1978), p. 209.

4. Ibid.

5. W. Michael Hoffman and Jennifer Moore, *Business Ethics, Readings and Cases in Corporate Morality* (New York: McGraw-Hill, 1984), "General Introduction," p. 6.

6. Paul T. Heyne, *Private Keepers of the Public Interest* (New York: McGraw-Hill, 1968), p. 55.

7. Ibid.

8. Richard J. Barnet and Ronald E. Muller, *Global Reach: The Power of the Multinational Corporations* (New York: Simon & Schuster, 1974), p. 264.

9. Randall Jarrell, "A Sad Heart at the Supermarket," in Norman Jacobs, ed., *Culture for the Millions* (Boston: Beacon Press, 1964), p. 101.

10. John Francis Kavanaugh, *Following Christ in a Consumer Society* (Maryknoll, New York: Orbis Books, 1982), p. 21.

11. Fred W. Graham, "America's Other Religion," *Christian Century* 17 March 1982, 306.

12. Jim Wallis, *The Call to Conversion* (San Francisco: Harper & Row, 1981), p. 49.

13. Ibid.

14. William W. May, "Dominating Spires of Business and Social Responsibility" in Donald C. Jones, ed., *Business, Religion and Ethics*, p. 169.

15. John Brooks, "The Money Machine," *The New Yorker*, 5 January 1981, 56.

16. William Langland, "Piers the Plowman," C. VII, lines 278–286, in Michael J. McTague, *The Businessman in Literature: Dante to Melville* (New York: Philosophical Library, 1979), p. 14.

17. Jacques Ellul, *The New Demons*, trans. C. Edward Hopkin (New York: Seabury Press, A Crossroad Book, 1975), p. 144.

18. Andrew M. Greeley, *No Bigger than Necessary* (New York: New American Library, 1977), p. 158.

19. Ibid., pp. 154ff.

20. Michael Schudson, *Advertising, The Uneasy Persuasion* (New York: Basic Books, 1984), p. 179.

21. Erich Fromm, *The Art of Loving* (New York: Harper & Row, 1956), p. 87.

22. Erich Fromm, *To Have or To Be?* (London: Jonathan Cape, 1976), pp. 3ff.

23. Ibid., p. 3.

24. Christopher Lasch, *The Culture of Narcissism* (New York: Warner Books, 1979).

25. Philip J. Lee, *Against the Protestant Gnostics* (New York: Oxford University Press, 1987), p. 198.

26. Alvin Toffler, *Future Shock* (New York: Random House, A Bantam Book, 1971), p. 14.

27. R. H. Tawney, *The Acquisitive Society* (New York: Harcourt Brace, 1920), p. 45.

28. J. Philip Wogaman, *Economics and Ethics* (Philadelphia: Fortress Press, 1986), p. 7.

29. Jim Wallis, *The Call to Conversion*, xiii; see also E. F. Schumacher, *Good Work* (London: Abacus, 1980), p. 26.

30. Brian A. Sullivan, "*Laborem Exercens*: A Theological and Philosophical Foundation for Business Ethics," *Listening* 20/2 (1985): 138.

31. Kavanaugh, *Following Christ*, p. 35.

32. Bernard Eugene Meland, *The Secularization of Modern Cultures* (New York: Oxford University Press, 1966), p. 26.

33. Erich Fromm, *To Have or To Be?*, p. 19.

34. Richard T. DeGeorge, *Business Ethics* (New York: Macmillan, 1986), p. 416.

35. Kavanaugh, *Following Christ*, p. 10.

36. Ibid., pp. 96f.

37. Peter Singer, "The Place of Nonhumans in Environmental Issues," in K. E. Goodpaster and K. M. Sayre, eds., *Ethics and Problems in the Twenty-first Century* (Notre Dame, Indiana: University of Notre Dame Press, 1979), pp. 191–198.

38. Lynn White, "The Historical Roots of our Ecological Crisis," *Science* 155 (1967): 1201–1207.

39. Fred Hirsch, *Social Limits to Growth* (Cambridge: Harvard University Press, 1978).

40. Christopher D. Stone, "Should Trees have Standing?—Toward Legal Rights for Natural Objects," in Tom L. Beauchamp and Norman E. Bowie, eds., *Ethical Theory and Business*, Second Edition (Englewood Cliffs, N.J.: Prentice Hall, 1983), p. 425.

41. Martin Buber, *I and Thou*, trans. Ronald Gregor Smith (New York: Charles Scribner 's Sons, 1958), p. 38.

42. Ibid., pp. 38f.

43. Ibid., p. 107.

44. Philip J. Lee, *Against Protestant Gnostics*, p. 248.

45. Rosemary Radford Ruether, *To Change the World* (London: SCM Press, 1981), p. 59.

46. John V. Taylor, *Enough is Enough* (Minneapolis: Augsburg Publishing House, 1977), p. 101.

47. Jim Wallis, *The Call to Conversion*, p. 51.

48. Meland, *Secularization of Modern Culture*, p. 113.

49. Kosuke Koyama, *No Handle on the Cross* (London: SCM Press, 1976), p. 96.

50. Greeley, *No Bigger than Necessay*, p. 158.

51. T. E. Hulme, *Speculations: Essays on Humanism and the Philosophy of Art* (Boston: Routledge & Kegan Paul, 1963) pp. 50f.

52. E. F. Schumacher, *Small is Beautiful* (London: Abacus, 1974), p. 99.

53. Taylor, *Enough*, p. 40.

54. Dorothee Soelle, *Suffering*, trans. Everett R. Kalin (London: Darton, Longman & Todd, 1975), p. 132.

55. Roland Barthes, *Camera Lucinda* (New York: Hill and Wang, 1981), p. 119, quoted in Schudson, *Advertising*, p. 229.

56. Wilfred Cantwell Smith, *Faith and Belief* (Princeton: Princeton University Press, 1979); and *Belief and History* (Charlottesville: University of Virginia Press, 1977).

57. Michael Novak, "Can a Chrisitan Work for a Corporation? The Theology of the Corporation," in Oliver F. Williams and John W. Houck, eds., *The Judeo–Christian Vision and the Modern Corporation* (Notre Dame, Indiana: University of Notre Dame Press, 1982), pp. 184ff.

58. Ralph Starr Butler, "What the Advertiser Owes the Public," in *The Ethical Problems of Modern Advertising* (New York: Arno Press, 1978), p. 28.

59. Charles Maurice and Charles W. Smithson, *The Doomsday Myth* (Stanford, Calif.: Hoover Institution Press, 1984), p. 25.

60. Mark Sagoff, "A Nonutilitarian Rationale for Preserving the Natural Environment," in Donald Scherer and Thomas Attig, eds., *Ethics and the Environment* (Englewood Cliffs, N.J.: Prentice Hall, 1983), p. 28.

61. J. Baird Collicott, "Animal Liberation: A Triangular Affair," in *Ethics and the Environment*, p. 61

62. Schumacher, *Small is Beautiful*, p. 31.

63. Paulos Gregarios, *The Human Presence, An Orthodox View of Nature* (Geneva: World Council of Churches, 1978), "Preface," p. 7.

64. Koyama, *No Handle on the Cross*, p. 20.

65. Ruether, *To Change the World*, p. 66.

66. Graham, "America's Other Religion," p. 308.

67. John Kenneth Galbraith, *The Affluent Society* (London: Andre Deutsch, 1958), pp. 213f.

68. Donella H. Meadows, Dennis L. Meadows, Jorgen Randers, William W. Behrens III, *The Limits to Growth* (New York: Universe Books, 1972).

69. See Taylor, *Enough Is Enough*, pp. 122f., n.5.

70. Frank Feather, ed., *Through the '80s: Thinking Globally, Acting Locally* (Washington, D.C.: World Future Society, 1980).

71. Kenneth E. Boulding, "The Economics of the Coming Spaceship Earth," in

Garrett De Bell, ed., *The Environmental Handbook* (New York: Ballantine Books, 1970), p. 96.

72. Schumacher, *Small is Beautiful*, pp. 150ff.
73. Soelle, *Suffering*, p. 39.
74. Taylor, , *Enough Is Enough*, p. 69.
75. Ibid., p. 50.
76. Gregarios, *The Human Presence*, p. 100.
77. Elie Wiesel, "Freedom and Gratitude," *Luther Magazine*, Dec. 1981, p. 6, in Robert S. Bachelder, "A Misplaced Hope and Its Misconceived Assumptions," in W. Michael Hoffman, Jennifer Mills Moore, and David A. Fedo, eds., *Corporate Governance and Institutionalizing Ethics* (Lexington, Mass. and Toronto: D.C. Heath & Co., 1984), p. 161.

Chapter 7. Salvation and Pluralism

1. D. T. Niles, "Karl Barth—A Personal Memory," *The South East Asia Journal of Theology* (Autumn 1969), 10-11, in Gerald H. Anderson, "Religion as a Problem for the Christian Mission," in Donald G. Dawe and John B. Carman, ed., *Christian Faith in a Religiously Plural World* (Maryknoll, N.Y.: Orbis Books, 1978), p. 114, n.l.
2. Wilfred Cantwell Smith, "The Christian in a Religiously Plural World," in John Hick and Brian Hebblethwaite, eds., *Christianity and Other Religions* (Glasgow: Collins, Fount Paperbacks, 1980), p. 91.
3. Ibid., pp.89f.
4. B. F. Streeter, *The Buddha and the Christ* (London: Macmillan, 1932), p. 186.
5. Hans Kung, *Eternal Life?* (Garden City, New York: Doubleday, 1984), pp. 55f.
6. Ninian Smart, "The Work of Buddha and the Work of Christ," in S. G. F. Brandon, ed., *The Saviour God* (New York: Barnes & Noble, 1963), p. 168.
7. John A. Hutchison, *Paths of Faith*, Second Edition (New York: McGraw-Hill, 1975), p. 144.
8. Ward J. Fellows, *Religions East and West* (New York: Holt, Rinehart and Winston, 1979), p. 435.
9. K. Sivaraman, "The meaning of *moksha* in contemporary Hindu thought and life," in S. J. Samantha, ed., *Living Faiths and Ultimate Goals* (Geneva: World Council of Churches, 1974), p. 5.
10. Brian Hebblethwaite, *Evil, Suffering and Religion* (London: Sheldon Press, 1976), p. 29.
11. Santosh Chandra Sengupta, "The Misunderstanding of Hinduism," in John Hick, ed., *Truth and Dialogue in World Religions: Conflicting Truth-Claims* (Philadelphia: Westminster Press, 1974), p. 97.
12. Ibid., p. 105.
13. Ward J. Fellows, *Religions East and West*, p. 85.
14. Santosh Chandra Sengupta, "Misunderstanding of Hunduism" p. 103.
15. R. C. Zaehner, "Salvation in the Mahabharata," in Brandon, ed., *The Saviour God*, p. 225.

16. K. Sivaraman, "The meaning of *moksha*," pp. 3f.

17. Trevor Ling, "Communalism and the Social Structure of Religion," in *Truth and Dialogue in World Religions*, p. 62.

18. Karl Barth, *Church Dogmatics*, vol. 1, pt. 2, trans. G. T. Thomson & Harold Knight (New York: Charles Scribner's Sons, 1956), pp. 340ff.

19. Edward Conze, "Buddhist Saviours," in *The Saviour God*, p. 68.

20. Ward J. Fellows, *Religions East and West*, p. 99.

21. K. Sivaraman, "The meaning of *moksha*," p. 9.

22. Ibid.

23. Kosuke Koyama, *No Handle on the Cross, An Asian Meditation on the Crucified Mind* (London: SCM Press, 1976), p. 88.

24. Clifford G. Hospital, *BREAKTHROUGH, Insights of the great religious discoverers* (Maryknoll, New York: Orbis Books, 1985), p. 165.

25. Donald G. Dawe, "Christian Faith in a Religiously Plural World," in *Christian Faith in a Religiously Plural World*, p. 16.

26. Harold Coward, *PLURALISM, Challenge to World Religions* (Maryknoll, New York: Orbis Books, 1985), p. 105.

27. Ibid., p. 105.

28. Eric J. Sharpe, "The Goals of Inter-Religious Dialogue," in *Truth and Dialogue in World Religions*, pp. 81ff.

29. Raymond Panikkar, "The Unknown Christ of Hinduism," in *Christianity and other Religions*, pp. 131f.

30. Donald G. Dawe, "Christian Faith", p. 17.

31. Rosemary Ruether, *To Change the World* (London: SCM Press, 1981), p. 39.

32. Ibid., p. 43.

33. Wilfred Cantwell Smith, "The Christian in a Religiously Plural World," p. 99.

34. Harold Coward, *Pluralism*, p. 80.

35. Raymond Panikkar, "The Unknown Christ of Hinduism," p. 136.

36. Alfred C. Krass, "Accounting for the Hope that is in Me," in *Christian Faith in a Religiously Plural World*, p. 165.

37. John V. Taylor, "The Theological Basis of Interfaith Dialogue," in *Christianity and other Religions*, p. 226.

38. Paul F. Knitter, *No Other Name? A Critical Survey of Christian Attitudes Toward the World Religions* (Maryknoll, New York: Orbis Books, 1986), pp. 207ff.

39. Harold Coward, *Pluralism*, p. 105.

40. Kosuke Koyama, *No Handle on the Cross*, p. 85.

41. Paul E. Knitter, *No Other Name?*, p. 18.

42. Gerardus van der Leeuw, *Religion in Essence and Manifestation*, trans. J. E. Turner (New York: Harper & Row, 1963), p. 682.

43. John Hick, "Jesus and the World Religions," in John Hick, ed., *The Myth of God Incarnate* (London: SCM Press, 1977), p. 182.

44. John Hick, "Whatever Path Men Choose is Mine," in *Christianity and other Religions*, pp. 180f.

45. John Hick, *Problems of Religious Pluralism* (London: Macmillan, 1985), p. 80.

46. John Hick, "Whatever Path Men Choose is Mine," p. 180.

47. Karl Rahner, "Christian and Non-Christian Religions," in *Christianity and other Religions*, p. 79.

48. Denis Edwards, *What are they saying about Salvation?* (New York: Paulist Press, 1986), p. 22.

49. John Hick, "Jesus and the World Religions," p. 176.

50. Geoffrey Parrinder, "Is the Bhagavad-Gita the Word of God?" in *Truth and Dialogue in World Religions*, p. 114.

51. John Hick, "The Outcome: Dialogue into Truth," in *Truth and Dialogue in World Religions*, pp. 152ff.

52. Frances Young, "Two Roots or a Tangled Mass?" in *The Myth of God Incarnate*, pp. 118f.

53. Clifford G. Hospital, *Breakthrough*, p. 29.

54. Nikolai Berdyaev, *The Destiny of Man* (New York: Harper Torch Books, 1960), p. 119.

55. Kazoh Kitamori, *Theology of the Pain of God* (London: SCM Press, 1966), p. 27.

56. Edward Conze "Buddhist Saviours," p. 79. Suzuki quote is from *Mysticism, Christian and Buddhist* (1957), p. 136.

57. Robert Lawson Slater, *Can Christians Learn from other Religions?* (New York: Seabury Press, 1963), pp. 22ff.

58. K.L. Seshagiri, A Hindu Response," in *Christian Faith in a Religiously Plural World*, p. 54.

59. Paul F. Knitter, *No Other Name?*, pp. 47ff.

60. Ernst Troeltsch, "The Place of Christianity among the World Religions," in *Christianity and other Religions*, p. 28.

61. Wilfred Cantwell Smith, "Conflicting Truth-Claims: A Rejoinder," in *Truth and Dialogue in World Religions*, p. 158.

62. Raymond Panikkar, "The Unknown Christ of Hinduism," p. 126.

63. Flannery O'Connor, *Mystery and Manners*, Occasional Prose, selected and edited by Sally and Robert Fitzgerald (London: Faber & Faber, 1972), p. 84.

64. Paul F. Knitter, *No Other Name?* p. 9.

65. Nathan Söderblom, *The Mystery of the Cross*, trans. A. G. Herbert (London: SCM Press, 1933), p. 33.

66. John B. Cobb, Jr., *Beyond Dialogue, Toward a Mutual Transformation of Christianity and Buddhism* (Philadelphia: Fortress Press, 1982), p. 48.

67. Paul Tillich, "Christianity Judging Itself in the Light of its Encounter with the World Religions," in *Christianity and other Religions*, p. 121.

Chapter 8. Social Salvation

1. Edward Norman, *Christianity and the World Order* (Oxford: Oxford University Press, 1979), p. 2.

2. Ibid., p. 59.

3. Gustavo Gutierrez, *A Theology of Liberation*, trans. and ed., Sister Carided Inda and John Eagleson (Maryknoll, New York: Orbis Books, 1973), p. 15.

4. J. Andrew Kirk, *Liberation Theology: An Evangelical View from the Third World* (Atlanta: John Knox Press, 1979), p. 206.

5. Chair. Duguoc, "Liberation and Salvation in Jesus Christ," in Rene Metz and Jean Schlick, eds., *Liberation Theology and the Message of Salvation*, trans. David G. Gelzer (Pittsburg: The Pickwick Press, 1978), p. 50.

6. José Miguez Bonino, *Doing Theology in a Revolutionary Situation* (Philadelphia: Fortress Press, 1975), p. 81.

7. Karl Marx and Friederick Engels, *The German Ideology*, Part I, ed. C. J. Arthur (New York: International Publishers, 1970), p. 47.

8. Gustavo Gutierrez, "Liberation Praxis and Christian Faith," in Rosino Gibellini, ed., *Frontiers of Theology in Latin America* (Maryknoll, New York: Orbis Books, 1979), p. 19.

9. Joseph Comblin, "What Sort of Service Might Theology Render?" in *Frontiers of Theology in Latin America*, p. 62.

10. Hugo Assmann, *Theology for a Nomad Church*, trans. Paul Burns (Maryknoll: New York: Orbis Books, 1976), p. 75.

11. Bonino, *Doing Theology in a Revolutionary Situation*, pp. 89f.

12. Assmann, *Theology for a Nomad Church*, p. 75.

13. Karl Marx, "Theses on Feuerbach," in Karl Marx and Friedrich Engels, *On Religion* (New York: Schocken Books, 1964), Thesis 11, p. 72.

14. Jon Sobrino, "The Following of Jesus and Faith in Christ," in Durstan R. McDonald, ed., *The Myth/Truth of God Incarnate* (Wilton, Connecticut: Morehouse-Barlow Co., 1979), p. 120.

15. Raul Vidales, "Methodological Issues in Liberation Theology," in *Frontiers of Theology in Latin America*, p. 315.

16. Kostas Axelos, *Alienation, Praxis, and Techne in the Thought of Karl Marx*, trans. Ronald Bruzina (Austin and London: University of Texas, 1976), pp. 49f.

17. Kirk, *Liberation Theology*, p. 167.

18. Assmann, *Theology for a Nomad Church*, p. 95.

19. Paulo Freire, *Pedagogy of the Oppressed*, trans. Myra Bergman Ramos (New York: Continuum, 1981), p. 53.

20. Axelos, *Alienation*, p. 172; see also George Lichtheim, *From Marx to Hegel* (New York: Herder & Herder, 1971), p. 78.

21. Edward Norman, *Christianity and the World Order*, p. 56.

22. Sheila Cassidy, *Audacity to Believe* (London: Collins, Fount Paperbacks, 1977), p. 305, quoted in Norman, *Christianity*, p. 16.

23. Cassidy, *Audacity*, pp. 306f.

24. Freire, *Pedagogy of the Oppressed*, p. 186.

25. Ibid., p. 84.

26. Ibid., pp. 102f.

27. Ibid., p. 101.

28. Ibid., p. 185.

29. Ibid., p. 85.

30. Ibid., p. 83.

31. Ibid., p. 167.

32. Matthew Lamb, *Solidarity with Victims* (New York: Crossroad Publishing Co., 1982) in Dermot A. Lane, *Foundations for a Social Theology: Praxis, Process and Salvation* (New York: Paulist Press, 1984), pp. 64f.

33. Peter Hinchliff, *Holiness and Politics* (Grand Rapids, Michigan: William B. Eerdmans, 1983), pp. 3f.

34. Paul van Buren, *Discerning the Way, A Theology of the Jewish-Christian Reality* (New York: Seabury Press, A Crossroad Book, 1980), p. 14.

35. Gregory Baum, *The Social Imperative* (New York: Paulist Press, 1979), pp. 125f.

36. John Wesley, *Works*, vol. 5, p. 296, in Theodore Runyon, "Introduction: Wesley and the Theologies of Liberation," in Theodore Runyon, ed., *Sanctifica-*

tion and Liberation: Liberation Theologies in the Light of the Wesleyan Tradition (Nashville: Abingdon, 1981), p. 42.

37. José Miguez Bonino, "Wesley's Doctrine of Sanctification from a Liberationist Perspective," in *Santification and Liberation: Liberation Theologies in the Light of the Wesleyan Tradition*, p. 55.

38. Assmann, *Theology for a Nomad Church*, p. 32.

39. Ibid., p. 77.

40. Baum, *The Social Imperative*, pp. 12f.

41. Bonino, *Doing Theology in a Revolutionary Situation*, p. 47.

42. Dow Kirkpatrick, "A Liberating Pastoral for the Rich," in *Sanctification and Liberation: Liberation Theologies In the Light of Wesleyan Tradition*, p. 211.

43. Ibid.

44. Jean Guichard, "Class Struggle and Proclamation of Salvation," in *Liberation Theology and the Message of Salvation*, p. 97.

45. Ibid., p. 98.

46. Joseph Comblin, "What Sort of Service," p. 61.

47. Baum, *The Social Imperative*, p. 101.

48. Bonino, *Doing Theology in a Revolutionary Situation*, p. 148.

49. Leonardo Boff, in Leonardo and Clodovis Boff, *Salvation and Liberation*, trans. Robert R. Barr (Maryknoll, New York: Orbis Books, 1985), p. 48.

50. Ibid., p. 13.

51. Assmann, *Theology for a Nomad Church*, p. 104.

52. Luis G. del Valle, "Toward a Theological Outlook Starting from Concrete Events," in *Frontiers of Theology in Latin America*, p. 98.

53. Assmann, *Theology for a Nomad Church*, pp. 62f.

54. Bonino, *Doing Theology in a Revolutionary Situation*, p. 78.

55. Michael Novak, *Will it Liberate?* (New York: Paulist Press, 1986), p. 127.

56. Jean Guichard, *"Class Struggle,"* pp. 90ff.

57. Ruether, *To Change the World*, p. 27.

58. Bonino, *Doing Theology in a Revolutionary Situation*, p. 167.

59. Ibid., p. 99.

60. André Dumas, *Political Theology and the Life of the Church*, trans. John Bowden (London: SCM Press, 1978), p. 119.

61. Baum, *The Social Imperative*, p. 77.

62. Ibid., p. 78.

63. Christopher Small, *Ariel like a Harpy: Shelly, Mary and Frankenstein* (London: Victor Gollancz Ltd., 1972), p. 300.

64. T. S. Eliot, "Choruses from 'The Rock'," in *The Complete Poems and Plays 1909–1950* (New York: Harcourt, Brace & Co., 1952), p. 106.

65. Alfred Lord Tennyson, "In Memoriam," in Jerome Hamilton Buckley, ed., *Poems of Tennyson* (Cambridge, Mass: The Riverside Press, 1958), p. 178.

66. Robin Gill, *The Social Context of Theology* (Oxford: Mowbrays, 1975), pp. 132f.

67. Michael Polanyi, *Personal Knowledge* (London: Routledge & Kegan Paul, 1958), p. 307.

68. Robert Bellah, *Beyond Belief* (New York: Harper & Row, 1970), p. 250.

69. Baum, *The Social Imperative*, p. 161.

70. Ibid., p. 112.

71. Bellah, *Beyond Belief*, pp. 251ff.

72. John Carmody, *Theology for the 1980s* (Philadelphia: Westminster Press, 1980), p. 28.

73. Assmann, *Theology for a Nomad Church*, p. 98.

74. Lonnie D. Kliever, *The Shattered Spectrum* (Atlanta: John Knox Press, 1981), p. 75.

75. Canaan Banana, *The Gospel according to the Ghetto* (Geneva: World Council of Churches, 1974), p. 9, in Edward Norman, *Christianity and the World Order*, p. 65.

76. Novak, *Will it Liberate?*, p. 109.

77. Gutierrez, *A Theology of Liberation*, p. 308.

78. Novak, *Will it Liberate?*, p. 31.

79. Carmody, *Theology for the 1980s*, p. 63.

80. Norman Snaith, *Mercy and Sacrifice* (London: SCM Press, 1953), p. 82.

81. Hinchliff, *Holiness and Politics*, p. 194.

82. James R. Bullock, *Whatever Became of Salvation?* (Atlanta: John Knox Press, 1979), p. 29.

83. Donald G. Bloesch, "Soteriology in Contemporary Christian Thought," *Interpretation* 35 (1984): 139.

84. José Miguez Bonino, "Wesley's Doctrine of Sanctification from a Liberationist Perspective," in *Sanctification and Liberation Theologies in the Light of Wesleyan Tradition*, p. 49.

85. Ibid., p. 50.

86. Carl E. Braaten, "The Christian Doctrine of Salvation," *Interpretation* 35 (1981): 127f.

87. Th. Wieser, "The Church: A Sign of Liberation and Salvation," in *Liberation Theology and the Message of Salvation*, p. 125.

88. Leonard Hodgson, *The Doctirne of the Atonement* (London: Nisbet & Co., Ltd., 1955), p. 94.

89. Ibid., p. 100.

90. Douglas John Hall, *Has the Church a Future?* (Philadelphia: Westminster Press, 1980).

91. Gutierrez, *A Theology of Liberation*, p. 256.

92. Dietrich Wiederkehr, *Belief in Redemption*, trans. Jeremy Moiser (Atlanta: John Knox Press, 1979), p. 54.

93. Assmann, *Theology for a Nomad Church*, p. 67.

94. Ibid., p. 35.

95. Gutierrez, *A Theology of Liberation*, p. 255.

96. Baum, *The Social Imperative*, p. 76.

97. Carl E. Braaten, *The Flaming Center* (Philadelphia: Fortress Press, 1977), p. 150.

98. Dennis P. McCann, *Christian Realism and Liberation Theology* (Maryknoll, New York: Orbis Books, 1981), p. 194.

99. Rupert E. Davies, "Justification, Sanctification, and the Liberation of the Person," in *Sanctification and Liberation: Liberation Theologies in Light of Wesleyan Tradition*, p. 77.

100. Clodovis Boff, *Salvation and Liberation*, pp. 95f.

101. Chair. Duquoc, "Liberation and Salvation," p. 55.

102. Clodovis Boff, *Salvation and Liberation*, p. 107.

103. Ibid., p. 98.

104. Bloesch, "Soteriology,"p. 138.

105. Gutierrez, *A Theology of Liberation*, p. 206.

106. Gustavo Gutierrez, *We Drink from our own Wells: The Spiritual Journey of a People*, trans. Matthew J. O'Connell (Maryknoll, New York: Orbis Books, 1984).

107. Gutierrez, *A Theology of Liberation*, pp. 36f.

108. Ibid., p. 176.

109. Kirk, *Liberation Theology*, p. 59.

110. Robert McAfee Brown, *Spirituality and Liberation* (Philadelphia: Westminster Press, 1988), p. 122.

111. McCann, *Christian Realism*, p. 192.

112. Norman, *Christianity and the World Order*, pp. 53f.

113. Leonardo Boff, *Salvation and Liberation*, p. 17.

114. Ibid., p. 44.

115. McCann, *Christian Realism*, p. 184.

116. Kirk, *Liberation Theology*, p. 59.

117. Jon Sobrino, "The Following of Jesus," p. 112.

118. Ajit Roy, "A Marxist View of Liberation," in Samartha, ed. *Living Faith and Ultimate Goals* (Geneva: World Council of Churches, 1974), p. 59.

119. Kosuke Koyama, *No Handle on the Cross* (London: SCM Press, 1976), "Preface."

120. Denis Edwards, *What are they Saying about Salvation?* (New York: Paulist Press, 1986), pp. 74f.

121. Leonardo Boff, *Salvation and Liberation*, p. 59.

Chapter 9. Personal Salvation

1. George Johnston, "Should the Church Still Talk About Salvation?" *International Review of Missions* 61 (1972): 48.

2. Philip J. Lee, *Against the Protestant Gnostics* (New York: Oxford University Press, 1987), p. 204.

3. Edward Norman, *Christianity and the World Order* (Oxford: Oxford University Press, 1979), p. 80.

4. Peter Hinchliff, *Holiness and Politics* (Grand Rapids, Michigan: William B. Eerdmans, 1983), p. 88.

5. Harvey Cox, *Religion in the Secular City, Toward a Postmodern Theology* (New York: Simon and Schuster, 1984), p. 146.

6. Paulo Freire, *Pedagogy of the Oppressed*, trans. Myra Bergman Ramos (New York: Continuum, 1981), p. 100.

7. Hinchliff, *Holiness and Politics*, p. 107.

8. Alfred North Whitehead, *Religion in the Making* (Cambridge: Cambridge University Press, 1927), p. 6; see also p. 37.

9. William James, *The Varieties of Religious Experience* (Garden City, New York: Doubleday Dolphin Books, n.d.), p. 37.

10. Gordon W. Allport, *The Individual and His Religion* (New York: Macmillan, 1968), p. 161.

11. Whitehead, *Religion in the Making*, p. 7.

12. Thomas Merton, *Contemplation in a World of Action* (Garden City, New York: Doubleday Image Books, 1973), p. 262.

13. Henri Nouwen, *The Wounded Healer* (Garden City, New York: Doubleday Image Books, 1979), p. 90.

14. Freire, *Pedagogy*.

15. James, *Varieties of Religions Experience*, p. 51.

16. Merton, *Contemplation*, p. 159.

17. Ibid., p. 389.

18. P. T. Forsyth, *The Work of Christ* (London: Collins, The Fontana Library, 1965), p. 112.

19. James, *Varieties of Religions Experience*, p. 448f.

20. Whitehead, *Religion in the Making*, p. 123.

21. Ibid., p. 37.

22. Carl Rogers, *On Becoming a Person* (Boston: Houghton Mifflin Co., 1961), p. 26.

23. Ibid.

24. James, p. 389.

25. In Martin Marty, *Righteous Empire, The Protestant Experience in America* (New York: The Dial Press, 1970), p. 177.

26. Ibid.

27. Ibid., p. 178.

28. Dorothee Soelle, *Suffering*, trans. Everett R. Kalin (London: Darton, Longman and Todd, 1975), p. 95.

29. See note 11 above.

30. George Herbert Mead, *On Social Psychology* (Chicago: University of Chicago Press, 1956), pp. 222f.

31. Harry Stack Sullivan, *Conceptions of Modern Psychiatry* (Washington: William Alanson White Psychiatric Foundation, 1947), xi.

32. Otto Klineberg, *Social Psychology* (New York: Henry Holt & Co., 1954), p. 68.

33. Mead, *On Social Psychology*, p. 244.

34. Nevitt Sanford, *Issues in Personality Theory* (San Francisco: Jossey-Bass Inc., 1920), p. 60.

35. Ibid., pp. 60f.

36. James R. Bullock, *Whatever Became of Salvation?* (Atlanta: John Knox Press, 1979), p. 41.

37. James Cone, *God of the Oppressed* (New York: Seabury Press, A Crossroad Book, 1975), p. 229.

38. Cecil Wayne Cone, *The Identity Crisis in Black Theology* (Nashville: The African Methodist Episcopal Church, 1975), pp. 83f.

39. Ibid., p. 122.

40. William H. Whyte, *The Organization Man* (New York: Simon and Schuster, A Touchstone Book, 1956), p. 255.

41. Ibid.

42. Ibid., p. 13.

43. Thomas à Kempis, *Of the Imitation of Christ*, trans. Abbot Jostin McCann (New York: New American Library, 1957). 1, 20. 1, p. 37.

44. Ibid., 1, 20. 6, p. 38.

45. Matthew Fox, *A Spirituality named Compassion and the Healing of the Globa Village, Humpty Dumpty and Us* (Minneapolis: Winston Press, 1979), p. 43.

46. Merton, *Contemplation*, p. 67.

47. Thomas Merton, *Faith and Violence* (Notre Dame, Indiana: University of Notre Dame Press, 1968), pp. 82f.

48. Victor A. Kramer, *Thomas Merton: Monk and Artist* (Kalamazoo, Michigan: Cistercian Publications, 1987), p. 109.

49. B. F. Skinner, *Beyond Freedom and Dignity* (London: Jonathan Cape, 1971).

50. Finley Carpenter, *The Skinner Primer, Behind Freedom and Dignity* (New York: Macmillan, 1974), p. 10.

51. Rogers, *On Becoming a Person*, p. 391.

52. Ibid., pp. 400f.

53. Ibid., p. 401.

54. P. T. Forsyth, *The Justification of God* (London: Independent Press Ltd., 1948), p. 18.

55. Arthur Koestler, "The Yogi and the Commissar (2)," in *The Yogi and the Commissar and Other Essays* (London: Hutchinson, 1965), pp. 230f.

56. Thomas Kuhn, *The Structure of Scientific Revolutions* (Chicago: University of Chicago Press, 1970).

57. Michael Polanyi, *Personal Knowledge* (London: Routledge and Kegan Paul, 1962).

58. Mihajlo Mesarovir and Eduard Pestel, *Mankind at the Turning Point* (New York: E.P. Dutton, & Co., 1974), p. 147.

59. Erich Fromm, *To Have or To Be?* (London: Jonathan Cape, 1976), p. 9.

60. Viktor E. Frankl, *Man's Search for Meaning, An Introduction to Logotherapy* (New York: Washington Square Press, 1963), pp. 153f.

61. Ibid., p. 175.

62. Henri Nouwen, *Creative Ministry* (Garden City, New York: Doubleday Image Books, 1978), p. 81.

63. Carl E. Krieg, "Bonhoeffer's Letters and Papers," *Religious Studies*, 9 (1973): 92.

64. Merton, *Contemplation in a World of Action*, p. 27.

65. Nouwen, *The Wounded Healer*, p. 38.

66. William F. Lynch, S.J., *Christ and Prometheus, A New Image of the Secular* (Notre Dame, Indiana: University of Notre Dame Press, 1970), p. 134.

67. Don Cupitt, *Taking Leave of God* (London: SCM Press, 1930), p. 101.

68. Bruce Matthews, *Craving and Salvation, A Study in Buddhist Soteriology* (Waterloo, Ontario: Wilfrid Laurier University Press, SR Supplements, 1983), p. 107.

69. Hugh T. Kerr and John M. Mulder, eds., *Conversion, The Christian Experience* (Grand Rapids, Michigan: William B. Eerdmans, 1983).

70. Sheila Cassidy, *Audacity to Believe* (London: Collins Fount Paperbacks, 1977), p. 121.

71. James, *Varieties of Religions Experience*, p. 342.

72. George A. Rawlyk, ed., *Henry Alline, Selected Writings* (New York: Paulist Press, 1987), p. 53.

73. "Journal of Henry Alline," in George Rawlyk, pp. 86f.

74. James, *Varieties of Religious Experience*, pp. 149, 161ff.

75. Paul Tournier, *The Meaning of Persons* (London: SCM Press, 1965), p. 167.

76. Carl E. Braaten, *The Flaming Center* (Philadelphia: Fortress Press, 1977), p. 149.

77. Thomas à Kempis, *Imitation of Christ*, 1, 23.5, p. 44.

78. In Marty, *Righteous Empire*, p, 256.

79. Fox, *A Spirituality*, p. 264.

80. Forsyth, *The Justification of God*, p. 64.

81. Soelle, *Suffering*, p. 53.

82. Nouwen, *Creative Ministry*, p. 20.

83. Hinchliff, *Holiness and Politics*, p. 139.

84. Arthur Koestler, "The Yogi and the Commissar," in *The Yogi and the Commissar and Other Essays*, p. 16.

85. Ibid., p. 17.

86. Tournier, *The Meaning of Persons*, p. 183.

87. Ibid., p. 182.

88. Cupitt, *Taking Leave God*, p. 100.

89. Ibid., p. 93.

90. Douglas John Hall, *Imaging God* (New York: Friendship Press, 1986).

91. Martin Buber, *I and Thou* (New York: Charles Scribner's Sons, 1958), p. 12.

92. Ibid.

93. Ibid., p. 28.

94. Ibid., p. 75.

95. Ibid., pp. 80f.

96. Ibid., p. 99.

97. Ibid., p. 95.

98. Ibid., p. 96.

99. Tournier, *The Meaning of Persons*, p. 233.

100. Merton, *Contemplation in a World of Action*, p. 35.

101. Ibid., p. 36.

Chapter 10. Eschatological Salvation

1. "Arius' Letter to Alexander," in *The Trinitarian Controversy*, ed. & trans., William G. Rusch (Philadelphia: Fortress Press, 1980), p. 31.

2. "Athanasius' Orations against the Arians," in *The Trinitarian Controversy*, p. 99.

3. "Nestorius' First Sermon Against the *Theotokos*," in *The Christological Controversy*, ed. & trans. Richard A. Norris, Jr. (Philadelphia: Fortress Press, 1980), p. 130.

4. "Cyril of Alexandria' s Second Letter to Nestorius," in *The Christological Controversy*, p. 133.

5. Hippolytus, *The Refutation of All Heresies*, trans. J. H. MacMahon, Ante-Nicene Christian Library, vol. 6 (Edinburgh: T. & T. Clarke, 1868), p. 335.

6. Ibid.

7. Tertullian, *Adversus Praxean*, Ante-Nicene Chrsitian Library, ed. Alexander Roberts & James Donaldson, vol. 15 (Edinburgh: T. & T. Clark, 1870), pp. 402f.

8. Richard Bauckham, "'Only the Suffering God can help': divine passibility in modern theology," *Themelios* 9 (1984): 6.

9. Karl Barth, *Church Dogmatics*, vol. 4, part 3, ed. G. W. Bromiley and T. F. Torrance (Edinburgh: T. & T. Clark, 1961), p. 414.

10. Dietrich Bonhoeffer, *Letters and Papers from Prison* (London: Collins, Fontana Books, 1953), p. 122.

11. Jürgen Moltmann, *The Crucified God* (New York: Harper & Row, 1974).

12. Kazoh Kitamori, *Theology of the Pain of God* (London: SCM Press, 1946, 1966).

13. Geddes MacGregor, *He Who Lets Us Be: A Theology of Love* (New York: Seabury Press, 1975).

14. Alfred North Whitehead, *Process and Reality*, Corrected Edition, ed. David Ray Griffin and Donald W. Sherburne (London: The Free Press, 1978), p. 351.

15. Charles Hartshorne, *The Divine Relativity* (New Haven and London: Yale University Press, 1948); and *Reality as Social Process* (Glencoe, Illinois: The Free Press, 1953).

16. Daniel Day Williams, *What Present-Day Theologians are Thinking* (New York: Harper & Row, 1952), p. 138.

17. Ronald Goetz, "The Suffering God: The Rise of a New Orthodoxy," *The Christian Century*, 16 April 1986, p. 385.

18. Jung Young Lee, *God Suffers for Us, A Systematic Inquiry into a Concept of Divine Passibility* (The Hague: Martinus Nijhoff, 1974), p. 1.

19. B. H. Streeter, *The Buddha and the Christ* (London: Macmillan, 1932), p. 224.

20. Whitehead, *Process and Reality*, p. 342.

21. Abraham Heschel, *The Prophets* (New York: Harper & Row, 1962).

22. Kazoh Kitamori, *Theology of the Pain of God*, p. 66.

23. Paul van Buren, *Discerning the Way, A Theology of the Jewish Christian Reality* (New York: Seabury Press, A Crossroad Book, 1980), p 36.

24. Ibid., p. 25.

25. Robert S. Paul, *The Atonement and the Sacraments* (London: Hodder & Stoughton, 1961), p. 292.

26. Kazoh Kitamori, *Theology of the Pain of God*, p. 45.

27. W. H. Vanstone, *Love's Endeavour, Love's Expense* (London: Darton, Longman & Todd, 1977), pp. 119f.

28. Geddes MacGregor, *He Who Lets Us Be: A Theology of Love.*

29. Ibid. p. 128.

30. Sheila Cassidy, *Audacity to Believe* (London: Collins, Fount Paperbacks, 1977), p. 89.

31. Ibid., p. 115.

32. Moltmann, *The Crucified God*, pp. 20ff., 265.

33. A. G. Herbert, "Preface" to Nathan Söderblom, *The Mystery of the Cross* (London: SCM Press, 1933), pp. 6f.

34. E. L. Mascall, *Existence and Analogy* (London: Libra Books, 1949), p. 142.

35. Ronald Goetz, "The Suffering God: The Rise of a New Orthodoxy," p. 388.

36. Ruth Page, "Human Liberation and Divine Transcendence," *Theology* 85 (1982): 184-190.

37. Sallie McFague, *Metaphorical Theology, Models of God in Religious Language* (London: SCM Press, 1983), p. 192.

38. Peter DeVries, *The Mackerel Plaza* (London: Victor Gollancz, 1958), pp. 7f.

Chapter 11. The Bottom Line for Salvation

1. Dorothy L. Sayers, *Christian Letters to a Post-Christian World* (Grand Rapids, Michigan: Eerdmans, 1969), p. 98.

2. Rudolph Otto, *The Idea of the Holy* (New York: Oxford University Press, 1958), p. 56.

3. Ibid., pp. 56–57.

4. James William McClendon, Jr., *Systematic Theology, Ethics* (Nashville: Abingdon Press, 1986), p. 356.

5. For one of the clearest statements of Hartshorne's position see his "Whitehead's Idea of God," in *The Philosophy of Alfred North Whitehead*, ed. Paul Arthur Schilpp (Evanston & Chicago: Northwestern University, 1941).

6. Alfred North Whitehead, *Religion in the Making* (Cambridge: Cambridge University Press, 1927), pp. 144f.

7. Philippa Foot,"Moral Arguments,"*Mind* (1958): 505f.

8. George Grant, *Time as History* (Toronto: Hunter Rose Co., 1970), p. 44.

9. Gordon Kaufman, *Theology for a Nuclear Age* (Manchester and Philadelphia: Manchester University Press and Westminster Press, 1985).

10. Ibid., p. 58.

11. Ibid., p. 59.

12. Ibid.

13. Ibid., pp. 62f.

14. Ibid., p. 61.

Bibliography

Adley, Lionel. *Hymns and the Christian "Myth"*. Vancouver: University of British Columbia Press, 1986.

Allport, Gordon. *The Individual and His Religion*. New York: Macmillan Co., 1968.

Altizer, Thomas J. J.,and William Hamilton. *Radical Theology and the Death of God*. New York: Bobbs-Merrill, 1966.

Anderson, Hugh. *Jesus and Christian Origins*. New York: Oxford University Press, 1964.

Anselm. *Cur Deus Homo*. Edinburgh: John Grant, 1909.

Aquinas, Thomas. *Summa Theologica*. London: Eyre and Spottiswoode, 1965.

Assmann, Hugo. *Theology for a Nomad Church*. Translated by Paul Burns. Maryknoll, New York: Orbis Books, 1976.

Aulen, Gustaf. *Christus Victor*. London: Society for Promoting Christian Knowledge (S.P.C.K.), 1970.

Axelos Kostas. *Alienation, Praxis, and Techne in the Thought of Karl Marx* Translated by Ronald Bruzina. Austin and London: University of Texas Press, 1976.

Barnet, Richard J., and Ronald E. Muller. *Global Reach: The Power of the Multinational Corporations*. New York: Simon and Schuster, 1974.

Barth, Karl. *Church Dogmatics*. Vol. 1, Pt. 2. Translated by G. T. Thomson and Harold Knight. New York: Charles Scribner's Sons, 1956.

————. *Church Dogmatics*. Vol. 4. Pt. 3. Edited by G. W. Bromiley and T. F. Torrance. Edinburgh: T and T Clark, 1961.

Bauckham, Richard. "'Only the Suffering God can help': divine passibility in modern theology." *Themelios* 9 (1984).

Baum, Gregory. *The Social Imperative*. New York: Paulist Press, 1979.

Beauchamp, Tom L., and Norman E. Bowie, eds. *Ethical Theory and Business*. Second Edition. Englewood Cliffs, N.J.: Prentice-Hall, 1983.

Bellah, Robert. *Beyond Belief*. New York: Harper and Row, 1970.

Berdyaev, Nikolai. *The Destiny of Man*. New York: Harper Torch Books, 1960.

Bloesch, Donald G. "Soteriology in Contemporary Christian Thought." *Interpretation* 35 (1981).

Bonhoeffer, Dietrich. *Letters and Papers from Prison*. London: Collins, Fontana Books, 1959.

Bonio, José Miguez. *Doing Theology in a Revolutionary Situation*. Philadelphia: Fortress Press, 1975.

Braaten, Carl E. "The Christian Doctrine of Salvation." *Interpretation* 34 (1981).

————. *The Flaming Center*. Philadelphia: Fortress Press, 1977.

381

Brandon, S. G. F. *The Saviour God*. New York: Barnes and Noble, 1963.

Brooks, John. "The Money Machine." *The New Yorker*, January 5, 1981.

Brown, Robert McAfee. *Spirituality and Liberation*. Philadelphia: Westminster Press, 1988.

Brunner, Emil. *The Christian Doctrine of the Church, Faith and the Consummation. Dogmatics* Vol. 3. Translated by David Cairns. London: Lutterworth Press, 1962.

―――. *The Mediator*. Translated by Olive Wyon. London: Lutterworth Press, 1934; New York: Charles Scribner's Sons, 1958.

Buber, Martin. *I and Thou*. Translated by Ronald Gregor Smith. New York: Charles Scribner's Sons, 1958.

Buckley, Jerome Hamilton, ed. *Poems of Tennyson*. Cambridge, Mass: The Riverside Press, 1958.

Bullock, James R. *Whatever Became of Salvation?* Atlanta: John Knox Press, 1979.

Bultmann, Rudolf. "Jesus and Paul." In *Existence and Faith*. Translated by Schubert M. Ogden. London: Collins, The Fontana Library, 1964.

―――. "New Testament and Mythology." In Hans Werner Bartsch and Reginald H. Fuller, eds., *Kerygma and Myth*. Vol. 1. London: Society for Promoting Christian Knowledge (S.P.C.K.), 1964.

―――. *Theology of the New Testament*. Vol. 1. Translated by Kendrick Grobel. London: SCM Press, 1952.

Cabasilas, Nicholas. *A Commentary on the Divine Liturgy*. Translated by J. M. Hussey and P. A. McNulty. London: Society for Promoting Chrisitian Knowledge (S.P.C.K.), 1983.

Cagley, John. *Religion in a Secular Age*. New York: New American Library, A Mentor Book, 1968.

Cahill, P. Joseph. "Rudolf Bultmann and Post-Bultmann Tendencies." In Martin E. Marty and Dean G. Peerman, eds., *New Theology*. No. 2. New York: Macmillan Co., 1965.

Carmody, John. *Theology for the 1980s*. Philadelphia: Westminster Press, 1980.

Carpenter, Finley. *The Skinner Primer, Behind Freedom and Dignity*. New York: Macmillan Co., 1974.

Cassidy, Sheila. *Audacity to Believe*. London: Collins, Fount Paperbacks, 1977.

Chadwick, Owen. *The Secularization of the European Mind in the Nineteenth Century*. Cambridge: Cambridge University Press, 1975.

Cobb, John B. *Beyond Dialogue, Toward a Mutual Transformation of Christianity and Buddhism*. Philadelphia: Fortress Press, 1982.

―――, and David Tracy. *Talking About God*. New York: Seabury Press, 1983.

Cone, Cecil Wayne. *The Identity Crisis in Black Theology*. Nashville: The African Methodist Episcopal Church, 1975.

Cone, James. *God of the Oppressed*. New York: Seabury Press, 1975.

Coward, Harold. *PLURALISM, Challenge to World Religions*. Maryknoll, New York: Orbis Books, 1985.

Cox, Harvey. *Religion in the Secular City, Toward a Postmodern Theology*. New York: Simon and Schuster, 1984.

―――. *The Secular City*. New York: Macmillan Co., 1965.

Cullmann, Oscar, and F. J. Leenhardt. *Essays on the Lord's Supper*. Richmond, Virginia: John Knox Press, 1958.

Cupitt, Don. *Taking Leave of God*. London: SCM Press, 1980.

Davies, D. J. *Meaning and Salvation in Religious Studies*. Leiden: E. J. Brill, 1984.

Davis, Keith. "An Expanded View of the Social Responsibility of Business." *Business Horizons* 18 (1975).

Davis, Stephen T.,ed. *Encountering Evil*. Atlanta: John Knox Press, 1981.

Dawe, Donald G., and John B. Carman, eds. *Christian Faith in a Religiously Plural World*. Maryknoll, New York: Orbis Books, 1978.

DeBell, Garrett, ed. *The Environmental Handbook*. New York: Ballantine Books, 1970.

DeGeorge, Richard T. *Business Ethics*. New York: Macmillan Co., 1986.

Delmore, J. et al. *The Eucharist in the New Testament, A Symposium*. Baltimore and Dublin: Helicon Press, 1964.

De Rougemont, Denis. *The Christian Opportunity*. New York: Holt, Rinehart and Winston, 1963.

DeVries, Peter. *The Mackerel Plaza*. London: Victor Gollancz, 1958.

Dillistone, F. W. "Atonement." In Alan Richardson and John Bowden, eds., *A New Dictionary of Christian Theology*. London: SCM Press, 1983.

———. *The Christian Understanding of Atonement*. Philadelphia: Westminster Press, 1968.

Dougherty, K. F. "Atonement." In *New Catholic Encyclopedia*. Vol. 1. Washington: The Catholic Univesity of America, 1967.

Dumas, André. *Political Theology and the Life of the Church*. Translated by John Bowden. London: SCM Press, 1978.

Early Christian Writings, The Apostolic Fathers. Translated by Maxwell Staniforth. Harmondsworth, Middlesex: Penguin Books, 1968.

Edwards, Denis. *What are they saying about Salvation?* New York: Paulist Press, 1986.

Eliot, T. S. "The Coctail Party," In *The Complete Poems and Plays 1909–1950*. New York: Harcourt, Brace and Co., 1952.

Ellul, Jacques. *The New Demons*. Translated by C. Edward Hophin. New York: Seabury Press, 1975.

Feather, Frank, ed. *Through the 80s: Thinking Globally, Acting Locally*. Washington, D.C.: World Future Society, 1980.

Fellows, Ward J. *Religions East and West*. New York: Holt, Rinehart and Winston, 1979.

Foot, Philippa. "Moral Arguments." *Mind* 67 (1958).

Forsyth, P. T. *The Justification of God*. London: Independent Press Ltd., 1948.

———. *The Work of Christ*. London: Collins, The Fontana Library, 1965.

Fox, Matthew. *A Spirituality named Compassion and the Healing of the Global Village, Humpty Dumpty and Us*. Minneapolis: Winston Press, 1979.

Frankl, Viktor E. *Man's Search for Meaning, An Introduction to Logotherapy*. New York: Washington Square Press, 1963.

Franks, Robert S. *The Work of Christ*. London: Thomas Nelson and Sons, 1962.

Freire, Paulo. *Pedagogy of the Oppressed*. Translated by Myra Bergman Ramos. New York: Continuum, 1981.

Fromm, Erich. *The Art of Loving*. New York: Harper and Row, 1956.

———. *To Have or To Be?* London: Jonathan Cape, 1976.

Fuchs, Ernst. *Studies of the Historical Jesus*. Naperville, Illinois: Alec R. Allenson, 1964.

Galbraith, John Kenneth. *The Affluent Society*. London: Andre Deutsch, 1958.

Garrison, Jim. *The Darkness of God: Theology after Hiroshima*. London: SCM Press, 1982.

Gaston, Lloyd. "Paul and Jerusalem." In Peter Richardson and John C. Hurd, eds., *From Jesus to Paul*. Waterloo, Ontario: Wilfrid Laurier University Press, 1984.

Gill, Robin. *The Social Context of Theology*. Oxford: Mowbrays, 1975.

Goetz, Ronald. "The Suffering God: The Rise of a New Orthodoxy." *Christian Century*, 16 April 1986.

Gollner, Andrew B. *Social Change and Corporate Strategy. The Expanding Role of Public Affairs*. Stamford, Connecticut: Issue Action Publications, 1983.

Goodpaster, K. E., and K. M. Sayre, eds. *Ethics and Problems in the Twenty-first Century*. Notre Dame, Indiana: University of Notre Dame Press, 1979.

Gough, Michael. *The Origins of Christian Art*. New York: Praeger Publishers, 1973.

Goulder, Michael, ed. *Incarnation and Myth; The Debate Continued*. London: SCM Press, 1979.

Graham, Fred W. "America's Other Religion." *Christian Century*, 17 March 1982.

Grant, George. *Time as History*. Toronto: Hunter Rose Co., 1970.

Greeley, Andrew M. *No Bigger than Necessary*. New York: New American Library, 1977.

Green, Michael, ed. *The Truth of God Incarnate*. London: Hodder and Stoughton, 1977.

Green, E.M.B. *The Meaning of Salvation*. London: Hodder and Stoughton, 1965.

Gregarios, Paulos. *The Human Presence, An Orthodox View of Nature*. Geneva: World Council of Churches, 1978.

Gutierrez, Gustavo. *A Theology of Liberation*. Translated by Sister Carided Inda and John Eagleson. Maryknoll, New York: Orbis Books, 1973.

———. *We Drink from our own Wells: The Spiritual Journey of a People*. Translated by Matthew J. O'Connell. Maryknoll, New York: Orbis Books, 1984.

Hahn, Ferdinand. *The Worship of the Early Church*. Translated by David E. Green. Philadelphia: Fortress Press, 1973.

Hall, Douglas John. *Has the Church a Future?* Philadelphia: Westminster Press, 1980.

———. *Imaging God*. New York: Friendship Press, 1986.

Hartshorne, Charles. *The Divine Relativity*. New Haven and London: Yale University Press, 1948.

———. *Reality as Social Process*. Glencoe, Illinois: The Free Press, 1953.

Hebblethwaite, Brian. *Evil, Suffering and Religion*. London: Sheldon Press, 1976.

Hengel, Martin. *The Atonement, The Origins of the Doctrine of the New Testament*. Translated by John Bowden. Philadelphia: Fortress Press, 1981.

Heschel, Abraham. *The Prophets*. New York: Harper and Row, 1962.

Heyne, Paul T. *Private Keepers of the Public Interest*. New York: McGraw-Hill, 1968.

Hick, John, ed. *The Myth of God Incarnate*. London: SCM Press, 1977.

————. *Problems of Religious Pluralism*. London: Macmillan and Co., 1985.

————, ed. *Truth and Dialogue in World Religions: Conflicting Truth-Claims*. Philadelphia: Westminster Press, 1974.

————, and Brian Hebblethwaite, eds. *Christianity and Other Religions*. Glasgow: Collins, Fount Paperbacks, 1980.

Higgins, A. J. B. *The Lord's Supper in the New Testament*. London: SCM Press, 1972.

Hinchliff, Peter. *Holiness and Politics*. Grand Rapids, Michigan: William B. Eerdmans, 1983.

Hippolytus. *The Refutation of All Heresies*. Translated by J. H. MacMahon. Ante-Nicene Christian Library. Vol. 6. Edinburgh: T and T Clark, 1868.

Hirsch, Fred. *Social Limits to Growth*. Cambridge: Harvard University Press, 1978.

Hodgson, Leonard. *The Doctrine of the Atonement*. London: Nisbet and Co., 1955.

Hoffman, W. Michael, and Jennifer Moore. *Business Ethics, Readings and Cases in Corporate Morality*. New York: McGraw-Hill, 1984.

Hospital, Clifford G. *BREAKTHROUGH, Insights of the great religious discoverers*. Maryknoll, New York: Orbis Books, 1985.

Hulme, T. *Speculations: Essays on Humanism and the Philosophy of Art*. Boston: Routledge and Kegan Paul, 1963.

Hutchison, John A. *Paths of Faith*. Second Edition. New York: McGraw-Hill, 1975.

Ice, Jackson Lee, and John J. Carey, eds. *The Death of God Debate*. Philadelphia: Westminster Press, 1967.

Jacobs, Norman, ed. *Culture for the Millions*. Boston: Beacon Press, 1964.

James, William. *The Varieties of Religious Experience*. Garden City, New York: Doubleday Dolphin Books, 1973.

Jeremias, Joachim. *The Eucharistic Words of Jesus*. London: SCM Press, 1966.

————. *The Problem of the Historical Jesus*. Translated by Norman Perrin. Philadelphia: Fortress Press, 1964.

Jersild, Paul. *Invitation to Faith*. Minneapolis: Augsburg Publishing House, 1978.

Johnston, George. "Should the Church still talk about Salvation?" *International Review of Missions* 61 (1972).

Jones, Donald C., ed. *Business, Religion, and Ethics*. Cambridge, Mass.: Oelgeschlager, Gunn and Hain, 1982.

Jung, Carl A. *Answer to Job*. Translated by R. F. C. Hull. London: Hodder and Stoughton, 1965.

Kähler, Martin. *The So-called Historical Jesus and the Historic, Biblical Christ*. Translated by Carl E. Braaten. Philadelphia: Fortress Press, 1964.

Kaufman, Gordon. *Theology for a Nuclear Age*. Manchester and Philadelphia: Manchester University Press and Westminster Press, 1985.

Kavanaugh, John Francis. *Following Christ in a Consumer Society*. Maryknoll, New York: Orbis Books, 1982.

Kee, Alistair. *Constantine versus Christ, The Triumph of Ideology*. London: SCM Press, 1982.

Kerr, Hugh T., and John M. Mulder, eds. *Conversion, The Christian Experience*. Grand Rapids, Michigan: William B. Eerdmans, 1983.

Kirk, J. Andrew. *Liberation Theology: An Evangelical View from the Third World*. Atlanta: John Knox Press, 1979.

Kitamori, Kazoh. *Theology of the Pain of God*. London: SCM Press, 1966.

Klauser, Theodor. *A Short History of the Western Liturgy*. Translated by John Halliburton. Oxford: Oxford University Press, 1979.

Kliever, Lonnie. *The Shattered Spectrum; A Survey of Contemporary Theology*. Atlanta: John Knox Press, 1981.

Klineberg, Otto. *Social Psychology*. New York: Henry Holt and Co., 1954.

Knitter, Paul F. *No Other Name? A Critical Survey of Chrisitian Attitudes Toward the World Religions*. Maryknoll, New York: Orbis Books, 1986.

Koestler, Arthur. *The Yogi and the Commissar and Other Essays*. London: Hutchison, 1965.

Koyama, Kosuke. *No Handle on the Cross*. London: SCM Press, 1976.

Kramer, Victor A. *Thomas Merton: Monk and Artist*. Kalamazoo, Michigan: Cistercian Publications, 1987.

Krieg, Carl E. "Bonhoeffer's Letters and Papers." *Religious Studies* 9 (1973).

Kuhn, Thomas. "Second Thoughts on Paradigms." In Frederick Suppe, ed., *The Structure of Scientific Theories*. Urbana: University of Illinois Press, 1977.

———. *The Structure of Scientific Revolutions*. Chicago: University of Chicago Press, 1962.

Kung, Hans. *Eternal Life?* Garden City, New York: Doubleday, 1984.

Lane, Dermot A. *Foundations for a Social Theology: Praxis, Process and Salvation*. New York: Paulist Press, 1984.

Lasch, Christopher. *The Culture of Narcissism*. New York: Warner Books, 1979.

Lee, Jung Young. *God Suffers for Us*. The Hague: Martinus Nijhoff, 1974.

Lee, Philip J. *Against the Protestant Gnostics*. New York: Oxford University Press, 1987.

Lichtheim, George. *From Marx to Hegel*. New York: Herder and Herder, 1971.

Lockman, Jan Milic. *Reconciliation and Liberation*. Translated by David Lewis. Philadelphia: Fortress Press, 1980.

Lynch, William F., S. J. *Christ and Prometheus, A New Image of the Secular*. Notre Dame, Indiana: University of Notre Dame Press, 1970.

McCann, Dennis P. *Christian Realism and Liberation Theology*. Maryknoll, New York: Orbis Books, 1981.

McClendon, James William, Jr. *Systematic Theology, Ethics*. Nashville: Abingdon Press, 1986.

Maccoby, Michael. *The Gamesman*. New York: Bantam Books, 1978.

McConnachie, John. *The Significance of Karl Barth*. London: Hodder and Stoughton, 1931.

McDonald, Durstan R., ed. *The Myth/Truth of God Incarnate*. Wilton, Connecticut: Morehouse-Barlow Co., 1979.

McFague, Sallie. *Metaphorical Theology*. London: SCM Press, 1983.

———. *Models of God, Theology for an Ecological, Nuclear Age*. Philadelphia: Fortress Press, 1987.

MacGregor, Geddes. *He Who Lets Us Be: A Theology of Love*. New York: Seabury Press, 1975.

MacKinnon, D. M. "Subjective and Objective Conceptions of Atonement." In F. G. Healey, ed., *Prospects for Theology: Essays in Honour of H. H. Farmer*. London: Nisbet and Co., 1966.

MacMillan, Alexander. *Hymns of the Church, A Companion to the Hymnary of the United Church of Canada*. Toronto: The United Church Publishing House, 1965.

MacMullen, Ramsay. *Christianizing the Roman Empire (A.D. 100–400)*. New Haven and London: Yale University Press, 1984.

McTague, Michael J. *The Businessman in Literature: Dante to Melville*. New York: Philosophical Library, 1979.

Martin, David. *The Religious and the Secular, Studies in Secularization*. London: Routledge and Kegan Paul, 1969.

Martin, Ralph P. *Worship in the Early Church*. Grand Rapids, Michigan: William B. Eerdmans, 1964.

Marty, Martin. *Righteous Empire, The Protestant Experience in America*. New York: The Dial Press, 1970.

Marx, Karl, and Friedrich Engels. *The German Ideology*. Part One. Edited by C. J. Arthur. New York: International Publishers, 1970.

———, and Friedrick Engels. *On Religion*. New York: Schocken Books, 1964.

Mascall, E. L. *Existence and Analogy*. London: Libra Books, 1949.

Matthews, Bruce. *Craving and Salvation, A Study in Buddhist Soteriology*. Waterloo, Ontario: Wilfrid Laurier University Press, SR Supplements, 1983.

Maurice, Charles, and Charles W. Smithson. *The Doomsday Myth*. Stanford, Calif.: Hoover Institution Press, 1984.

Mead, George Herbert. *On Social Psychology*. Chicago: University of Chicago Press, 1956.

Meadows, Donella H., Dennis L. Meadows, Jorgens Randers, William W. Behrens III. *The Limits to Growth*. New York: Universe Books, 1972.

Meland, Bernard Euqene. *The Secularization of Modern Cultures*. New York: Oxford University Press, 1966.

Merton, Thomas. *Contemplation in a World of Action*. Garden City, New York: Doubleday Image Books, 1973.

———. *Faith and Violence*. Notre Dame, Indiana: University of Notre Dame Press, 1968.

Mesarovir, Mihajlo, and Eduard Pestel. *Mankind at the Turning Point*. New York: E. P. Dutton and Co., 1974.

Metz, Rene, and Jean Schlick, eds. *Liberation Theology and the Message of Salvation*. Translated by David G. Gelzer. Pittsburgh: The Pickwick Press, 1978.

Miller, Donald G. "Expository Article on Jh. 3:1–21." *Interpretation* 35 (1981).

Moberly, Elizabeth R. *Suffering, Innocent and Guilty*. London: Society for Promoting Christian Knowledge (S.P.C.K.), 1978.

Moeller, Charles. *Man and Salvation in Literature*. Translated by Charles Underhill Quinn. Notre Dame, Indiana: University of Notre Dame Press, 1970.

Moltmann, Jürgen. *The Crucified God*. Translated by R. A. Wilson and John Bowden. London: SCM Press, 1974.

Moule, C. F. D. *Worship in the New Testament*. Richmond, Virginia: John Knox Press, 1961.

Mozley, J. K. *The Doctrine of the Atonement*. London: Gerald Duckworth & Co. Ltd., 1962.

Munby, Denys. *The Idea of a Secular Society*. Oxford: Oxford University Press, 1963.

Munck, Johannes. *PAUL and the Salvation of Mankind*. Richmond, Virginia: John Knox Press, 1959.

Newlands, George M. *Theology of the Love of God*. London: Collins, 1980.

Niebuhr, Reinhold. *An Interpretation of Christian Ethics*. Cleveland & New York: World Publishing Co., Meridian Books, 1963.

Norman, Edward. *Christianity and the World Order*. Oxford: Oxford University Press, 1979.

Norris, Richard A. *The Christological Controversy*. Philadelphia: Fortress Press, 1980.

Nouwen, Henri. *Creative Ministry*. Garden City, New York: Doubleday Image Books, 1978.

———. *The Wounded Healer*. Garden City, New York: Doubleday Image Books, 1979.

Novak, Michael. *Will it Liberate?* New York: Paulist Press, 1986.

O'Connor, Flannery. *Mystery and Manners*. London: Faber and Faber, 1972.

Oden, Thomas. *Agenda for Theology*. San Francisco: Harper and Row, 1979.

Ogden, Schubert. *Faith and Freedom*. Belfast: Christian Journals, 1979.

Otto, Rudolf. *The Idea of the Holy*. New York: Oxford University Press, 1958.

Page, Ruth. "Human Liberation and Divine Transcendence." *Theology* 85 (1982).

Paul, Robert S. *The Atonement and the Sacraments*. London: Hodder and Stoughton, 1961.

Pittenger, Norman. *The Meaning of Being Human*. New York: Pilgrim Press, 1982.

Polanyi, Michael. *Personal Knowledge*. London: Routledge and Kegan Paul. 1958.

Premasagar, Peddi Victor. "Crisis for Salvation Theology!" *The International Review of Missions* 61 (1972).

Rashdall, Hastings. *The Idea of the Atonement in Christian Theology*. London: Macmillan and Co., 1919.

Rauschenbusch, Walter. *A Theology of the Social Gospel*. New York: Abingdon Press, 1945.

Rawlyk, George A., ed. *Henry Alline, Selected Writings*. New York: Paulist Press, 1987.

Redeker, Martin. *Schleiermacher: Life and Thought*. Translated by John Well-hausser. Philadelphia: Fortress Press, 1973.

Richmond, James. *Ritschl: A Reappraisal*. London: Collins, 1978.

Ricoeur, Paul. "Biblical Hermeneutics." *Semia* 4 (1975).

Ritschl, Albrecht. *The Christian Doctrine of Justification and Reconciliation*. Translated by H. R. Mackintosh and A. B. MacAulay. Edinburgh: T. and T. Clark, 1900.

Robinson, James M. *A New Quest of the Historical Jesus*. London: SCM Press, 1970.

Robinson, John A. T. *Exploration into God*. London: SCM Press, 1967.

———. *Honest to God*. London: SCM Press, 1963.

Rogers, Carl. *On Becoming a Person*. Boston: Houghton Mifflin Co., 1961.

Routley, Erik. *Hymns Today and Tomorrow*. London: Darton, Longman and Todd, 1964.

Ruether, Rosemary Radford. *To Change the World*. London: SCM Press, 1981.

Runyon, Theodore, ed. *Sanctification and Liberation; Liberation Theologies in the Light of Wesleyan Tradition*. Nashville: Abingdon Press, 1981.

Rusch, William G., ed. *The Trinitarian Controversy*. Philadelphia: Fortress Press, 1980.

Samantha, S. J., ed. *Living Faiths and Ultimate Goals*. Geneva: World Council of Churches, 1974.

Sanford, Nevitt. *Issues in Personality Theory*. San Francisco: Jossey-Bass Inc., 1920.

Sayers, Dorothy L. *Christian Letters to a Post Christian World*. Grand Rapids, Michigan: William B. Eerdmans, 1969.

Scherer, Donald, and Thomas Attig, eds. *Ethics and the Environment*. Englewood Cliffs, N.J.: Prentice-Hall, 1983.

Schilpp, Paul Arthur, ed. *The Philosophy of Alfred North Whitehead*. Evanston and Chicago: Northwestern University Press, 1941.

Schleiermacher, Friedrich. *The Christian Faith*. Edited by H. R. Mankintosh and J. S. Stewart. Edinburgh: T. and T. Clark, 1928.

Schudson, Michael. *Advertising, The Uneasy Persuasion*. New York: Basic Books, 1984.

Schumacher, E. F. *Good Work*. London: Abacus, 1980.

———. *Small is Beautiful*. London: Abacus, 1974.

Schweitzer, Albert. *The Quest of the Historical Jesus*. Translated by W. Montgomery. London: A. and C. Black, 1931.

Skinner, B. F. *Beyond Freedom and Dignity*. London: Jonathan Cape, 1971.

Slater, Robert Lawson. *Can Christians Learn from other Religions?* New York: Seabury Press, 1963.

Small, Christopher. *Ariel like a Harpy: Shelley, Mary and Frankenstein*. London: Victor Gollancz Ltd., 1972.

Smith, Wilfred Cantwell. *Belief and History*. Charlottesville: University of Virginia Press, 1977.

———. *Faith and Belief*. Princeton: Princeton University Press, 1979.

Snaith, Norman. *Mercy and Sacrifice*. London: SCM Press, 1953.

Snook, Lee E. *The Anonymous Christ, Jesus as Saviour in Modern Theology*. Minneapolis: Augsburg Publishing House, 1986.

Sobrino, Jon. *Christology at the Crossroads: A Latin American Approach*. New York: Orbis Books, 1978.

Söderblom, Nathan. *The Mystery of the Cross, Thoughts for Holy Week and Other Weeks*. Translated by A. G. Herbert. London: SCM Press, 1933.

Soelle, Dorothee. "*Brief.*" In Robert A. Evans and Thomas D. Parker, *Christian Theology; A Case Study Approach*. London: Society for Promoting Christian Knowledge (S.P.C.K.), 1977.

————. *Suffering*. Translated by Everett R. Kalin. London: Darton, Longman and Todd, 1975.

Streeter, B. H. *The Buddah and the Christ*. London: Macmillan and Co., 1932.

Sullivan, Harry Stack. *Conceptions of Modern Psychiatry*. Washington: William Alanson White Psychiatric Foundation, 1947.

Sullivan, Brian A. "*Laborem Exercens*: A Theological and Philosophical Foundation for Business Ethics." *Listening* 20 (1985).

Tamke, Susan. *Make a Joyful Noise unto the Lord: Hymns as a Reflection of Victorian Social Attitudes*. Athens: Ohio University Press, 1978.

Tawney, R. H. *The Acquisitive Society*. New York: Harcourt Brace, Joranovich, 1920.

Taylor, John V. *Enough is Enough*. Minneapolis: Augsburg Publishing House, 1977.

Tertullian. *Adversus Praxea*. Edited by Alexander Roberts and James Donaldson. Ante-Nicene Christian Library. Vol. 15. Edinburgh: T. and T. Clark, 1870.

Thomas à Kempis. *Of the Imitation of Christ*. Translated by Abbot Jostin McCann. New York: New American Library, 1957.

Tillich, Paul. *Systematic Theology*. Combined volume. Digswell Place: James Nisbet and Co., 1968.

Toffler, Alvin. *Future Shock*. New York: Random House/Bantam Books, 1971.

Tournier, Paul. *The Meaning of Persons*. London: SCM Press, 1965.

Updike, John. *Roger's Version*. New York: Alfred A. Knopf, 1986.

Van Buren, Paul. *Discerning the Way*. New York: Seabury Press, 1980.

————. *The Secular Meaning of the Gospel*. Harmondsworth, Middlesex: Penguin Books, 1963.

Van der Leeuw, Gerardus. *Religion in Essence and Manifestation*. Translated by J. E. Turner. New York: Harper and Row, 1963.

Vanstone, W.H. *Love's Endeavour, Love's Expense*. London: Darton, Longman and Todd, 1977.

Volz, Carl A. *Faith and Practice in the Early Church*. Minneapolis: Augsburg Publishing House, 1983.

Von Harnack, Adolf. *History of Dogma*. Vol. 1. Translated by Neil Buchanan. New York: Dover Publications, 1961.

————. *What is Christianity?* Translated by Thomas Bailey Saunders. New York: G. P. Putnam's Sons, 1904.

Wainwright, Geoffrey. *Eucharist and Eschatology*. New York: Oxford University Press, 1981.

Wallis, Jim. *The Call to Conversion*. San Francisco: Harper and Row, 1981.

Westermann, Claus. *BLESSING, In the Bible and the Life of the Church*. Translated by Keith Crim. Philadelphia: Fortress Press, 1978.

White, Lynn. "The Historical Roots of our Ecological Crisis." *Science* 155 (1967). (1967).

Whitehead, Alfred North. *Process and Reality*. Corrected edition. Edited by David Ray Griffin and Donald W. Shelburne. London: The Free Press, 1978.

———. *Religion in the Making*. Cambridge: Cambridge University Press, 1927.

Whyte, William H. *The Organization Man*. New York: Simon and Schuster, 1956.

Wiederkehr, Dietrich. *Belief in Redemption*. Translated by Jeremy Moiser. Atlanta: John Knox Press, 1979.

Wiesel, Elie. "Freedom and Gratitude." *Luther Magazine*, Dec. 1981.

Wiles, Maurice. *Faith and the Mystery of God*. London: SCM Press, 1982.

Williams, Daniel Day. *The Spirit and the Forms of Love*. New York: Harper and Row, 1968.

———. *What Present-Day Theologians are Thinking*. New York: Harper and Row, 1952.

Williams, Oliver F., and John W. Houck, eds. *The Judeo-Christian Vision and the Modern Corporation*. Notre Dame, Indiana: University of Notre Dame Press, 1982.

Wogaman, J. Philip. *Economics and Ethics*. Philadelphia: Fortress Press, 1986.

Wrede, William, *Paul*. Translated by Edward Lummis. Lexington, Kentucky: American Theological Library Association, 1962.

Young, Frances M. *Sacrifice and the Death of Christ*. London: Society for Promoting Christian Knowledge (S.P.C.K.), 1975.

———. "Salvation Proclaimed." *Expository Times* 94 (1983).

Ziesler, J. A. *Pauline Christianity*. Oxford: Oxford University Press, 1983.

Index

393